Selections from the Letters and Speeches of the Hon. James H. Hammond

*Available from the Simms Initiatives and the
University of South Carolina Press*

The Army Correspondence of Colonel John Laurens, ed.
As Good as a Comedy and Paddy McGann
Beauchampe
Border Beagles
Carl Werner, 2 vols.
The Cassique of Kiawah
Castle Dismal
Charlemont
The Charleston Book, ed.
Confession
Count Julian
The Damsel of Darien, 2 vols.
Dramas: Norman Maurice, Michael Bonham, and Benedict Arnold
Egeria
Eutaw
The Forayers
The Geography of South Carolina
The Golden Christmas
Guy Rivers
Helen Halsey
Historical and Political Poems (*which includes* Monody, The Vision of Cortes, The Tri-Color, Donna Florida, and Charleston and Her Satirists)
The History of South Carolina
Joscelyn
Katherine Walton
The Letters of William Gilmore Simms, Vol. 1
The Letters of William Gilmore Simms, Vol. 2
The Letters of William Gilmore Simms, Vol. 3
The Letters of William Gilmore Simms, Vol. 4
The Letters of William Gilmore Simms, Vol. 5
The Letters of William Gilmore Simms, Vol. 6 (exp. ed.)
The Life of Captain John Smith
The Life of the Chevalier Bayard
The Life of Francis Marion
The Lily and the Totem
Marie de Berniere
Martin Faber and Other Tales, 2 vols.
Mellichampe
The Partisan
Pelayo, 2 vols.
Poems, Descriptive, Dramatic, Legendary, and Contemplative, 2 vols.
The Remains of Maynard Davis Richardson
Richard Hurdis
Sack and Destruction of the City of Columbia
The Scout
Selections from the Letters and Speeches of the Hon. James H. Hammond, ed.
Simms's Poems Areytos
Social and Political Prose: Slavery in America/Father Abbot
South Carolina in the Revolutionary War
Southward Ho!
Stories and Tales
A Supplement to the Plays of William Shakespeare
Vasconselos
Views and Reviews in American Literature, History and Fiction, 2 vols.
Voltmeier
War Poetry of the South
The Wigwam and the Cabin
Woodcraft
The Yemassee

Selections from the Letters and Speeches of the Hon. James H. Hammond

William Gilmore Simms

Critical Introduction by Alexander Moore
With a Biographical Overview by David Moltke-Hansen

The University of South Carolina Press

New material © 2015 University of South Carolina

Cloth original published by John F. Trow & Co., 1866
Paperback published by the University of South Carolina
Columbia, South Carolina 29208

www.sc.edu/uscpress

Manufactured in the United States of America

24 23 22 21 20 19 18 17 16 15
10 9 8 7 6 5 4 3 2 1

ISBN 978-1-61117-480-9 (pbk)

Published in cooperation with the Simms Initiatives, a project of the University of South Carolina Libraries with the generous support of the Watson-Brown Foundation.

William Gilmore Simms: A Biographical Overview

David Moltke-Hansen

Introduction

Harper's Weekly put it succinctly in its July 2, 1870, issue: "In the death of Mr. Simms, on the 11th of June, at Charleston, the country has lost one more of its time-honored band of authors, and the South the most consistent and devoted of her literary sons" (qtd. In Butterworth and Kibler 125–26). Indeed no mid-nineteenth-century writer and editor did more than William Gilmore Simms to frame white southern self-identity and nationalism, shape southern historical consciousness, or foster the South's participation and recognition in the broader American literary culture. No southern writer enjoyed more contemporary esteem and attention, at least after Edgar Allan Poe moved north. Among American romancers (or writers of prose epics), only New Yorker James Fenimore Cooper was as successful by the 1840s. In those same years, Simms was the South's most influential editor of cultural journals. He also was the region's most prolific cultural journalist and poet, publishing an average of one book review and one poem per week for forty-five years.

Before his death Simms saw his national reputation fall along with the Confederacy he had vigorously supported and with the slave regime that many in the North had come to despise. Nevertheless reprints of most of the twenty titles in the selected edition of his works, first published between 1853 and 1860, appeared up until World War I. Thereafter only *The Yemassee*, an early romance about an Indian war in South Carolina, continued in print. The tide began to turn in the 1950s, when five volumes of Simms's letters appeared and a growing number of his works were issued in new editions. Publication in 1992 of the first literary biography, by John C. Guilds, and establishment of the William Gilmore Simms Society and the *Simms Review* the next year at once reflected and fostered this revived interest. Yet not until the 2011 launch of the digital Simms edition of the South Caroliniana Library of the University of South Carolina did scholars of southern, American, and nineteenth-century culture have the prospect of ready access to all of Simms's separately published works. With the University of South Carolina Press's cooperation, readers also will have access to sixty works in paperback editions by the end of 2014. Simms himself never saw nearly so many of his works in print at one time.

Clearly the decline in the critical standing of, and historical attention to, Simms and his oeuvre in the century after his death has reversed in the years since. The last three decades of the twentieth century saw more published on Simms than the previous hundred years (Butterworth and Kibler 126–200; MLA International). The last decade of the twentieth and first decade of the twenty-first centuries saw more dissertations and theses on him (forty-one) than had appeared in all the years before. This is not to say that Simms is yet given the attention directed to some of his contemporaries. For the first decade of the twenty-first century, the Modern Language Association International Bibliography lists roughly four times as many scholarly publications on James Fenimore Cooper, more than ten times as many on Nathaniel Hawthorne, and sixteen times as many on Edgar Allan Poe. Not surprisingly, therefore, Simms is not yet included in most anthologies of American literature, although he is a subject or a source in an expanding and ever more diverse body of scholarship.

To prepare to read Simms, it is important to see his writings in multiple contexts. He rarely wrote about himself outside of his more personal poems and his letters (some fifteen hundred of the many thousands of which survive). Yet he systematically drew on his background, personal experience, and relationships in his work. He also shaped that work through a progressively developed poetics and philosophy of life, history, and art. He did so in the context of his very broad reading of both contemporary and earlier Western literature and in the midst of multiple professional engagements and responsibilities. The richness and variety of these writings and involvements make Simms a key figure for future understanding of the literary culture, issues, and networks in mid-nineteenth-century America.

Background

Simms's family history reflected the dynamics that fueled the spread southward and westward of the populations, plantation economy, and society of the South Atlantic states. Simms's ancestry also reflected the Scots-Irish and English roots of what became identified as southern culture by the 1830s, a generation after the end of most immigration to the region. Two of Simms's grandparents, William and Elisabeth Sims, were Scots-Irish and migrated to South Carolina from Ulster. One, John Singleton, was an American-born son of putatively English immigrants, who had come to South Carolina from Virginia. The fourth, Jane Miller, was daughter of two Scots-Irish and Irish descended people—John Miller, of North and then South Carolina, and Jane Ross. Ross's family also migrated to South Carolina from western Virginia, where members lived cheek by jowl with other Scots-Irish families, who migrated to the Carolinas (White, *Ross*). Simms's father and Uncle James migrated in 1808 from Charleston to Tennessee, then to Mississippi. This was after the bankrutpcy of the elder William's business and the deaths of his wife and their other two sons. Following the last of these losses, the elder Simms's hair turned white in a week. To his anguished eyes, Charleston appeared "a place of tombs" (qtd. in Guilds 6, 12).

For the son, however, Charleston was home—so much so that he refused to leave his maternal grandmother and move to Mississippi when his uncle came to get him in 1816. Then the fifth largest and by far the wealthiest city, as well as one of the greatest ports, in America, Charleston was at the peak of its influence (Moltke-Hansen, "Expansion" 25-31; Rogers). Cotton culture on the sea islands to the south, begun in 1790, and rice culture in impounded lowcountry tidal marshes meant that the port was filled not only with sailors of many lands and languages, but also with enslaved people of many African and Creole cultures and speech ways (slaves continued to be imported legally in large numbers until 1808). This street life made vivid the transnational nature of plantation agriculture and the fact that the developing region's dramatically expanding borders "were not just geographic; they also were human, historical, and intellectual" (Moltke-Hansen, "Southern" 19).

Even more important for the future author, the expanding region's borders and nature were taking imaginative shape. The West of the senior William Gilmore Simms and the first Creek War in which he fought, the Revolutionary War of the young Simms's maternal grandfather, the backcountry of many related Scots-Irish settlers, all these became grist for a lonely, energetic boy, who spent as much time with books as he could (Simms, *Letters* 1:161). The possibilities of such settings, incidents, and characters were not confined to history alone. Simms reported that he "used to glow and shiver in turn over 'The Pilgrim's Progress,'" while "Moses' adventures in 'The Vicar of Wakefield' threw [him] into paroxysms of laughter" (Hayne 261-62). Sir Walter Scott's Border and medieval romances and James Fenimore Cooper's Leatherstocking tales also deeply colored his imagination (Simms, *Views* 1:248, and Moltke-Hansen, "Southern" 6-15). As affecting were the ghost stories and Revolutionary War tales of his grandmother and the verses sent, and tales told, by his father.

These diverse tales became reasons to explore—in books, but also on the ground. As a boy, Simms ranged through the city and along the banks of the Ashley River, which fed into Charleston Harbor. He did so in search of scenes of colonial and Revolutionary battles and incidents (*Letters* 1:lxii). He first heard his uncle's and father's many Irish and frontier stories when they visited in Charleston in 1816 and 1818, respectively. He heard more on his trips to Mississippi during the winter of 1824 through the spring of 1825 and again in 1826. The first trip took him through Georgia and Alabama, where he saw elements of the Creek and Cherokee nations. At the time, Simms later reported, he was a boy "cumbered with fragmentary materials of thought, . . . choked by the tangled vines of erroneous speculation, and haunted by passions, which, like so many wolves, lurked, in ready waiting, for their unsuspecting prey" (*Social* 6). When he first got to Mississippi, traveling partly by stage, partly by riverboat, and partly by horse, Simms learned that his father had just come back from "a trip of three hundred miles into the heart of the Indian country" (Trent 15). Later father and son "rode together on horseback to various settlements on the frontier of Alabama and Mississippi" (Guilds 10-11, 17-18). Simms recalled as well "having traveled 150 miles beyond the Mississippi" (Shillingsburg, "Literary Grist" 120). The next year he returned to the Southwest by ship. "During this [second] trip he carried a 'note book.'" There he jotted episodes, encounters, stories heard, characters seen, and descriptions of the landscapes unfolding around him. He also wrote "at least sixteen poems" (Kibler, "First"; Shillingsburg, "Literary Grist" 123).

Simms took a third western trip five years later, writing letters back to the newspaper that by then he was editing (*Letters* 1:10-38). Together these three trips provided materials for his writings over more than forty years. "The first . . . produced mainly short fiction; the second inspired much poetry; . . . the first and third . . . yielded three novels written in the 1830s" (Shillingsburg, "Literary Grist" 119). This was, in part, because of the trips' timing. Sixteen years after the first trip, Simms told students at the University of Alabama that in the interval their world had changed from a howling wilderness into a place of growing civilization (Simms, *Social* 5-6). Had he not gone when he did, he would have been too late to see the frontier. Later travels took him many other places and also provided much grist for his writing. Never again, however, did he experience the frontier firsthand. Furthermore, on these later trips Simms was a practiced professional writer, no longer that boy haunted by passions.

Personal Life

After the ten-year-old boy's momentous refusal to leave Charleston, his grandmother sent Simms for two years to the grammar school taught on the campus and by the faculty of the nearly moribund College of Charleston. By then he already was "versifying the events of the war [of 1812]," just concluded, publishing "doggerel" in the local papers, and learning to read in several languages (*Letters* 1:285). His trip west a decade later helped him decide to pursue both literature and a career in law, but back in Charleston—this despite his father's urging that he stay in Mississippi. Upon his return home, he began to read law and also launched a literary weekly, the *Album*, which ran for a year. He became engaged as well to Anna Malcolm Giles, daughter of a grocer and former state coroner.

A year later the young couple married. This was six months before Simms was admitted to the South Carolina bar, on his twenty-first birthday, not long before he was appointed as a city magistrate. Although living up the Ashley River in the more healthful, less expensive village of Summerville, Simms kept a law office in the city. Shortly after using his maternal inheritance to buy the *City Gazette* at the end of 1829 and moving down to Charleston Neck, just north of the city limits where he had lived as a boy, Simms lost both his father and his maternal grandmother. He also found himself attacked because of his Unionist stance in the Nullification crisis resulting from South Carolina's rejection of a federal tariff. Then, in early 1832, Simms's wife died. Soon after, he took his four-year-old daughter back to Summerville to live and determined to sell his newspaper and leave the state for a literary life in the North.

Fueling his ambition was the correspondence Simms had begun several years earlier with an accountant whom he had published in his *City Gazette* but not yet met—Scots immigrant James Lawson. At the time Lawson, seven years Simms's senior, edited a New York City newspaper and, in addition to writing plays and poetry, was a friend (and, later, informal literary agent) to a wide circle (McHaney, "An Early"). Simms's trip north in the summer of 1832 saw the two begin a lifelong friendship, cemented as they squired ladies about and interacted with Lawson's literary circle. In subsequent years Simms multiplied the number of his friendships, in both the North and the South, making them in some measure a replacement for the family that he had lost. Lawson remained the closest of his northern friends, while James Henry Hammond, a future governor and U.S. senator, became his closest friend in South Carolina.

Late in 1833, after his Summerville house burned, Simms wrote Lawson to say that he was enamored of "a certain fair one" (*Letters* 1:73). Seventeen-year-old Chevillette Eliza Roach was the daughter of "a literary-minded aristocrat of English descent" with two plantations on the banks of the Edisto River in Barnwell District (later County) (Guilds 70). The courtship was protracted, as Simms felt it necessary first to clear debts that friends had bought up on his behalf. He also was determined "to marry no woman" before he was "perfectly independent of her resources, and her friends" (*Letters* 1:78). Therefore he did not propose until the spring of 1836. The nuptials took place seven months later, and as a result, Simms came to call the four thousand acres of Woodlands Plantation, with its seventy slaves, home. It was twenty years, however, before he took over management of the plantation and, then, only in the wake of his father-in-law's final sickness and death. Five years after that, he lost his wife, the mother of fourteen of his fifteen children. Nine of the children Chevillette bore him had already died, devastating Simms repeatedly. Five were still living (three sons and two daughters), as was Simms's daughter by his first marriage, who helped raise the youngest of her siblings. Those remaining children—even Gilly, who fought in the Confederate army—all outlived their father. Gilly and a brother-in-law ran Woodlands after the war, when Simms, though dying of cancer, was earning what he could by writing again for publications in the North and editing one or another South Carolina newspaper.

Career

The trip north in 1832 did not result in Simms moving there. Except during the Civil War, however, he returned almost every year. This was because the contacts he made, and the exposure to literary culture that he enjoyed, helped him define his future as an author. Earlier he had written fiction and criticism as well as journalism, filling the pages of several short-lived cultural journals and his newspaper, but between the ages of nine and twenty-six Simms had focused his literary efforts primarily on poetry. Beginning with his first book of verse in 1825, he had published five small volumes in Charleston. A couple had received positive notice in New York, and in the fall of 1832, J. & J. Harper issued the sixth anonymously from there, *Atalantis: A Story of the Sea*. Coming back the following summer, Simms had in hand for the Harpers a gothic novella, *Martin Faber*, and after his return south, he also would send the manuscript of his first two-volume border romance, *Guy Rivers: A Tale of Georgia*.

The reception of these and the romances and short stories that followed quickly made Simms one of the nation's most successful fictionists. He continued to issue poetry as well—roughly a collection every three years over the thirty-seven years that he worked as a professional author. But this output was dwarfed by the fiction—on average a title every year (counting several serialized works but not counting the many revised editions). Then there were the two dozen separately published orations, histories, and biographies as well as edited collections of documents and dramas and a geography of South Carolina. Add to these the revised editions and the further printings and issues of his own works and it appears that Simms saw a title coming off the presses at the rate of one every three months or so. Making that figure all the more astounding is the fact that, during more than a dozen of those years (the early-to-mid 1840s, the late 1840s-to-early 1850s, and the mid-to-late 1860s), he also was editing a cultural journal or newspaper. Furthermore he contributed reams of reviews and poems, hundreds of op-ed pieces and columns, and dozens of short stories and public addresses, which were never collected and published in volume form.

His career mapped an arc. It ascended meteorically in the 1830s and peaked in the early-to-mid 1840s, before beginning to descend. One reason was the popularity of the historical fiction that Simms began to write. When he left behind the law, his first newspaper, and the Nullification controversy, as well as his sadness, historical fiction was all the rage. Sir Walter Scott had fueled the craze, beginning with the publication of his first Border romance in 1814. He died in September 1832. Seventeen years Simms's senior, James Fenimore Cooper, the closest America had to a Scott at the time, was at the peak of his reputation and success, having started publishing his romances in 1820. Thus the way had been prepared for a writer of Simms's historical imagination and preoccupations. Within five years of his first trip north, moreover, Lawson's (and now his) circle became loosely affiliated with a nationalistic and Democratic group, self-styled Young America, this after Young Italy and similar ethnic, nationalist, European, cultural and political movements (Moltke-Hansen, "Southern"). Edgar Allan Poe and other members gave Simms's first fictions positive, if not uncritical, attention.

By the end of the 1830s, paradoxically, Simms, like Cooper, found his success attracting unauthorized editions of his works because Britain and America did not have an international copyright agreement. Further, in the wake of the panic of 1837, Americans bought fewer books. Simms's response was to diversify his portfolio. He turned to biography and history, including his hugely successful *Life of Francis Marion* (1844). He also returned to the editor's chair, overseeing one and then another cultural journal. These were unlike the ones he had edited in the 1820s: they included contributions by numerous authors, not just those from Charleston, but from the region and also the North. The ambition motivating the journals was to connect and promote Charleston intellectually. Consequently the journals more closely resembled metropolitan quarterly reviews in their offerings.

The mid-1840s saw Simms involved in politics, even serving a term in the South Carolina legislature. By the middle of the Mexican-American War in 1847, he had concluded that the South needed to become an independent nation. Thereafter, although he maintained ties with many in the Young America circle, he no longer promoted his writings as fostering Americanism in literature (*Views*). Instead he increasingly emphasized the ways in which his three romance series—the colonial, the Revolutionary, and the border—were making tangible and meaningful the origins and development of the future southern nation and the sad but inevitable consequences for Native Americans (Watson, *From Nationalism*; compare Nakamura).

Sectional politics colored more and more of Simms's perceptions, speeches, and private communications. The rising tide of abolitionism had him aghast. It also fed his growing sense that his position in American letters was slipping. He returned to editing, and his poetry, which was more often explicitly about the South, became increasingly patriotic in tone. Although his first biographer, William Peterfield Trent, insisted that Simms's declining standing reflected the change in literary fashion from historical romances to realistic novels, Simms in fact wrote more and more as a social realist in the 1850s (Wimsatt, "Realism").

The Civil War consumed Simms. As he wrote Lawson, "Literature, especially poetry, is effectually overwhelmed by the drums, & the cavalry, and the shouting" (*Letters* 4:369–70). He did manage to editorialize often and to rework and finish things long on his desk, including poems, a novel, and a dramatic treatment of Benedict Arnold, the northern traitor in the Revolutionary War. Then, in the wake of the Confederacy's loss and the failure of his vision for the South, he found himself recording the loss in a new newspaper, dealing with the trauma in his poetry, and becoming more existential and psychological in his fictional treatments. Simms's old New York friends tried to help. He did edit and see through publication a volume of Confederate war poetry. Yet it is a measure of his reduced stature that the several new romances he published appeared only in serial form. In part this may have been because he was in a sense competing with himself. Publishers were beginning to reprint volumes out of the selected edition of his writings. Many of Simms's works were available in book form, just not new works.

Associations

As the *Letters* testify, Simms had complex, overlapping networks of friends and colleagues. As a boy and young man, he received the friendship, patronage, and commendation of a variety of well-placed people in Charleston, including Charles Rivers Carroll. It was Carroll with whom he read law, to whom he dedicated his first romance, and after whom he named a son. Both men were Unionists during the Nullification controversy. So were Hugh Swinton Legare (later U.S. attorney general) and the considerably older William Drayton, as well as lawyer and editor Richard Yeadon and Greenville, South Carolina, newspaper editor Benjamin Franklin Perry. Also considerably older was James Wright Simmons, who had joined with Simms to launch the *Southern Literary Gazette* in 1828, when Simms was twenty-two. Through him Simms had direct contact with such British literary figures as Leigh Hunt and Byron (Kibler, *Poetry* 15).

The next group of influential friends and collaborators that Simms acquired were members of the Lawson circle and included such figures as Edwin

Forrest, the Shakespearean actor, and Evert Duyckinck, who published several of Simms's volumes in Wiley and Putnam's series Library of American Books, which he edited. Among the many others were poets and editors William Cullen Bryant and Fitz-Greene Halleck. Simms also made nonliterary friends in New York and Philadelphia, such as John Jacob Bockee and William Hawkins Ferris, the cashier at the U.S. Treasury office in New York who, after the war, helped Simms, Henry Timrod (poet laureate of the Confederacy), and others.

As a Barnwell planter, Simms met a widening circle of South Carolina's leaders and literati. For instance his acquaintance with James Henry Hammond began in the late 1830s and deepened into a friendship in the early 1840s. It was in the early 1840s, too, when he again was editing cultural journals, that Simms became friends with many southern writers. He regarded several of them, including Virginians George Frederick Holmes, Edmund Ruffin, and Nathaniel Beverley Tucker as members, together with Hammond and himself, in a "sacred circle." Uniting the circle were members' devotion to the South and a shared sense of the marginal status and critical importance of the life of the mind in a largely rural and unintellectual region (Faust, *Sacred*). Others of Simms's wide connections in the region did not interact as much with each other, but Simms long corresponded with Maryland novelist and lawyer John Pendleton Kennedy, Irish-born Georgia poet Richard Henry Wilde, Alabama lawyer and writer Alexander Beaufort Meek, and Louisiana historian and assistant attorney general Charles Gayarré, among others. By the 1850s, when Simms once more returned to editing a cultural journal, many of the writers whom he recruited were members of a younger generation. Poets Paul Hamilton Hayne and Henry Timrod were two. Often they and a half dozen others of Simms's and their generations met in John Russell's Charleston Book Shop and adjourned to dinner at Simms's Smith Street home, "dubbed 'The Wigwam'" (*Letters* 1:cxxxvi). Shortly before his death fifteen or so years later, Simms wrote Hayne, "I am rapidly passing from the stage, where you young men are to succeed me" (*Letters* 5:287).

Thought

The welter of Simms's works disguises unities and dynamics of the thought underlying them. From early on Simms was convinced that art ennobles or transforms, as well as gives voice to individuals and societies; therefore it must be cultivated assiduously. Without the potential for high artistic attainment, he insisted, societies are not ready for the independence and regard of free peoples. This is where Simms the historian joined Simms the poet. Societies develop, he argued (using the stadialism of the Scottish historical school), from imitation through self-assertion to achievement and also from savagery through strife to settled agricultural communities and, ultimately, to a hierarchical civilization supporting a rich artistic life. It was the job of the artist to help envision the goal, inspire the pursuit, and inform the process. That process was at once progressive and dialectical. Order, without dynamism, stifled development, as did the obverse—the dominance by ungoverned impulses or uncontrolled license. This was true in the individual, but also in societies as a whole. War was necessary for civilization, but its success was measured in the securities of the home, the center of cultural production and reproduction.

Whether in the public or in the domestic arena, "the true governor, as [Thomas] Carlyle call[ed] him—the king man—" guided rather than impeded the forces of change and progress (Simms, "Guizot's" 122). There were few such men with the capacity to lead. The same was true of nations. Neither all people nor all peoples were equal in either capacity or attainment. That was why Native Americans were overrun and Africans had been enslaved by European peoples in the New World. Indeed, Simms argued, "slavery in all ages has been found the greatest and most admirable agent of Civilization," giving education and examples to less evolved peoples (*Letters* 3:174). The degree to which a people had evolved mattered. That was why, he held, Americans had won independence from the most powerful empire in the world. They had done so through their Revolution, led by an elite that felt correctly its time had come (Simms, "Ellet's" 328). By mid-1847 that also was Simms's judgment for the South: the region had evolved enough to become independent (*Letters* 2:332). The hope inspired and then failed him and the people he sought to lead.

While not all men could rise to the highest rank, they all had the same responsibility at home. There the father was patriarch, protector, and head, while the mother was nurturer, moral instructor, and heart. There, too, children's characters and minds were formed by age twelve ("Ellet's"). Children's upbringing was critical to citizenship, and it was through her sons and the support of her husband, father, and brothers that a woman shaped the public sphere. The culture and character instilled in the child expressed and informed not just the household, but the larger society—the people.

"The history of peoples and their embodiments in institutions, states, and artistic productions—these were the great subjects" in Simms's view (Moltke-Hansen, "Southern" 120). Yet "poets were the only class of philosophers who had recognized" this until his own day, when at last "we now read human histories. We now ask after the affections as well as the ceremonies of society" ("Ellet's" 319-20). Peoples or races—that is, ethnic groups—were not unchanging any more than were their politics and their cultures. They either advanced or were overrun by history. Further, new peoples emerged, and old identities were submerged. The Spanish conquistadors were the creation of centuries of conflict with the Moors: their motivation was the glory of conquest, not the routine of trade or the plow. On the other hand, the English settlements in North America reflected the impulse to transform the wilderness into verdant farms and build society (*Views* 64, 178-85; *Social* 8). The same impulse drove Americans westward in Simms's own day and gave Americans their Manifest Destiny.

To explore these facts of the South's settlement and its place in international conflicts, Simms wrote all together, between 1833 and 1863, two romances set in eighth-century Spain, two set during the Spanish exploration and conquest of the Americas and two during the later English colonization of South Carolina, seven set during the American Revolution, and—depending on how one counts—perhaps eight set on the borders of the nineteenth-century South. After the war he published one more Revolutionary romance and two more that, like it, were set beyond the boundaries of civilization. He also left two unfinished romances, also set beyond society's normal reach. These late works, however, no longer had as their framing justification the cultivation of the South's future and civilization.

White southerners had their independence foreclosed by the war. In his last works, therefore, Simms found himself exploring the psychological, philosophical, and historical impulses that led to the Confederacy's demise and what, in the aftermath, it meant to be a good man and to build for the future, however impoverished. On the first score, he argued that the impulse to idealism behind abolitionism ignored historical realities, becoming inhuman in its consequences. On the latter score, he affirmed responsibility for one's dependents and the virtues of stoicism, as well as a continued commitment to the beauty and truth of art and the impulses to the cultivated life and fields. Therefore, in the face of the burning of his Woodlands home and library in February 1865—during Sherman's march and in the midst of desperate circumstances—he insisted that home, or the ideals and past characterizing its potential, still was at the center of true civilization, but only if elevated by art (*Sense* 8, 17). It was wrong to measure civilization by the getting, spending, and mad dashing, or material progress and utilitarianism, characteristic of both a capitalistic North and also many southerners. These traits he often had attacked even before the war, insisting that "the work of the Imagination, which is the Genius of a race, is only begun when its material progress is supposed to be complete" (*Poetry* 12).

Writings

Simms expressed many of his ideas most personally in letters and most cogently in essays, speeches, and occasional introductions to his books. But he illustrated them most fully in his fiction and poetry. By the time he arrived in New

York in 1832, he had formed many of the core ideals and beliefs that would shape his work. His application of them, however, modified his understanding over time. Growing as a writer and growing in knowledge and experience, he also grew as a thinker.

In his hierarchy of values, poetry came first. It was a prophetic calling as well as evocative of the deeply felt (or, sometimes, the fleeting) and thus testimony to the perdurance and transcendence of the beautiful and the human spirit. Yet, as Simms often ruefully reflected, prose spoke to many more people. That was a principal reason why he turned to writing prose epics or romances. He gave his most concerted consideration of poetry's value and roles in three lectures in Charleston in 1854. Over the prior three years he had given portions of them in Augusta, Georgia, Washington, D.C., and Richmond and Petersburg, Virginia. Entitled *Poetry and the Practical*, they did not see print until 1996, as Simms never found the time to expand them as he wanted. On the other hand, his last address on the same themes, *The Sense of the Beautiful*, was issued soon after he delivered it, also in Charleston.

Many of his important reviews have not yet been gathered, but Simms collected some in 1845–46, and *Views and Reviews in American Literature, History and Fiction* came out in 1846 and 1847 in two "series." Beginning with a consideration of "Americanism" in literature, the first series explored the themes and periods of American history for treatment by the novelist. Simms argued there, and in forewords to several of his romances, that fiction rendered the past more truthfully, interestingly, and tellingly than histories and biographies could because fiction—like poetry—required imagination to look beyond what is not known or expressed. The second series examined additional American writers and what distinguished them, for instance, in their humor.

Despite their early success, Simms's romances, novellas, and stories provoked mixed reviews. Poe eventually concluded that Simms had become "the best novelist which this country has, on the whole, produced" but also insisted that "he should never have written 'The Partisan,' nor 'The Yemassee.'" This was in a review of *Confession*. That novel, like the gothic *Martin Faber*, demonstrated, Poe contended, that Simms's "genius [did] not lie in the outward so much as in the inner world." Yet he nevertheless wrote of Simms's short-story collection *The Wigwam and the Cabin* that "in invention, in vigor, in movement, in the power of exciting interest, and in the artistical management of his themes, he has surpassed, we think, any of his countrymen." Other critics, especially in the genteel and Whiggish Knickerbocker circle, joined Poe in condemning what they considered to be the excessively graphic and vulgar qualities of many characters and scenes, and Simms's prolixity and sententiousness, in his romances (Butterworth and Kibler 64, 50).

The violent realism and earthiness of the romances did not result in realistic novels. Although Simms received early praise for his characterizations (particularly of women), he used the romance formula, with its stereotypic heroes and heroines, predictable themes, and conventional polarities. People were on quests or had lost their way or were fighting long odds or were carrying forward the banner of (and modeling) civilization or were mired in the slough of despond or were resisting all the claims of civilized society and behavior or were pursuing love interests. Deceitfulness, selfishness, and greed opposed honor, high-mindedness, and honesty against the backdrop of the South's development from the earliest days of Spanish exploration to the westward movement in Simms's own youth.

It was only gradually that Simms married the psychological acuity of some of his portraits of the interior struggles of his gothic characters and fiction to the historical romance. Helping him think through how to do so were the biographies he wrote in the mid-1840s, but also the incidents on which he focused particular fictions, such as the murder in *Beauchampe; or, The Kentucky Tragedy* (1842). However incomplete the blending of realism and romanticism or of stereotypical and socially individuated renderings through the 1840s, by the 1850s Simms fundamentally had made the transition to social realism in such works as *Woodcraft* and *The Cassique of Kiawah*. Indeed some scholars have considered *Woodcraft* the first realistic novel in America (Bakker; Wimsatt, "Realism").

In some sense disguising the transition is the fact that Simms also increasingly wrote as a humorist and, in so doing, often rendered his late narratives fabulistically, when not writing social comedy or stories of manners. This dimension of Simms's work was largely hidden, however, until the 1974 publication of *Stories and Tales*, volume 5 in the Centennial Simms edition. There, for the first time, readers had access in print to "Bald-Head Bill Bauldy." There, too, for the first time one could read together that story, "Legend of the Hunter's Camp," and "How Sharp Snaffles Got His Capital and Wife," which was published posthumously in *Harper's Magazine* in October 1870. These and other stories and tales made it clear that Simms was a fecund contributor to southern and American humor.

Humor let Simms take up issues that he could not otherwise address in print and still expect to be well received. He did so both during and after the war. The war also pushed Simms past the emerging fashion of social realism. Having destroyed the familiar, the preoccupation of much realistic fiction, the war made the liminal central (Shillingsburg, "Cub"). While his romances and tales had often explored life on the edge or in extreme circumstances, whether in war or on the frontier or on the verge of madness or in fanciful realms, it had done so against a backdrop of, and with the goal of affirming, social norms and development. In the war's wake that goal seemed absurd. Mythologized memories of a healthy past might nurture a sense of the beautiful but could not help one deal with the present. Thus Simms's conclusion, in a March 1869 letter to Paul Hamilton Hayne: "Let us bury the Past lest it buries us!" (*Letters* 5:214). Fifteen months later he lay dead in the 13 Society Street, Charleston, home of his oldest daughter, with the shell holes in the walls of the bedroom he had shared with several children.

Posthumous Reputation

The twenty years after Simms's death saw him often respectfully treated, first in obituaries, later in memoirs and columns, and also in literary dictionaries and encyclopedias. Yet Charles Richardson's 1887 *American Literature: 1607-1885* proved a harbinger of a shift: Simms, Richardson observed, was "more respected than read," having "won considerable note because he was so sectional" and then having "lost it because he was not sectional enough," although he showed "silly contempt for his Northern betters" (qtd. in Butterworth and Kibler 130). Five years later Trent's biography of Simms appeared. It was the first full-length, scholarly treatment. Its central thesis was that Simms's environment frustrated his abilities: the South was inimical to art and the life of the mind, and Charleston high society's hauteur marginalized Simms despite his talent and character. Trent's second thesis was that Simms's commitment to the romance and his romanticism meant that his works had become largely unreadable in an age of literary realism. Although Vernon Parrington and later scholars recognized Simms's impulses to realism, the two theses long shaped Simms criticism and, indeed, also helped frame study of antebellum southern literature and intellectual life (Parrington 119-30).

A Virginian born in 1862, Trent was a progressive who wanted a New South radically different from the old. He saw his pioneering study of Simms as an opportunity to criticize what the Civil War had made untenable. From his perspective the Old South was not the expanding and rapidly developing environment, with a deep history, that Simms portrayed, but a place where slavery stultified and stunted the growth and progress displayed by the North. Southern—especially South Carolinian—writers occasionally challenged Trent's agenda and conclusions, but those critiques had little impact. Not until after publication of the Simms letters in the 1950s did scholars begin to consider the author in the historical and contemporary contexts that he had rendered in his poetry and fiction. And not until after the centennial of his death did a growing number of scholars, having concluded that southern intellectual history was not an oxymoron, begin to study in detail the culture in which Simms participated and to which he contributed so voluminously and variously.

Some of these scholars also have had agendas: they have wanted to see Simms included in the American literary canon, for instance, or they have wanted to defend the heritage that in their view Trent, and so many others, inappropriately belittled or ignorantly dismissed. More fruitfully, other scholars have begun to reframe the understanding of nineteenth-century American intellectual life by stripping away preconceptions that characterized earlier evaluations of Simms and his contemporaries. They are closely examining the historical record and transatlantic and other contemporary contexts and developments in the process. Although the pursuit of canonical status in a postcanonical age seems quixotic at this point, the explosion of the canon is leading to more varied fare being offered and may, therefore, mean that Simms, once his work is widely available, will be more often anthologized as well as studied. Defensiveness about Simms and the antebellum South may warm the hearts of like-minded people, just as critics of the Old South have been encouraged by shared presuppositions and disdain. Yet dueling cultural ideologies do not advance comity and may only reinforce mutual incomprehensions. Continued, deep research in original sources and the theoretical reframing that Atlantic history, the history of the book, and other perspectives offer—these approaches promise most for further study of Simms, his works, and his world.

Works Cited

For amplified readings by and on Simms and on his world, go to http://simms.library.sc.edu/bibliography.php.

Bakker, Jan. "Simms on the Literary Frontier; or, So Long Miss Ravenel and Hello Captain Porgy: *Woodcraft* Is the First 'Realistic' Novel in America." In *William Gilmore Simms and the American Frontier,* edited by John Caldwell Guilds and Caroline Collins, 64–78. Athens: University of Georgia Press, 1997.

Butterworth, Keen, and James E. Kibler Jr. *William Gilmore Simms: A Definitive Guide.* Boston: G. K. Hall, 1980.

Faust, Drew Gilpin. *A Sacred Circle: The Dilemma of the Intellectual in the Old South, 1840–1860.* Baltimore: Johns Hopkins University Press, 1977.

Guilds, John C. *Simms: A Literary Life.* Fayetteville: University of Arkansas Press, 1992.

Hayne, Paul Hamilton. "Ante-Bellum Charleston." *Southern Bivouac* 1 (October 1885): 257–68.

Kibler, James E. "The First Simms Letters: 'Letters from the West' (1826)." *Southern Literary Journal* 19 (Spring 1987): 81–91.

———. *The Poetry of William Gilmore Simms: An Introduction and Bibliography.* Columbia: Southern Studies Program, University of South Carolina, 1979.

McHaney, Thomas L. "An Early 19th-Century Literary Agent: James Lawson of New York." *Publications of the Bibliographical Society of America* 64 (Spring 1970): 177-92.

Moltke-Hansen, David. "The Expansion of Intellectual Life: A Prospectus." In *Intellectual Life in Antebellum Charleston*, edited by Michael O'Brien and David Moltke-Hansen, 3-44. Knoxville: University of Tennessee Press, 1986.

———. "Southern Literary Horizons in Young America: Imaginative Development of a Regional Geography." *Studies in the Literary Imagination* 42, no. 1 (2009): 1-31.

Nakamura, Masahiro. *Visions of Order in William Gilmore Simms: Southern Conservatism and the Other American Romance.* Columbia: University of South Carolina Press, 2009.

Parrington, Vernon L. *The Romantic Revolution in America, 1800-1860.* Vol. 2 of *Main Currents in American Thought.* New York: Harcourt, Brace and Company, 1927.

Rogers, George C., Jr. *Charleston in the Age of the Pinckneys.* Columbia: University South Carolina Press, 1980.

Shillingsburg, Miriam J. "The Cub of the Panther: A New Frontier." In *William Gilmore Simms and the American Frontier*, edited by John Caldwell Guilds and Caroline Collins, 221-36. Athens: University of Georgia Press, 1997.

———. "Literary Grist: Simms's Trips to Mississippi." *Southern Quarterly* 41, no. 2 (2003): 119-34.

Simms, William Gilmore. *Atalantis: A Story of the Sea: In Three Parts.* New York: J. & J. Harper, 1832.

———. *Beauchampe; or, The Kentucky Tragedy.* 2 vols. Philadelphia: Lea and Blanchard, 1842.

———. *The Cassique of Kiawah: A Colonial Romance.* New York: Redfield, 1859.

———. *Confession; or, The Blind Heart. A Domestic Story.* 2 vols. Philadelphia: Lea and Blanchard, 1841.

———. "Ellet's 'Women of the Revolution.'" *Southern Quarterly Review*, n.s. 1 (July 1850): 314-54.

———. "Guizot's Democracy in France." *Southern Quarterly Review* 15, no.29 (1849): 114-65.

———. *Guy Rivers: A Tale of Georgia.* 2 vols. New York: Harper & Brothers, 1834.

———. *The Letters of William Gilmore Simms.* Edited by Mary C. Simms Oliphant, Alfred Taylor Odell, and T. C. Duncan. 6 vols. Columbia: University of South Carolina Press, 1952-82.

———. *The Life of Francis Marion.* New York: Henry G. Langley, 1844.

———. *Martin Faber, the Story of a Criminal; and Other Tales.* 2 vols. New York: Harper & Brothers, 1837.

———. *Poetry and the Practical.* Edited by James E. Kibler. Fayetteville: University of Arkansas Press, 1996.

———. *The Sense of the Beautiful: An Address . . . before the Charleston County Agricultural and Horticultural Association, May 3, 1870.* Charleston: Charleston County Agricultural and Horticultural Association, 1870.

———. *The Social Principle: The Source of National Permanence. An Oration, Delivered before the Erosophic Society of the University of Alabama . . . December 13, 1842*. Tuscaloosa: Erosophic Society, University of Alabama, 1843.

———. *Stories and Tales*. Vol. 5 of *The Writings of William Gilmore Simms*. Centennial edition; introductions, explanatory notes, and texts established by John Caldwell Guilds. Columbia: University of South Carolina Press, 1974.

———. *Views and Reviews in American Literature, History and Fiction*. 2 vols. New York: Wiley and Putnam, 1845 (1846).

———. *The Wigwam and the Cabin*. 2 vols. New York: Wiley and Putnam, 1845–46.

———. *Woodcraft, or Hawks about the Dovecote: A Story of the South, at the Close of the Revolution*. New York: Redfield, 1854.

Trent, William Peterfield. *William Gilmore Simms*. Boston: Houghton, Mifflin, 1892.

Wakelyn, Jon L. *The Politics of a Literary Man: William Gilmore Simms*. Westport, Conn.: Greenwood Press, 1973.

Watson, Charles S. *From Nationalism to Secessionism: The Changing Fiction of William Gilmore Simms*. Westport, Conn.: Greenwood Press, 1993.

White, William B., Jr. *The Ross-Chesnut-Sutton Family of South Carolina*. Franklin, N.C.: Privately printed, 2002.

Wimsatt, Mary Ann. "Realism and Romance in Simms's Midcentury Fiction." *Southern Literary Journal* 12, no. 2 (1980): 29–48.

Critical Introduction

SELECTIONS FROM THE LETTERS AND SPEECHES OF THE
HON. JAMES H. HAMMOND, OF SOUTH CAROLINA

Alexander Moore

In December 1861, nine months after the American Civil War had begun William Gilmore Simms received a letter from his great friend James Henry Hammond. Formerly Governor of South Carolina and United States Senator, Hammond had considered Simms's suggestion that he publish a volume of his literary "Remains"; that is, his speeches, public letters, and other original documents. Hammond envisioned the book to be "a very select & rather undersized Volume & I would cheerfully make any compensation to the Publisher that you might think right."[1] Simms planned the book to become a volume for inclusion in a larger publishing enterprise close to Simms's heart, a "Library of the Confederate States." Soon thereafter the author revealed to John Reuben Thompson, poet and former editor of the *Southern Literary Messenger*, that he was "revising Hammond's Essays & Speeches for the Press" as a title in the new series: "The volumes to average 400 pp. each, & sold at 1.00 or 1.25 according to bulk. New works to be interspersed as prepared, and wholesome variety to be sought in History, Biography, Statesmanship, Poetry & Fiction" (*Letters* 6: 223). Simms then elaborated his plan to William Porcher Miles:

> I have been suggesting a scheme of a Library of the Confederate States, to include only Southern writers in all departments, publishing a <u>single vol.</u> monthly. It will comprise Lives, with selections, of & from [John C.] Calhoun, [George] McDuffie, [Robert Y.] Hayne, [Nathaniel] Bev[erly] Tucker, [Thomas] Jefferson, [George] Washington, [John] Randolph, &c. with the miscellaneous writings of Hammond, [William J.] Grayson, &c. and be interspersed with original writings as they offer. I merely propose & will not edit. (*Letters* 4: 397)

By then Simms had already contradicted his statement to Miles that he would not edit the series; for, he was at work "revising Hammond now for the Press" (ibid.). *Selections from the Letters and Speeches of the Hon. James H. Hammond, of South Carolina* was published by John F. Trow in New York City in early 1866 under circumstances far different from those Hammond and Simms had anticipated four years earlier. Hammond had been deceased for nearly two years and the Confederacy had been extinguished in April 1865.

From the start of his literary career Simms had exhorted native writers to create an American national literature different in content and character from that of Europe and Great Britain. As sectional conflict between North and South worsened and eventually divided the Union, he shifted that advocacy to creating a distinctive southern literature—different in character and content from the literature of the northern states. Simms intended the Library of the Confederate States to be the vehicle by which the Confederacy would take its place on the world's literary stage. The Civil War and defeat of the short-lived Confederate republic prevented Simms from fulfilling his ambitious plan.

Book Plans

Sometime between December 1861 and his death in November 1864 Hammond composed a draft table of contents and began assembling copies of his pamphlet publications and official papers to use as texts for the anthology. Simms was at work early in 1862 on at least three speeches; so, it is likely that Hammond composed his list in late 1861 or early 1862. Hammond's list contained twelve items to be published "in one volume — large type — good paper.... It will make with large print an Octavo vol. of 250 or 300 pages."[2] When published in 1866 *Selections* was an octavo volume of 368 pages and contained eleven of the twelve items on Hammond's list, arranged chronologically in the order that he had proposed. However, by early 1862 preparation of Hammond's texts may have reached an impasse as the two men disagreed on some editorial issues.

At the close of 1861 Simms began editing and "correcting" pamphlet versions of three speeches. When he sent his texts to Hammond he received a reply on 18 February 1862, that revealed resistance to his editorial tinkering:

> I have read only the first page of the "Kansas speech." The corrections seem to be improvements, but glancing further over the pages, they appear to be so elaborate that when adopted it may be as much your speech as mine. I don't know how that would look as our styles are very different. My aim has always been <u>clearness</u> first, then *vigor* & for these I sacrifice elegance when necessary & sometimes grammar.... I will see whenever I can bring my self to the ungrateful task of looking over those Speeches again, how it stands & how far the adoption of your Corrections will estrange the style of these from my other productions.[3]

In other words Simms and Hammond differed on some elements of preparing the *Selections* text. To compare the *Selections* version of Hammond's "Speech on the Admission of Kansas ... March 4, 1858" with the pamphlet version published in Washington, DC by Lemuel Towers reveals the sort of emendations that had caught Hammond's eye. Simms introduced qualifying words and phrases, changed capitalizations, and italicized some words for emphasis. These emendations may have tempered the "vigor" of Hammond's expressions but their effect was to clarify subject and verb agreement, eliminate superfluous punctuation, and to link accurately pronouns with their antecedent nouns.

James Henry Hammond's health had been declining through 1864 and he died on November 13 at Redcliffe, his Edgefield District plantation (Faust, *Hammond* 376-9). Amid his own wartime and personal losses, Simms mourned Hammond's demise. Writing to Edward Spann Hammond, Simms stated that "[Y]our father was my most confidential friend for near twenty years. Never were thoughts more intimate than his & mine. We had few or no secrets from each other.... There was something kindred in our intellectual nature." Simms then turned his thoughts to his friend's literary remains and intellectual legacy:

> Preserve all his papers. I hope some day to render a proper tribute to his memory. We have no chance for this now. There is no organ. There are no means. Do not suffer his revised publications to be mislaid. Have them carefully preserved, compactly put up & sealed against mischance. With God's blessing, I hope to put on record my appreciation of his claims and to illustrate them by his works. (*Letters* 4: 469-70)

Among his various accomplishments Hammond was foremost a politician and would-be statesman, who served South Carolina as governor and legislator in the United States House of Representatives and Senate. His activities in Congress — attendance, committee memberships, and voting record — are part of the public records of the nation. They were published in the official journals of the Senate and House of Representatives.[4] Hammond was elected to the Twenty-fourth Congress. He took his House seat on 18 December 1835 and resigned in February 1836 due to failing health. His House speeches and remarks are found in volumes of the *Congressional Globe*, and *Register of Debates in Congress*.[5] Hammond's Senate term was longer and more noteworthy. He was elected to the Thirty-fifty Congress and took his seat in December 1857. Reelected to the Thirty-sixth Congress, he resigned on 11 November 1860, in response to the presidential election of Abraham Lincoln.[6] The *Congressional Globe* contains his Senate speeches and remarks.

In that era important Congressional speeches were widely published in newspapers and as pamphlets to reach a broad readership. Newspaper readers had insatiable appetites for lengthy columns of political speeches set in small type sizes. *Globe* texts were disseminated throughout the nation when they were reprinted in national and regional newspapers. Publishers occasionally gave Congressional orators opportunities to correct and revise their texts, thereby lending pamphlet versions greater literary authority than *Globe* versions. Hammond's Congressional speeches, especially those included in *Selections*, had also been published in the *Charleston Mercury* and other South Carolina newspapers. Newspapers were the chief tools in disseminating political views, establishing political party loyalties, and creating public opinion. As a young man Hammond had briefly edited the *Southern Times*, a pro-nullification newspaper in Columbia, South Carolina. Scrapbooks in the Hammond Papers at the South Caroliniana Library and Library of Congress contain clippings from newspapers throughout the nation reporting Hammond's political activities in Washington and South Carolina and printing his speeches with regularity. His other publications expand his legacy beyond the sphere of southern politics. Among those were speeches on southern politics and culture delivered on special occasions, periodical essays, and even some juvenile works of literary pretension (Tucker, "Hammond" 485-86).

Hammond's pamphlets, journal articles, and newspaper essays ranged from scientific farming and plantation management to politics but the cornucopia of his diaries, plantation records, commonplace books, and thousands of letters is his chief legacy. Simms had known from their earliest acquaintance that Hammond was a consummate letter writer and diligent keeper of his personal and business papers. Even as Union forces devastated South Carolina in 1864-65, Simms persisted in his goal to preserve Hammond's papers and to publish a volume of letters to complement the planned *Selections*. A volume of Hammond's letters would add another title to the Library of the Confederate States and immortalize his late friend's talents.

Two months after Hammond's death Simms elaborated to Harry Hammond, his friend's eldest son, his plans for the volume of letters. He returned to Catherine Fitzsimons Hammond a bundle of her late husband's letters and encouraged other Hammond correspondents to return their letters to the family (*Letters* 4: 482-83). During 1865 Hammond's widow began to seek a publisher for the speeches and public letters volume. She wrote to her brother-in-law Marcellus C.M. Hammond that she had entrusted to her son-in-law James Gregg some pamphlets her deceased spouse had "corrected and arranged for publication" to her son-in-law James Gregg to carry to Great Britain in hopes of finding a publisher. These were likely texts that Hammond and Simms had labored upon in 1862 augmented by others edited since then. Gregg made the attempt, "but he writes that upon inquiry it could be published on better terms at the North. Spann advises that we defer as this is not the time to do it. He is deeply interested in it and will probably give it more attention than [my sons]

Paul or Harry as his tastes are more in that line. I can't trust myself with the past" (Bleser, *Hammonds* 145).

As late as 1868 — two years after *Selections* had been published — Simms described to M.C.M. Hammond his desire to publish an essay on Hammond "when I shall be able to undertake the article on J.H.H. for the present that must be delayed." He wished to thanks Edward Spann Hammond for sending a copy of *Selections*. An inscription in that copy was dated July 1866 with a note that "his [Simms's] name & that date in it."[7] This inscription is useful in narrowing the publication date of the volume.

Simms's counsel was heeded regarding the value of Hammond's papers. The James Henry Hammond Papers, Hammond-Bryan-Cumming Collection, and papers of other family members survive as a rich archive of the history of South Carolina and the South. First preserved by Hammond, his friends and supporters, then by family members and descendants, those collections are now entrusted to public institutions to preserve and make them available for study. The Library of Congress, South Caroliniana Library, and Southern Historical Collection at the University of North Carolina contain the majority of Hammond and Hammond-related collections. The major collections have been microfilmed and are available in published microform editions.[8]

Several published documentary editions contain Hammond's correspondence and diaries. Carol K. Rothrock Bleser's *Secret and Sacred* edition of Hammond's private diaries and her *Hammonds of Redcliffe* edited letters have demonstrated the value of Hammond's papers. Drew Gilpin Faust comprehended their breadth and depth to write an authoritative biography, *James Henry Hammond and the Old South: A Design for Mastery* and *A Sacred Circle: The Dilemma of the Intellectual in the Old South, 1840-1860*.[9]

A Measure of the Man

James Henry Hammond had a mercurial personality. Intellectually gifted and omnivorous in his interests, he struggled unsuccessfully to curb his appetites for wealth, public display, fame, and sexual license. His "design for mastery" was foremost a hopeless struggle for self-mastery. Simms once told his friend that "Were you as rarely good as you are rarely endowed, you would be the one of the most perfect men living" (*Letters* 1: cxii). To this lack of self-control Hammond added a near-obsession to record on paper every aspect of his life and personality. In his introduction to the 1978 edition of *Selections* Clyde Wilson sought to give a context to Hammond's excesses and to rescue him from becoming a stereotype:

Like any other man of strong intelligence, physical vigor, ambition, and sensitivity, Hammond suffered bouts of melancholy, indolence, self-pity, discouragement, indecisiveness, and lust. That his bouts are better documented than those of most of us does not necessarily prove anything in particular about Hammond or about his society — except that they were human. (xii)

Hammond or his heirs concealed some of the most revealing and embarrassing episodes in the man's life by redacting his most personal diaries. However, the obvious sparseness of these redactions suggests that just as his ego and sense of his place in history drove Hammond to document even his most foolish acts, that same self-regard prevented him from censoring those incriminating documents. What might he bother to conceal when he indifferently doctored his "secret & sacred" account of his sexual dalliances with his teen-age nieces and his liaisons with Sally and Louisa Johnson, a mother and daughter enslaved at Redcliffe?[10]

Those episodes damaged Hammond's political career and family life. In addition, they undermined — at least for modern readers — many of his publicly-expressed views on society and culture. Perhaps the most glaring discrepancies between his public expressions and his private behavior related to the subject of sexual relations between enslaved women and their white owners. Sally Johnson and her daughter Louisa Johnson were acknowledged concubines of Hammond and his sons. He had purchased the mother and her two-year-old daughter in 1838. They both bore enslaved Hammond-fathered offspring. Henderson Johnson, his enslaved son by Sally Johnson, was fourteen years of age in 1856 (Faust, *Hammond* 317-18). His liaison with Sally was underway when Hammond asserted in a public letter to Thomas Clarkson that "some intercourse of the sort does take place. Its character and extent, however, are grossly and atrociously exaggerated. No authority divine or human has yet been found sufficient to arrest all such irregularities among men. But it is a known fact, that they are perpetrated here, for the most part, in the cities. Very few mulattoes are reared on our plantations" (136-37). He continued his remarks: "it is well known that this intercourse is regarded in our society as highly disreputable. If carried on habitually it seriously affects a man's standing, so far as it is known; and he who takes a colored mistress — with rare and extraordinary exceptions — loses caste at once" (ibid.). As Wilson suggested, few people can truthfully claim that their private lives and public utterances seamlessly complement one another. Likewise, Hammond's hypocrisies may have been no greater than those of most men. Yet he documented his own so well that he has become an easy example of the vices that contemporaneous abolitionists and later generations of historians have ascribed to southern slaveholders.

The 1866 Edition

The contents of *Selections* conform to Hammond's undated draft outline. However, the final arrangements for its 1866 publication remain unknown. Whether Simms or Hammond's sons had signed the publishing agreement and prepared the printer's copy text is also unknown. Perhaps Catherine Hammond or her son-in-law James Gregg was an active agent in New York City on behalf of the project. Harry Hammond had some role in the publication; for, he added a biographical essay on his father and began it with the statement,

> at a period when the entire obliteration of everything at the South seemed imminent and inevitable, these papers were hurriedly sent to the publishers in the hope of preserving some trace of what had been. One hundred copies were printed without preface, note, comment or correction. To remedy in part, these defects, the following sketch has been prepared for insertion in these volumes. (preface)

Hammond then summarized his father's life and highlighted some features of each document in the book. He characterized him as an industrious, successful planter who was attentive to the physical and spiritual needs of his slaves:

> Lightly tasked, well clothed, well fed, their lives and persons protected, their sufferings alleviated by the kindest care, their domestic affections cherished with conscientious delicacy, a church built for them, Christian preaching with religious instruction in a Sunday School furnished, it would have been difficult to find a happier or more progressive body of agricultural laborers with greater local attachments, more trusting in, and trusted by those they worked for, than the slaves on his plantations. (ibid.)

Edward Spann Hammond's apparent ignorance of decisions regarding the book and, indeed, its publication date strikes a note of confusion on his part. On 13 November 1866, the second anniversary of his father's death and five months or more after *Selections* was published, he wrote to his mother his ideas for a book of his father's writings:

> While the great mass catch only at floating paragraphs in daily papers, there are great minds in their closets eager for the original and profound. These are the men that must soon be brought conspicuously before our people. It is those who would welcome a publication of Father's works, and would set store upon them if they possess the merit which he and we have

always thought they possessed, and which has been accorded to them universally when an opinion upon them has been expressed. I would therefore suggest that steps be taken to have a carefully corrected edition. Of considerable size, with picture and a brief biographical sketch, published at an early day. I have but little doubt that so far from its costing any thing, that several of the first publishing houses of the country would readily undertake it and pay to the family a percentage on every copy sold, or a handsome sum for the edition, for the privilege of making the publication.... I would suggest that Uncle M[arcellus] and Mr. Simms be consulted before doing any thing. (Bleser, *Hammonds* 155)

Living in Lynchburg, Virginia, E. Spann had perhaps not been kept up to date on efforts to publish *Selections*. By 1868 he had located and sent to Simms a copy of the work inscribed to him and dated July 1866. In three years he had not seen his father's letters that Simms had returned to the family in 1865 because his brother Harry had not shared them. E. Spann's apparent isolation might explain his post-publication remarks on its inclusions and omissions:

Among Father's writings I must confess I fail to find the merit I hoped for in the first article in the book. A sentence here and there might be saved but the bulk of it seems to me dross to his other writings. There are some fine short passages in Anti-Debt and the Institute Speech. The last paragraph of the College Address is perhaps the finest he ever wrote. The last 10 lines of the Kansas speech nearly equal it in its prophetic solemnity. The exhortation in the Calhoun and Barnwell addresses are very fine—classic and polished—while the character in the former is intense in its vigor and thoroughness. (Bleser, *Hammonds* 157)

Selections contains eleven speeches and public letters. The earliest is from 7 July 1834, and the last is dated 21 May 1860. All had been published in some form during Hammond's lifetime, usually soon after they were written or uttered. A few were issued in more than one edition. Collected in a single anthology, they provided a primer to the political tenets and cultural values of the antebellum South, beginning with nullification and state sovereignty in the wake of the Compromise of 1833 and concluding with a Senate speech in May 1860 that reflected upon the failed promises of the Compromise of 1850. Clyde Wilson's introduction and textual endnotes to his 1978 edition elaborated the contexts of the items in the volume. These notes are reproduced in this Simms Initiatives edition. However, the 1978 edition lacked bibliographical information on some of the more significant selections. This new introduction adds to the textual information in that earlier edition. Some other facsimile editions of *Selections* have been published in the twentieth century. It was copied in microfiche by Lost Cause Press in 1976 and reprinted in a cloth-bound facsimile in 1985 by Reprint Company of Spartanburg, South Carolina. The Hathi Trust Digital Library Record 000407865 has made available online copies of the 1866 edition housed in the libraries of Harvard University, Library of Congress, University of Michigan, and New York Public Library. An inscription in the Harvard Library copy reads "Gift of Harry Hammond, Beech Island, So. Carolina Ap. 11. 81." One of the South Caroliniana Library's copies was owned by Simms and later by his granddaughter, the author and editor Mary Simms Oliphant.

Speeches and Essays

The first item in *Selections* was "Report at a Meeting of the State Rights and Free Trade Party of Barnwell ... July 7th, 1834." This address had its proximate context as a response to the June 1834 South Carolina Court of Appeals decision in the case of McCrady v. Hunt, the "test oath controversy." The decision upheld a lower court ruling that the state's 1833 oath of allegiance was unconstitutional. The Compromise of 1833 had defused the confrontation between South Carolina and the federal government respecting the Force Act of 1832 and the state's Ordinance of Nullification. In the aftermath of the controversy the state had required officeholders to take an oath that affirmed state sovereignty. Hammond was twenty seven years of age when he delivered this speech to the Barnwell District State Rights and Free Trade Party members. The Barnwell speech placed Hammond among the nullifier party allied with John C. Calhoun. It demonstrated his mastery of the constitutional and political issues involved in the crisis and his ability to express them in a clear, convincing manner. In October 1834 he was elected to the United States House of Representatives, his first elected office and the start of his political career on the national stage. Drew Faust observed, "It is significant that Hammond chose this as the first important statement of his political career when he was considering a collection of his works. In accordance with his wishes, it appears as the first item in the posthumous compilation of his works" (*James Henry Hammond* 154, n31).

Hammond's 1 February 1836, "Speech on the Justice of Receiving Petitions for the Abolition of Slavery in the District of Columbia" was one of his last acts in the Twenty-fourth Congress. On 26 February 1836 he resigned his seat for health reasons. This speech aligned Hammond with Calhoun in opposition to Representative Henry Laurens Pinckney on the issue of how Congress should respond to growing numbers of petitions from organizations and individuals seeking to abolish slavery. In the House Pinckney instituted a policy called the "gag rule" in which abolition petitions were immediately tabled without discussion. The conflict was ostensibly a narrow one about House rules of procedure. However, Hammond and Calhoun recognized that the gag rule was inadequate to deter agitation in Congress. For, if the House had the power to table a petition it could later take it up from the table for consideration. Their position was that Congress had no authority whatsoever to receive these petitions or to take any action whatsoever upon them.

Hammond expostulated on the beneficial character of southern slavery. He contrasted the stabilizing role of slavery in human society with the chaotic consequences of abolition in the British West Indies and of unbridled industrial capitalism in Great Britain, the chief source of anti-slavery agitation during the 1830s. In addition to its publication in the *Congressional Globe*, Hammond's speech was published in pamphlet form as *Remarks of Mr. Hammond, of South Carolina, on the Question of Receiving Petitions for the Abolition of Slavery in the District of Columbia*.

Hammond's governor's messages of November 1843 and 1844 to the South Carolina General Assembly ranged widely in the number and variety of his recommendations for changes in the organization and operation of state government. In 1843 he recommended reorganization of state government by consolidating state offices in Columbia to obviate the "dual executive" maintenance of duplicate treasurer, state attorney, and secretary of state offices in Charleston. He also proposed eliminating the state surveyor general's post and permitting local districts to maintain their own land records. In both messages Hammond — a former teacher and a teacher's son — sought to strengthen public education by establishing state-funded academies in each election district. The state system would provide uniform standards and funding: "Every dollar which can be spared from the absolute want of the State, should be first offered to this great cause" (71). Wilson observed that Hammond's messages demonstrate that "the antebellum South Carolina ethos was not pervasively hostile to progress.... Nor do these messages, closely read, confirm the portrait of Hammond the haughty aristocrat. They exhibit as sincere an interest in the welfare of all citizens as could be found anywhere at the time" (xviii).

Ninety-eight of the 368 pages in *Selections* were devoted to defending African American slavery in principle and practice. As such, these were the most frequently reprinted and widely distributed of Hammond's public pronouncements. His 21 June 1844 public letter to Reverend Thomas Brown of Glasgow framed part of its argument on his governor's pardon of John L. Brown, who had aided his enslaved mistress to escape from her owner. Brown's conviction and death sentence for slave stealing had become an international *cause célèbre*, eliciting appeals for clemency from British abolition societies. The letter was published in pamphlet form as *Letter of His Excellency Governor Hammond to the Free Church of Glasgow, on the Subject of Slavery*.[11]

His letters to Thomas Clarkson, dated 28 January and 24 March 1845 constituted a review of the history and present state of slavery in the American South, a defense of that institution from attacks by British and northern abolition societies, plus a review of biblical and constitutional justifications for slavery in human society. The author sought to demonstrate that slavery-based societies promoted stability and offered benefits to all classes in these societies. He criticized industrial capitalism in Great Britain and in the North because that system promoted conflict between social and economic classes unlike the natural, close-knit relationships between slaves and owners in the South. Turmoil in capitalist societies engendered reform movements — temperance, women's rights, workers' movements — that were anathema in the South. He wrote, "We have been so irreverent as to laugh at Mormonism and Millerism, which have created such commotions farther North; and modern prophets have no honor in our country. Shakers, Rappists, Dunkers, Socialists, Fourierists and the like keep themselves afar off" (134).

Three pamphlet editions of Hammond's letters to Clarkson have been identified: *Two Letters on Slavery in the United States: Addressed to Thomas Clarkson, Esq. by J.H. Hammond*; *Gov. Hammond's Letters on Southern Slavery: Addressed to Thomas Clarkson, the English Abolitionist*; and *Cartas del Gobernador Hammond [sobre la esclavitud del Sur, dirigidas a Thomas Clarkson]*. The letters were also included in the influential anthology *The Pro-Slavery Argument: As maintained by the Most Distinguished Writers of the Southern States Containing the Several Essays, on the Subject, of Chancellor Harper, Governor Hammond, Dr. Sim[m]s, and Professor Dew*.

Hammond's "Oration Delivered before the Two Societies of the South Carolina College, 4th of Dec., 1849" extolled education as the means for developing moral beings and good citizens, not simply as a means for training individuals to enter professions. An excerpt was published as "Intellectual Power" in Evert A. and George L. Duyckinck's *Cyclopedia of American Literature: Embracing Personal and Critical Notices of Authors, and Selections from their Writings*.

John Caldwell Calhoun died in Washington, DC, on 31 March 1850 and was interred in Charleston's Saint Philip's Churchyard on 26 April 1850. Testimonials, orations, and plans to create monuments to the deceased statesman's memory continued for several years after his death. Commemorative services gave politicians and political parties opportunities to appropriate Calhoun's life and views to their own uses. At seventy pages, Hammond's oration is the lengthiest item in *Selections*. Hammond examined the man's political career, demonstrating that Calhoun's views on the South and the nation had evolved from his youthful support of the Union and the tariff system that proved so destructive to southern planters. The longtime editor of *The Papers of John C. Calhoun*, Clyde Wilson observed that Hammond's oration was the "best concise account of Calhoun's career and also the best statement in brief compass of the history of antebellum American politics from the Carolina viewpoint" (xxi). It was published as *An Oration on the Life, Character and Services of John Caldwell Calhoun: Delivered on the 21st Nov., 1850, in Charleston, S.C. at the Request of the City Council* and a variant text was included among twenty five other orations and testimonials in *The Carolina Tribute to Calhoun*, edited by J. P. Thomas.

The "Speech on the Admission of Kansas ... March 4, 1858" ranged over issues of popular sovereignty and the powers of Congress to regulate the admission of territories to the Union. In it Hammond boasted that the South could survive as an independent nation if the Union were divided by secession. The speech is famous because it contained two statements for which Hammond is most remembered. His challenge to British and northern industrialists became a slogan for Southern nationalists: "What would happen if no cotton was furnished for three years? I will not stop to depict what every one can imagine, but this is certain: England would topple headlong and carry the whole civilized world with her save the South. No, you dare not make war on cotton. No power on earth dares to make war upon it. Cotton *is* king" (316-17). Hammond's second "quotable quote" was his expression of a "mud-sill" theory of human society:

> In all social systems there must be a class to do the menial duties, to perform the drudgery of life.... Such a class you must have, or you would not have the other class which leads progress, civilization, and refinement. It constitutes the very mud-sill of society and of political government; and you might as well attempt to build a house in the air, as to build either the one or the other, except on this mud-sill. (318)

The South's mud-sill was African American slavery; that of the North was "your whole hireling class of manual laborers and 'operatives,' as you call them" (319). According to Hammond, slaves in the South had been raised from African barbarism to the higher status of mud-sills while in the North white women and men were degraded from their natural dignity to the mud-sill class by economic and social oppression. The North's mud-sill was "galled by their degradation" but, despite their misery, possessed the power of the ballot box. When they discovered their power, they would revolutionize the North as thoroughly as abolitionists sought to revolutionize the South (320).

The *Congressional Globe* version of this speech enjoyed considerable distribution in American newspapers. It was published in pamphlet form as *Speech of*

Hon. James H. Hammond, of South Carolina, on the Admission of Kansas, under the Lecompton Constitution. Delivered in the Senate, of the United States, March 4, 1858. Excerpts were published in *To the People of the South: Senator Hammond and the Tribune* by "George Michael Troup" and *Are Working Men Slaves?: The Question Discussed by Senators Hammond, [David C.] Broderick and [Henry] Wilson.*

Commenting on Hammond's 29 October 1858 speech at the Barnwell Court House, Wilson suggested that "The moderate tone of the speech lends itself to the suspicion that on the eve of secession the lifelong Southern nationalist had come to accept the Calhounian vision of a united South within the Union. Noteworthy is his desire to do justice to those Northerners who had withstood the anti-Southern currents of the time" (xxiii). Two pamphlet versions were published: *Speech of Hon. James H. Hammond, delivered at Barnwell C[ourt] H[ouse], October 29th, 1858* and *Speech of Hon. James Hammond, delivered at Barnwell Court House, October 29, 1858.*

Because Hammond resigned from the United States Senate on 11 November 1860 in the wake of Abraham Lincoln's presidential election, his "Speech on the Relations of the States, ... May 21, 1860" was one of his last public utterances on the sectional crisis. The immediate subject was another examination of the politics of admitting territories to the United States. Hammond disparaged "squatter sovereignty" which had turned Kansas Territory into a proxy war between pro- and antislavery settlers. He recapitulated his remarks on sovereignty and the defense of slavery with the telling observation that "The Senate is weary of it, the country is weary of it, and I, myself, am so weary of it that I have not listened or read, when it was the topic, for months" (365).

Hammond's weariness in 1860 did not afflict Simms or most of the Confederate South. The eleven states of the Confederacy and much of its white population asserted (and most must have believed) that the dissolution of the Union was the third American Revolution, one that recognized that revolution had already occurred and that it was time to recognize the fact. The North had revolutionized itself economically, culturally, and ideologically in ways that the South had not. The South had clung to a self-serving vision of the American Republic that bore little resemblance to the nation in 1860. Was the Civil War a "modern" nineteenth-century political revolution spurred on by the evolution of nationalism? Or, was it a rebellion driven by conservatives aiming to preserve an "original intention" version of the American Republic? No matter what lens was used to view the Civil War, by 1862, "weariness" was the pervasive squint. Simms and Hammond wrote each often during the last years of Hammond's life, exchanging lengthy letters on life, politics, and the pervasive "war news" that few could call optimistic by 1862.

Hammond never shook off his weariness with secession and war. He wasted declining energy to complain about Confederate taxes and confiscations and the ineptitude of Confederate generals on the battlefield. For Simms the weariness arrived in waves of misfortune in 1862: his infant daughter Hattie died in January 1862 and his beloved Woodlands Plantation was nearly destroyed by fire on 29 March 1862. The cause of the fire was never reported and may well have been an accident. Simms described the effects of the fire in letters to William Porcher Miles and Hammond, dated April 10, from "Woodlands in Ruins." With the assistance of his slaves he was able to save nearly all of his library and the manuscripts collections — his own writings and historical documents — and many of the house furnishings (*Letters* 4: 399-405).

"Woodlands in Ruins" concludes this introduction because it demonstrated Hammond's last act of benevolence to his life-long friend. Along with other friends of Simms, Hammond created a subscription fund to rebuild Woodlands. That effort was a gesture of support for the man who had stood by him for more than thirty years, defending his honor amid Hammond's dishonorable acts, and trumpeting Hammond's genius to the state and nation for those same decades. Despite the damage, Simms and his slaves saved most of the library, original and historical manuscripts, some furniture and household furnishings. On 10 April 1862 Simms wrote to Hammond lamenting the "Demonology" and misfortune that "haunts his steps & dogs his career, as tenaciously as ever the Furies clung to the heels of Orestes" (*Letters* 4: 402). Hammond and others lost little time starting a subscription to assist the author.

J. Dickson Bruns, David F. Jamison, George Sass, George A. Trenholm, William Gregg, and Hammond prepared a circular "to raise a purse to be placed at [Simms's] disposal."[12] By June they had raised $3,600 and a neighbor, John S. Jennings, had donated sufficient lumber from his nearby sawmill to enable Simms to begin rebuilding his home on a reduced scale. Simms publicly acknowledged these men's generous acts in a letter of 27 June 1862 published in the *Charleston Mercury* and *Daily Courier* of 8 July 1862. In it he boasted of the strength of his friendships and managed to express some of his characteristic optimism in the face of calamity (*Letters* 4: 409-12).

That optimism perished slowly but inevitably in the coming three years. James Henry Hammond died in November 1864. Three months later the rebuilt Woodlands was pillaged and destroyed by Union troops and stragglers on 18 February 1865. Columbia and Charleston had surrendered the previous day, and Columbia suffered a catastrophic fire on February 17-18. War weariness became desolation.

Notes

1. James Henry Hammond to William Gilmore Simms, 12 December 1861, James Henry Hammond Papers, Library of Congress, reel 238o, item 24798.

2. James Henry Hammond, undated, Hammond Papers, Library of Congress, reel 238p, item 25271.

3. Hammond to Simms, 18 February 1862, Library of Congress, reel 238o, item 24808.

4. *House Journal*, 25th Congress, 1st Session (Serial Set No. 285); *House Journal*, 24th Congress, 2nd Session (Serial Set No. 300); *Senate Journal*, 36th Congress, 1st Session and Special Session (Serial Set No. 1022); *Senate Journal*, 36th Congress, 2nd Session and 37th Congress, Special Session (Serial Set No. 1077).

5. *Congressional Globe*, 24th Congress, 1st Session, *Volume III*, 27-33; *Congressional Globe*, 24th Congress, 1st Session, *Volume III, Appendix*, 565-7; and *Register of Debates in Congress*, *Volume XI, Part 2*, 2492-500.

6. The *Congressional Globe*, 35th Congress, 1st Session, *Appendix*, 69-71, and *Congressional Globe*, 36th Congress, 1st Session, 1633, contain his Senate speeches and remarks.

7. Simms to Marcellus C.M. Hammond, 28 March 1868, *Letters*, 5: 121, n.57; E. Spann Hammond to M.C.M. Hammond, 2 March 1868, Bleser, ed., *Hammonds of Redcliffe*, 156.

8. Kenneth M. Stampp, ed., *Records of Ante-bellum Southern Plantations from the Revolution through the Civil War. Series A, Selections from the South Caroliniana Library, University of South Carolina* (Frederick, MD: University Publications of America, 1985) contains 15 reels of Hammond family material. Reels 13-15 include Hammond plantation journals and scrapbooks from the Library of Congress. Ira Berlin and others, eds., *Records of Southern Plantations from Emancipation to the Great Migration. Series C, Selections from the South Caroliniana Library, University of South Carolina* (Bethesda, MD: UPA Collection from LexisNexis, 2004), Part One contains 22 reels of Hammond family material from six collections. The James Henry Hammond Papers, 1774-1875, Library of Congress Collection MSS24695, fill 20 reels of microfilm available for purchase.

9. Carol Bleser, editor, *The Hammonds of Redcliffe* (New York: Oxford UP, 1981; Columbia: U of South Carolina P, 1997) and *Secret and Sacred: The Diaries of James Henry Hammond, A Southern Slaveholder* (New York: Oxford UP, 1988; Columbia: U of South Carolina P, 1997); *The Papers of John C. Calhoun*, 28 volumes, edited by Robert L. Meriwether and others (Columbia: U of South Carolina P, 1959-2003); *The Letters of William Gilmore Simms*, 6 volumes, edited by Mary C. Simms Oliphant *et al* (Columbia: U of South Carolina P, 1952-2012); James F. Jameson, ed., "Letters on the Nullification Movement in South Carolina, 1830-1834," *American Historical Review* 6, no. 4 (July 1901): 736-52 all contain Hammond correspondence. Drew Gilpin Faust, *A Sacred Circle: The Dilemma of the Intellectual in the Old South, 1840-1860* (Baltimore, MD: Johns Hopkins UP, 1977); *James Henry Hammond and the Old South: A Design for Mastery* (Baton Rouge: Louisiana State UP, 1982).

10. Bleser, ed., *Secret and Sacred*, 169 (Hamptons), 17-9, 231, 234 (Johnsons); Bleser, ed., *Hammonds of Redcliffe*, 9-10, 29-33 (Hamptons), 10-11 (Johnsons); Faust, *James Henry Hammond*, 241-5, 288-91, 302, 313 (Hamptons), 85-8, 303, 315-20 (Johnsons).

11. Recent scholarship on the Brown case includes Betty DeRamus, *Freedom by Any Means: True Stories of Cunning and Courage on the Underground Railroad* (New York: Atria Books, 2009), "Romeo Must Live," 51-67; and Caleb W. McDaniel, "The Case of John L. Brown: Slavery, Sex, South Carolina, and the Whispering Gallery of Transatlantic Abolition," unpublished essay presented at "Civil War — Global Conflict," Carolina Lowcountry and Atlantic World Conference, College of Charleston, 4 March 2011 (http://scholarship.rice.edu/handle/1911/37261, accessed 4 July 2013).

12. J. Dickson Bruns to Hammond, 20 April 1862, Hammond Papers, Library of Congress, reel 238o, item 24822-3.

Works Cited

Bleser, Carol, ed. *The Hammonds of Redcliffe*. New York: Oxford UP, 1981; Columbia: U of South Carolina P, 1997.

———, ed. *Secret and Sacred: The Diaries of James Henry Hammond, A Southern Slaveholder*. New York: Oxford UP, 1988; Columbia: U of South Carolina P, 1997.

Faust, Drew Gilpin. *James Henry Hammond and the Old South: A Design for Mastery*. Baton Rouge: Louisiana State UP, 1982.

Hammond, James Henry. *An Oration, Delivered at Capt. Lorick's, in Lexington District, S.C. on the Fifth of July, 1830*. Columbia: Printed at the Times & Gazette Office, 1830.

———. *Remarks of Mr. Hammond, of South Carolina, on the Question of Receiving Petitions for the Abolition of Slavery in the District of Columbia*. Washington, DC: D. Green, [1836].

———. "Overseers." *Carolina Planter* 1.2 (August 1844): 25-30.

———. *Letter of His Excellency Governor Hammond to the Free Church of Glasgow, on the Subject of Slavery*. Columbia: A.H. Pemberton, 1844.

———. *Two Letters on Slavery in the United States: Addressed to Thomas Clarkson, Esq. by J.H. Hammond*. Columbia: Allen, McCarter, 1845.

———. *Gov. Hammond's Letters on Southern Slavery: Addressed to Thomas Clarkson, the English Abolitionist*. Charleston: Walker & Burke, 1845.

———. *Cartas del Gobernador Hammond [sobre la esclavitud del Sur, dirigidas a Thomas Clarkson]*. New Orleans, 1845.

———. *An Oration on the Life, Character and Services of John Caldwell Calhoun: Delivered on the 21st Nov., 1850, in Charleston, S.C. at the Request of the City Council*. Charleston: Walker & James, 1850 and a variant text in *The Carolina Tribute to Calhoun*, edited by J.P. Thomas (Columbia, SC: Richard L. Bryan, 1857), 283-325.

———. *The Pro-Slavery Argument: As maintained by the Most Distinguished Writers of the Southern States Containing the Several Essays, on the Subject, of Chancellor Harper, Governor Hammond, Dr. Sim[m]s, and Professor Dew*. Philadelphia: Lippincott, Grambo, & Co., 1853.

———. *Marl. A Letter Addressed to the Agricultural Society of Jefferson County, Georgia*. Augusta: Printed by J. McCafferty, 1846.

———. "Anniversary Oration, of the State Agricultural Society of South Carolina. . . . 25th November, 1841," in *Proceedings of the Agricultural Convention of the State of South Carolina from 1839 to 1845 Inclusive* (Columbia: Summer and Carroll, 1846), 175-92.

——. *The Railroad Mania and A Review of the Bank of the State of South-Carolina: A Series of Essays by Anti-Debt*. Charleston, SC: Burges, James & Paxton, 1848, originally published in the *Charleston Mercury*.

——. *The North and the South: A Review of the Lecture on the Same Subject, delivered by Mr. Elwood Fisher, before the Young Men's Mercantile Association, of Cincinnati, Ohio*. Charleston: Printed by James S. Burges, 1849. "Reprinted from the *Southern Quarterly Review* July 1849."

——. *Speech of Hon. James H. Hammond, of South Carolina, on the Admission of Kansas, under the Lecompton Constitution. Delivered in the Senate, of the United States, March 4, 1858*. Washington: Lemuel Towers, 1858.

——. *Speech of Hon. James H. Hammond, delivered at Barnwell C[ourt] H[ouse], October 29th, 1858*. Charleston: Walker & Evans, 1858 and Washington [DC]: Henry Polkinghorn, 1858.

——. *The Regina Coeli: Correspondence between the Hon. James H. Hammond and John H.B. Latrobe*. Baltimore: Printed by J.D. Toy, 1858 on the African slave trade originally published in the *Baltimore American*, 20 December 1858, pp. 39-47.

——. *To the People of the South: Senator Hammond and the Tribune*. Charleston: Evans & Cogswell, 1860 by "George Michael Troup."

——. *Are Working Men Slaves?: The Question Discussed by Senators Hammond, [David C.] Broderick and [Henry] Wilson*. Washington: Buell & Blanchard, 1860.

——. *Cyclopedia of American Literature: Embracing Personal and Critical Notices of Authors, and Selections from their Writings*. 2 vols. Philadelphia: Wm. Butler & Co., 1875. 2: 263-65.

——. *Selections from the Letters and Speeches of James Henry Hammond*. Ed. Clyde N. Wilson. Columbia, SC: Southern Studies Program, 1978, a facsimile reprint of the 1866 edition published by John F. Trow & Co., New York City.

Simms, William Gilmore. *The Letters of William Gilmore Simms*. Ed. Mary C. Simms Oliphant et al. 6 vols. Columbia: U of South Carolina P, 1952-2012.

Tucker, Robert Cinnamond. "James Henry Hammond, South Carolinian." University of North Carolina, doctoral dissertation 1958.

SELECTIONS

FROM THE

LETTERS AND SPEECHES

OF THE

HON. JAMES H. HAMMOND,

OF SOUTH CAROLINA.

With An Introduction And Notes

By Clyde N. Wilson

Published for the Southern Studies Program
University of South Carolina

THE REPRINT COMPANY, PUBLISHERS
SPARTANBURG, SOUTH CAROLINA
1978

CONTENTS

Acknowledgments ix
Introduction xi
Sketch of James Henry Hammond by "H.H."
following page xxv
Selections from the Letters and Speeches of the
  Hon. James H. Hammond, of South Carolina
Explanatory Notes 369
Index 385

ACKNOWLEDGMENTS

This reprint of a rare volume of South Caroliniana, *Selections from the Letters and Speeches of the Hon. James H. Hammond, of South Carolina*, was made possible by a grant from the Norris Foundation to the Southern Studies Program of the University of South Carolina. For her interest in the volume and her aid in making possible its publication, we are particularly indebted to Mrs. Mary C. Simms Oliphant. Mr. Alexander Moore, a graduate student in the Southern Studies Program, provided assistance in the preparation of the notes and index. For other help we should like to thank Mr. E. L. Inabinett, Director of the South Caroliniana Library, and Mr. Charles E. Lee, State Archivist of South Carolina.

C.N.W.
J.B.M.

INTRODUCTION

Posterity has not been kind to James Henry Hammond, a fate he was fully capable of anticipating. To those nineteenth-century historians who took their cue from the winning side in the sectional conflicts in which he engaged he was a prime example of the Southern grandee—that arrogant, moody, nouveau riche, rash, hypersensitive class of men who, according to the dominant political mythology of the nineteenth century, brought down well-deserved destruction upon themselves by their malevolent efforts to destroy the American republic. More recently derogatory emphasis has shifted from the externals of his career to the interior. One of the leading historians of the antebellum South has put Hammond on the couch, portraying him as "the Hamlet of the Old South"— vain, indecisive, lazy, in a word: neurotic.[1]

Whatever element of truth these characterizations may contain, both depend ultimately on the standpoint of the observer—they are matters of perspective. Sir Herbert Butterfield has reminded us that moral judgments are treacherous for historians—that what we think are moral judgments are really aesthetic judgments, that is, statements of taste or preference.[2] The first characterization represents a conqueror's taste, and if convention insists that we find the Old South unlovely to behold, then it follows that its spokesmen must be ugly, too.

As for the psychopathological approach, it is one that Hammond lent himself to and is a risk that must be run by any man who combines (as Hammond did) a capacity for self-analysis, a talent for vivid self-expression, and the habit of putting his intimate thoughts on paper.[3] Like any other man of strong intelligence, physical vigor, ambition, and sensitivity, Hammond suffered bouts of melancholy, indolence, self-pity, discouragement, indecisiveness, and lust. That his bouts are better documented than those of most of us does not *necessarily* prove anything in particular about Hammond or about his society—except that they were human.

So far as the public man revealed by this collection of papers is concerned, Hammond's most obvious characteristic was a realistic and independent intelligence. Whatever the subject or the occasion, Hammond had the capacity to get to first principles and to face inexpedient facts, to size up his enemy without wishful thinking. The frankness and realism with which he faced the slavery conflict is impressive. In his speech on the abolition petitions we find him remarking to the House of Representatives: "It is indeed natural that a people not owning slaves should entertain a strong aversion to domestic servitude." And a little further on: ". . . I am not one of those who permits himself to trust that the conflict will be at an end. No, sir, we shall have to meet it elsewhere." It is not difficult to agree with his Carolina political opponent Benjamin F. Perry that Hammond's "views were those of a statesman and not a mere politician."[4]

His versatile intelligence did not confine itself to the political. Hammond's oration before the two literary societies of South Carolina College, an erudite attack on utilitarianism and materialism, may startle those who normally think of the Old South as an intellectual desert.

INTRODUCTION   xiii

The only thing lacking in the selection here reprinted for a display of Hammond's full range is one of his essays or orations on agriculture. Perhaps the best example is his address in 1849 at the first state fair of South Carolina, which combines a celebration of the soil with a candid examination of the socioeconomic prospects of the state.[5] But the compiler of *Selections from the Letters and Speeches of the Hon. James H. Hammond, of South Carolina* decided, wisely no doubt, that the oration was just a bit too narrow in interest for a collection that was designed to include the cream of Hammond's public papers.[6]

And who was this judicious compiler?

The facts of the original editing and publication of this volume are not certain, but there is good reason to believe that William Gilmore Simms, prolific man of letters and close friend of Hammond, was involved. In a letter of 1862 to John Reuben Thompson, the Richmond editor, Simms proposed publication of a volume of Hammond's papers as part of a projected "Library of the Confederate States" and commented, "I am now revising Hammond's Essays & Speeches for the press." The format of the volume in hand resembled the format Simms planned for the abortive patriotic library described in that letter.[7]

Early in 1865, two months after Hammond's death, Simms wrote to Hammond's son Harry. (Harry Hammond was the "H. H." whose initials were affixed to the biographical sketch which accompanied this volume.) He would gladly assist in collecting good examples of James H. Hammond's personal correspondence, Simms said, "whenever the family shall deem it a proper time to prepare an additional volume." In regard to such private papers, Simms added that "we should reserve his correspondence for some future volume."[8] From the evidence of these two letters of Simms it seems reasonable to assume that the volume in hand was compiled by him during the war. Be that as it may, the book appeared in 1866 with the imprint of John F. Trow and Company of New York in an edition of only 100 copies, according to Harry Hammond's introductory sketch. That untitled, undated sketch, obviously written and printed later than the manufacture of the volume itself, was tipped into some copies at the end, into others immediately preceding the text (where it has been placed in this reprint). It does little to clarify the circumstances of the editing and publishing of the volume, informing us only that "at a period when the entire obliteration of everything at the South seemed imminent and inevitable, these papers were hurriedly sent to the publishers in the hope of preserving some trace of what had been." Ironically, a work conceived as providing a hallowed text for an independent South ended as a tattered relic of a Lost Cause, preserved on the sufferance of a Northern publisher.

Making allowance for its filial origins, Harry Hammond's sketch is an adequate if too brief account of his father's public career. Clearly James Henry Hammond would have risen to the top wherever fate had placed him, although two factors aided his ascent. One was the openness of the Carolina society of his time to talent. The sketch does not mention, for instance, that while still in his early twenties Hammond, the son of a schoolteacher who had immigrated from Massachusetts, was entrusted by men like John C. Calhoun, Robert Y. Hayne, and James Hamilton, Jr., with the editorship of their party newspaper in the capital city and then with key appointments in the militia. The other factor that assisted his rise was a good marriage which laid the basis for his fortune, though Hammond's talent and energy improved upon that good luck.

INTRODUCTION xv

As it was, Hammond filled capably every role provided by his society—planter, lawyer, editor, orator, scholar, militia leader, governor, representative, senator. One wishes that H. H. had rounded out the account of his father's accomplishments by mentioning the art collection and the library at Silver Bluff, the Hammond estate on Beech Island near Augusta. Of course, the son could not be expected to have mentioned the Hammond descendants who have provided useful members of the commonwealth down to the fourth generation.[9] And for different reasons he could not be expected to explore the less appealing side of the biography, the vanity and sexual indiscretions that have been treated by Clement Eaton and others. "Were you as rarely good as you are rarely endowed," Simms remarked to Hammond, "you would be one of the most perfect men living."[10]

The earliest paper selected for this collection, the report "at a meeting of the State Rights and Free Trade Party of Barnwell District . . . July 7th, 1834," written when Hammond was twenty-six, arose out of the "test oath" controversy. In the interest of a united front, the South Carolina General Assembly of 1833, confirming an act of the Nullification Convention of 1832, had required an oath of "true allegiance" to the state from all officeholders, as well as initiated a constitutional amendment requiring such an oath of all voters. The "test oath" was vigorously opposed by the "union party" within the state, and in the case of McCrady vs. Hunt, brought by a militia officer who refused to take the oath, a majority of the Court of Appeals ruled the provision unconstitutional. Hammond's paper is a formulation of the response of the "Nullifiers" to the Court. In our cynical age such position papers are considered merely tactical rationalizations, but in antebellum South Carolina arguments hashed out at public meetings and the resolutions and reports that ensued were an integral part of the process of forming democratic consensus. It often took physical courage as well as political dexterity to fight out such matters on the hustings.

In this paper Hammond chastizes the judiciary for exceeding its authority and intruding into the main issue of the nullification controversy, an issue which could only be decided by the people—that is, "whether . . . sovereignty, or the last power of decision in all civil and political questions, from which there can be no appeal, resides in the States, respectively, or in the Federal Government." In the course of his report Hammond made a distinction between society and government, giving the precedence to the former. To this theme he would return repeatedly. The paper indicates that the Nullifiers placed themselves squarely within the traditions of American republicanism. South Carolinians, as Hammond remarks in a later selection, were loyal to the union, but not blindly so. Having escaped "the divine right of Kings," they had no intention of submitting to "the divine right of Union."

The speech delivered in the U.S. House of Representatives in 1836 on the abolition petitions concerned the question of whether abolitionism should be ignored or should be met at the threshold. In 1836 conventional politicians, North and South, deprecated the agitation of the slavery issue, apparently on the theory that if the agitation were ignored it would go away. Such conventional politicians contended that the proper response to the flood of abolitionist petitions that suddenly inundated the Congress in the early thirties was to receive and immediately table them. To Hammond, speaking for the predominant South Carolina opinion, this response was inadequate. The petitions must be unequivocally rejected. What was at stake was non-negotiable—the survival of the South as a self-governing society. He was in no mood to minimize the size or significance of the threat. While a certain aversion to slavery was natural among people with different habits and traditions than the South's, Hammond remarked, that was not sufficient to explain the sudden appearance in the thirties of abolitionism. Rather, "other causes are at work. This excitement belongs to the spirit of the age." The new spirit, according to Hammond, was not related to the American Revolution, which he regarded as a part of the "war of intelligence against political oppression." Rather, a new egalitarianism had sprung from the French Revolution. "Since that period, man appears no longer to be the being that he was." Hammond is for the people, that self-governing community of independent citizens who carried out the American Revolution, but not for the mob, that "ignorant, uneducated, semi-barbarous mass which swarms and starves upon the face of Europe." Because the New World lacked any hereditary privileged class like the old, the Jacobinical spirit had here selected the slave-holding class as its most convenient target.

His two annual messages to the legislature while Governor perhaps display Hammond in his best light. The Governor in South Carolina had relatively little constitutional power but considerable influence and discretionary authority, since the legislature met for only about a month each year and local government was weak. As Governor, Hammond courageously took on the vested interest of the Bank of the State of South Carolina which was entangled in the affairs of the state in the same way the second Bank of the United States had been in national affairs a decade before. In this he was essentially a Jeffersonian Republican interested in minimizing public debt and in avoiding exploitation of the public treasury by private institutions, however plausibly they were presented as essential to the public welfare. His second major gubernatorial theme, education, also has a Jeffersonian ring. "Here [in education]," Hammond wrote, "indeed a liberal expenditure enriches and adorns, while a narrow economy impoverishes and degrades." He recommended publicly supported academies in each district of the state (as opposed to the private schools and public "poor schools" that then existed). Hammond lost both of his major battles, but as these two messages make clear, the antebellum South Carolina ethos was not pervasively hostile to progress. But the progress had to be of the South Carolinians' own choosing and in their own hands. Nor do these messages, closely read, confirm the portrait of Hammond the haughty aristocrat. They exhibit as sincere an interest in the welfare of all citizens as could be found anywhere at the time.

The letter to the Free Church of Glasgow and the two letters to Thomas Clarkson, most famous of the British abolitionists, all written while Hammond was Governor, constitute possibly the ultimate apologia for the slave system of the Old South. Calhoun, speaking for a generation cast in the mold of the republicanism of the Revolution and early national period, did not so much defend slavery as he defended the idea of an organic Southern community immune from outside political meddling. Hammond is clearly within that tradition, but has diversified his strategy to meet new developments. Unlike Calhoun, Hammond is willing to employ not only analysis and authority but description and comparison. Hammond is aware of the power of propaganda, the rise of a mass reading public in the urban society of the North and Europe. It was this audience that the abolitionists had addressed—an audience for which sentimental novels rather than classical orations provided the imagery of public discourse.

For such an audience it was necessary to paint pictures, and this Hammond did. The picture he drew was of Southern society as a patriarchy, of the plantation as family—"our patriarchal scheme of domestic servitude," a hierarchical order with an unequal distribution of rights and duties but incorporated for the welfare of the whole. The portrait was seldom drawn with more artistry and conviction than by Hammond.

By the use of irony he succeeded in good measure in turning the rhetorical tables on the abolitionists. They simply did not know what they were talking about, he argued. They were agitated not about slavery as it existed in the South but about what they imagined existed. Foreign abolitionists "in denouncing our domestic slavery, denounce a thing of which they know absolutely nothing—nay, which does not even exist." They had convinced themselves and sought to convince the world that slavery had made Southerners violent, lazy, sexually immoral, unprogressive, irreligious, and bad credit risks. In countering this onslaught Hammond admitted that slavery is an evil in the abstract. He did not hesitate to admit the existence of corporal punishment and occasional sexual exploitation. But he insisted upon rejecting the wholesale stereotype of a hellishly dark and evil South which had been, implicitly, counterpoised by the antislavery forces against an impossibly angelic "free" society. In so doing he made noteworthy (and perhaps still applicable) suggestions about the religious life of the South (pages 133–134), and he warned that the abolitionists have accumulated "a balance of invective which, with all our efforts, we shall not be able to liquidate much short of the era in which your [British] National debt will be paid."

As Hammond portrays them, the methods and goals of the abolitionists were simply not appropriate to the question at hand. In an ironic passage he argues that Clarkson, chiefly responsible for the British efforts to stamp out the slave trade, had actually increased the sum total of human misery. And the context of Hammond's argument makes clear a neglected aspect of the controversy. The abolitionist movement was an international movement, the center of which was coterminous with the center of British imperialism, a fact which made it doubly suspect to Americans. And, perhaps for idiosyncratic reasons, Hammond was unusually sensitive to the strong overtones of suppressed sexuality that suffused the propaganda of the abolitionists, a theme which he played upon effectively. "Such rage without betrays the fires within," he remarked.

His arguments against the abolitionists also told when he emphasized that the Southern form of slavery was, after all, merely one variation of universal hierarchy and servitude. "You think it a great 'crime' that we do not pay our slaves 'wages,' and on this account denounce us as 'robbers.'" This, said Hammond, was to give a status to the mere receiving of wages that was unjustified, for wages did not constitute freedom or prove that the toilers of industrial England or the coolie laborers of the Empire were any freer than Southern slaves. The emphasis only revealed how deeply the abolitionists were embroiled in "the prevailing vice and error of the age," bringing everything to the single standard of money. In this Hammond premeditated the most recent and most profound student of the antislavery movement, who can be interpreted as arguing that the abolitionists were not so much interested in abolishing human servitude and exploitation as they were in abolishing a particular form of servitude which had come to be regarded as archaic—a stance which provided a rationale for participating in other, more fashionable forms of exploitation.[11]

The oration delivered by Hammond at age forty-two before the two societies of South Carolina College goes a long way toward illuminating the best aspects of the particular synthesis of liberal and conservative values that made up the culture of the Old South. While giving a full and sincere praise to the material progress of the nineteenth century, Hammond entered a gentle demurrer to the spirit of that era. He reminded the flower of the youth of South Carolina that the accumulation of wealth and of technological mastery are results, not causes, results which depend ultimately upon the striving human spirit. The "energetic selfishness" of the utilitarian was insufficient even for material progress. This oration and the Plutarchian essay on Calhoun which follows show the extent to which the ancient classics permeated the Southern world-view.

The latter remains the best concise account of Calhoun's career and also the best statement in brief compass of the history of antebellum American politics from the Carolina viewpoint. The celebration of the greatest Carolinian once more displays Hammond's refusal to take the easy path around facts. He pointed out what to his generation was Calhoun's "superstitious" attachment to the Union, his lack of humor, and his carelessness in the construction of sentences. He stated that if Calhoun's early career were examined "with the sternness of the historian . . . we cannot fail to perceive that . . . his views, in many most important particulars, were essentially erroneous." To point this out was "due to truth, to history, and to him." Summing up Calhoun, Hammond found him, by the Carolina calculus, to be a progressive: a "merely negative and stolid conservatism did not at all suit the genius of Mr. Calhoun, which was essentially active and ever looking forward to the improvement of mankind."

The speech of March 4, 1858, on the Kansas question, was delivered three months after Hammond entered the Senate, at the height of the controversy over slavery in the territories when men came armed to Congress. This forthright statement of Southern nationalism is the source of two famous quotations, both of which underwent severe distortion on the political hustings. In his inventory of the assets of the South in contest with any potential enemy, one of the points Hammond touched upon was the role of its commodities in world commerce, staples for which the North and England were dependent upon the South. "No," Hammond declared, "you dare not make war on cotton. No power on earth dares to make war upon it. Cotton *is* king. Until lately [the panic of 1857] the Bank of England was king; but . . . the last power has been conquered." Hammond did not contend that cotton was the only or the greatest asset of the South, but merely the one to which its enemies, being men for whom the economic motive was uppermost, were vulnerable. The statement was more defensive than arrogantly assertive.

In this speech, too, Hammond made his "Mud-sill" remarks. Every society must be built on a mud-sill class, "a class to do the menial duties, to perform the drudgery of life," a class which the South had found in its slaves. The mud-sill class of the North was its "whole hireling class of manual laborers" who were "essentially slaves." The rising Republican party made effective use of this statement, portrayed as proof of the contempt of arrogant Southern grandees for the laboring men of the North. Read in context, the statement may be more reasonably seen as one of sympathetic alliance with the labor of the North. It is the capitalists that Hammond regards as his enemy and undertakes to insult. It is the capitalists to whom the peroration is directed, a peroration which, as H.H. suggests, might be the epitaph of the planter class. You capitalists of the North are demanding to seize the helm of the republic from the planters of the South who have thus far guided it, Hammond declared. You may well succeed. But reflect that, after seventy years, we will turn over to you a government strong, prosperous, and honorable. Will you be able to say as much when your turn comes to yield?

The speech at Barnwell Court House, October 29, 1858, while he was Senator, is designed to explain to Hammond's constituents the maneuverings of the previous session of Congress. It is a well-considered review of the position of the South at that point. To Hammond the explosive issue of slavery in the territories had arisen not out of the demands or requirements of the South but out of the demagogic party maneuverings of the North. The moderate tone of the speech lends itself to the suspicion that on the eve of secession the lifelong Southern nationalist had come to accept the Calhounian vision of a united South *within* the Union. Noteworthy is his desire to do justice to those Northerners who had withstood the anti-Southern currents of the time.

The last selection, a speech in the Senate seven months before the secession of South Carolina, is, like the first selection and the speech on Kansas, concerned with the question of sovereignty. Specifically at issue was power to prohibit slavery in the territories, for Southerners a complex constitutional question. Granted that Congress enjoyed the constitutional right to regulate the territories, only a sovereign people could create a state. Congress may admit states to the Union, but the creation of a state is an act of sovereignty that must be exercised by a given community of people, and it was only that people at or after the act of creation who could decide the question of slavery. So Hammond ends with the same question—Where does the ultimate allegiance of the American lie?—and the same answer that he began with—Sovereignty in America was that organic body of the people of a state in plenary convention assembled.

The sentiments and concerns recorded here may be remote from today. Yet given the range, versatility, and subtlety of the intellect displayed by these papers, it is perhaps not too much to assert that no student of antebellum American intellectual life can safely disregard James Henry Hammond. At the least their republication can be an occasion to re-examine the individuality here represented and the larger Southern society reflected in it—a society which, centering in Hammond's South Carolina after the 1820's, still remains to be fully comprehended despite all the attention that has been devoted to it.

NOTES

[1] Clement Eaton, *The Mind of the Old South* (Baton Rouge: Louisiana State University Press, c. 1964), pp. 21–42.

[2] Sir Herbert Butterfield, "Moral Judgments in History," reprinted in Hans Meyerhoff, ed., *The Philosophy of Hitory in Our Time* (Garden City, N.Y.: Doubleday & Co., Inc., c. 1959), pp. 237–238.

[3] Hammond is among the best-documented personalities of the Old South. The James Henry Hammond Papers at the South Caroliniana Library of the University of South Carolina contain an estimated 4,720 items and 106 manuscript volumes. The Library of Congress's James Henry Hammond Papers are described as being

contained in 17 boxes and 33 volumes. There are also significant Hammond documents in other collections in these depositories and in other depositories such as the Southern Historical Collection of the University of North Carolina and the College of William and Mary. This body of manuscript material includes personal correspondence, diaries, plantation journals, business papers, and scrapbooks.

[4] Benjamin F. Perry, *Reminiscences of Public Men* (Philadelphia: John D. Avil & Co., 1883), p. 107.

[5] James Henry Hammond, *An Address Delivered Before the South-Carolina Institute at Its First Annual Fair, on the 20th November 1849* (Charleston: Walker and James, 1849).

[6] Robert Cinnamond Tucker, "James Henry Hammond, South Carolinian" (Doctoral dissertation: University of North Carolina, 1958), contains a bibliography of Hammond's published works and is the best available general account of his life.

[7] Simms to Thompson, January 16, 1862, typescript in possession of Mrs. Mary C. Simms Oliphant. To be published in the forthcoming Volume 6 of Mary C. Simms Oliphant, Alfred Taylor Odell, and T. C. Duncan Eaves, eds., *The Letters of William Gilmore Simms*, 5 vols. to date (Columbia: University of South Carolina Press, 1952–1956).

[8] Simms to Harry Hammond, January 25, 1865, in *The Letters of William Gilmore Simms*, vol. 4, pp. 482–483. (ALS in the Hammond, Bryan, Cumming Papers, South Caroliniana Library.)

[9] Hammond's descendants in each generation have included persons who have achieved prominence, down to his great-grandson, John Shaw Billings, who was editorial director of Time-Life, Inc.

[10] Quoted in *The Letters of William Gilmore Simms*, vol. 1, p. cxii.

[11] See David Brion Davis, *The Problem of Slavery in the Age of Revolution, 1770–1824* (Ithaca, N.Y., and London: Cornell University Press, c. 1975), p. 251.

At a period when the entire obliteration of everything at the South seemed imminent and inevitable, these papers were hurriedly sent to the publishers in the hope of preserving some trace of what had been. One hundred copies were printed without preface, note, comment or correction. To remedy in part these defects, the following sketch has been prepared for insertion in these volumes.

JAMES HENRY HAMMOND was born in the District of Newberry, S. C., November 15, 1807. His father was the sixth in descent from William Hammond, of London, whose son, Benjamin, came to Massachusetts in 1634. The family resided in that State, until the father of the subject of this sketch, moved to South Carolina in 1803. There he married Catharine Fox Spann of Edgefield, and became Professor of Languages in the South Carolina College in 1805. Young Hammond graduated with distinction from this college in 1825, when, under the presidency of Thomas Cooper, it was one of the foremost institutions of learning in America. He was admitted to the bar in 1828, and entered at once upon a lucrative practice of the law. In 1831 he married Catherine Fitzsimons, daughter of Christopher Fitzsimons, who had accumulated a fortune in Charleston, then one of the chief centres of commerce in the United States. They took up their residence on the Silver Bluff plantation, on the left bank of the Savannah River. His life was that of a Southern planter. Living in the solitude of the open country, with only a semi-weekly mail, he toiled daily in his fields, surveying, levelling, and directing in person the operations of clearing, draining, manuring, and improving the methods of tillage. He succeeded largely, sustaining the thrift of the soil, and reducing several thousand acres to cultivation, including large bodies of swamp never before penetrated by the foot of man. From one field of six hundred acres he gathered a crop of thirty-seven thousand bushels of corn, in a section thought then, and since, little adapted to this crop. These things he accomplished by his labor, out of his limited resources, in the face of all obstacles, without once borrowing money. Devoted to his family, he was scarcely less so to his slaves. Lightly tasked, well clothed, well fed, their lives and persons protected, their sufferings alleviated by the kindest care, their domestic affections cherished with conscientious delicacy, a church built for them, Christian preaching with religious instruction in a Sunday School furnished, it would have been difficult to find a happier or more progressive body of agricultural laborers with greater local attachments, more trusting in, and trusted by those they worked for, than the slaves on his plantations.

His leisure hours were given to a broad and patriotic consideration of public affairs. Self-contained, with his life work about him, he neither sought, nor desired public office. But when the occasion required it, or his fellow citizens called on him for help, he was never backward in doing what his hands found to do with all his might. Believing in State sovereignty, he held that the undivided *allegiance* of the citizen belonged to this transcendant power, however much his *obedience* might be due to any member of coordinate governments. Throughout his life, his earliest public utterances (see report of a meeting of the States Rights and Free trade party of Barnwell, S. C., 7th July, 1834), and his latest (see speech on the Relation of the States, U. S. Senate, 21st May, 1860), bear witness to the strength of this faith. In 1834 he was elected to Congress, but his health failing, he was forced to resign before the close of the first session he attended. His physicians advised him to travel, and after spending some time in Europe, he returned to his home at Silver Bluff and his agricultural pursuits. He was elected Governor of South Carolina in 1842. His administration was marked by its rigid economy. He asked that the appropriations for arms which he left unexpended be withdrawn, as the State had more munitions of war than it would ever probably require. He proposed plans for the immediate liquidation of the State debt, although her bonds stood higher in the English market than those of any other State save one; he advised steps looking to a practical approximation of universal free trade; he systematized the first agricultural survey of the State; consolidated the two State arsenals into the military academy, and organized it after the model of West Point; urged that every dollar that could be spared from the wants of the State be expended on education, especially in the establishment in each district of an academy of high grade; recommended a reduction and consolidation of State offices. He was assailed in voluminous petitions, circulars and letters, on account of the conviction of one John L. Brown for abducting a negro slave. Brown was tried and condemned under an English colonial law; Governor Hammond had pardoned him before any of these documents arrived; he however replied to them in a letter to the Presbytery of Glasgow and in two letters to Thomas Clarkson, Esq.

These letters were translated in France, and had a wide European circulation, as the fullest argument in defence of Southern slavery. Opposed to slavery in the abstract, opposed to the reopening of the African slave trade, opposed to the extension of slavery by propagandism in this country (see Barnwell speech, 26th October, 1858), he defended the peculiar domestic slavery of the South, against the denunciations of Abolitionists from all quarters, asserting that they denounced a thing of which they knew absolutely nothing—nay, which did not even exist. During a long period of retirement and labor on his plantations that followed, he made numerous contributions to the literature of the day, notably a series of articles against the railroad system and the Bank of the State; an oration before the Mechanics Institute of

Charleston; another before the two societies of the South Carolina College, and one at the invitation of the City Council of Charleston, on the Life, Character and Services of John C. Calhoun. Very unexpectedly to himself, in 1857, he was elected United States Senator from South Carolina. In a speech delivered the 4th of March, 1858, in reply to Mr. Seward, on the admission of Kansas to the Union, he closed with these words: "You complain of the rule of the South; that has been another cause that has preserved you. We have kept the Government conservative to the great purposes of the Constitution. We have placed it, and kept it, upon the Constitution; and that has been the cause of your peace and prosperity. The Senator from New York says that that is about to be at an end; that you intend to take the Government from us; that it will pass from our hands into yours. Perhaps what he says is true; it may be; but do not forget—it can never be forgotten—it is written on the brightest page of human history, that we, the slaveholders of the South, took our country in her infancy, and after ruling her for sixty out of the seventy years of her existence, we surrendered her to you, without a stain upon her honor, boundless in prosperity, incalculable in her strength, the wonder and the admiration of the world. Time will show what you will make of her; but no time can diminish our glory or your responsibility." Early (U. S. House of Representatives, 1836), lifting his voice in warning against the avowed disunion sentiments of the Abolitionists; fully sensible of the advantages of the Union; with a profound veneration for the institutions established by the Constitution; appreciating the glory of remaining an integral part of the great republic; opposed to the secession movement in 1852; advising against that of 1860; he nevertheless held the autonomy of his native State paramount to all other considerations, and after the passage of the ordinance of secession, by the convention of South Carolina, he resigned his seat in the United States Senate. Broken in health by his sojourn in Washington, he was too feeble to take an active part in the conflict that followed. Anxious to maintain the financial stability of the Confederacy, he devised and proposed to the Confederate authorities a plan for prohibiting the private export of cotton; for purchasing it with bonds of the new government and holding it abroad and at home as a basis of credit. As the sequel showed it might have added a value amounting to two billion of dollars in gold to the resources of the Confederacy. To the last he sustained the failing fortunes of his country's cause, animis opibusque. He died November 13th, 1864, just three days before Sherman started on his march to the sea, which swept away with the besom of war the homes and institutions of the South, Free Trade and State Sovereignty, in defence of which, the life here recorded, had been spent. H. H.

SELECTIONS

FROM THE

LETTERS AND SPEECHES

OF THE

HON. JAMES H. HAMMOND,

OF SOUTH CAROLINA.

NEW YORK:
JOHN F. TROW & CO., PRINTERS, 50 GREENE STREET.
1866.

Entered according to Act of Congress in the year 1866, by

JOHN F. TROW & CO.,

In the Clerk's Office of the District Court of the United States, for the Southern District of New York.

CONTENTS.

PAGE

REPORT AT A MEETING OF THE STATE RIGHTS AND FREE TRADE PARTY OF BARNWELL DISTRICT, SOUTH CAROLINA, HELD AT BARNWELL COURT-HOUSE, ON MONDAY, JULY 7TH, 1834, ... 5

SPEECH ON THE JUSTICE OF RECEIVING PETITIONS FOR THE ABOLITION OF SLAVERY IN THE DISTRICT OF COLUMBIA, . 15

MESSAGE TO THE SENATE AND HOUSE OF REPRESENTATIVES OF THE STATE OF SOUTH CAROLINA, NOV. 28, 1843, . . 51

MESSAGE TO THE SENATE AND HOUSE OF REPRESENTATIVES OF THE STATE OF SOUTH CAROLINA, NOV. 26, 1844., . . 79

LETTER TO THE FREE CHURCH OF GLASGOW, ON THE SUBJECT OF SLAVERY, ... 105

TWO LETTERS ON THE SUBJECT OF SLAVERY IN THE UNITED STATES, ADDRESSED TO THOMAS CLARKSON, ESQ., . . 114

AN ORATION DELIVERED BEFORE THE TWO SOCIETIES OF THE SOUTH CAROLINA COLLEGE, ON THE 4TH OF DEC., 1849, . 199

CONTENTS.

                                                                                         PAGE

AN ORATION ON THE LIFE, CHARACTER, AND SERVICES OF JOHN CALDWELL CALHOUN, DELIVERED ON THE 21ST NOVEMBER, 1850, IN CHARLESTON, S. C., AT THE REQUEST OF THE CITY COUNCIL, ... 231

SPEECH ON THE ADMISSION OF KANSAS, UNDER THE LECOMPTON CONSTITUTION, DELIVERED IN THE SENATE OF THE UNITED STATES, MARCH 4, 1858, ... 301

SPEECH DELIVERED AT BARNWELL C. H., S. C., OCTOBER 29, 1858, ... 323

SPEECH ON THE RELATIONS OF THE STATES, DELIVERED IN THE SENATE OF THE UNITED STATES, MAY 21, 1860., . . 358

STATE RIGHTS AND FREE TRADE.

AT A MEETING OF THE STATE RIGHTS AND FREE TRADE PARTY OF BARNWELL DISTRICT, SOUTH CAROLINA, HELD AT BARNWELL COURT-HOUSE, ON MONDAY, JULY 7TH, 1834, COL. JAMES H. HAMMOND MADE THE

REPORT.

THE Committee, appointed by the Meeting of the Citizens of Barnwell on the 4th of June, have reflected maturely on the subject referred to their consideration. Few occasions have occurred in the history of our State, requiring more serious deliberation, and dispassionate decision. An honest and independent Judiciary is the safest check upon the accumulation of power in the Legislative and Executive Departments of the Government. Unfortunately, the manner of their appointment, compensation, and promotion, is too apt to lead the Judges, if not directly to sanction, at least to connive at, the usurpations of the coördinate Departments. Whenever, therefore, in the exercise of their acknowledged functions, they throw themselves in opposition to and arrest the hand of legitimate power, it becomes a people, jealous of their rights, and justly prejudiced in favor of too weak rather than too strong a Government, to sustain them in their judgment, unless it should be clear that they have been influenced by unworthy motives, or have made an unjust and dangerous decree. Entertaining this view, had the majority of the Court of Appeals, in the present instance, following the safe judicial precedent of adjudging no point not necessarily involved in determining the rights of the parties before the Court, confined themselves to the proper construction of the Constitution of the State, this Committee would, without hesitation, have recommended, as the wisest course, a silent submission to their decision, until the Constitution could be amended by the action of the people, so as to obviate every obstacle to their wishes. But, as they have gone further, and, after conclusively settling the rights of parties by deciding the Oath, required by the recent Military Bill, to be against the Constitution of the State, and, therefore, void; with great candor as men, but doubtful discretion as Judges, have unnecessarily discussed, and judicially decided, the great fundamental question which lies at the bottom of our system of State and Federal Governments, involving, essentially, all their relations with one another, as well as the political rights of every individual in America—it becomes the duty of the people, in the opinion of this Committee, to look fully into the matter, and inquire into the reasons of such an important and extraordinary step. Indeed, to permit a question so interesting, so vital to their rights and liberties, which, in some form or other, has agitated this confederacy from its origin to the present day, which they themselves have long discussed with the most intense anxiety, and decided for this State by a majority of two thirds; in support of which decision, they have actually taken up arms, and pledged life, fortune, and honor: to be finally adjudged and settled against them, by the mere dicta of two men, no matter how great their worth, or how dignified their station, without freely examining their motives and their arguments, would exhibit an inconsistency and apathy too great to be expected or believed: And this examination the Committee proposes briefly to make.

The discussion of this great question has, necessarily, divided the State into two parties; its vital importance of itself, its connection with some of the most interesting measures of the day, and the length and ardor of the discussion, have produced much exasperation. It is well known that the two Judges, who constitute the majority of the Appeal Court, are members of that party which has opposed the measures of the majority of the people constituting the State. They have been active partisans, taking part, publicly, in the discussion before the people—confidentially consulted, it is supposed, on all the movements of the party, and members of the Convention of that party, which met at the most critical moment of affairs, and resolved not to sustain the State, when it was evident that a contest for its existence was at hand. Whatever may be our respect for the private worth, or our veneration for the public dignity, of these Judges, it is impossible to close our minds to the conviction, that from these facts should be traced the motives which induced them to depart from the rules ordinarily observed in their decisions, and to discuss unnecessarily the question constituting the basis of the difference between the two parties of the State; and (following, no doubt, the sincere conviction of their minds), to throw the weight of their judicial influence into the scale of the party in the minority.

The real question put at issue, and determined by the Judges, in that part of their decision which may justly be considered *ultra* judicial, is, whether, according to our confederated system, sovereignty, or the last power of decision in all civil and political questions, from which there can be no appeal, resides in the States, respectively, or in the Federal Government. The paramount allegiance of the citizen, or obligation to obey without further question, is due of course to that last power or sovereignty. The Oath in the Military Bill required every Officer to swear allegiance to the State of South Carolina; in other words, to acknowledge her his sovereign. Although the Court of Appeals, on other grounds, decided the Oath to be void, yet they have chosen to make a dictum against it on this ground also; and by a course of reasoning as extraordinary as original. They argue thus: Allegiance, in its feudal origin, meant the duty which a vassal owed his Chief—the subject his King; to follow them in war, and to pay tax and homage to them in peace, for which he was protected in both; that, in this country, where there are no Kings or Chiefs, but all power resides in the People, this duty is due to them; that in a state of nature they cannot exact it, nor give what is required in return for it, *protection*. It is, therefore, due only to *their government*, which they regard as the first state of a popular organization. It then means nothing but obedience. But we have two Governments, State and Federal. We now, therefore, owe allegiance, or obedience, to two powers. Neither has a right to claim it exclusively. Judge O'Neale understands the Oath prescribed by the Legislature, to require exclusive allegiance to the State, and, therefore, not to be enforced. Judge Johnson does not so understand it, but concurring in the train of reasoning above stated, puts it beyond doubt, that if such be the true meaning of the Oath (which it clearly is) he must concur in this conclusion also. This is the substance of the argument of the majority of the Appeal Court fairly stated, in few words. We admit, on our part, that we have two Governments. We admit, that we owe obedience to both. We admit, that obedience is all that Government can now require of us, and *if* the highest duty which we owe, is to the *Government* of the people, we admit the consequence that *allegiance* and *obedience* are the same, and the conclusions of the Court correct. But the highest duty which we owe is not to the Government. On this point we take our issue, and draw the dividing line, which, however slight it may appear, at first glance, in the opinion of this committee, separates right and wrong, justice and oppression, liberty and bondage. Upon what ground can Government claim from us this paramount obligation? Because, says the Court, it gives us in return the highest possible equivalent, protection. Protection? How? Can Government, of itself, by virtue of any inherent power it possesses, *create* men, money, and arms, to protect us against foreign or domestic war? Can it give spontaneous force and vigor to its laws, to protect our lives, or liberty, or property, from the assaults of our fellow-men? Nay; can it, by any elementary vitality, any independent self-action, maintain its own existence for a single hour? If it cannot do these things, and that it cannot is the first principle of Republicanism, how can it *protect* us? The argument is not only superficial, but dangerous. The Court, while pretending to discard the idea of allegiance as foreign in its origin, and anti-republican in its nature, has fallen into the very error which it reprobated, and founded its whole theory upon the exploded doctrines of the old world. It is there taught, that Governments can do everything. It is there that Kings, acting by "divine right," have unlimited control over the destinies of their subjects; and Governments universally punish it as treason to question their possession of sovereign and unlimited power, by virtue of which they bind the conscience, seize the property, sacrifice the lives, and "protect" the rights of the people. Here, we have a power *above the Government*. A power which sustains and "protects" the Government, gives it existence, energy, legality, the command of resources, and the power to exact the "obedience" of the citizen. This transcendent power is SOVEREIGNTY, and belongs to the people only. Not to the people in a "state of nature," which is one of those philosophic dreams with which political science has nothing to do; but to the people in a state of society in which they have been found from the foundation of the world. In other words, it belongs to the true first state of popular organization called the SOCIAL COMPACT. A compact which, from the nature of things, necessarily arises whenever a number of individuals meet and form a distinct community, whether large or small, the principle of whose existence is, that they will adhere together, on their own soil, against all the world; and the first law of which is, that every member must submit implicitly to the will of the majority, so long as he continues with them. It is this high and exclusive obligation which we dignify with the name of "allegiance," in return for which, the individual receives the substantial protection of the compact, not only from external and internal foes, but from all invasions of his right by Government itself, which it creates, limits, checks, and alters at discretion. The duty which we owe that Government, while it exists, in all its various departments, is called "obedience."

If this view be correct, it follows that the Court of Appeals has entirely mistaken the nature of allegiance, and the authority to which it is due—that there is a clear distinction between allegiance and obedience; and that since an individual cannot be at the same time a member of two social compacts, his allegiance cannot be divided, though his obedience may be due to any number of coördinate authorities. By applying these conclusions to the question drawn before the Court, it will be perceived, that to determine the true ultimate relations of the American citizen to his two Governments, it is only necessary to ascertain to what Social Compact he belongs. There his allegiance is due, and in all conflicts for power, to that he must adhere; or, by abandoning it, deprive himself of all its privileges. Where then does his compact lie? It is well known, that in every instance of the formation of a Colony in this country, whether by direct emigration from the mother-country, or by separation from other Colonies, a new and distinct community was created, independent of every other in America; which constituted a separate Social Compact, and gave rise to a separate Government. It is true, each Social Compact considered itself a part of the Social Compact, and each Government depended on the Government of England. This anomalous condition is what is termed, among nations, the Colonial state. And it is only necessary to regard it in this point of view, to perceive how intolerable it must be to the free spirit, and how impossible it was, and *is*, to maintain it among the Sons of Liberty on this side of the Atlantic. The Revolution severed this connection, and each Colony was declared a Sovereign and Independent State. They afterwards formed the present Union, and created a new Government by the Constitution of the United States. Did they dissolve their separate Social Compacts, and consolidate them into one, and revive their colonial condition with a change of masters only, by this act? There is no evidence of the fact in the Constitution, nor in the history of the times. There has always been a party in this country, led more by their instinct for power than any force of reason, who have attempted to confuse the relation of the State and Federal Governments, and, practically, to consolidate all power in a Federal Head; but this clear elementary fact of the amalgamation of the compact, without which all their attempts at reasoning must fall, has not, that we know of, ever been contended for.—No such event took place. A new *Government* was created—not a *State*—a new body *politic*—not *social*. A new authority was called into existence, empowered to require the "obedience" of the citizen, but not to claim his "allegiance;" in short a new *agency*, not a *sovereignty*, arose. The different Social Compacts parted with no portion of their transcendent dominion, but only made a new division of their delegated power between the State and the new Government, retaining, unimpaired, their sovereign right to limit and control the action of both within their geographical boundaries. The farthest they did go, was to agree not to *alter* the Constitution of the Federal Government, without the consent of three fourths of the compacts. But in this they yielded up no real power, since any one of them can secede and throw off its obligations to the whole, whenever it sees fit; and, consequently, is not necessarily bound to submit finally to the alterations which may be made, against its wishes, even by three fourths. Thus it appears to this Committee, that the Social Compacts of each of the States remain perfect and unimpaired by their connection with the other States, and as the highest known human authority within their respective limits, is entitled to claim the allegiance of every individual, so long as he remains a citizen thereof; and to withhold not only power, but protection from every one who refuses to acknowledge it. In support of this view, and the whole argument, we might cite the express reservation in the Constitution of the United States, and the Oaths of exclusive Allegiance required by a large number of the States. We might also add to this mere sketch of the argument, in favor of State Sovereignty, many other views and illustrations to meet those of the Court, and strengthen our position; but the Committee forbear to urge them on the patience of this meeting, believing they have said enough to place their opinions upon incontestible grounds. They might also go on to show, that from the principles here laid down, results inevitably the right of State interposition to check the unconstitutional acts of the Federal Government, with all its salutary consequences; while from those laid down by the Court, follows as certainly the consolidation and colonial dependency of the States, with all its train of evils, the first of which must be dissolution of the Union. But this would again lead us into discussion, foreign to the immediate purpose of the meeting.

Upon a calm review of the whole matter, the Committee are of opinion, that the Constitution of the State ought to be amended, in conformity with the Bill introduced at the last session of the Legislature, so as to require an oath of Allegiance from all persons hereafter taking Office under the State of South Carolina. As it is evident, from the opinions of a majority of the Court of Appeals, that no oath requiring exclusive allegiance to the State will be enforced by that Court, it would be nugatory to amend the Constitution, without also remodelling the Court, so as to secure the full and effectual execution of the will of the People. The Committee regard it, therefore, as absolutely necessary that that should be done in such manner as to the Legislature may seem best.

J. H. HAMMOND, *Chairman.*

SPEECH

ON THE JUSTICE OF RECEIVING PETITIONS FOR THE ABOLITION OF SLAVERY IN THE DISTRICT OF COLUMBIA.

THE motion of Mr. Cushing, of Massachusetts, to receive the petition of sundry inhabitants of Massachusetts praying for the abolition of Slavery and the Slave-trade in the District of Columbia being under consideration:

Mr. Hammond said, that when he had first demanded the preliminary question of reception on the presentation of a similar petition some weeks ago, it was his hope and expectation that it would be decided without debate. On every subsequent occasion when he had felt it his duty to make a similar demand, he had entertained the same desire, and had himself refrained from taking any part in the discussions which had arisen. It was obvious, however, that gentlemen presenting these petitions were determined to discuss them; and after what had occurred on last petition-day, he concluded that no petition would be offered to the House hereafter, without a preliminary speech as well as motion. As much, therefore, as he felt indisposed to block the proceedings of the House on this important day, he thought perhaps he had as well say at once what he had to say on this subject in its present stage, and by so doing he might facilitate the business of the House.

I listened, sir, with much pleasure to the address of the gentleman from Massachusetts (Mr. Cushing) who presented this petition, and I believe I can say that I concur in every principle which he laid down. I am sure that he cannot have a greater regard for the right of petition than I entertain. But, really, I cannot see what the discussion of that right can have to do with the question before the House.

No one here desires to "pass a law" depriving "the people of the right of peaceably assembling, and petitioning for a redress of grievances." They have so assembled. They have petitioned for the redress of their imaginary grievances. The petition has been presented to the House. Its contents have been stated. If it had been requested, the petition itself might have been read by the Clerk. We are, sir, in full possession of its character and object—the petitioners and their representatives having performed their part without "let or hindrance;" and it is now our duty to perform that which devolves on us. We may refuse to receive the petition, and record the refusal on our journals; or we may receive and instantly reject; or commit, and, on a report, reject the prayer of the petitioners; or we may grant their prayer. Any of these courses it is fully competent for this House to adopt; and none of them, in my opinion, impugn in the slightest degree the right of petition which has been so justly denominated "sacred."

I think, sir, that this House should not receive the petition, and that is the course which I suggest. The gentleman says it is not disrespectful in its terms. I pass that by, then. But I think we should not receive it still, because it asks us to do what we have no constitutional power to do; and what, if we had the power, it would be ruinous to a large portion of this confederacy, and ultimately destructive to all our institutions, for us to do.

The constitutional power to abolish Slavery and the Slave-trade in this District, is claimed by virtue of the clause which gives to Congress "exclusive legislation" here. I admit at once, that under that clause Congress has full power, so far as "legislation" is concerned, over this District, except where it is limited by the letter or the spirit of the Constitution in other portions of that instrument, or by the contracts made with the States of Virginia and Maryland in the acts of cession by those States. As this point has been ably, and I think satisfactorily, discussed, both in this House and another portion of the Capitol, I will take but a single view of it at this time. All the powers given by the Constitution are trust powers, and should be construed in connection with each other, and in reference to the great objects they were intended to accomplish. Now, I ask, if any member of this House, having before him these clauses of the Constitution forbidding the passage of laws, even by the States, to prevent the arrest of "persons held to labor" in the other States—forbidding "Congress to take private property" even "for public uses without just compensation," and recognizing slaves as *property*, entitled to representation only as three fifths, and not as *persons* entitled to full representation,—can say that it will not be a violation of the letter and the whole spirit of the Constitution to assume the power which you are now called on to exercise—as much a violation of it as to pass an *ex post facto* law or bill of attainder here?

I ask gentlemen if they believe this Constitution would ever have received the sanction of a single Slave-State, if it had been suspected for a moment that this power now claimed was given to Congress by it?

But, sir, admitting for the sake of argument that the Constitution places no limitation to the power of "legislation" in the District of Columbia: I ask how far that power will, of itself, extend? What are the great objects of all human legislation? To *protect* life, liberty, and *property*. Can we, under this definition, assume the power wantonly to *destroy* them? It is true property is sometimes seized as a penalty for misdemeanors; and liberty, and even life, are forfeited for crimes. But does this warrant Congress, or any legislative body in this country, *at its free will and pleasure* to confiscate the estate of a peaceful and unoffending citizen, or imprison him or take away his life without offence?—Sir, monstrous as these propositions are, they are not more monstrous, nor would they be more fatal in their consequences, than that which these petitioners ask us now to adopt.—And here let me say, in answer to the gentleman from Massachusetts (Mr. Cushing), that I can see no difference between the constitutional power to abolish the internal Slave-trade and the power to abolish Slavery itself. If the slave-owner is deprived of the full use of his property, unless that use impairs the rights of others, you can as well deprive him of the property itself. The principle in both cases is the same. But for the reasons I have already mentioned, I will not dwell on this branch of the subject.

Mr. Speaker, I object to the reception of these petitions, in the next place, because they are sent here by persons who are pursuing a systematic plan of operations, intended to subvert the institutions of the South, and which, if carried into effect, must desolate the fairest portion of America, and dissolve in blood the bonds of this Confederacy. It has been said upon this floor, that the Abolitionists of the North are very few in number, and of so little influence as to be unworthy of our attention. It has been said here, on the other hand, that they constitute a majority north of Mason and Dixon's line, and that their influence is "tremendous." Amid this conflicting testimony, permit me to call the attention of the House to some important facts connected with the subject.

It will be recollected that during this session, in consequence of the course which has been taken in the matter, on but a single day has an opportunity occurred for a free presentation of petitions of the character of that before us. On that day, although it could not have been expected that the occasion would occur, fifty-eight of these petitions were presented—a number considerably larger than the average number presented during the last four sessions. These petitions are signed by between seven and eight thousand persons, male and female; some of them signing as representatives of large Societies. I have been informed that three hundred petitions of this kind have been forwarded to Congress, and I do not doubt the fact. If they are as numerously signed, we shall have the names of some forty thousand persons petitioning Congress at this session to abolish Slavery and the Slave-trade in the

District of Columbia. This, sir, is no slight evidence of the strength of the Abolition party.

But let us trace the history of the formation of the Societies to which I have alluded. In 1832, less than four years ago, the New England Anti-Slavery Society was formed. This, I believe, was the first noticeable Society of this kind created on this side of the Atlantic. I remember well the ridicule with which it was covered when it was known that it had been formed by a meeting of *eleven* persons. Sometime in the year 1833 the New York Anti-Slavery Society was formed by a meeting composed of two and twenty men, and *two females*. I remember, also, the contempt with which this annunciation was greeted; but, sir, they grew in spite of indifference and contumely.

On the 4th of December, 1833, at a Convention of Abolitionists in the city of Philadelphia, the great American Anti-Slavery Society was formed, and a bold " DECLARATION OF THEIR SENTIMENTS " was given to the world. They announced that "all slaves should instantly be set free" " without compensation to their owners;" " that the paths of preferment, of wealth, and of intelligence, should be as widely opened to them as to persons of a white complexion;" and that to effect these purposes they pledged themselves "to organize Anti-Slavery Societies everywhere;" "to send forth agents to remonstrate, warn, and rebuke; to circulate periodicals and tracts;" "to enlist the pulpit and the press;" "to purify the Churches of the crime of slavery;" "and to encourage the labor of freemen rather than that of slaves, by giving a preference to their productions."

From this moment the infection spread with unparalleled rapidity. In May following (1834) there were SIXTY Anti-Slavery Societies. By May, 1835, the number had increased to TWO HUNDRED. By October, 1835, it had swollen to THREE HUNDRED. And by a document which I hold in my hand purporting to be a "protest of the American Anti-Slavery Society" against certain sentiments expressed on this subject, by the President of the United States, in his last Annual Message, it appears that there were known to be THREE HUNDRED AND FIFTY Anti-Slavery Societies in the United States on the 25th day of December last.

Some of these societies contain as many as four thousand members, and none of them, I believe, less than fifty. On a fair calculation it may be presumed that not less than one hundred thousand persons in the non-slaveholding States are united in these societies, and their numbers are increasing daily with a rapidity almost beyond conception—a disciplined corps, who have pledged life and fortune to the great purpose of emancipation.

That the spirit, means, purposes, and plans of these societies may appear more fully, I will refer to the "Address of the American Anti-Slavery Society," at its last annual meeting, which I have in my hand, and ask permission of the House that the Clerk may read.

"Address to the Auxiliaries and Friends of the American Anti-Slavery Society.

"DEAR BRETHREN: At the last annual meeting of the American Anti-Slavery Society, it was 'Resolved, That an effort be made to raise 30,000 dollars for the use of the Society the present year, and that the Abolitionists present pledge themselves to raise such sums as they may respectively offer.'

"Donations and pledges were immediately obtained, amounting to 14,500 dollars.

"Additional pledges have since been obtained in Boston, to the amount of 4,000 dollars. The sum of 11,500 dollars remains to be raised. As there are known to be more than two hundred Anti-Slavery Societies, on kindred principles with the American, we have no doubt that this sum can speedily be made up. Each Society has only to raise 150 dollars, and the work is done. We believe that those Societies which remain unpledged will joyfully come forward to do their proportion as soon as called on.

* * * * * *

"The plan proposed at the annual meeting, and now adopted by the Executive Committee, in the confident belief that the means will be furnished, is this:

"1. To increase the number of Agents, by appointing as many able, efficient, and thorough-going men as can be obtained.

"2. To commence the distribution of publications on a new and extended scale.

"The following publications will be issued monthly, viz.:

"1. On the first week of each month, a small folio paper, entitled 'Human Rights,' to be filled with facts and arguments on the subject of Slavery and its remedy, written in a plain and familiar style. Of this twenty thousand copies will be printed, to be increased to fifty thousand or more, as soon as arrangements can be made to have them promptly and judiciously distributed among the reading population.

"2. On the second week, the 'Anti-Slavery Record,' a small magazine, with cuts, will be printed, to the number of twenty-five thousand copies.

"3. On the third week, the 'Emancipator' will be printed on a large imperial sheet, of the size of the 'New York Observer,' or the 'New York Evangelist.' This will contain more extended essays and descriptions, on points connected with the cause. It is expected that from fifteen to twenty-five thousand copies will be printed monthly this year.

"4. On the fourth week will be issued twenty-five thousand copies of the 'Slave's Friend,' a juvenile magazine, with cuts, adapted especially for circulation among children and youth.

"All these publications will be distributed gratuitously, by the aid of the auxiliaries, to those who are not Abolitionists, or will be sold at the office, to friends of the cause, at a very low rate.

* * * * * *

"The present is the time for action.

* * * * * *

"Let Female Societies be formed. Female Societies probably did more for the abolition of slavery in Great Britain than those of the other sex. They scattered anti-slavery tracts, handbills, pamphlets, and books, everywhere. They circulated petitions; they covered articles of furniture or apparel, such as pincushions, work-boxes, handkerchiefs, boxes, baskets, purses, portfolios, etc., etc., with devices and mottoes reminding the users of the poor slaves. They made the matter a topic of conversation on almost all occasions. Several societies of ladies in this country have already commenced the same course with good success. Let the female sex, then, throughout the land, emulate the efforts made by their sisters over the ocean, in this work of benevolence.

"Juvenile Societies, too, may be engaged in the same work. Children are all Abolitionists.
* * * * * *

"We hope Abolitionists will everywhere make it a personal business to distribute the publications; that they will not let them be thrown away, but put them in the hands, only, of those who will read and think. Let no Abolitionist, at home or abroad, ever be without a supply, and be ready to embrace every favorable opportunity.

"Petitions to Congress for the abolition of Slavery in the District of Columbia should be put in circulation immediately. The minds of the members of Congress should, if possible, be enlightened as to the real design of the American Anti-Slavery Society, and their prejudices should be removed, as in many it may easily be, by personal interviews with Abolitionists. The way may thus be prepared for a more favorable hearing before the representatives of the people. * * *

(Signed) "ARTHUR TAPPAN,
JOHN RANKIN,
LEWIS TAPPAN,
JOSHUA LEAVITT,
SAMUEL E. CORNISH,
WILLIAM GOODELL,
ABRAHAM L. COX,
THEODORE S. WRIGHT,
SIMEON S. JOCELYN,
ELIZAR WRIGHT, Jr.
Executive Committee of the American Anti-Slavery Society."

Here, Sir, is a number of the paper entitled "Human Rights"—a neat, well-printed sheet. Here are several numbers of the "Anti-Slavery Record," on the outside of each of which is a picture representing a master flogging naked slaves, and each of which contains within pictures equally revolting. Here is a handful of the little primer called the "Slave's Friend." On the covers, and within each of these, are also pictures calculated to excite the feelings, and to nurture the incendiary spark in the tender bosom of the child. And here, Sir, is "The Emancipator," a large and handsome paper. And that you may understand the spirit and principles which it inculcates, I will read to the House a paragraph from a number dated New York, Nov., 1835.

"THE ALTERNATIVE.—William Wertenbaker, Assistant P. M. and Librarian of the University of Virginia, gives notice that he has committed to the *flames* a copy of 'Human Rights' we sent him, and very gravely asks, 'Which of the two do you prefer—*a perpetuity of slavery, or a dissolution of the Union?*' The latter, we say, by all odds, if we must choose. We are for union, but not with slavery. We will give the Union for the abolition of slavery, if nothing else will gain it; but if we cannot gain it at all, then the South is welcome to a dissolution—the sooner the better. The slaveholders may as well understand, first as last, that 'The Union' may have other uses to them than that of a *lash* to shake over the heads of Northern freemen."

It speaks for itself. I make no commentary. Here, Sir, is a pamphlet called the "Anti-Slavery Reporter," published monthly, I believe, by this Society. Here is a "Quarterly Anti-Slavery Magazine," of very respectable size, edited by Elizar Wright, Jr. Here is a pamphlet entitled "Anti-Slavery Hymns," of which there are nineteen. They purport to be for the use of the "Monthly Concerts for the Enslaved" in the city of New York, and the publication of a more copious collection in Boston is announced. Here is a small book entitled "Juvenile Poems." It contains, besides a great number of doggerel articles of the most inflammatory character, some nine or ten disgusting prints, all of which are designed "for the use of free American children of every complexion." Here is a pamphlet written by a "*Man of Color*," and here are a quantity of Sermons, Essays, Reports, Letters, &c., &c., all intended for the same incendiary purposes.

I hold also in my hand, that most powerful engine in party warfare, an "Anti-Slavery Almanac for 1836." From this allow me to read two short extracts. The following will show the political tendency of this abolition agitation: "*We are rewarding slaveholders for their usurpation and injustice, by allowing them to send 25 Representatives to Congress to represent their slave property.*" It has been said that "the petitioners have no further object than merely to wipe from the national escutcheon the stain affixed to it by permitting slavery to exist at the seat of government of the United States." In answer to that allow me to quote the following passage; and there is scarcely a publication that I have exhibited here to day in which the same sentiment is not expressed: "*Should you abolish slavery in the District of Columbia alone, it would heave the foundation of the system in every State of the Union.*" Nor is this work without its pictures, libelling the slaveholders with its vile caricatures. To illustrate more fully the political tendency of the extraordinary excitement on this subject, although I do not intend on this occasion to discuss that branch of the question, I will refer the House to an extract from the "Anti-Slavery Circular," printed at Medina, Ohio, December, 1835, which I hold in my hand, and which I again ask the favor of the House to permit the Clerk to read.

"There are now about half a million that still have the *liberty* of holding slaves; their slaves now amount to upwards of two millions, and their landed estates are of vast extent; they have entire control over eleven States—the poorer classes of the white people are well trained to subjection, and occupy a grade a little above that of the slaves. Few nobles in Europe can command so great a retinue of servants—and no king on earth possesses more absolute authority. Indeed, such is their dignity, wealth, and influence, that although but half a million, they are able to control twelve and a half millions, and do in fact govern the Union; and the plan is now laid to keep up and increase their dignity, wealth, and power, to future generations. They have managed so wisely as to get the whole Union bound by the Constitution to keep their slaves in subjection, and allow them a representation in the General Government in proportion to the number of their slaves. The increase of these, already 54,000 a year, will soon give the increase of one Representative every year. By the aid of the rest of the Union, the slaves can be kept in subjection until they shall have become much more numerous than the white people, provided they are prevented from learning to read, and thus kept in total ignorance. And for this purpose, laws are passed with heavy penalties against teaching slaves to read. Now it is obvious, that by those means Slavery might be extended to remote posterity, especially with what assistance the Colonization Society might be able to give them, by carrying off occasionally a little of the surplusage. Every one can easily see that these Southern gentlemen have before them a magnificent prospect of wealth and power, provided the rest of the Union will continue to be their humble servants in enabling them to keep their slaves in subjection. Now the avowed design of the Abolitionists is to abolish Slavery—not indeed by force of arms, but by forming against it public opinion, which will be even more powerful. They have combined together to propagate the doctrine, that 'all men are made of one blood,' and of course are 'treated equal.' Vast sums of money are now pledged to propagate the sentiment throughout the whole land. Agents are lecturing, papers are circulating, societies are forming, and thousands continually joining them. It seems as if the world will soon be on fire. What is to be done? Argument has been tried and exhausted in vain! Mobs have been tried with little effect! The heresy spreads like fire in the whirlwind. The last remedy is now demanded—Extermination entire,—nothing less will do! If matters go on as they are, the result is obvious:—Every man who does not hold slaves will set his face against Slavery—and then, how will half a million of men continue to hold more than two millions in bondage? Mark the design! All force is disavowed; but then, the slaveholder must, so soon as the tide of public opinion rolls against him, yield up his slaves: he cannot hold them without aid; much less can he bear the reproach that will be heaped upon him.

"It is not to be disguised, Sir, that war has broken out between the South and the North, not easily to be terminated. Political and commercial men, for their own purposes, are industriously striving to restore peace. But the peace which they may accomplish will be superficial and hollow. True and permanent peace can only be restored by removing the cause of the war—that is, slavery. It can never be established on any other terms. The sword now drawn will not be sheathed till victory, entire victory, is ours or theirs; not until that deep and damning stain is washed out from our nation, or the chains of Slavery are riveted afresh where they now are, and on our necks also. It is idle, criminal, to speak of peace on any other terms."

Sir, while we are discussing the question of the reception of these petitions, movements are making at the north, and societies are springing up like mushrooms. Here are the proceedings of a meeting held within a few weeks past, at Lowell, Massachusetts, the centre of the tariff interest, at which was formed a "Young Men's Anti-Slavery Society," the preamble of whose constitution I will read:

"PREAMBLE.

"WHEREAS, unconditional slavery exists to a fearful extent amongst us as a nation, in violation of those principles that moved our fathers to the dreadful struggle of the Revolution—'that all men are created equal, that they are endowed by their Creator with certain unalienable rights, that among these are life, liberty, and the pursuit of happiness.'

"WHEREAS, the aristocracy of the South are determined to perpetuate it by means scarcely less dreadful than the tortures of the Inquisition, and the [bastard] aristocracy of the North are aiding their 'chivalrous' compeers of the South in their inhuman endeavors by misrepresenting, slandering, threatening, and imprisoning those who boldly espouse the cause of universal freedom, and further by circulating publications and making speeches so highly incendiary as to excite mobs, and impel them to their ruthless work of terror and destruction.

"WHEREAS, the *crisis* has arrived at which the descendants of the pilgrims must determine whether they will establish the shameful and cowardly precedent of surrendering their most sacred rights at the nod of an arrogant, domineering, and self-constituted aristocracy, or in the spirit of their fathers manfully maintain them.

AND WHEREAS, if we remain silent and inactive we effectually surrender *those rights*, and with them the hopes of the slave, till the prediction of Jefferson shall be realized, and the slave, fearless and free, shall till the land of his thraldom enriched with the blood of his master.

THEREFORE, RESOLVED, under a deep sense of duty to ourselves, to the slave, to our country, and to God, that 'sink or swim, live or die, survive or perish,' we will exercise the right of discussing the subject of slavery; that we will use all constitutional and peaceful means for its speedy termination—and to act the more efficiently, form ourselves into a society and adopt the following, &c.

Here is a circular, dated "Pautucket, Rhode Island, Jan. 12, 1836," calling a "Rhode Island Anti-Slavery Convention," to meet shortly at Providence. It is signed by eight hundred and forty persons. I will read from it the following remarkable passage, from which it may be seen how deep the roots of this hostility to our institutions have struck into the foundations of society.

> "Our *country* friends, we hope, will attend as numerously as they have signed the circular. The wealth and aristocracy of our cities are against us. They sympathize not with the 'poor and needy,' but with 'the arrogant and him of high looks.' Let our laboring men, then, the mechanics and the farmers, attend the Convention. They can easily arrange their business so as to make it convenient to be in Providence at that time."

Here, Sir, is the Prospectus of the *sixth volume* of the "LIBERATOR," published at Boston by Isaac Knapp. Prefixed to it is an incendiary picture, and it contains the following passage, which exhibits, possibly with some exaggeration, in a strong point of view, the extent of the agitation on this subject throughout the non-slaveholding States.

> "The sixth volume of the 'Liberator' commences on the first of January, 1836. During the term of its existence, it has succeeded, in despite of calumny and a strong opposition, in dispelling the apathy of the nation, creating an extraordinary and most auspicious interest for the oppressed, inducing a rigid investigation of the subject, and securing a host of mortal combatants who are pledged never to retreat from the field. The wrongs of the slaves—the danger of keeping them longer in bondage—the duty of giving them immediate freedom—are the topics of conversation or discussion in all debating societies—in lyceums—in stages and steamboats—in pulpits and in periodicals—in the family circle, and between a man and his friend. The current of public sentiment is turning, and soon it will roll a mighty river, sweeping away in its healthful and resistless career all the pollutions of slavery."

This prospectus is accompanied by an anonymous communication, for which of course I cannot vouch, which states that Dr. Channing has softened the asperity of his remarks on Thompson, the *foreign* Anti-Slavery missionary, in his late work on slavery; that the work has, in consequence, been stereotyped by the Abolitionists, and that the demand for it is insatiable.

As the last evidence which I shall offer of the extent of the excitement at the North upon the Slave question, I will read the following extracts from a letter from the western part of the State of New York. It is dated 12th January, 1836. The writer of it is a gentleman who has been a close and shrewd observer of events passing around him. He is a man of talents and of strict integrity, and is one who has done and suffered something for his country. He says:

"The madness which influences our Northern people on the subject of slavery, is well calculated to fill the stoutest with dismay. The spirit which followed the Utica and Peterboro' Convention of Abolitionists has totally changed the question from that of the emancipation of the slave to that of the continuance of the Union.

* * * * * *

"The North is now laboring to unite her people against you. The effort is immense and continual. The enclosed anti-slavery pamphlets and some 'Emancipators' were distributed at a Presbyterian prayer meeting in my neighborhood the other day, by the president of the anti-slavery society of this county, and were handed to me by the Deacon of the church, through the hands of one of the men in my employ. The object is to unite the Northern people in hatred of the people of the South, by false representations of the condition of their slaves, and by charges of cruelty, immorality, and irreligion. I endeavor to convince my neighbors that these pamphlets are false in every particular, and that if they join in the cry of abolition, they must partake of the enormous sin of bringing on a civil war, of destroying our Union, and of causing a renewal of the horrors of St. Domingo. And for what do they labor to bring on their country and their fellow-citizens of the South these dreadful calamities? It is for the liberty of the slave; and in gaining that liberty, or in the attempt, they inevitably lose their own. But this view has no weight; the effort to free your slaves will be made; and Congress will be the ultimate scene of the struggle. Our next elections will mainly turn on this question, unless you settle it now and forever; that is, before this session expires. If you adjourn without so settling it, you will have to resort to the bayonet to adjust it."

[Mr. Granger and Mr. Lee, of New York, demanded the name of the author. Mr. H. said, I cannot give it. I will vouch for his character. But such is the state of society around him, I fear it would prove dangerous, if not fatal to him, to disclose his name.]

Mr. Speaker, I believe what I have just read. Sir, there can no longer be a doubt of the deep, pervading, uncontrollable excitement which shakes the anti-slave States on this subject, nor of the energy and power with which the Abolitionists are pressing their mad and fatal schemes. Every mail from the North brings fresh news of agitation, every breeze is tainted with it. It spreads like wild-fire in the prairies, and throws its red glare up to heaven, that all may see while it sweeps with resistless fury everything before it. I call on every slaveholder in this House, and in this country, to mark its fearful progress and prepare to meet it. He who falters here or elsewhere, he who shrinks from taking the highest and the strongest ground at once, is a traitor! A traitor to his native soil! A traitor to the memory of those from whom he has inherited his rights! A traitor to his helpless offspring, who call upon him for protection! And on his head be the blood which his treachery or cowardice may cause to flow.

Allow me now, Sir, to examine more closely the real designs of those Abolitionists, the means by which they will attempt to effect them, and the probable es ult. Their designs are very succinctly stated in the volume which I hold in my hand. It is a treatise on this subject entitled "Jay's Inquiry"—written by William Jay, a judge, I believe, of the State of New York, and a son of the distinguished John Jay. More than five thousand copies of this work, I am told, have been sold. He says, "*the Society aimed at effecting the following objects, viz.:*

"1st. The immediate Abolition of Slavery throughout the United States.

"2d. As a necessary consequence, the suppression of the American Slave-Trade.

"3d. The ultimate elevation of the black population to an equality with the white in civil and religious privileges."—p. 141.

Sir, the abolition of slavery can be expected to be effected in but three ways: through the medium of the slaveholder—or the Government—or the slaves themselves.

I think I may say that any appeal to the slaveholders will be in vain. In the whole history of the question of Emancipation in Europe or America, I do not remember a dozen instances of masters freeing their slaves, at least during their own lifetime, from any qualms of conscience. If they are seized with these qualms, they usually sell their slaves first, and then give in their adhesion to the cause, as has been the case with many whom I could mention.

The Abolitionist can appeal only to the hopes or fears or interest of the slaveholder to induce him to emancipate his slaves. So far as our hopes are concerned, I believe I can say we are perfectly satisfied. We have been born and bred in a slave-country. Our habits are accommodated to them, and so far as we have been able to observe other states of society abroad, we see nothing to invite us to exchange our own; but on the contrary, everything to induce us to prefer it above all others.

As to our fears, I know it has been said by a distinguished Virginian, and quoted on this floor, "that the fire-bell in Richmond never rings at night, but the mother presses her infant more closely to her breast in dread of servile insurrection." Sir, it is all a flourish. There may be nervous men and timid women, whose imaginations are haunted with unwonted fears among us, as there are in all communities on earth, but in no part of the world have men of ordinary firmness, less fear of danger from their operatives than we have. The fires which in a few years have desolated Normandy and Anjou, the great machine-burning in the heart of England, the bloody and eternal struggles of the Irish Catholics, and the mobs which for some years past have figured in our Northern States, burning convents, tearing down houses, spreading dismay and ruin through their cities, and even taking life, are appropriate illustrations of the peace and security of a community whose laborers are all *called* free. On the other hand, during the two hundred years that slavery has existed in this country, there has, I believe, been but one serious insurrection, and that one very limited in its extent.

The appeal, however, to our interest, is that which might appear to promise much success, for whatever it is the interest of a community to do, that (sooner or later) it will be sure to do. If you will look over the world, you will find that in all those countries where slavery has been found unprofitable, it has been abolished. In northern latitudes, where no great agricultural staple is produced, and where care, skill, and a close economy enter largely into the elements of production, free labor has been found more valuable than that of slaves. You will there find labor usually exercised in small combinations under the immediate eye of a watchful and frugal master. I speak more particularly of those who cultivate the soil; but the large masses of mechanical operatives who are brought together form no exception to the principle. They are classified. There is an accurate division of their labor; each branch of it requires peculiar art, and in the higher departments a degree of skill must be attained, to produce which, stronger stimulants are necessary than can be ordinarily applied to slaves.

In such countries the dominant classes have found it to their advantage to permit each individual to accumulate for himself, and to deprive him of a portion of his earnings sufficient for their purposes through the operations of the government. Hence the partial emancipation of the serfs of the continent of Europe. Hence the abandonment of villeinage in England. And hence the emancipation of slaves in the free states of this Union. But in southern latitudes, where great agricultural staples are produced, and where not only a large combination of labor under the direction of one head is required, but it is also necessary that the connection between the operatives and that head should be absolute and indissoluble, domestic slavery is indispensable. To such a country it is as natural as the clime itself—as to the birds and beasts to which that climate is congenial. The camel loves the desert; the reindeer seeks the everlasting snows; the wild fowl gather to the waters; and the eagle wings his flight above the mountains. It is equally the order of Providence that slavery should exist among a planting people, beneath a southern sun. There the laborer must become a fixture of the soil. His task is not from day to day, nor from month to month, but from season to season, and from year to year. He must be there to clear, to break up, to plant, to till, to gather, and to clear again; and he must be kept there by a never-ceasing, unavoidable, and irresistible force. The system of " *strikes* " so universally practised in all other kinds of labor would desolate a planting country in a few years. If, in the heat of the crop, when the loss of one or two days even may irreparably ruin it, the laborers were to abandon the fields and demand higher wages, the owner would have no other alternative than to say to them, " Work, and take enough to satisfy yourselves "—which would, of course, be all. Sir, it is not the interest of the planters of the South to emancipate their slaves, and it never can be shown to be so.

Slavery is said to be an evil; that it impoverishes the people, and destroys their morals. If it be an evil, it is one to us alone, and we are contented with it—why should others interfere? But it is no evil. On the contrary, I believe it to be the greatest of all the great blessings which a kind Providence has bestowed upon our favored region. For without it, our fertile soil and our fructifying climate would have been given to us in vain. As it is, the history of the short period during which we have enjoyed it has rendered our Southern country proverbial for its wealth, its genius, and its manners.

Failing as the Abolitionists must do in every appeal to the slaveholder, let us see with what probability of success they can call upon the Government to emancipate our negroes. There are about 2,300,000 slaves at this moment in the United States, and their annual increase is about 60,000. Sir, even the British Government did not dare to emancipate the slaves of its enslaved West India subjects without some compensation. They gave them about 60 per cent. of their value. It could scarcely be expected that this Government would undertake to free our slaves without paying for them. Their value, at $400 average (and they are now worth more than that), would amount to upwards of nine hundred millions. The value of their annual increase, alone, is twenty-four millions of dollars; so that to free them in one hundred years, without the expense of taking them from the country, would require an annual appropriation of between thirty-three and thirty-four millions of dollars. The thing is physically impossible.

But it is impossible for another reason: the moment this House undertakes to legislate upon this subject, it dissolves the Union. Should it be my fortune to have a seat upon this floor, I will abandon it the instant the first decisive step is taken, looking towards legislation on this subject. I will go home to preach, and if I can, to practise disunion, and civil war, if needs be. A revolution must ensue, and this Republic sink in blood.

The only remaining chance for the Abolitionists to succeed in their nefarious schemes will be by appealing to the slaves themselves; and, say what they will, this is the great object at which they aim. For this are all their meetings, publications, lectures, and missions; to excite a servile insurrection, and, in the language of the miscreant Thompson, to "*teach the slave to cut his master's throat.*" This will be no easy task. Sir, it is a proverb, that no human being is perfectly contented with his lot, and it may be true that some strolling emissary may extract, occasionally, complaints from Southern slaves and spread them before the world. But such instances are rare. As a class, I say it boldly, there is not a happier, more contented race upon the face of the earth than our slaves. I have been born and brought up in the midst of them, and so far as my knowledge and experience extend, I should say they have every reason to be happy. Lightly tasked, well clothed, well fed—far better than the free laborers of any country in the world, our own and those perhaps of the other States of this confederacy alone excepted—their lives and persons protected by the law, all their sufferings alleviated by the kindest and most interested care, and their domestic affections cherished and maintained—at least so far as I have known, with conscientious delicacy.

A gentleman from Massachusetts (Mr. ADAMS) has introduced upon this floor the abolition cant of wives and husbands, parents and children, torn from each other's arms, and separated forever. Such scenes but rarely, very rarely happen. I do not believe such separations are near so common among slaves, as divorces are among white persons where they can be with much facility obtained. I am very sure that children and parents do not so often part, as in the ordinary course of emigration in this country they do among the freest and proudest of our land. Sir, our slaves are a peaceful, kind hearted and affectionate race, satisfied with their lot, happy in their comforts, and devoted to their masters. It will not be an easy thing to seduce them from their fidelity. But if by an artful and delusive appeal to his excited passions the Abolitionist should succeed in drawing the slave into his fiendish purposes, our never sleeping watchfulness would speedily detect every conspiracy that might be formed. Our habits in this respect have become a second instinct. Our vigilance is as prompt and personal as our courage—as faithful a guardian, and not more troublesome. It does not arise from fear, but from the fact that we ourselves, to a great extent, constitute our own police, and in guarding against minor evils will not fail to discover every danger of great magnitude. Such has been and such will always be the case. Every insurrection which has yet been meditated,—and there have been but very few,—when not discovered by some faithful slave, has been soon discovered by the whites, the unfortunate occurence at Southampton only excepted—if that can be called an insurrection which was the bloody outbreaking of six drunken wretches. I believe that every appeal to the slave to assist, through the horrid process of burning and assassination, in his own emancipation, much as it is (in secret at least) cherished, will be without success.

Sir, I feel firmly convinced that, under any circumstances, and by any means, emancipation, gradual or immediate, is impossible. We may be disturbed in our comforts, harassed, injured, perhaps some partial sufferings may be the consequences of their mad and savage projects, but slavery can never be abolished. The doom of Ham has been branded on the form and features of his African descendants. The hand of fate has united his color and his destiny. Man cannot separate what God hath joined.

But, Mr. Speaker, admitting for a moment that the Abolitionist could accomplish all his objects. Suppose the bonds of the slave were broken peacefully, and he was turned loose to choose his life and occupation on the face of the earth, what would probably be his actual state? Sir, we have some experience on this subject. I hold in my hand a paper containing an account of the situation of a colony of free blacks in Brown county, in Ohio, which I ask permission for the Clerk to read.

ABOLITION.

From the Cincinnati Gazette.

"Some forty miles from Cincinnati, to the East, are two settlements of free negroes—probably near a thousand—men, women and children, of the true ebony color; with a very little mixture of the mahogany or lighter shades. The negroes own the land occupied by them, but without the power to sell. Each family has a small farm. They are emancipated slaves, and these lands were purchased expressly for them, and parcelled out among them about fifteen years ago.

"Their lands are not of the best quality of Ohio lands; but, by good management could be made very good—they are particularly well adapted to grass, either meadow or pasture.

"Having been formerly slaves and compelled to work, one would suppose they ought to have industrious habits. They have had every inducement to industry and good conduct held out to them. The experiment was to test the merits of the negro race under the most favorable circumstances for success.

"Has this experiment succeeded? No it has not. In all Ohio, can any white settlement be found equally wretched, equally unproductive?

"Farms given to them fifteen years ago, instead of being well improved, and the timber preserved for farming, have been sadly managed—small, awkward clearings, and those not in grass, but exhausted and worn out in corn crops—the timber greatly destroyed—wretched log houses, with mud floors; with chimneys of mud and wood—with little timber for further farming.

"They are so excessively lazy and stupid, that the people of Georgetown (near by their camps) and the neighboring farmers will not employ them as work hands to any extent. They do not raise produce enough on their own lands to feed their families, much less do they have a surplus for sale abroad. They pass most of their time in their little sorry cabins; too listless even to fiddle and dance. One may ride through the "negro camp," as they are called, passing a dozen straggling cabins with smoke issuing out of the ends, in the middle of clearings, without seeing a soul either at work or play. The fear of starvation makes them work the least possible quantity, while they are much too lazy to play.

"Why do not the zealous Abolitionists go there and see the experiment in all its beauty—the slave changed into a free, but wretched savage! Why not make something of these thousand negroes? There are not more than two or three families out of the whole who are improved by the change from slavery to freedom.

"The negro settlements are a dead weight upon Brown county, as to any productive benefit from the negro lands, or from negro labor; and that space of country might as well, to this day, have remained in possession of the Indians.

"If Southern wealth can be applied to buy and colonize among us such a worthless population, what farmer in Ohio is safe? Has he any guarantee that a black colony will not be established in his neighborhood.

"Let any one who wishes to learn the operation of emancipated negroes, visit the Brown county camps. As they sink in laziness, poverty and filth, they increase in numbers—their only produce is children. They want nothing but cowries to make them equal to the negroes of the Niger."

Such, Sir, are the blessed fruits of Abolition; and to make such miserable and degraded wretches as these are we called on to give up our happy, industrious, and useful slaves—to strike out of existence nine hundred millions of active and inestimable capital, and impoverish and desolate the fairest region of the globe? But it is said that this is the dark side of the picture, and that emancipation—"*gradual* emancipation," would produce far better consequences. Although I am perfectly satisfied that no human process can elevate the black man to an equality with the white—admitting that it could be done—are we prepared for the consequences which then must follow?

Are the people of the north prepared to restore to them two-fifths of their rights of voters, and place their political power on an equality with their own? Are *we* prepared to see them mingling in our legislation? Is any portion of this country prepared to see them enter these halls and take their seats by our sides, in perfect equality with the white representatives of the Anglo-Saxon race—to see them fill that chair—to see them placed at the heads of your Departments; or to see perhaps some Toussaint, or Boyer, grasp the Presidential wreath and wield the destinies of this great Republic? From such a picture I turn with irrepressible disgust.

But, Sir, no such consequences as either of these views exhibit can take place with us. There is no such thing as gradual emancipation, even if we were to consent to it. Those who know the negro character cannot doubt, what the recent experiments in the West Indies fully prove, that the first step you take towards emancipation bursts at once and forever the social ties of the slave. In our country, where the two classes of population are so nearly equal, such a state of things as now exists in Jamaica would not last a day—an hour. Sir, any species of emancipation with us would be followed instantly by civil war between the whites and the blacks. A bloody, exterminating war, the result of which could not be doubtful, although it would be accompanied with horrors such as history has not recorded. The blacks would be annihilated, or once more subjugated and reduced to slavery. Such a catastrophe would be inevitable.

Permit me now, Sir, for a moment to look into the causes of this vast and dangerous excitement, for it is intimately connected with the true merits of this important question. I am not disposed to attribute it to any peculiar feelings of hostility entertained by the North against the South, arising from position merely. It is indeed natural that a people not owning slaves should entertain a strong aversion to domestic servitude. It is natural that the descendants of the Puritans, without any deep investigation of the subject, should have an instinctive hostility to slavery in every shape. It is natural that foreigners, with whom the North is crowded—just released themselves from bondage—extravagant in their notions of the freedom of our institutions, and profoundly ignorant of the principles on which society and government are organized—should view with horror the condition of the Southern operatives. And here let me say that these opinions, so natural, so strong, and so distinctly marking the geographical divisions of our country, indicate differences which, if pushed much further, will inevitably separate us into two nations; a separation which I should regard as a calamity to the whole human race, and which we of the South will endeavor to avert by every means save the sacrifice of our liberties, or the subversion of our domestic institutions.

But other causes are at work. This excitement belongs to the spirit of the age. Every close observer must perceive that we are approaching, if we have not already reached, a new era in civilization. The man of the nineteenth century is not the man of the seventeenth, and widely different from him of the eighteenth. Within the last sixty years there have been greater changes—not on the face of the earth, but in the history of civilized man, than had taken place before, perhaps, since the reign of Charlemagne. The progress and the philosophy of the events which have brought us to this state may be readily perceived and stated. Formerly all learning was confined to the clergy—all political power to the hereditary rulers of the people. The invention of printing dispersed knowledge among the middle classes. The clergy could no longer absorb it all. The first effect of this was the destruction of ecclesiastical despotism, which was consummated by the Reformation. The next, a war of intelligence against political oppression. But the glittering temptations of power seduced it from its purposes—allured it to its assistance, and used its energies to rivet more closely their chains upon the people. At length, Government could no longer absorb all the talents and acquirements and ambition of the world. Then the effects of the contest began to show themselves. The tremendous conflicts for political ascendancy which took place in the British Parliament during the reign of George the Second, were followed by the American Revolution, which was initiated by the great intellects of this country, whom the mother government could neither conciliate to its abuses, nor purchase, nor intimidate. Next came that terrible tragedy, the French Revolution, which was confessedly brought about by the writings of the great philosophers of France. Since that period, man appears no longer to be the being that he was. His moral nature seems to have been changed as by some sudden revelation from the lips of the Almighty; although the close observer sees that the great cause which had been so long and so silently, but surely working to effect this purpose, was the wide increase of knowledge. Bursting from the trammels of centuries of ignorance and sloth, he has been pressing onward for good and evil, with an energy tremendous and terrific. All nature has felt the impulse. The thin air has been converted into a resistless power. Steam, whose every definition was an useless vapor, has been made the most tremendous engine which has ever yet been placed in human hands —overcoming in its infancy time, space, and resistance with a celerity and ease just not supernatural. Railroads have been thrown over swamps, rivers, lakes and mountains, which, connecting new and distant points, open vast channels for intercourse and commerce. Labor-saving machinery of every kind has been incalculably improved: much of it perfected. In one word, we have reached a period when physical impossibilities are no longer spoken of. What was visionary yesterday, is planned, estimated and resolved upon to-day —to-morrow it is put in execution, and the third day superseded by something more wonderful and more important still.

During the period of this mighty change, the great struggle between the rulers and the ruled has been carried on with corresponding vigor; through the thousand channels which genius has opened, wealth has flown in to aid it in its contest with the strong arm of power. The two combined, finding themselves still unable to cope with the time-hardened strength of hereditary government, and eager, impatient, almost frenzied to achieve its conquest, have called in to their assistance another ally—*the people*. Not the " people " as we have hitherto been accustomed in this country to define that term, but the MOB—THE SANS-CULLOTTES. Proclaiming as their watchword that now prostituted sentiment "that all men are born free and equal," they have rallied to their standard the ignorant, uneducated, semi-barbarous mass which swarms and starves upon the face of Europe! Unnatural and debasing union! Hereditary institutions are gone. Already have the nobility of France been overthrown. Their days are numbered in the British Empire. Let them go. I am not their advocate. What next? *Confiscation has begun!* The result is as obvious as if it were written on the wall. The hounds of Acteon turned upon their master. Genius and wealth, stimulated by "an ambition that o'erleaps itself," have called these spirits from the vasty deep; but they will down no more. The spoils of victory are theirs, and they will gorge and batten on them.

In this country we have no heriditary institutions to attract the first fury of this tempest, which is also brewing here, for the electric fluid has crossed the ocean, and the elements denote that it is expanding over the northern arch of our horizon. The question of Emancipation, which in Europe is only a collateral issue, a mere ramification of the great controversy between hereditary power and ultimate agrarianism, has become with us the first and most important question; partly because the levellers here have not yet felt the heavy pressure of political oppression, and partly because they have regarded our institutions of slavery as most assimilated to an aristocracy. In this they are right. I accept the terms. *It is a government of the best,* combining all the advantages, and possessing but few of the disadvantages of the aristocracy of the old world. Without fostering to an unwarrantable extent the pride, the exclusiveness, the selfishness, the thirst for sway, the contempt for the right of others, which distinguish the nobility of Europe—it gives us their education, their polish, their munificence, their high honor, their undaunted spirit. Slavery does indeed create an aristocracy—an aristocracy of talents, of virtue, of generosity and courage. In a slave country *every freeman* is an aristocrat. Be he rich or poor, if he does not possess a single slave, he has been born to all the natural advantages of the society in which he is placed and all its honors lie open before him, inviting his genius and industry. Sir, I do firmly believe that domestic slavery regulated as ours is produces the highest toned, the purest, best organization of society that has ever existed on the face of the earth.

Against this institution war has been commenced. A crusade is proclaimed. The banner has been hoisted, and on it is inscribed that visionary and disastrous sentiment, "Equality to all mankind;" although there is no analogous equality in the moral or physical creation, in earth, air, or water—in this world, or in the world to come, if our religion be not altogether wrong! The sans-culottes are moving. On the banks of the Hudson, the Ohio and the Susquehannah—on the hills, and in the vales, and along the "iron-bound coast" of *immaculate* New England, they are mustering their hosts and preparing for their ravages. Let them come! we will be ready. Standing on our institutions, which of themselves give us a strength almost impregnable, and rallying around them as one man, with the help of God I believe we shall be able to roll back the frantic tide to whence it came. But woe unto the men of substance in the North whose infatuation may impel them to join this fatal crusade. The bloodhounds they are setting upon us, successful or unsuccessful, will in due time come back from the chase; and come back to wring from them the accumulations of their industry, to overturn their altars and desolate their household.

Mr. Speaker, I have touched on topics to-day which have not heretofore been broached within these walls. In thus departing from the usual silence of the South upon this subject, it may be thought that I have gone too far. But times have changed. They change before our eyes with the rapidity of thought. Painful as it is, the truth should now be told, for shortly it will speak itself, and in a voice of thunder. We cannot, in my judgment, avoid this danger longer, by closing our eyes upon it and lulling our people into a false security. Nor can we justify ourselves before the world for the course which we may be compelled to take in order to maintain our rights, without boldly declaring what those rights are, defining them and showing that they are inestimable. All minor considerations must give way to effect those all-important objects. These have been my motives for the course I have taken here. I leave it to the approaching crisis to determine whether I am right or wrong.

Sir, if I were asked what it is, under existing circumstances, the South desires the North to do, I should say, "Pass laws in your different States forbidding, by the severest penalties, the publication or circulation of such incendiary pamphlets as I have exhibited here to-day." This your Legislatures are fully competent to do without infringing on freedom of speech, or freedom of the press. That freedom means well-regulated, legal freedom, and not unrestrained licentiousness.

Have you not laws to punish libel and slander? If a citizen of the State of New York were to say of another citizen that he was a "land pirate," "a murderer," and a "man-stealer," would he not be liable to an action of slander? If he were to write these things of him, or caricature him by infamous and disgusting pictorial representations, would he not be indictable for libel? What violation, then, of social or constitutional right, would it be to extend the benefit of these same laws to us?

We ask nothing more than the recognition of a well-known principle of international law, a striking illustration of which has happened within the memory of many who now hear me. It will be recollected that just before the war between France and England, which broke out in 1803, the English presses teemed with abuse of the First Consul. Bonaparte complained to the English Ministers. They indicted Peltier, tried, and convicted him. The declaration of war only prevented him from receiving his punishment. If England, where there have been more battles fought for the liberty of speech, and of the press, than in any portion of the world, felt herself bound to indict a journalist for libelling her greatest enemy, the enemy, as she deemed, of the whole human race, on the very eve of war with him, is it unreasonable to require you to extend the same justice to the grossly slandered and deeply injured people of the South; brethren as you call us of one great confederacy, devoted to the same great principles of constitutional liberty, and who have so often mingled our blood with yours, on the same glorious battle field?

Sir, I cannot believe gentlemen are sincere when

they urge here this slang about the right of petition, and the freedom of speech and of the press, as though any one here had the remotest desire to curtail them. When Tappan and Garrison, and Gerrit Smith, and such as they are, use this cant, I understand them: they wish to inflame the popular passions by false appeals to popular rights. But when such men as the gentlemen from Massachusetts (Messrs. Adams and Cushing), and the gentleman from New York (Mr. Granger), who favored us the other day with eulogiums on certain Abolitionists, introduce it on this floor, I do not—yes, I do understand them. But I will not press that point, for I wish to connect this question with no political intrigues or discussions.

I will say frankly that I do not believe we shall be able to obtain the passage of such laws as I have alluded to in any non-slaveholding States. Sir, there is not a man of any note, or at least of any political aspiration, who will dare to make such propositions. He would be prostrated, and forever. He would be covered with a mountain of public odium under which he could never rise again. And I want no stronger evidence of the true state of public sentiment in those States than this single fact.

What, Sir, does the South ask next? She asks, and this at least she has a right to demand, that these petitions be not received here and recorded on your journals. This House at least ought to be a sanctuary, into which no such topic should be allowed to enter. Representatives from every section of the Republic ought to be permitted to come here faithfully to perform their duties to their constituents and their country, without being subjected to these incendiary attacks—

their feelings insulted, their rights assaulted, and the falsest calumnies of themselves and those they represent thrown on them daily, and perpetuated to their posterity, and all the world, among the archives of the Union. Is this demanding anything unreasonable, unjust, unkind? Sir, we cannot endure it. If these things are to be permited here you drive us from your councils. Let the consequences rest on you.

But, Mr. Speaker, even if this House should refuse to receive these petitions, I am not one of those who permits himself to trust that the conflict will be at an end. No, sir, we shall still have to meet it elsewhere. We will meet it. It is our inevitable destiny to meet it in whatever shape it comes, or to whatever extremity it may go. Our State Legislatures will have to pass laws regulating our police with a strict hand. They will have to pass and to enforce laws prohibiting the circulation of incendiary pamphlets through the mail within their limits. We may have to adopt an entire non-intercourse with the free States, and finally, Sir, we may have to dissolve this Union. From none of these measures can we shrink as circumstances may make them necessary. Our last thought will be to give up our Institutions. We were born and bred under them, and will maintain them or die in their defence. And I warn the Abolitionists, ignorant, infatuated barbarians as they are, that if chance shall throw any of them into our hands he may expect a FELON'S DEATH. No human law, no human influence can arrest his fate. The superhuman instinct of self-preservation, the indignant feelings of an outraged people, to whose hearth-stones he is seeking to carry death and desolation, pronounce his doom; and if we failed to accord to him ignominious death, we should be unworthy of the forms we wear, unworthy of the beings whom it is our duty to protect, and we should merit and expect the indignation of offended Heaven.

MESSAGE

TO THE SENATE AND HOUSE OF REPRESENTATIVES OF THE STATE
OF SOUTH CAROLINA, NOV. 28, 1843.

EXECUTIVE DEPARTMENT,
Columbia, *Nov.* 28, 1843.

Gentlemen of the Senate and House of Representatives:

SINCE your adjournment the late long continued depression of financial affairs throughout the world has reached and passed what we have much reason to believe was its final crisis. During the last Spring prices of every description fell to the lowest point ever known, but have since continued steadily, though gradually, to advance. The revival of business has not been the effect of accidental causes, or speculative operations, or expansion of the paper currency; nor is it owing to any act of legislation in any part of the world, favorable to trade. It has been the natural result of industry, economy, and time, which have swept off a large proportion of the embarrassments created by the disasters of the past, and accumulated at all the great commercial points, in safe hands, a vast and unexampled amount of sound *metallic* capital. We have, therefore, good reason to indulge the hope that it will be permanent, and to felicitate ourselves on the dawn of a new era in trade and finance.

There is but one serious obstacle, now apparent, that can arrest and roll back, in any short period, the returning tide of our prosperity; and that is, the narrow and delusive idea, which still seems to prevail with a majority of those who rule the world, that they can promote the interests of their respective countries, by fettering trade and building up monopolies. Until we seriously approximate to universal Free Trade—to an unrestricted exchange of the surplus production of one country for the surplus of another, by which means, the wants of all will be supplied in the cheapest manner, and commerce, currency, and credit are established in natural and enduring channels, the periodical recurrence of speculations, fluctuations and disasters that will convulse the world, must be looked for with perfect certainty.

It is a matter for congratulation, that England, the source and centre, from which have directly or indirectly sprung nearly all the great improvements of modern times, has given evidence of a serious change on this great question. Her recent legislation has been decidedly directed towards a relaxation of her prohibitory and protective laws. It is to be regretted, at the same time, that nearly every other important power in Europe, has within a few years past, in its convulsive efforts to throw off the embarrassments of the time, increased restrictions upon trade. Whilst our own government, recurring to that policy which is every where else regarded as one of the most odious features of aristocratic and despotic power, and held in abhorrence by the people, has re-enacted its tariff laws, and made them more rigorous and oppressive than they have ever been before. That a government like ours, purporting to be based on perfect freedom and equality, should perpetrate such laws; and that a people so intelligent as ours—so distrustful of their rulers—so ready to resist injustice and oppression—four-fifths of whom are agriculturists, all deeply injured by restrictions upon foreign commerce—should permit such an execrable system to be fastened on them, is one of the most extraordinary events in the history of the age. To the enlightened views so rapidly gaining ground among those who control the English government—to the progress of true knowledge among the other States of Europe, and to the change of power into other hands which is just about to be realized in our country, I look with confidence for a vast amelioration and early abandonment of the whole system of protective duties.

In the meantime it should be borne constantly in mind, that any departure from the great principles of industry and economy, and a steady faith that with the practice of these two cardinal virtues time will do the rest, must be attended with the most serious consequences to our future welfare. And perhaps no occasion could be more auspicious than the present for you to institute a close and searching examination into the precise condition of our State, in all its departments, and introduce such alterations and reforms as will enable her to take the tide of prosperity to most advantage, and maintain it longest.

Her financial condition claims, perhaps, at this especial moment, your first attention. The public debt of the State may be put down in round numbers at three millions and a half of dollars ($3,500,000).

The following is a correct Statement of the items, viz.:

Date.	Amount outstanding.	Rate of interest.	When reimbursable.	Object of the loan.
1794–5	$193,501 85	3 per cent.	At will	Payment of Revolutionary claims.
1824	250,000 00	5	January 1845	Internal improvements.
1826	300,000 00	5	1846	Do. do.
"	10,000 00	6	1850	Benefit of Mrs. Randolph.
1838	141,662 50	5	1858	Subscription to S. Western R. R. Bank.
"	1,035,555 55	5	1860	Rebuilding city of Charleston.
"	964,444 44	6	1870	Do. do. do.
1839	200,000 00	6	1848	Loans and subs'tion to L. C. &. C. R. R. Co.
"	200,000 00	6	1850	Do. do. do. do.
"	200,000 00	6	1852	Do. do. do. do.
	$3,495,164 35			

$1,051,422 00—Amount of surplus revenue deposited with the State by the U. S.
2,000,000 00—Amount of loan by the L. C. & C. R. R., guaranteed by the State.

It is highly probable the State will never be called on to refund the surplus revenue, though her liability for it should never be forgotten, in an estimate of her debt. It is to be hoped that her guarantee of the railroad bonds is only nominal, and that in due season they will be discharged by the railroad company. I therefore deduct these items in stating the public debt, for which certain and early provision must be made, at three millions and a half.

It will be perceived that the payments of this debt run through a period of twenty-six years, and that the heaviest instalments are the last. Admitting that the State will punctually discharge it as it falls due, without creating another, it is yet a serious question whether she should not use every effort in her power to discharge it earlier. A public debt is no longer regarded anywhere as a public blessing, and such a mass of it, hanging over her for such a period, must press heavily upon the enterprise and resources of the State.

I feel called on, however, to declare, that I do not believe the debt will be paid even as it falls due, without creating a fresh one in lieu of it, or a large portion of it, unless important changes are made in the financial arrangements of the State. And as these changes might, if effected at all, be so made as to discharge it at a much earlier period, it seems to me the wisest policy to relieve the people as speedily as possible of this immense pressure. The debt can be *bona fide* paid only by levying taxes to the amount of it, or by using the funds of the State already in existence. Although I have not the least doubt that the people would, without a murmur, submit to be taxed to any amount, rather than that the slightest imputation should rest upon the good faith of the State; yet while there exists any other means of meeting her obligations, I presume no one will propose to resort to onerous taxation. The alternative is to use the funds of the State now committed to the management of the bank.

The idea has been often, and recently gravely, put forth, that the bank would pay the debt as it became due, out of the profits arising from the operations of banking. To show the fallacy of such an idea, it is only necessary to compare the interest on the debt with the profits of the bank. The interest amounts at this time to one hundred and eighty-six thousand, six hundred and thirty-one dollars and ninety-six cents ($186,631 96) per annum, exclusive of expenses, which must raise the expenditure for this purpose to at least one hundred and ninety thousand dollars ($190,000) annually. The net profits of the bank, for the fiscal year of 1842, were reported at two hundred and ten thousand, seven hundred and sixty-nine dollars and forty-two cents ($210,769 42), leaving a balance of twenty thousand seven hundred and sixty nine dollars and forty-two cents ($20,769 42). The net profits of the last fiscal year amounted to two hundred and twenty-six thousand, seven hundred and thirty-two dollars and seventeen cents ($226,732 17), leaving a balance in favor of the bank, of thirty-six thousand, seven hundred and thirty-two dollars and seventeen cents ($36,732 17). It is obvious that an annual accumulation to the amount of the largest of these sums, would not discharge the debt in much less than a century. Nor is there any just ground for anticipating a great increase of profits for the future. The period for immense returns from banking operations has passed away and, it is to be hoped, forever. Such is especially the case with this bank, since the monopoly which it so long enjoyed in this State has ceased, by the incorporation of other banks, and cannot be revived again.

It is also said that the State has received and still retains equivalents for a large proportion of her debt which can be converted at the proper time for paying it. She possesses eight thousand (8,000) shares of railroad and railroad bank stock, which it is gratifying to state is rising rapidly in value and, it is to be hoped will one day be worth to her the eight hundred thousand dollars ($800,000) which it cost. She holds also the obligation of the railroad company for upward of $400,000 more, which is doubtless perfectly secure. But these investments could hardly be made available to meet a crisis and, unless converted very gradually, can only be done at a heavy loss. Nor do the small dividends declared materially assist in paying the interest of the stock issued to make them. For the rest—the sinking fund, the fire loan, and the surplus revenue—they are all *banked on*, and, although separate accounts are kept of them in the bank books, they are as essentially a part of the bank capital as the comparatively small portion which is acknowledged to be such. They have been loaned out, and to be used to pay the public debt, must, like other discounts, be collected from the debtors of the bank. In short, what are supposed to be equivalents for the State debt, are securities of no higher value than those in which all the other funds of the State have been invested by the bank, nor are they more readily convertible into money, and the interest on them is now included in the annual return of the bank.

It is said again, that one million ($1,000,000) of our internal improvement debt has been redeemed, and this is taken as proof of the capacity of the bank to redeem the whole debt. It is true, that one million has been paid, but it has been made the pretext for issuing stock to the amount of one million seven hundred and six thousand, one hundred and six dollars, and ninety-four cents ($1,706,106 94), thus actually increasing the public debt seven hundred thousand dollars, instead of diminishing it.

This can be readily made to appear. In a moment of generous enthusiasm, worthy of the character of the State and her citizens, a bill was passed at an extra session in 1838, almost by universal consent, to borrow two millions of dollars ($2,000,000) for rebuilding the City of Charleston, after the calamitous fire of that year. Of this amount, one million and thirty-five thousand, five hundred and fifty-five dollars and fifty-five cents ($1,035,555 55), was obtained in London, on 5 per cent. bonds. This was loaned to the citizens of

Charleston for building purposes, and supplied all their wants. Faith and justice to the people of State required that the balance of the bonds not sold for the purpose for which they were issued, and not wanted for it, should have been destroyed. The bank, however, obtained the Governor's consent to raise them to 6 per cent. bonds, to the amount of nine hundred and sixty-four thousand, four hundred and forty-four dollars and forty-four cents ($964,444 44), and took possession of them as a loan from the State to itself, and merely charged itself debtor to the State in that amount on the books of the bank, though it still continues to report the whole two millions as the "Fire Loan." The pretext for this, was to pay the instalments of the debt of eight hundred thousand dollars ($800,000) which fell due in 1840; and of two hundred thousand dollars ($200,000) which fell due in 1842. And on that ground the Legislature afterward, in 1841, sanctioned the conduct of the bank, by laying on the table a resolution to cancel this remainder of the Fire Loan Bonds. But this was not all. At the regular session, in December, 1838, the Legislature passed an Act confirming the subscription of the Governor to the Rail Road Bank and authorizing the Comptroller General to pay it by drafts upon the Bank of the State, or by an issue of 5 per cent., in case the President and Directors of the Bank found it embarrassing to advance the funds. Although the Sinking Fund at that time amounted to eight hundred and twenty-four thousand dollars ($824,000), and the Surplus Revenue to nine hundred and fifty-one thousand dollars ($951,000), and the large balance of the Fire Loan Bonds before mentioned was absorbed by the

Bank during the current fiscal year, the 5 per cent. stock was issued to the amount of two hundred thousand dollars ($200,000), though afterwards reduced to one hundred and forty-one thousand, six hundred and sixty-two dollars and fifty cents ($141,662 50). And again, at the Session of 1839, the Legislature transferred to the Sinking Fund, to aid in the liquidation of the public debt, six hundred thousand dollars ($600,000) of the Surplus Revenue, which had been pledged to the payment of the subscription of the State to the Rail Road Company, and issued for that purpose the same amount of 6 per cent. stock. The operation in both these instances was precisely the same as if these stocks had been created to pay the public debt, the appropriate funds in the Bank being withheld on that account. Thus, in the whole, was seventeen hundred thousand dollars borrowed to pay the one million of internal improvement bonds; and that at a period when the Sinking Fund and Surplus Revenue—funds specially applicable to such a purpose exceeded not only the debt paid, but even the enormous sum borrowed, and would have covered both the instalments of the debt and the subscription to the Rail Road Company and Bank, had they been so applied. If the history of the past is to furnish any criterion by which to judge of the future, I fear that whenever an instalment of the public debt becomes due, some scheme will be devised to induce the Legislature to issue new stock to redeem it; and if at every payment the whole, and seventy per cent. more than is paid, is borrowed, it requires no gift of prophecy to foresee that this process of redemption will overwhelm the State in debt. I fear, too, that it may be considered as certain that the bank will never, unless forced to do it, part with a dollar of its capital, or of the funds used as capital, to pay any portion of the principal of the debt. To diminish its funds would be to curtail its power and influence; and though history does record some rare instances of men—exceptions to the general rule—who have voluntarily resigned power, I do not remember a single one of a corporation of any kind having done it.

Being fully assured that the bank can never pay the public debt by the profits arising from its operations, and being equally convinced that it never will, voluntarily, pay any part of it out of its capital, I suggest to you the propriety of requiring it, under penalty of forfeiting its charter, to purchase annually, and at some period in each year to cancel, in the presence of the Comptroller General, State Bonds to the amount of five hundred thousand dollars, besides paying the interest on the balance. By such an arrangement the whole debt would be paid in seven, instead of twenty-six years.

It may be doubted by some, whether the bank will be able to withdraw so large a sum from her debtors annually, without producing great distress in the State. It might be answered, that according to its own report, the bank collected and paid out, during the single fiscal year of 1840, upwards of twelve hundred thousand dollars; and the pressure on the money market at that time was incomparably heavier than it now is, or is likely soon to be. There could not, in fact, be a more favorable juncture than the present, to commence the operation I suggest. Money is abundant among capitalists, interest extremely low, and safe investments scarce; and a season of prosperity is evidently about to open on us.

I think, however, it can be made manifest, that these purchases can be effected without serious inconvenience to any class of the bank's debtors. There is now, and is usually due the bank on notes discounted, over two millions of dollars ($2,000,000). The Bonded Debt exceeds six hundred thousand dollars ($600,000). The Suspended Debt, and Debt in Suit, amount to upwards of four hundred thousand dollars ($400,000), and the Fire Loan discounts to above a million of dollars ($1,000,000), making an aggregate amount now due the bank, of more than four millions of dollars ($4,000,000). With its specie and other funds, including its investments in other than State Stocks, and five hundred thousand dollars ($500,000) of these debts, it should be fully able to redeem its circulation and deposits, and pay all other demands upon it at any time—leaving three and a half millions applicable to the public debt. Besides this, the bank owns, or did own on the 30th Sept. last, upwards of four hundred and fifty thousand dollars ($450,000) in stock of this State. This stock, with only fifty thousand dollars invested in the same way, might constitute the redemption of the first year; and for that period no debtor need be disturbed. It is understood that one million of the amount of Notes Discounted, consists of accommodation paper, at short dates. These accommodations might be curtailed during the second and third years without inconvenience to the customers of the bank, who could readily obtain discounts elsewhere in the present redundant condition of the Bank Capital in this State. In the mean time the Fire Loan Discounts would be falling due to a considerable amount, and if, after three years' notice, the debtors on Stationary Discounts and Bonds could not be prepared to liquidate their liabilities at the rate of twenty-five per cent. per annum, a longer indulgence would not only be unsafe, but extremely unwise.

Whenever it has been heretofore suggested that the bank should curtail its discounts, or call in its debts, the reply has been promptly made that the planters will be distressed, and that this is a planters' bank. When a planter borrows money, it is almost always for speculation, or to pay the losses of speculation, or of profligate self-indulgence. He never needs a loan to carry on his legitimate planting operations; and when he becomes a borrower, even if it be to hold his produce, or to purchase lands and laborers, he becomes as much a speculator as the merchant or broker, and is entitled to no more indulgence. The only bank which could really benefit the planters would be a Savings Bank, where the cash balances from their crops might be deposited on interest until required.

It will probably be said that the scheme I have proposed for paying the Public Debt will virtually throw the bank into a state of liquidation. Not so, however. Its present actual capital amounts to four millions of dollars ($4,000,000)—the debt to three millions and a half ($3,500,000), which, if paid, will leave the handsome sum of five hundred thousand dollars ($500,000) for banking purposes. To this might be added the shares of the State in the Rail Road Company and Bank, and also their obligation. This would raise the nominal capital to one million, seven hundred thousand ($1,700,000), and would give it one intrinsically worth considerably more than its present acknowledged, permanent capital, which amounts to only eleven hundred and fifty-six thousand, three hundred and forty-eight dollars and forty-eight cents ($1,156,348 48).

But even if the operation of paying the Public Debt should absorb the Bank entirely, it would, in my opinion, constitute no objection to the scheme. The State would get rid of two evils at once. It is at least a question whether all banks are not evils. That a bank operating like ours exclusively on the funds and credit of the State is, seems to be generally conceded. The best proof of it is, that almost all other banks so framed, save ours, have failed—producing incalulable embarrasment and suffering. An equally clear proof of the opinion of the people of this State, is the unexampled unanimity with which they have, for several years past, waged an unremitted warfare against the establishment of a similar, and not more objectionable institution, by the Federal Government. That our bank has neither failed nor produced any great political crisis, is owing to our extreme good fortune, in having always had at its head men of the highest character and uncommon ability. Its other officers and directors, too, have been, almost without exception, gentlemen of intelligence and strict integrity. The character of the people of our State is also opposed to extensive speculations, and perhaps nowhere in the world is a default in a public trust regarded with such universal and utter abhorrence. All these necessary elements of past success cannot be expected to co-exist forever. As men, we may be permitted to indulge the hope that they may; as Legislators, you would be forgetful of history and human nature to calculate upon it. Was it now an original question, few voices I apprehend would be found in favor of a bank of the State. Having run a career of thirty years, might it not be wise to apply at this time an active and searching test to its success and soundness? I have not the slightest reason to doubt its present soundness. But too much depends upon the fact, to admit of much longer delay in ascertaining it beyond all question. Nor is it a matter for less grave consideration, whether the State is to borrow money forever, in order to loan it out at the same, or nearly the same rates of interest, subject to all the expenses, fluctuations and disasters of banking—a business which of all others has proved the most uncertain and ruinous to States and individuals.

The strongest objection that I see to the plan I have suggested for the speedy payment of the public debt, is the doubt whether the State stock can be purchased at such amounts at par. Within the next seven years, however, nine hundred and sixty thousand dollars ($960,000) of debt will be redeemable, at par. Of the stock now held by the bank, there was, on the 30th of September, certainly sixty-four thousand dollars ($64,000), perhaps more, not redeemable within that time, but already obtained at par. A million more, redeemable in 1860, is held in Europe, and is there quoted below par; though it is matter of pride for us to know that it stands higher than the stock of any other State, save one. In the present condition of American credit abroad, this stock might probably be purchased at par. Could so much be obtained, four-sevenths of the debt would be extinguished, and time and circumstances might place the balance within reach. On most of these stocks the State obtained a premium, and it would not be unfair for her to pay a similar one to redeem them.

Should the attempt to purchase all the debt, however, fail, the next best that could be done, short of actual payment, would be to shift the balance of it on the other States of the Union, by purchasing the stocks of such as are undoubtedly sound and faithful to their engagements. It is probable that an abundance of such stocks may be obtained at any time, within the next seven years, below or at par. And provision might be made for procuring them instead of our own stock, if it rises much above par.

If the scheme I have recommended for paying the debt of the State should not meet your approbation, it seems to me important that you should at least make arrangements for a Sinking Fund, in fact, as well as in name. The fund now distinguished by that name does not differ practically, in the slightest respect, from any portion of the bank capital. It is kept as a separate item in the books of the bank; the surplus profits are nominally turned over to it, and the interest of the State debt subtracted from it. But to keep up this distinction is all unnecessary labor, since the whole fund is loaned out precisely on the same terms as the other bank funds. The fundamental principle of a real Sinking Fund is compounding interest for a special purpose. It should be set apart, its dividends reinvested as they are declared, and the whole of it sacredly pledged for the redemption of the principal of the debt; the interest being paid in the mean time from other resources. It is manifest that a Sinking Fund, which is expected to pay both the principal and interest of the debt, must be as large as the debt itself, or far more profitably invested. Our Sinking Fund amounts at present to little over one-fifth of the State debt, and if you do not think proper to pay the debt as I have proposed, I suggest the expediency of withdrawing that fund from the bank, and with it the two hundred thousand dollars of surplus revenue still on deposit there; that the whole amount be placed in the hands of commissioners, to be invested, and made to accumulate by compound interest for the discharge of the principal of the public debt, not including any instalments due within the next seven years, unless rendered absolutely necessary from the want of other means; and that, in the mean time, the bank shall be required to pay the interest on the whole debt, and such instalments of the principal as shall fall due in seven years. To the Sinking Fund thus constituted, all the surplus funds of the State Treasury might be added. These measures would draw from the vortex of the bank such a portion of the resources of the State as would enable it certainly to meet the greater part of the public debt; and if combined with a judicious system of economy, and an unalterable resolution never under any circumstances to issue more stock until the debt was wholly discharged, would furnish safe ground for the hope that there would ultimately be an end to our present burdens.

The receipts of the State Treasury, during the past fiscal year, have amounted to two hundred and ninety-nine thousand, one hundred and ninety-six dollars and sixteen cents ($299,196 16), and the expenditures, during the same period, amounted to two hundred and seventy-seven thousand, eight hundred and thirty-three dollars and seventy-seven cents ($277,833 77); leaving a balance on the transactions of the year, of twenty-one thousand, three hundred and sixty-two dollars and thirty-nine cents ($21,362 39). This balance, added to the balance accruing during the year 1842, will leave, after due allowance for undrawn appropriations, about forty-eight thousand dollars ($48,000) at the disposal of the Legislature. This amount will be further increased by nine thousand dollars, being the unexpended balance of the two contingent funds committed to my hands. Before any extraordinary appropriations are made out of this sum, it should be considered that there will be no further receipts into the Treasury until June next, when the taxes become due, and that it is wholly inadequate to defray the ordinary expenses of the State up to that period. Notwithstanding a similar balance reported to you in 1842, the bank was in advance to the Treasury, to the amount of twenty-four thousand dollars ($24,000) by the first of December of the same year, and to the amonnt of thirty thousand ($30,000) at the same period of the year before, and thereafter it continued to advance all the moneys required by the Treasury until the taxes were paid in. These advances are heavy drafts upon the bank, and it becomes the State to make arrangements to dispense with them, either by ordering the taxes to be collected at an earlier period, or by such a system of economy, as will speedily secure a sufficient balance at the close of the fiscal year, to defray expenses until the first of June following.

Among the undrawn appropriations is the sum of twenty-five hundred dollars ($2,500), which was at your last session, in conformity with the provisions of the Act of 1833, placed in the hands of the Executive, for the purchase of arms and military equipments. I have had no occasion to use this fund. The arsenals and magazines already contain more munitions of war than the State will probably ever require for service; and the Federal Government annually furnishes a quota of arms valued at from six to eight thousand dollars. This quota is rated in muskets; but by a provision in the Act of Congress these may be commuted, on application of the Executive of the State, for other arms and equipments. A judicious use of this resource will enable the State always to keep up a proper assortment of munitions of war without the expenditure of a dollar. I have this year taken advantage of it to equip the Marion Artillery Company in Charleston, by commuting about a thousand dollars which would otherwise have been expended out of this appropriation. I recommend that the appropriation be withdrawn, and the portion of Act of 1833 authorizing it, repealed.

In his last annual Message, my immediate predecessor urged on you the necessity of a reorganization of the Executive Department of the State. I invite you to a re-perusal of his remarks. In all that he has said I give my entire and cordial concurrence, and earnestly recommend a serious consideration of the subject. I think, too, that a reorganization of all the officers connected with the Executive Department is as imperatively required. The circumstances which led to a division of them between the Seat of Government and the City of Charleston having ceased to exist, the division should cease also. The Rail-Road has brought them so near together that they might be reunited with little inconvenience to any one, and much to the advantage of the State at large. There can be no necessity for two Treasurers within six or eight hours ride of each other. There is very little, if any ungranted land in the State, and the Surveyor General's office might with propriety be finally closed. It is now chiefly an instrument for perpetrating frauds, and increasing litigation. Such duties of the Surveyor General, as it would be beneficial to the State to have performed, might be confided to a clerk in the Secretary of State's Department. The present incumbent has voluntarily made to me a Report, which gives a very candid statement of the condition of his office, and I transmit it to you as worthy of your consideration. There might be constitutional difficulties in the way of closing the office during his term, but provision could be made for doing so hereafter. The Comptroller General should be near the Treasurer and the Executive. There are still stronger reasons for reorganizing the office of Secretary of State, and locating it entirely at the seat of Government. The whole salary of this office is derived from fees, and no trifling portion of it is paid by the State for small and occasional services. He should at least be put upon the footing of a State officer, by having a fixed salary, in lieu of all charges against the State, and for taking care of the records. A large portion of these records are in a wretched condition. Many have entirely gone to decay, and others are fast mouldering away; while some important papers are altogether lost. These are the necessary consequences of a divided office, and an officer without a salary. The most important duties of the Secretary of State are connected with the Executive Department, and he should be fixed near it. The private records in this office might be transferred to the Register's office in the Districts to which they properly belong. It was a Colonial regulation which placed them in the Secretary of State's office, and the reason for it has long ceased. I recommend the appointment of a Commissioner to reorganize all the offices to which I have alluded, and to reunite them at the Seat of Government. It will, however, require a constitutional amendment to effect the latter purpose, and if you approve the recommendation it will be necessary to pass an Act to that effect at your present Session.

In making this recommendation, I trust I shall not be regarded as aiming a blow at the compromises of the Constitution. On the contrary, I would regard it as one of the greatest calamities which could happen to the State, that the present ascendency of one section of it in the Senate, and the other in the House of Representatives, should be in the slightest degree disturbed. And, imperatively as I think the interest of the State demands that all the chief officers should be assembled at this place, I would not propose it, if I could believe that it would have a tendency to produce such an effect.

In accordance with a Resolution passed at your last Session, I appointed Commissioners to meet at Limestone Springs, to enquire into the expediency of establishing a High School there. I have not yet received their Report. The first duty of a government, after providing for the security of its constituents, is to take proper measures for their education. The benefits they derive from facilitating commerce, by digging canals, clearing out rivers, constructing roads, and opening new channels of intercourse, are great; but they sink into insignificance in comparison with the vast importance of pouring out upon them in every direction copious streams of knowledge—expanding their intellects, elevating and purifying their morals, and training them up to a high and noble cast of thought. Under a government like ours, where no aristocracy of birth or wealth is tolerated, or can ever take root, the only hope we can have of the harmonious action or lasting duration of our institutions, is by resting them on the solid foundation of a people imbued with lofty sentiments, and deeply versed in all the lore of learning; who will be capable of comprehending all the blessings they confer, watchful of distant danger, and prepared to meet and overcome it, not less by power of intellect, than by force of arms. Every dollar which can be spared from the absolute wants of the State, should be first offered to this great cause. Here indeed a liberal expenditure enriches and adorns, while a narrow economy impoverishes and degrades. It is to be feared that education has been stationary in this State, if it has not retrograded, during the last quarter of a century. The College, founded and sustained by the wise munificence of the State, has done and continues to do more than was expected of it. But the Academies have not kept pace. There are comparatively few in the country, where young men can be well prepared to enter the higher classes of colleges. The consequence is, that many are yet sent abroad to inferior institutions, and return home with educations less complete, and without the advantage of that intimate association with the youth of every section of the State, which can only be formed here, and which is of such lasting advantage to themselves, and to the country. I recommend to your serious consideration, the propriety of establishing, at some healthy and central spot in each District, an Academy endowed in the same manner as the College. The sparseness of our population, and the want of concentrated wealth in the country, will postpone, for an indefinite period, such establishments by the people themselves. And in such a matter, the loss of time is absolutely fatal. If the means of the State will not permit such an expenditure, in addition to that already incurred for purposes of education, I submit to you the expediency of diverting the present Free School Fund to that object. The Free School System has failed. This fact has been announced by several of my predecessors, and there is scarcely an intelligent person in the State, who doubts that its benefits are perfectly insignificant in comparison with the expenditure. Its failure is owing to the fact, that it does not suit our people or our government, and it can never be remedied. The paupers, for whose children it is intended, but slightly appreciate the advantages of education; their pride revolts at the idea of sending their children to school as "*poor scholars*," and besides, they need them at home, to work. These sentiments and wants can in the main only be countervailed by force. In other countries where similar systems exist, force is liberally applied. It is contrary to the principles of our institutions to apply it here, and the Free School System is a failure. The sum which is annually appropriated for the support of Free Schools, if equally divided for one year among the twenty-eight Districts of the State, giving two portions to Charleston District, will be sufficient to build in each a good Academy. If, thereafter, one thousand dollars a year were appropriated to each Academy, a teacher of the highest qualifications might be secured for every one, and a saving of about eight thousand dollars per annum effected by the State. If, in addition to this salary, the profits of his School were also given to the Teacher, the rates of tuition could be reduced, to the advantage of the tax-payers, and he might be required to instruct, free of charge, such poor scholars as should be sent to him. The details of such a system cannot be dwelt on here. The immense advantages of it over the present one, are obvious, at a glance. The opportunity of giving a thorough academical education to his children would be placed in the hands of every parent of ordinary means, while such of the poor as really desired to educate theirs, might still have it in their power. The common schools would be vastly improved, under the superintendence of those who had passed through these Academies, while the standard of education would be immensely elevated throughout the State, and the College receive a new impulse in the dispensation of its incalculable blessings. Its Professorships could always be readily and ably supplied from among the accomplished teachers the Academies would develop, and its graduates of high attainments, but slender means, would in turn find useful and profitable employment in taking charge of the Academies, instead of crowding, as they now usually do, the other professions. In short, under such a system, it would be scarcely possible for any young man to grow up in our State in ignorance and idleness, or fail in obtaining a respectable settlement at home, if he possessed energy and worth. Should it not meet your approbation, and the Free School System be continued, I renew the recommendation of my immediate predecessor for the appointment of a Superintendent of these Schools.

In obedience to another of your Resolutions of the last Session, I have made very particular inquiries into the condition of the Catawba Indians. I visited their neighborhood myself, during the summer, and conversed with most of their head men. There is quite a misapprehension as to the diminution of their number, since the last treaty. It arose probably from the circumstance, that a considerable portion of them have removed to North Carolina, and taken up their residence, for the present, among the Cherokees of that State. It would undoubtedly be better for them, if all could go there and become absorbed in that well-regulated and flourishing remnant of the Cherokee tribe. But to this the authorities of North Carolina object, and it would be manifestly improper for us to send them into a sister State against her wishes. Unless they could be prevailed on to allow themselves to be removed beyond the Mississippi, to lands to be procured for them by the State, I know of no better arrangement, for the present, than to continue the experiment now going on. A Farm has been purchased for them, on which nearly all now in the State have settled. Your annual appropriation supplies all their necessary wants, and whatever they make by their own labor, is clear gain to them. I transmit herewith two Memorials which have been furnished at my request, giving an interesting history of this Tribe, from its emigration from Canada in 1860, to the present day, and also detailing the manner in which the present land owners have derived their titles; which will serve to correct the general, but unfounded belief, that these lands have been acquired without consideration. There is not a more respectable or more valuable population in any part of the State, than the residents on the Indian Land; nor any more entitled to every reasonable indulgence at your hands.

The Arsenals at Charleston and Columbia have been converted into Military Academies, in conformity with the Act of the Legislature. The change is unquestionably a great improvement on the former system.

The appointment of State Agricultural Surveyor was accepted by EDMUND RUFFIN, Esq., a distinguished Agriculturist of Virginia. He has been engaged during the year, with assiduity and zeal, in the performance of his duties in various parts of the State, and I have no doubt that his labors will be attended with the most beneficial and important results. I expect to be able to lay his Report before you in a few days.

The Court of Errors, at its last Term, decided the appeal in the case of the State against the Banks which refused to accept the provisions of the Act of 1840; and established the important principle, that suspension of specie payments is sufficient cause for the forfeiture of their charters. I can scarcely suppose that it was the intention or desire of the State to punish the Banks for past offences by the Act referred to, but simply to provide against future suspensions. Nor can they be thought worthy of punishment for appealing to the Judiciary, as they certainly had the right to do, to decide a question of vital consequence to them and to the country. Having obtained a decisive and important victory, it appears to me that it would not only be magnanimous, but wise, to forgive the past, and look only to the future. I took the responsibility of instructing the Attorney General and the Solicitors not to press the suits against the Banks to trial at the fall term of the Common Pleas, for the purpose of leaving you free to take such a course as you might deem most consistent with the dignity and interest of the State. I suggest to you the propriety of repealing the Act of 1840, and passing a new one, founded on the decision of the Court of Errors, declaring that any future suspension of specie payments shall cause the forfeiture of the charter of the suspending Bank, and requiring the Executive, in all such cases, immediately to institute proceedings for that purpose. The Act of 1840 is too indulgent to the Banks, in permitting them to suspend, on payment of a trifling penalty; and as to the monthly returns which it requires, experience has everywhere proved that they are worse than useless. I have recently received communications from the Bank of South Carolina and the State Bank, notifying me that they would no longer contest the validity of this Act, and asking to be allowed to conform to its provisions. I refer the matter to your consideration.

I have received, and transmit to you, a communication from Hon. BAYLIS J. EARLE, resigning his seat upon the Bench, in consequence of ill health. His retirement from a station which he has filled with such eminent ability, is a serious public loss, and the cause of it, a source of deep regret.

I transmit to you Resolutions on various subjects, from a number of our sister States, and also letters referring to documents received from the Federal Government. I need not suggest to you to give them a respectful consideration.

It has been rumored, and some remarks of the English Minister for Foreign affairs in the House of Lords have given countenance to the rumor, that a Treaty is on foot, between Great Britain and Texas, by which the former is to bind herself to guarantee the Independence of Texas, on condition of the abolition of Slavery in that country. Our most vital interests would be involved in such a Treaty. It is scarcely possible that Texas can make a compact so absolutely suicidal. The true interests of Texas, and of this country, demand that she should be annexed to this Union; and it is to be hoped that ere long this will be done. If it is not, the Federal Government should resist the ratification of any such Treaty with Great Britain, as an aggression upon the United States. Possessed of Canada, and the West Indies, claiming Oregon, seeking to obtain a foothold in Texas, and looking with a covetous eye to Cuba, this great Naval Power is evidently aiming to encircle us in her arms. We should not, perhaps, permit ourselves to doubt, at this time, that Texas cannot be so blind to her own welfare as to make a Treaty stipulating for the abolition of Slavery, nor that the Federal Government, in such an event, would fail to assert the rights and dignity of the United States. But an expression of your opinion on the annexation of Texas to the Union, might not be improper.

I have, in the discharge of my duty, given you the best information I possess of the condition of the State, and recommended to your consideration such measures as I deem necessary and expedient. It remains for your better judgment to approve or disapprove. May the Great Ruler of the Universe, who alone is Wise and Perfect, so influence your deliberations, that whatever you do may redound to the welfare and honor of our country.

J. H. HAMMOND.

MESSAGE

TO THE SENATE AND HOUSE OF REPRESENTATIVES OF THE STATE OF SOUTH CAROLINA, NOV. 26, 1844.

The following Message was read by the Executive Secretary, Col. BEAUFORT T. WATTS:

EXECUTIVE DEPARTMENT,
Columbia, *Nov.* 26, 1844.

Gentlemen of the Senate and House of Representatives:

IN my last annual Message to your predecessors, I congratulated them on the apparent dawn of a new era in our prosperity, which I hoped might be permanent. The currency had reached, and I am happy to say, has continued to maintain a sound condition. Commerce, trade, and manufactures were flourishing, as they yet flourish in most parts of the civilized world; and it was natural to suppose that agriculture must also revive. But we have been disappointed. Against the pressure of laws everywhere adopted to encourage manufactures, agriculture seems destined to struggle in vain. And as these laws are chiefly directed against the manufacturing supremacy of England, they fall with peculiar weight upon that great agricultural staple on which our prosperity depends. The price of cotton throughout the world is, and must for our time, in all probability, continue to be regulated by the price in Liverpool. Its value in that market depends upon the condition of the cotton manufacturers in England; and the tariff laws of other countries, which check the foreign demand for English cotton goods, must necessarily lower the price of the raw material in Liverpool, while it rises nowhere else; but, on the contrary, falls everywhere with the fall in that great mart, through which passes two-thirds of the crop of the whole world. No matter, then, where cotton manufactures flourish, unless they flourish in England, cotton cannot bear a fair price; and every attempt to build them up artificially elsewhere, is at the immediate cost of the cotton grower. Did they naturally spring up under a system of universal free trade, and in wholesome competition with England, they would indicate an actual increase of consumption, and prove highly beneficial to us. But tariff laws, though they may alter the channels of trade, and in doing so produce, as they invariably do, much mischief, have no power to increase consumption. On the contrary, by increasing the manufacturers' prices where they are in force, they necessarily diminish it, and thereby depreciate the raw material. Such laws may take from one and bestow upon another, to the injury of the whole, but they cannot *create* wealth. How long the present state of things will continue, and in what it will terminate, cannot be foreseen; but the fact appears to be clearly established, for the first time in the history of the world, that, by the skill of political jugglery, trade, commerce, and manufactures may be made to flourish, and a sound currency exist, while agriculture, the acknowledged mother of them all, and particularly that branch of agriculture which furnishes them with their life-blood, is sunk to the lowest point of depression.

The income of the State, from all sources, during the past year, amounts to three hundred and six thousand, eight hundred and thirty-one dollars and sixty-three cents ($306,831 63). The expenditures during the same period have reached the sum of three hundred and forty-seven thousand, seven hundred and four dollars and sixty-three cents ($347,704 63); of which, however, fifty-six thousand, four hundred and eighty-three dollars and seventy-three cents ($56,483 73) have been applied to the reduction of the principal of the public debt. The current income has therefore exceeded the ordinary expenses of the State, by the sum of fifteen thousand, six hundred and ten dollars and twenty-three cents ($15,610 23). The balance in the Treasury at the close of the year (a portion of it, however, subject to undrawn appropriations) amounted to seventy thousand, five hundred and six dollars and fifty-nine cents ($70,506 59), to which may be added about eight thousand dollars, being the unexpended balance of the contingent funds placed in the hands of the Executive.

The direct taxes levied and collected for the use of the State, amounted this year to two hundred and seventy-seven thousand, five hundred and sixty-two dollars and forty cents ($277,562 40). And during the same period there has been also collected from the people the additional sum of one hundred and one thousand, four hundred and twenty-eight dollars and ninety-two cents ($101,428 92); and during the year 1843, one hundred and three thousand, seven hundred and twenty-nine dollars and ninety-two cents

($103,729 92), or about an average of thirty-seven per cent. of the State taxes annually, which has been assessed by the Commissioners of the Poor, of Public Buildings, and of Roads and Bridges, in the different Districts. I have had accurate accounts kept of the taxes thus levied and collected for these years, that I might apprise you of their great amount, and call your attention to the propriety of providing for a more strict accountability for their appropriation than has been hitherto exacted. These Commissioners have been required to report, some of them to the Comptroller General, and some to the Clerks of the Courts, and account with them for the monies received and expended; but I am not aware that it is regularly done. If it was required of the Commissioners to publish such reports, and circulate them through their respective Districts, so that the people might be informed of the purposes to which their money was applied, it would be nothing more than is proper and consistent with the spirit of our institutions. It is the right of every citizen to know for what he is taxed; to judge of the propriety of it; and to be assured that the money has been used with discretion and economy. And it is a right which cannot be too jealously watched over.

I recommended to the last Legislature to take speedy and effective measures for the payment of the public debt, then amounting to three and a half millions of dollars ($3,500,000), the interest on which, including charges, exceeded one hundred and ninety thousand dollars per annum ($190,000). I proposed that the Bank of the State should be directed to redeem it, at the rate of five hundred thousand dollars a year. An act was passed requiring the Bank to provide for the payment of the instalments of the debt falling due on the first of January, 1845—6 amounting to five hundred and fifty thousand dollars ($550,000), and to deliver to the Comptroller General, to be cancelled, the evidences of State debt in its possession, to the amount of four hundred and fifteen thousand, two hundred and seventy dollars ($415,270). Of the evidences of State debt held by the Bank, one hundred and sixty-three thousand, four hundred and sixty-eight dollars ($163,468) fell due in 1845—6, so that the whole amount of debt, the liquidation of which was provided for by the act of last session, was eight hundred and one thousand, eight hundred and two dollars ($801,802), or about four hundred thousand dollars per annum for two years. I am happy to say that the Bank surrendered to the Comptroller General, in January last, and that he cancelled, four hundred and seventeen thousand, and eight dollars and twenty-nine cents ($417,008 29) of the public debt, being something more than was required of it; and I do not doubt that it will provide for the punctual payment of the instalments of 1845—6 as they become due.

I will not repeat to you the reasons which induced me to make to your predecessors the recommendations referred to. They are stated at large in my last annual Message. I feel bound, however, to say, that nothing has occurred since to change the opinions then expressed. As far as regards the Bank, the President of that institution, in a report made to the Legislature near the close of the last session, has painted in such strong colors its power, and the evils it might cause, as justly to increase the apprehensions previously felt upon that subject. Objecting to the collection and payment of three and a half millions, with a capital of more than four millions, at regular intervals during seven years, he says that, "so large a creditor going at once into the courts, would alarm all other banks and individual creditors, compel them in a measure to suspend the usual accommodations, draw in their circulation, contract their business, and also sue in every case where they are distrustful of their debts. Their customers, thus checked and pressed, would in turn sue those indebted to them, and an universal state of alarm would pervade the country. The dockets of the courts would be crowded with cases, and the Sheriffs would transfer vast amounts of property at incalculable sacrifices; the value of all other property would be greatly depreciated, and slaves would be run off, or many of them bought up by the people of other States, and would be transferred to improve their condition, leaving heavy taxation to this State, and less property to bear it. Lands abandoned and houses deserted by a ruined and bankrupted people, would everywhere remain the monuments of an erroneous and precipitate legislation."

If such disastrous consequence would arise from a liquidation not complete, and protracted through a period of seven years, how much depends on the perfect management of the Bank, and to what calamities would we be subjected by its failure—a fate from which it has no chartered immunity, and which, involved as it is in the vortex of trade, may overtake it suddenly, when the people least expect, and are worst prepared for a catastrophe so terrible. Is it wise for us to slumber on such a volcano? Does not a just regard for the safety and welfare of the community require that efficient measures should be taken to remove from it, at the earliest possible period, an engine so destructive, which fraud, accident, or oversight might at any moment put in fatal operation? It is at least worthy your consideration, whether we are to incur the risk of it forever; and if not, as its charter has but twelve years to run, there is little time to be lost, since it cannot be closed up in seven without desolating the State.

The Bank of South Carolina, and the State Bank, have accepted the provisions of the act of 1840, and the suits against them have been withdrawn.

It affords me great pleasure to inform you that the militia of the State are completely organized, and are, for militia, in excellent training. There are few officers of any grade who are not familiar with, and competent to instruct the men in the different schools of infantry tactics, and in camp duties. The artillery on the coast is in fine condition, and the cavalry throughout the State numerous, well mounted, and well drilled in the sword exercise, and the manœuvres appropriate to that arm of service. The whole number of the militia amounts to near fifty-five thousand, officers and men.

There are now in the State arsenals, in order for service, ten thousand five hundred muskets, rifles and carbines; one hundred and two pieces of artillery; thirty thousand pounds of powder; and twenty-five thousand pounds of lead, besides a large quantity of balls and cartridges. The other military stores and equipments are in proportion. The number of public arms in the hands of the militia cannot easily be ascertained, but it is not short of five thousand muskets and rifles, and twenty-five cannon, mostly brass. The State may therefore be regarded as prepared to arm, at any moment, nearly or quite one-half of her whole militia force, and to furnish them with ammunition for perhaps a campaign, without incurring any new expense; while the men she can bring into the field are probably better qualified to render efficient service than any citizen soldiery in the world. And it will cost nothing but your firm adherence to the present military system to maintain her in this position for the future.

In fact, the military expenses of the State might, I think, be materially reduced, and the benefits of one valuable branch of the present system greatly extended, by a change which can be readily effected. There are no good reasons why there should be two Arsenals in the State, or that they should be placed at the two most expensive points in it—Charleston and Columbia. A few hundred stands of arms, given in charge to the City Councils of these places, would be all that could be required, if, indeed, they would be necessary for their protection in an emergency; while in such an event the arsenals containing all our military stores, unprovided as they are with a guard capable of affording the slightest protection to them, must necessarily fall into the hands of any active foe. Prudence, therefore, dictates that the arsenals should be removed from locations where they may be subjected to surprises, and established at some spot in the interior, less accessible, and at the same time cheaper and more healthy. Such a spot might be found on one or the other branch of the rail-road, which now affords such facilities for transportation that a position anywhere upon it would be as convenient for military purposes as at Charleston or Columbia. The sale of the arsenal and magazine buildings and grounds, at these places, would, I have little doubt, furnish ample funds for erecting a brick arsenal and extensive wooden barracks in the country, without requiring a dollar from the Treasury. The consolidation of the two schools would enable you to dispense with one set of Professors and other officers, which, with the cheapness of living, and the number of pay students that might be expected if the situation was known to be perfectly healthy, would in all probability reduce the expenditure to one-half the sum now appropriated to their support. That amounts, at present, to about twenty-eight thousand dollars. In suggesting this plan, I by no means desire to be understood as recommending any change as regards the school system. It is a great improvement on that of a hired guard, and the cadets are as efficient protectors of the arsenals as the guards were; neither being anything more than nominally so. The cadets, united in one body, and increased by an unlimited number of pay students, would afford ample protection; while so fine a school, at a healthy location in the country, would induce a large proportion of the rising generation to prepare themselves for future service, both military and civil, by embracing its advantages. The policy heretofore pursued, of repairing damaged arms, is questionable. They are, for the most part, not worth the expense. The appropriation of two thousand dollars per annum, for repairing arms and arsenal purposes, may, I think, in any event, be henceforth judiciously curtailed one-half.

I transmit to you a report made to me by our very efficient Adjutant General, whose recommendations are entitled to your serious attention; and also interesting Reports from the military schools.

Permit me to renew to you a recommendation which I made to your predecessors, to establish a central academy at some suitable point in every District in the State, with an endowment of a thousand dollars a year to each. If you are unwilling to abandon the free-school system, and appropriate the funds to this object, I see no reason why twenty-eight thousand dollars additional might not be annually devoted to this important purpose. Our expenditure would then be far short of that made by many of the States in this Union, and in none of them is a more liberal one required than in ours. We have but a few well-conducted academies, and these, as soon as they acquire any reputation, are inconveniently crowded; and depending as they do for their success upon the accidental circumstance of having a competent Principal, properly appreciated, they seldom dispense their advantages to the same degree, for a length of time. Our common schools are, for the most part, a disgrace to an enlightened people. A system of permanent academies, liberally endowed, one of which would be within the reach of every citizen, conducted by such men as your appropriation, and the tuition funds would attract, and teaching uniformly a course prescribed by the Trustees of the College, would produce a revolution in the education of the State in a few years. The annual expenditure would not equal that now incurred for military purposes. While I am far from censuring that expenditure, and trust that the apathy of a long peace may not be allowed to delude us into false security, still it is certain that, under God, the world is now mainly governed by the force of intellect; and it is the duty of a wise Government to bestow its highest care upon the mental culture of its people. We have expended millions for internal improvements, which have never yielded a dollar of clear revenue to the Treasury, nor perhaps brought a valuable emigrant or preserved a useful citizen to us. The interest of a single half million appropriated to the establishment and support of central academies, will give an impulse to education which in a short time would be felt in every artery of our political, mercantile, and agricultural systems. You have liberally and wisely provided for the education of the more wealthy by establishing a College, which has done, and continues to do, more for the State than every other corporation put together, within her limits; and you bestow annually a large sum for the mental improvement of the poor, which I wish I could say produced corresponding benefits. But for that large and substantial body, constituting here, as it does in all countries, the broad and solid foundation on which rests the frame-work of the political system—that middle class, who may not take advantage of your free schools, and cannot conveniently take advantage of your College—you have done nothing. These central academies would meet their wishes, or at least their wants. The necessity of turning your most serious attention to education is pressing; and it is incalculably important. We are engaged in the experiment of Governments, simple and federative, upon principles as new as they are grand; and propose to solve the great political and moral problem of how far Freedom and Security are compatible. Sixty years—which constitute but a brief portion of a nation's cycle—have not convinced the world, nor wholly satisfied ourselves. The momentous question yet remains, Will our institutions endure? They have passed to three generations—they may fail in the fourth or fifth, or tenth. They certainly will fail, and with them the best hopes of mankind, unless the most anxious and unremitted care is bestowed on the education of those, on whom it will devolve to sustain them. Ignorance and free institutions cannot co-exist. An ignorant people can never long have any other than a despotic government. They are not fit to be free; and though they may possibly achieve, they cannot maintain their liberty. It is an old and trite saying, that the price of freedom is eternal vigilance. It is, nevertheless, profoundly true. It is usually interpreted to mean that the people must watch over their rulers. This is important. But in this country, where the people are truly and practically the source of all power, the application must go farther. They must watch themselves. They must guard against their own prejudices and passions; against local and narrow views; against party spirit; against their proverbial love of change; in short, they must guard against their own ignorance, which is the fruitful parent of all these dangers, and which will otherwise speedily degrade them, from the rank of a people, to that of a populace.

In obedience to a resolution of the last session, I have had the repairs made in the Secretary of State's office, which were indispensably necessary for the preservation of the records. There are still many improvements which might be made in that office, and also in the Surveyor General's, that would be both useful and convenient. The expense of them was greater than I felt authorized to incur, without consulting the Legislature. I think it highly expedient that a Commission should be appointed to examine the condition of these offices, and report to you in detail upon them. I have heretofore recommended that all the State offices should be consolidated at the Seat of Government; that the Executive Department should be properly organized; that a stated salary should be given to the Secretary of State, in lieu of perquisites, which are now his only compensation, and that the Land Office should be closed. The experience of another year has confirmed my opinion of the propriety and importance of these measures, and I suggest them again for your consideration.

The power of appointing Notaries Public has been immemorially exercised by the Executive. I can find no law conferring that power; nor can I, indeed, find any statute creating such an office. It is recognized in some acts, and its authority is sometimes specially limited; but none of them prescribe its powers and duties, or fix its term of duration. The office originated in the Civil Law, was handed down with it to all modern nations, and probably has no other authority here than that derived from usage. As it is held by hundreds in the State, and is more and more sought after, I think you would do well to legalize its existence, and regulate its appointment, powers, and tenure.

Much inconvenience, and sometimes serious evils, arise from the ignorance of the common Magistrates, and their irregular distribution in the Districts for which they are commissioned. They are also undoubtedly too numerous. If one Magistrate, and only one, was appointed in each beat company in the State, the number, I apprehend, would be sufficient, the location more convenient, and the chances of procuring the most intelligent citizens to fill a station so responsible greatly increased. As, however, but few of the Magistrates can be expected to be lawyers, or to have a law library at their command, I believe it to be indispensable to the regular administration of the law within their jurisdiction, that a Manual should be compiled and published, by the authority of the State, explaining in a clear manner the powers and duties of Magistrates, and prescribing the proper forms of proceedings in their courts; to which might be added a codification of the common and statute laws, and reported decisions, with which it is necessary that they should be familiar. The expense of such a work would bear but a small proportion to its value to the people at large, as well as to the Magistrates. The law strikes many of its severest blows through the agency of the common Magistracy; and it is but fair that the humblest as well as the highest citizen should be dealt with by the same rule, well defined and thoroughly understood by those who are its ministers.

The act of 1839, prescribing the manner of electing District officers, requires some amendment. In case of the death of the Clerk of the Court, the mode of filling the vacancy is not distinctly stated. To prevent great and pressing inconvenience and loss, I have been compelled to make an appointment under the act of 1815, which it was probably the intention of the Legislature of 1839 to supersede. Its requisitions, as regards the commissioning of sheriffs, are extremely inconvenient and uncertain, if not incompatible.

A title to the Mount Dearborn lands has been at length acquired for the State, and it is recorded in the office of the Secretary of State, and of the Register of Mesne Conveyance in Lancaster District.

Duplicates of the weights and measures established by the Federal Government have been received, and deposited with the Collector of the Port of Charleston for safe-keeping, until you can make some disposition of them.

I transmit to you the supplementary report of Mr. RUFFIN, our late able and indefatigable State Agricultural and Geological Surveyor. In consequence of his resignation of that appointment at the close of the year, I offered it to M. TUOMEY, Esq., of Virginia, an accomplished Geologist and Botanist, who accepted it. His very valuable and interesting report is herewith submitted. It has been found impossible to traverse every portion of the State within the year. Many important localities remain unexplored, and many require to be visited again to render perfect even a general view of the Geology of the State. I would not recommend a minute and detailed geological survey at the public expense. I do not think it called for at this time, or likely, in the present state of that science, to supersede the necessity of other surveys at no very remote period; but it is due to science, and the character of the State, that, since the survey has been instituted, it should be completed on the scale on which it is commenced. That can probably be done in one year more, and I recommend its continuation for that length of time.

I know of no measure better calculated to improve our agriculture than one which has been heretofore suggested to the Legislature—the exemption of land from executions for debt, other than that contracted for its purchase. If a law was passed to that effect, to go into operation at a given time hereafter, I can perceive but little injury or inconvenience that would be likely to result from it, while the advantages to be derived are numerous and important. It would enhance the value of land, induce investments in it, and insure substantial and extensive improvements of every kind. It would probably check emigration, diminish speculation, and in many ways conduce to the stability and permanence of all our institutions. The subject is at least worthy of your attention.

I cannot omit to invite you to an earnest consideration of federal affairs, and the peculiar relations of this State to the Federal Government, which have become highly interesting and important. The proceedings of the last session of Congress form an epoch in our history. With the events which preceded, and the circumstances under which the Act of Congress, called the Compromise Act, was passed, you are familiar. That Act was in fact a treaty, made between belligerent parties—with arms in their hands—solemnly ratified by the Federal Government on the one part, and a Convention of the State of South Carolina on the other, and deposited among the archives of our country. No treaty was ever made more important in its character, or more sacredly binding in its obligations. By that treaty South Carolina bound herself to submit for nine years longer to an unconstitutional and most oppressive Tariff, in consideration that its exactions should be gradually reduced during that period, and that after the expiration of it no higher Tariff should again be levied than was necessary to defray the expenses of an economical administration of the Government; and that the rate of duties should in no event, but the emergency of war, exceed twenty per cent. ad valorem. Our State faithfully adhered to the compact, and patiently bore the heavy burden which had been imposed upon her. In 1842 the period arrived for the Federal Government to fulfil its stipulations, and reduce the Tariff to twenty per cent. ad valorem, or lower, if so much was not requisite for the support of an economical administration. But instead of reducing them, the rate of duties was increased—actually increased to a point higher than the Tariff which South Carolina had declared null and void within her limits in 1832; which declaration led to the Compromise Act. History furnishes no instance of a grosser, or more insulting breach of faith, while perhaps no law has ever been enacted by the regular government of a civilized country, so subversive of the rights and destructive to the interests of any respectable portion of its people, as the Tariff Act of 1842, considered in all its bearings, is to the rights and interests of the Planting States of this Confederacy. It might naturally have been supposed, and probably it was expected, that this State, in conformity with the principles she had so long professed, and on which she had heretofore acted, would immediately nullify this Act; but she did not. Closely united at the time with the great Democratic party of the Union on the general principles of government, and on certain questions of federal policy of the utmost moment—seeing that this party had carried the elections to the House of Representatives by a large majority—and justly regarding it as pledged to free trade, and bound to repeal this exorbitant Tariff, she paused, and determined to await the action of another Congress; thus furnishing a fresh example of her patriotic forbearance, and sincere devotion to the peace and integrity of the Union. The new Congress met, and has terminated its first session. Propositions were made in both branches to modify the Tariff, and signally defeated. In the House, where the Democratic majority was large, the proposition was disposed of almost without debate, and a majority of the Democrats from the States north of the Potomac actually voted against it; while in the Senate, some of the leaders of that party from the same section did so likewise. There seems, therefore, to be no reasonable, or even plausible ground, on which to rest a hope that this law, so unconstitutional, and so ruinous to us, will ever be repealed, or reduced to the standard of the Compromise. The friends of the Tariff do not appear to entertain the slightest idea of such a thing. They have distinctly proclaimed it to be the settled policy of the Federal Government; and, in fact, they scarcely conceal that they regard our further remonstrances on the subject as intrusive and impertinent. Nor could we, after the utter contempt which they have manifested for their plighted faith, repose with safety upon any concessions which they might, by circumstances, be forced again to make.

With what confidence we may rely, on the other hand, upon the Northern section of the Democratic party to carry out the free trade principles which they profess, we are well admonished by the history, not only of the last session of Congress, but of the protective policy itself. The act of 1828, the most stringent of the Tariff acts, save that of 1842, was carried by the votes of the Democratic leaders of the State of New York, given under very peculiar circumstances; and this last act, by the votes of Democratic leaders from the same State, and from Pennsylvania. And it may be regarded as certain, that the friends of the protective system will be able, at all times, to command as many votes among the Northern Democrats as may be necessary for their purposes.

Nor can we, I fear, anticipate any demonstration of such a fixed, determined, and combined resistance to that policy on the part of the South, as will force the North to abandon it entirely. For this apprehension there are many reasons, but one is paramount. Unfortunately, the Electors of President and Vice-President are chosen by the people, in all the Southern States except our own. They are, in consequence, at all times almost equally divided about men; and interested politicians spare no pains to impress it on the voters, that the salvation of the country depends upon the elevation of this or that individual to the Presidential chair. In this exciting contest, measures and principles become matters of minor consequence; and though it is well known that no President, whatever may have been his political creed, has yet had firmness to veto a Tariff bill, however monstrous, and that no anointed candidate even, has ever been able fully and consistently to declare himself against the protective policy, they still persist in the pernicious delusion that everything will be secured by the triumph of their favorite. While every other question, however vital to liberty and the Constitution, continues to be made subordinate to this, and to be estimated solely by its influence on the Presidential election; and while that election continues to be made directly by the masses, it is almost vain to expect that the people of any State can be united among themselves, or the States of any section combine, unless under extraordinary impulses, to resist effectually the usurpations of the Federal Government.

Under these circumstances, it devolves on South Carolina to decide what course she will pursue in reference to the Tariff. The period has arrived when she can no longer postpone her final decision. It is due from her. It is expected of her. And if she fails to announce it, her silence will nevertheless be conclusive. Whatever may be the technical validity, or legal force, of the opinions on this important question which your predecessors have placed upon your records, it appears clear to me that our State is bound by her past history, and the principles she professes; and owes it to the country and herself, to adopt such measures as will at an early period bring all her moral, constitutional, and, if necessary, physical resources, in direct array against a policy, which has never been checked but by her interposition, and which impoverishes our country, revolutionizes our Government, and overthrows our liberties. The expediency, the manner, and the precise time of doing this, are for your grave deliberation.

The last session of Congress was also signalized by the rejection of a treaty for the annexation of Texas to the United States. The cause assigned for this rejection was, that Mexico not having yet acknowledged the independence of Texas, it would be a violation of our treaty of amity and peace with that power to receive Texas into the Union. It is at least a question, whether the United States has not a claim to Texas paramount to any to which Mexico can pretend. It may also be questioned, whether the terms on which Texas united with the Mexican Republic, and formed a Department of it, did not entitle her of right to withdraw whenever she saw proper. Be that as it may, she has in fact dissolved the connection, and has been recognized as an Independent Power, by the United States, England, France, Belgium, and Holland. A jury of nations has pronounced a divorce, and Mexico has abstained for eight years from attempting to revive the union by the ordinary means of force of arms. Her claims cannot now be regarded as anything short of frivolous. That the political sensibility of the United States should now hang a point of honor on these claims, and thereby throw away an empire, must appear to all the world extremely romantic, if not ridiculous. While Russia is by incessant war extending her overgrown dominion into the rugged steppes of Tartary; while France sheds torrents of blood, and spends millions of treasure, to conquer a foothold on a sterile coast of Africa, and, stretching across two oceans, opens her batteries on the female sovereign of a petty island at the antipodes, to establish her supremacy there; and while England with rapacious hand despoils Eastern princes of province after province, and even condescends to accept a kingdom on the Musquito shore, as a legacy from a barbarian chief; that the United States should, from mere delicacy, refuse a proffered territory of three hundred thousand square miles, embracing the most fertile soil on the globe, and peopled by her own children, cannot be otherwise regarded than as absolutely Quixotic. Europe, while rejoicing at such an unexpected event, is so utterly incapable of appreciating these sublimated notions of national faith, as not to hesitate to ascribe it solely to the influence of party spirit, and note it as a fresh evidence of the instability of our institutions. That party spirit may have had some influence in the rejection of this treaty, is probable. But the main, and most powerful reason, undoubtedly was the deadly animosity of a portion of this Union to our domestic slavery, and the fear of extending and perpetuating it. This reason has been openly avowed by nearly the whole press of the non-slaveholding States; by their public lecturers, by their most distinguished orators, and by the Legislatures of several States—particularly that of Massachusetts—whose resolutions I transmit to you, in which is strongly intimated the expediency of dissolving the Union of these States, on this very ground, if Texas is annexed.

Scarcely any circumstance could have furnished so striking a proof of the deep-seated hostility of every portion, and almost every individual, of the North, to our system of Slavery, and their fixed determination to eradicate it, if possible, as the rejection of this treaty, and the arguments by which they justify it. In every point of view, save one, the acquisition of Texas was of more consequence to the North than to the South. To them it gave an increase of commerce; a fresh market for their manufactures; another vent for population; new subjects on whom to levy tribute. To us, security, only; and security at an immense sacrifice in the value of our lands and of our staples. But the pride of increased dominion, the thirst of wealth; ambition, and avarice—long supposed to be the two strongest passions of our nature—have sunk before their fanatical zeal to uproot an institution with which is linked forever, and inseparably, the welfare, and almost the existence, of five millions of their fellow-citizens.

Nor is the refusal to ratify this treaty, so vitally important to the South, the only extraordinary proof which the past year has furnished, of the exuberant and rancorous hostility of the North to our domestic slavery. At a meeting in May last, of the General Conference of the Methodist denomination—whose ecclesiastical constitution and government bear, in some respects, a striking resemblance to the political Constitution and Government of this Confederacy—a pious Bishop of the South was virtually deposed from his sacred office, because he was a slaveholder. It was openly and distinctly stated, that the Methodist congregations in the non-slaveholding States, embracing a much larger proportion of the masses than any others, would no longer tolerate a slave-holder in their pulpits; a fact which has been since exemplified. With becoming spirit, the patriotic Methodists of the South dissolved all connexion with their brethren of the North. And for this they are entitled to lasting honor and gratitude from us. Other instances might be cited, not so striking, but equally decisive of the fact, that the abolition phrenzy is no longer confined to a few restless and daring spirits, but has seized the whole body of the people in the non-slaveholding States, and is rapidly superseding all other excitements, and trampling on all other interests. It has even been thought that the organized Abolition vote might decide the pending Presidential election; and both parties at the North have been charged with endeavoring to conciliate it for their candidate. While England, encouraged by these movements, and exasperated by our Tariff laws, is making avowed war on us, that she may strike a blow at those who are more our enemies than hers.

Though all these efforts may fail to coerce Congress to pass an Act of Emancipation, and can hardly succeed in organizing an extensive insurrection among our slaves, it cannot be disguised that they are doing mischief here, and may soon effect irreparable injury. They must be arrested. It is indispensably necessary that they should be arrested in the shortest possible period of time. The question is, How is this to be done? Argument and remonstrance are clearly useless. All appeals to sympathy, to interest, and to the guarantees of the Bond of Union, have failed, as yet, and will, I have no doubt, continue to fail. Seeing, as we of the South do, the naked impossibility of emancipation, without the extermination of one race or the other, through crimes and horrors too shocking to be mentioned—leaving a devastated land covered with ashes, tears, and blood—I cannot doubt that you will be justified by God and future generations, in adopting any measures, however startling they may appear, that will place your rights and property exclusively under your own control, and enable you to repel all interference with them, whatever shape it may assume. And as you incur a danger of no ordinary character—one so subtle and insidious in its approaches that there is no ascertaining how soon it may be too late to resist it

—I believe you will be equally justified in taking these measures as early and decisively as in your judgment you may deem proper.

The State of South-Carolina has been charged, and sometimes from high quarters, with entertaining a desire to dissolve the Union of these States; and the expression of a sentiment looking that way, by any of her citizens, is widely denounced as treasonable, if not blasphemous. There is no State which has given, in its times of trial, a more ardent or effective support to the Union than our own. There is no State which has less to gain by anarchy and revolution, or that is less disposed to plunge into them wantonly. Neither her fundamental institutions, nor her legislation, betray a love of change. Her people are steady in their principles, and loyal to their customs, laws, and constitutions. But their devotion is not blind. They are not to be defrauded of their rights under prostituted forms, however sacred in their origin, nor deterred, either by obloquy or danger, from maintaining them. They are by no means insensible of the advantages of the Union. They are not wanting in those sentiments which teach them to venerate the institutions founded, in part, by their own wise and heroic ancestors; nor in that pride which would lead them to appreciate the glory of continuing members of a republic extending over two millions and a half of square miles, and which might one day number five hundred millions of enlightened citizens. But the Union was a compact for justice, liberty, and security. When these fail, its living principles are gone. South-Carolina can have no respect for an empty name—still less for one which becomes synonymous to her with oppression, vassalage and danger. It is vain to sound it in our ears, and claim for it our allegiance. Our ancestors in the old world, waged a successful war against the divine right of Kings; and our fathers of the Revolution broke the yoke of Lords and Commons. Little has been gained for us, by these two noblest struggles which history records, if we are now to be overawed by the divine right of Union, and steeped in wretchedness under its violated character. The illustrious man who has been called, by universal consent the Father of our Country, did indeed leave it to us, as his parting admonition, that we should cling to the Union as our ark of safety. But, much as we reverence his precept, his example is still dearer to us. Sacred as we hold his last words, we cannot throw them into the scale against the history of his life; and that teaches us to resist oppression, from whatever quarter it may come, and whatever hazard is incurred.

Coming for the first time together, having duties to perform which to some of you are new, and holding in your hands the destinies of South-Carolina, you cannot be too strongly impressed with the necessity of reflecting maturely on the important questions that devolve upon you, and of reverentially invoking to your aid that Almighty Power, who searches all hearts, weighs all motives, and metes out to all human efforts a just measure of success.

J. H. HAMMOND.

LETTER

TO THE FREE CHURCH OF GLASGOW, ON THE SUBJECT OF SLAVERY.

EXECUTIVE DEPARTMENT,
South Carolina, 21st *June*, 1844.

SIR:—The last post brought me your communication, accompanying the memorial of the Presbytery of the Free Church of Glasgow, in behalf of John L. Brown, convicted in this State of aiding a slave in escaping from her master, and sentenced to be hung in April last. It will be gratifying to you, seeing the interest you have taken in the matter, to learn that I have pardoned Brown. In consequence of representations made to me in December last by Judge O'Neall, speaking for himself and the judges of the Court of Appeals, I commuted his punishment to thirty-nine lashes. Facts, not known to the jury, nor to the judges, were afterward brought to my knowledge, which satisfied me that Brown had no criminal design in what he did; and in the month of March I transmitted to him a full pardon. I was not at all aware, at that time, of the great interest taken abroad in behalf of one whose case I had never heard mentioned here, except on the occasions referred to; and I was astonished to find myself overwhelmed soon after with voluminous petitions for his pardon from the non-slaveholding States of this Union; and to perceive that his sentence was commented on, not only by the English newspapers, but in the English House of Lords. The latest, and I trust the last communication to me on the subject, is your memorial.

The interference of foreigners, or any person beyond our boundaries, in the execution of the municipal laws of a sovereign State, even if in respectful terms, is certainly a violation of all propriety and courtesy; and if carried to any extent, must become wholly intolerable. I pass that by, however. The law under which Brown was convicted, was enacted during our colonial existence, and is emphatically British law. It is also a good law. I pardoned him, not because I disapproved the law, but because I did not think he violated it. It would be the most absurd thing in the world to recognize by law a system of domestic slavery, and yet allow every one to free, not merely his own slaves, but those of his neighbor, whenever instigated to do so by his own notions of propriety, his interest, or his caprice. What sort of security would we have for property held on such terms as these? You cannot but perceive, that to permit others to take our slaves from us at pleasure with impunity, would amount to a total abolition of slavery. There would be no real difference between this, and allowing the slaves to go free themselves. Your Presbytery, and all the petitioners for Brown, and agitators of his case, must have seen the matter in this light; and it is attributing to us but a small share of common sense, to suppose that we would not take the same view of it ourselves.

Whether death should be inflicted for such an offence is another question. We have modified in a great degree the sanguinary code of law left us by our British ancestors; but we have not gone the length to which some philosophers, both here and in your country, would have all governments to go—of abolishing the punishment of death. Nor do I believe the success your government has met with in endeavoring to diminish crime by abolishing this punishment in so many cases, will encourage them to press the matter much farther at this time. Considering the value of a slave; the facility of seducing him from his owner; the evil influence which frequent seduction might exercise on an institution, the destruction of which must speedily and inevitably strike from the roll of civilized States nearly the whole slaveholding section of this country, as it has already done St. Domingo and Jamaica; and the enthusiastic and reckless enemies of this institution by whom we are surrounded, it seems to me that if any offence affecting property merits death, this is one.

Your memorial, like all that have been sent to me, denounces slavery in the severest terms; as "traversing every law of nature, and violating the most sacred domestic relations, and the primary rights of man." You and your Presbytery are Christians. You profess to believe, and no doubt do believe, that the laws laid down in the Old and New Testaments for the government of man, in his moral, social and political relations, were all the direct revelation of God himself. Does it never occur to you, that in anathematizing slavery, you deny this divine sanction of those laws, and repudiate both Christ and Moses; or charge God with downright crime, in regulating and perpetuating slavery in the Old Testament, and the most criminal neglect, in not only not abolishing, but not even reprehending it, in the New? If these Testaments came from God, it is impossible that slavery can "traverse the laws of nature, or violate the primary rights of man." What those laws and rights really are, mankind have not agreed. But they are clear to God; and it is blasphemous for any of His creatures to set up their notions of them in opposition to His immediate and acknowledged Revelation. Nor does *our* system of slavery outrage the most sacred domestic relations. Husbands and wives, parents and children, among our slaves, are seldom separated, except from necessity or crime. The same reasons induce much more frequent separations among the white population in this, and, I imagine, in almost every other country.

But I make bold to say that the Presbytery of the Free Church of Glasgow, and nearly all the abolitionists in every part of the world, in denouncing our domestic slavery, denounce a thing of which they know absolutely nothing—nay, which does not even exist. You weep over the horrors of the Middle Passage, which have ceased, so far as we are concerned; and over pictures of chains and lashes here, which have no existence but in the imagination. Our sympathies are almost equally excited by the accounts published by your Committees of Parliament—and therefore true; and which have been verified by the personal observation of many of us—of the squalid misery, loathsome disease, and actual starvation, of multitudes of the unhappy laborers—not of Ireland only, but of England—nay, of Glasgow itself. Yet we never presume to interfere with your social or municipal regulations—your aggregated wealth and congregated misery—nor the crimes attendant on them, nor your pitiless laws for their suppression. And when we see by your official returns, that even the best classes of English agricultural laborers can obtain for their support but seven pounds of bread and four *ounces* of meat per week, and when sick or out of employment, must either starve or subsist on charity, we cannot but look with satisfaction to the condition of our slave laborers, who usually receive as a weekly allowance, fifteen pounds of bread, and three *pounds* of bacon—have their children fed without stint, and properly attended to—are all well clothed, and have comfortable dwellings, where, with their gardens and poultry yards, they can, if the least industrious, more than realize for themselves the vain hope of the great French king, that he might see every peasant in France have his fowl upon his table on the Sabbath—who, from the proceeds of their own crop, purchase even luxuries and finery—who labor scarcely more than nine hours a day, on the average of the year—and who, in sickness, in declining years, in infancy and decrepitude, are watched over with a tenderness scarcely short of parental. When we contemplate the *known* condition of your operatives, of whom, that of your agricultural laborers is perhaps the least wretched, we are not only not ashamed of that of our slaves, but are always ready to challenge a comparison, and should be highly gratified to submit to a reciprocal investigation, by enlightened and impartial judges.

You are doubtless of opinion that all these advantages in favor of the slave, if they exist, are more than counterbalanced by his being deprived of his freedom. Can you tell me what *freedom* is—who possesses it, and how much of it is requisite for human happiness? Is your operative, existing in the physical and moral condition which your own official returns depict—deprived too of every political right, even that of voting at the polls—who is not cheered by the slightest hope of ever improving his lot or leaving his children to a better, and who actually seeks the four walls of a prison, the hulks, and transportation, as comparative blessings—is *he* free—*sufficiently* free? Can you say that this sort of freedom—the liberty to beg or steal—to choose between starvation and a prison—does or ought to make him happier than our slave, situated as I have truly described him, without a single care or gloomy forethought?

But you will perhaps say, it is not in the Thing, but in the Name, that the magic resides—that there is a vast difference between being *called a slave* and being *made one*, though equally enslaved by law, by social forms, and by immutable necessity. This is an ideal and sentimental distinction which it will be difficult to bring the African race to comprehend. But if it be true, and freedom is a name and idea, rather than reality, how many are there then entitled even to that name, except by courtesy; and how many are able to enjoy the idea in perfection? Does your operative regard it as a sufficient compensation for the difference between four ounces and three *pounds* of bacon? If he does, he is a rare philosopher. In your powerful kingdom social grade is as thoroughly established and acknowledged as military rank. Your commonalty see among themselves a series of ascending classes, and, rising above them all, many more, composed of men not a whit superior to themselves in any of the endowments of nature, who yet in name, in idea, and in fact, possess greater worldly privileges. To what one of all these classes does *genuine* freedom belong? To the duke, who fawns upon the prince—to the baron, who knuckles to the duke, or to the commoner, who crouches to the baron?

Doubtless you all boast of being ideally free; while the American citizen counts *your* freedom slavery, and could not brook a state of existence in which he daily encountered fellow mortals, acknowledged and privileged as his superiors, solely by the accident of birth. He, too, in turn, will boast of his freedom, which might be just as little to your taste. I will not pursue this topic farther. But I think you must admit that there is not so much in a name; and that ideal or imputed freedom is a very uncertain source of happiness.

You must also agree, that it would be a bold thing for you or any one to undertake to solve the great problem of good and evil—happiness and misery, and decide in what worldly condition man enjoys most, and suffers least. Your profession calls on you to teach that his true happiness is seldom found upon the stormy sea of politics, or in the mad race of ambition, in the pursuits of mammon, or the cares of hoarded gain; that, in short, the wealth and honors of this world are to be despised and shunned. Will you then say, that the slave must be wretched, because he is debarred from them? or because he does not indulge in the dreams of philosophy, the wrangling of sectarians, or the soul-disturbing speculations of the skeptic?

or because, having never tasted of what is *called* freedom, he is ignorant of its ideal blessings, and as contented with his lot, such as it is, as most men are with theirs?

You and your Presbytery doubtless desire, as we all should, to increase the happiness of the human family. But since it is so difficult, if not impossible, to determine in what earthly state man may expect to enjoy most of it, why can you not be content, to leave him in that respect where God has placed him; to give up the ideal and the doubtful, for the real; to restrict yourselves to the faithful fulfilment of your great mission of preaching " the glad tidings of salvation" *to all classes and conditions ;* or, at the very least, sacredly abstain from all endeavors to ameliorate the lot of man by revolution, bloodshed, massacre, and desolation, to which all attempts at abolition in this country, in the present, and, so far as I can see, in any future age, must inevitably lead?

Be satisfied with the improvement which slavery has made, and which nothing but slavery could have made to the same extent, in the race of Ham. Look at the negro in Africa—a naked savage—almost a cannibal, ruthlessly oppressing and destroying his fellows; idle, treacherous, idolatrous, and such a disgrace to the image of his God, in which you declare him to be made, that some of the wisest philosophers have denied him the possession of a soul. See him here—three millions at least of his rescued race—civilized, contributing immensely to the subsistence of the human family, his passions restrained, his affections cultivated, his bodily wants and infirmities provided for, and the true religion of his Maker and Redeemer taught him. Has slavery been a curse to him? Can you think God has ordained it for no good purpose? or, not content with the blessings it has already bestowed, do you desire to increase them still? Before you act, be sure your heavenly Father has revealed to you the means. Wait for the inspiration which brought the Israelites out of Egypt, which carried salvation to the Gentiles.

I have written you a longer letter than I intended. But the question of slavery is a much more interesting subject to us, involving, as it does, the fate of all that we hold dear, than anything connected with John L. Brown can be to you; and I trust you will read my reply with as much consideration as I have read your memorial.

I have the honor to be, very respectfully,
Your obedient servant,
J. H. HAMMOND.

To the Rev. Thomas Brown, D.D., Moderator of the Free Church of Glasgow, and to the Presbytery thereof.

TWO LETTERS

ON THE SUBJECT OF SLAVERY IN THE UNITED STATES, ADDRESSED TO
THOMAS CLARKSON, Esq.

         Silver Bluff, South Carolina,
           January 28, 1845.

 Sir:—I received a short time ago, a letter from the Rev. WILLOUGHBY M. DICKINSON, dated at your residence, "Playford Hall, near Ipswich, 26th Nov., 1844," in which was inclosed a copy of your Circular Letter addressed to professing Christians in our Northern States, having no concern with Slavery, and to others there. I presume that Mr. DICKINSON's letter was written with your knowledge, and the document inclosed with your consent and approbation. I therefore feel that there is no impropriety in my addressing my reply directly to yourself, especially as there is nothing in Mr. DICKINSON's communication requiring serious notice. Having abundant leisure, it will be a recreation to devote a portion of it to an examination and free discussion of the question of Slavery as it exists in our Southern States; and since you have thrown down the gauntlet to me, I do not hesitate to take it up.

 Familiar as you have been with the discussions of this subject in all its aspects, and under all the excitements it has occasioned for sixty years past, I may not be able to present much that will be new to you. Nor ought I to indulge the hope of materially affecting the opinions you have so long cherished, and so zealously promulgated. Still, time and experience have developed facts, constantly furnishing fresh tests to opinions formed sixty years since, and continually placing this great question in points of view, which could scarcely occur to the most consumate intellect even a quarter of a century ago; and which may not have occurred yet to those whose previous convictions, prejudices and habits of thought have thoroughly and permanently biassed them to one fixed way of looking at the matter; while there are peculiarities in the operation of every social system, and special local as well as moral causes materially affecting it, which no one, placed at the distance you are from us, can fully comprehend or properly appreciate. Besides, it may be possibly, a novelty to you to encounter one who conscientiously believes the Domestic Slavery of these States to be not only an inexorable necessity for the present, but a moral and humane institution, productive of the greatest political and social advantages, and who is disposed, as I am, to defend it on these grounds.

I do not propose, however, to defend the African Slave Trade. That is no longer a question. Doubtless great evils arise from it as it has been, and is now conducted: unnecessary wars and cruel kidnapping in Africa; the most shocking barbarities in the Middle Passage; and perhaps a less humane system of slavery in countries continually supplied with fresh laborers at a cheap rate. The evils of it, however, it may be fairly presumed, are greatly exaggerated. And if I might judge of the truth of transactions stated as occurring in this trade, by that of those reported as transpiring among us, I should not hesitate to say, that a large proportion of the stories in circulation are unfounded, and most of the remainder highly colored.

On the passage of the Act of Parliament prohibiting this trade to British subjects rests what you esteem the glory of your life. It required twenty years of arduous agitation, and the intervening extraordinary political events, to convince your countrymen, and among the rest your pious King, of the expediency of the measure; and it is but just to say, that no one individual rendered more essential service to the cause than you did. In reflecting on the subject, you cannot but often ask yourself: What after all has been accomplished; how much human suffering has been averted; how many human beings have been rescued from transatlantic slavery? And on the answers you can give these questions, must in a great measure, I presume, depend the happiness of your life. In framing them, how frequently must you be reminded of the remark of Mr. Grosvenor, in one of the early debates upon the subject, which I believe you have yourself recorded, "that he had twenty objections to the abolition of the Slave Trade: the first was, *that it was impossible*—the rest he need not give." Can you say to yourself, or to the world, that this *first* objection of Mr. Grosvenor has been yet confuted. It was estimated at the commencement of your agitation in 1787, that forty-five thousand Africans were annually transported to America and the West Indies. And the mortality of the Middle Passage, computed by some at 5, is now admitted not to have exceeded 9 per cent. Notwithstanding your Act of Parliament, the previous abolition by the United States, and that all the powers in the world have subsequently prohibited this trade—some of the greatest of them declaring it piracy, and covering the African seas with armed vessels to prevent it—Sir Thomas Fowel Buxton, a coadjutor of yours, declared in 1840, that the number of Africans now annually sold into slavery beyond the sea, amounts, at the very least, to one hundred and fifty thousand souls; while the mortality of the Middle Passage has increased, in consequence of the measures taken to suppress the trade, to 25 or 30 per cent. And of the one hundred and fifty thousand slaves who have been captured and liberated by British men-of-war since the passage of your Act, Judge Jay, an American Abolitionist, asserts that one hundred thousand, or two-thirds, have perished between their capture and liberation. Does it not really seem that Mr. Grosvenor was a Prophet? That though nearly all the "impossibilities" of 1787 have vanished, and become as familiar *facts* as our household customs, under the magic influence of Steam, Cotton and universal peace, yet this wonderful prophecy still stands, defying time and the energy and genius of mankind. Thousands of valuable lives and fifty millions of pounds sterling have been thrown away by your government in fruitless attempts to overturn it. I hope you have not lived too long for your own happiness, though you have been thus spared to see that, in spite of all your toils and those of your fellow laborers, and the accomplishment of all that human agency could do, the African Slave Trade has increased threefold under your own eyes—more rapidly, perhaps, than any other ancient branch of commerce—and that your efforts to suppress it have effected *nothing more* than a threefold increase of its horrors. There is a God who rules this world—All powerful—Farseeing: He does not permit His creatures to foil His designs. It is He who, for His allwise, though to us often inscrutable purposes, throws "impossibilities" in the way of our fondest hopes and most strenuous exertions. Can you doubt this?

Experience having settled the point that this Trade *cannot be abolished by the use of force*, and that blockading squadrons serve only to make it more profitable and more cruel, I am surprised that the attempt is persisted in, unless it serves as a cloak to other purposes. It would be far better than it now is, for the African, if the trade was free from all restrictions, and left to the mitigation and decay which time and competition would surely bring about. If kidnapping, both secretly and by war made for the purpose, could be by any means prevented in Africa, the next greatest blessing you could bestow upon that country would be to transport its actual slaves in comfortable vessels across the Atlantic. Though they might be perpetual bondsmen, still they would emerge from darkness into light—from barbarism to civilization—from idolatry to Christianity—in short from death to life.

But let us leave the African slave trade, which has so signally defeated the *Philanthropy* of the world, and turn to American slavery, to which you have now directed your attention, and against which a crusade has been preached as enthusiastic and ferocious as that of Peter the Hermit—destined, I believe, to be about as successful. And, here let me say, there is a vast difference between the two, though you may not acknowledge it. The wisdom of ages has concurred in the justice and expediency of establishing rights by prescriptive use, however tortious, in their origin, they may have been. You would deem a man insane, whose keen sense of equity would lead him to denounce your right to the lands you hold, and which perhaps you inherited from a long line of ancestry, because your title was derived from a Saxon or Norman conqueror, and your lands were originally wrested by violence from the vanquished Britons. And so would the New England Abolitionist regard any one who would insist that he should restore his farm to the descendants of the slaughtered Red men, to whom God had as clearly given it as he gave life and freedom to the kidnapped African. That time does not consecrate wrong, is a fallacy which all history exposes; and which the best and wisest men of all ages and professions of religious faith have practically denied. The means, therefore, whatever they may have been, by which the African race now in this country have been reduced to slavery, cannot affect us, since they are our property, as your land is yours, by inheritance or purchase and prescriptive right. You will say that man cannot hold *property in man*. The answer is, that he can and *actually does* hold property in his fellow all the world over, in a variety of forms, and *has always done so*. I will show presently his authority for doing it.

If you were to ask me whether I am an advocate of slavery in the abstract, I should probably answer, that I am not, according to my understanding of the question. I do not like to deal in abstractions. It seldom leads to any useful ends. There are few universal truths. I do not now remember any single moral truth universally acknowledged. We have no assurance that it is given to our finite understanding to comprehend abstract moral truth. Apart from Revelation and the Inspired Writings, what ideas should we have even of God, Salvation and Immortality? Let the Heathen answer. Justice itself is impalpable as an abstraction, and abstract liberty the merest phantasy that ever amused the imagination. This world was made for man, and man for the world as it is. We ourselves, our relations with one another and with all matter are real, not ideal. I might say that I am no more in favor of slavery in the abstract, than I am of poverty, disease, deformity, idiocy or any other inequality in the condition of the human family; that I love perfection, and think I should enjoy a Millennium such as God has promised. But what would it amount to? A pledge that I would join you to set about eradicating those apparently inevitable evils of our nature, in equalizing the condition of all mankind, consummating the perfection of our race, and introducing the Millennium? By no means. To effect these things, belongs exclusively to a Higher Power. And it would be well for us to leave the Almighty to perfect His own works and fulfil His own covenants; especially, as the history of the past shows how entirely futile all human efforts have proved, when made for the purpose of aiding Him in carrying out even his revealed designs, and how invariably he has accomplished them by unconscious instruments, and in the face of human expectation. Nay more, that every attempt which has been made by fallible man to extort from the world obedience to his "abstract" notions of right and wrong, has been invariably attended with calamities, dire and extended, just in proportion to the breadth and vigor of the movement. On slavery in the abstract, then, it would not be amiss to have as little as possible to say. Let us contemplate it as it is. And thus contemplating it, the first question we have to ask ourselves is, whether it is contrary to the Will of God, as revealed to us in His Holy Scriptures—the only certain means given us to ascertain His Will. If it is, then slavery is a sin; and I admit at once that every man is bound to set his face against it, and to emancipate his slaves should he hold any.

Let us open these Holy Scriptures. In the twentieth chapter of Exodus, seventeenth verse, I find the following words: "Thou shalt not covet thy neighbor's house, thou shalt not covet thy neighbor's wife, nor his man-servant nor his maid-servant, nor his ox, nor his ass, nor anything that is thy neighbor's"—which is the Tenth of those commandments that declare the essential principles of the Great Moral Law delivered to Moses by God Himself. Now, discarding all technical and verbal quibbling as wholly unworthy to be used in interpreting the word of God, what is the plain meaning, undoubted intent, and true spirit of this commandment? Does it not emphatically and explicitly forbid you to disturb your neighbor in the enjoyment of his property; and more especially of that which is here specifically mentioned as being lawfully and by this commandment made sacredly his? Prominent in the catalogue stands his "man-servant and his maid-servant," who are thus distinctly *consecrated as his property* and guaranteed to him for his exclusive benefit in the most solemn manner. You attempt to avert the otherwise irresistible conclusion, that slavery was thus ordained by God, by declaring that the word "slave" is not used here, and is not to be found in the Bible. And I have seen many learned dissertations on this point from Abolition pens. It is well known that both the Hebrew and Greek words translated "servant" in the Scriptures, mean also and most usually "slave." The use of the one word instead of the other was a mere matter of taste with the Translators of the Bible, as it has been with all the commentators and religious writers; the latter of whom have I believe for the most part adopted the term "slave," or used both terms indiscriminately. If, then, these Hebrew and Greek words include the idea of both systems of servitude, the conditional and unconditional, they should, as the major includes the minor proposition, be always translated "slaves," unless the sense of the whole text forbids it. The real question, then, is, what idea is intended to be conveyed by the words used in the commandment quoted? And it is clear to my mind that as no limitation is affixed to them, and the express intention was to secure to mankind the peaceful enjoyment of every species of property, the terms "Men servants and Maid servants" include all classes of servants, and establish a lawful, exclusive and indefeasible interest equally in the "Hebrew Brother who shall go out in the seventh year" and "the yearly hired servant," and those "purchased from the Heathen round about," and were to be "Bondmen forever," *as the property of their fellow man.*

You cannot deny that there were among the Hebrews "Bond-men forever." You cannot deny that God especially authorized his chosen people to purchase

"Bond-men forever" from the Heathen, as recorded in the 25th *Chap. of Leviticus*, and that they are there designated by the very Hebrew word used in the Tenth commandment. Nor can you deny that a "BOND-MAN FOREVER" is a "SLAVE;" yet you endeavor to hang an argument of immortal consequence upon the wretched subterfuge, that the precise word "slave" is not to be found in the *translation* of the Bible; as if the Translators were canonical expounders of the Holy Scriptures, and *their words*, not *God's meaning*, must be regarded as His Revelation.

It is vain to look to Christ or any of his Apostles to justify such blasphemous perversions of the word of God. Although slavery in its most revolting form was everywhere visible around them, no visionary notions of piety or philanthropy ever tempted them to gainsay the LAW, even to mitigate the cruel severity of the existing system. On the contrary, regarding slavery as an *established* as well as *inevitable condition of human society*, they never hinted at such a thing as its termination on earth, any more than that "the poor may cease out of the land," which God affirms to Moses shall never be; and they exhort "all servants under the yoke" to "count their masters as worthy of all honor;" "to obey them in all things according to the flesh; not with eye-service as men-pleasers, but in singleness of heart, fearing God;" "not only the good and gentle, but also the froward;" "for what glory is it if when ye are buffeted for your faults ye shall take it patiently? but if when ye do well and suffer for it ye take it patiently, this is acceptable of God." St. Paul actually apprehended a runaway slave and sent him to his master! Instead of deriving from the Gospel any sanction for the work you have undertaken, it would be difficult to imagine sentiments and conduct more strikingly in contrast than those of the Apostles and the Abolitionists.

It is impossible therefore to suppose that slavery is contrary to the Will of God. It is equally absurd to say that American slavery differs in form or principle from that of the chosen People. *We accept the Bible terms as the definition of our slavery, and its precepts as the guide of our conduct.* We desire nothing more. Even the right to " buffet," which is esteemed so shocking, finds its express license in the Gospel. 1 *Peter ii.* 20. Nay, what is more, God directs the Hebrews to " bore holes in the ears of their brothers" to *mark* them, when under certain circumstances they become *perpetual slaves. Ex. xxi.* 6.

I think, then, I may safely conclude, and I firmly believe, that American slavery is not only not a sin, but especially commanded by God through Moses, and approved by Christ through His Apostles. And here I might close its defence; for what God ordains and Christ sanctifies should surely command the respect and toleration of Man. But I fear there has grown up in our time a Transcendental Religion which is throwing even Transcendental Philosophy into the shade— a Religion too pure and elevated for the Bible; which seeks to erect among men a higher standard of Morals than the Almighty has revealed, or our Saviour preached; and which is probably destined to do more to impede the extension of God's Kingdom on earth than all the Infidels who have ever lived. Error is error. It is as dangerous to deviate to the right hand as the left. And when men professing to be holy men, and who are by numbers so regarded, declare those things to be sinful which our Creator has expressly authorized and instituted, they do more to destroy his authority among mankind, than the most wicked can effect by proclaiming that to be innocent which he has forbidden. To this self-righteous and self-exalted class belong all the Abolitionists whose writings I have read. With them it is no end of the argument to prove your propositions by the text of the Bible, interpreted according to its plain and palpable meaning, and as understood by all mankind for three thousand years before their time. They are more ingenious at construing and interpolating to accommodate it to their new-fangled and etherial code of morals, than ever were Voltaire & Hume in picking it to pieces to free the world from what they considered a delusion. When the Abolitionists proclaim " man-stealing" to be a sin, and show me that it is so written down by God, I admit them to be right, and shudder at the idea of such a crime. But when I show them that to hold "bond-men forever" is ordained by God, *they deny the Bible, and set up in its place a Law of their own making.* I must then cease to reason with them on this branch of the question. Our religion differs as widely as our manners. The Great Judge in the day of final account must decide between us.

Turning from the consideration of slave-holding in its relations to man as an accountable being, let us examine it in its influence on his political and social state. Though, being foreigners to us, you are in no wise entitled to interfere with the civil institutions of this country, it has become quite common for your countrymen to decry slavery as an enormous political evil to us, and even to declare that our Nothern States ought to withdraw from the Confederacy rather than continue to be contaminated by it. The American Abolitionists appear to concur fully in these sentiments, and a portion at least of them are incessantly threatening to dissolve the Union. Nor should I be at all surprised if they succeed. It would not be difficult, in my opinion, to conjecture which region, the North or South, would suffer most by such an event. For one I should not object, by any means, to cast my lot in a confederacy of States whose citizens might all be slave-holders.

I endorse without reserve the much-abused sentiment of Gov. M'Duffie, that "slavery is the corner stone of our Republican edifice;" while I repudiate, as ridiculously absurd, that much-lauded but nowhere accredited dogma of Mr. Jefferson, that "all men are born equal." No Society has ever yet existed, and I have already incidentally quoted the highest authority to show that none will ever exist, without a natural variety of classes. The most marked of these must, in a country like ours, be the rich and the poor, the educated and the ignorant. It will scarcely be disputed that the very poor have less leisure to prepare themselves for the proper discharge of public duties than the rich; and that the ignorant are wholly unfit for them at all. In all countries save ours these two classes, or the poor rather, who are presumed to be necessarily ignorant, are by law expressly excluded from all participation in the management of public affairs. In a Republican Government this cannot be done. Universal suffrage, though not essential in theory, seems to be in fact a necessary appendage to a Republican system. Where universal suffrage obtains, it is obvious that the government is in the hands of a numerical majority; and it is hardly necessary to say that in every part of the world more than half the people are ignorant and poor. Though no one can look upon poverty as a crime, and we do not generally here regard it as any objection to a man in his individual capacity, still it must be admitted that it is a wretched and insecure government which is administered by its most ignorant citizens, and those who have the least at stake under it. Though intelligence and wealth have great influence here as everywhere in keeping in check reckless and unenlightened numbers, yet it is evident to close observers, if not to all, that these are rapidly usurping all power in the non-slave-holding States, and threaten a fearful crisis in Republican institutions there at no remote period. In the slave-holding States, however, nearly one-half of the whole population, and those the poorest and most ignorant, have no political influence whatever, because they are slaves. Of the other half a large proportion are both educated and independent in their circumstances; while those who unfortunately are not so, being still elevated far above the mass, are higher toned and more deeply interested in preserving a stable and well ordered Government, than the same class in any other country. Hence, slavery is truly the "corner stone" and foundation of every well-designed and durable "Republican edifice."

With us every citizen is concerned in the maintenance of order, and in promoting honesty and industry among those of the lowest class who are our slaves; and our habitual vigilance renders standing armies, whether of soldiers or policemen, entirely unnecessary. Small guards in our cities, and occasional patrols in the country, ensure us a repose and security known nowhere else. You cannot be ignorant that, excepting the United States, there is no country in the world whose existing Government would not be overturned in a month, but for its standing armies, maintained at an enormous and destructive cost to those whom they are destined to overawe—so rampant and combative is the spirit of discontent wherever nominal Free labor prevails, with its ostensive privileges and its dismal servitude. Nor will it be long before the "*Free States*" of this Union will be compelled to introduce the same expensive machinery to preserve order among their "free and equal" citizens. Already has Philadelphia organized a permanent Battalion for this purpose; New York, Boston and Cincinnati will soon follow her example; and then the smaller towns and densely populated counties. The intervention of their militia to repress violations of the peace is becoming a daily affair. A strong Government, after some of the old fashions—though probably with a new name—sustained by the force of armed mercenaries, is the ultimate destiny of the non-slave-holding section of this confederacy, and one which may not be very distant.

It is a great mistake to suppose, as is generally done abroad, that in case of war slavery would be a source of weakness. It did not weaken Rome, nor Athens, nor Sparta; though their slaves were comparatively far more numerous than ours, of the same color for the most part with themselves, and large numbers of them familiar with the use of arms. I have no apprehension that our slaves would seize such an opportunity to revolt. The present generation of them, born among us, would never think of such a thing at any time, unless instigated to it by others. Against such instigations we are always on our guard. In time of war we should be more watchful and better prepared to put down insurrections than at any other periods. Should any foreign nation be so lost to every sentiment of civilized humanity as to attempt to erect among us the standard of revolt, or to invade us with Black Troops for the base and barbarous purpose of stirring up servile war, their efforts would be signally rebuked. Our slaves could not be easily seduced, nor would anything delight them more than to assist in stripping Cuffee of his regimentals to put him in the Cotton-field, which would be the fate of most black invaders, without any very prolix form of " apprenticeship." If, as I am satisfied would be the case, our slaves remained peaceful on our plantations, and cultivated them in time of war under the superintendence of a limited number of our citizens, it is obvious that we could put forth more strength in such an emergency, at less sacrifice, than any other people of the same numbers. And thus we should, in every point of view, "out of this nettle danger, pluck the flower safety."

How far slavery may be an advantage or disadvantage to those not owning slaves, yet united with us in political association, is a question for their sole consideration. It is true that our Representation in Congress is increased by it. But so are our Taxes; and the non-slave-holding States, being the majority, divide among themselves far the greater portion of the amount levied by the Federal Government. And I doubt not that, when it comes to a close calculation, they will not be slow in finding out that the balance of profit arising from the connection is vastly in their favor.

In a social point of view the Abolitionists pronounce slavery to be a monstrous evil. If it was so, it would be our own peculiar concern, and superfluous benevolence in them to lament over it. Seeing their bitter hostility to us, they might leave us to cope with our own calamities. But they make war upon us out of excess of charity, and attempt to purify by covering us with calumny. You have read and assisted to circulate a great deal about affrays, duels and murders occurring here, and all attributed to the terrible demoralization of slavery. Not a single event of this sort takes place among us, but is caught up by the Abolitionists and paraded over the world with endless comments, variations and exaggerations. You should not take what reaches you as a mere sample, and infer that there is a vast deal more you never hear. You hear all, and more than all the truth.

It is true that the point of honor is recognized throughout the slave region, and that disputes of certain classes are frequently referred for adjustment to the "trial by combat." It would not be appropriate for me to enter, in this letter, into a defence of the practice of duelling; nor to maintain at length that it does not tarnish the character of a people to acknowledge a standard of honor. Whatever evils may arise from it, however, they cannot be attributed to slavery; since the same custom prevails both in France and England. Few of your Prime Ministers, of the last half century even, have escaped the contagion, I believe. The affrays, of which so much is said, and in which rifles, bowieknives and pistols are so prominent, occur mostly in Frontier States of the South-West. They are naturally incidental to the condition of society as it exists in many sections of these recently settled countries, and will as naturally cease in due time. Adventurers from the older States and from Europe, as desperate in character as they are in fortune, congregate in these wild regions, jostling one another and often forcing the peaceable and honest into rencontres in self-defence. Slavery has nothing to do with these things. Stability and peace are the first desires of every slave-holder, and the true tendency of the system. It could not possibly exist amid the eternal anarchy and civil broils of the ancient Spanish dominions in America. And for this very reason domestic slavery has ceased there. So far from encouraging strife, such scenes of riot and bloodshed as have within the last few years disgraced our Northern cities, and as you have lately witnessed in Birmingham and Bristol and Wales, not only never have occurred, but I will venture to say never will occur in our slave-holding States. The only thing that can create a mob (as you might call it) here, is the appearance of an Abolitionist, whom the people assemble to chastise. And this is no more of a mob, than a rally of shepherds to chase a wolf out of their pastures would be one.

But we are swindlers and repudiators! Pennsylvania is not a slave State. A majority of the States which have failed to meet their obligations punctually are non-slave-holding; and two-thirds of the debt said to be repudiated is owed by these States. Many of the States of this Union are heavily encumbered with debt—none so hopelessly as England. Pennsylvania owes $22 for each inhabitant—England $222, counting her paupers in. Nor has there been any repudiation, definite and final, of a lawful debt, that I am aware of.

A few States have failed to pay some instalments of interest. The extraordinary financial difficulties which occurred a few years ago account for it. Time will set all things right again. Every dollar of both principal and interest owed by any State, North our South, will be ultimately paid; *unless the abolition of slavery overwhelms us all in one common ruin.* But have no other nations failed to pay? When were the French assignats redeemed? How much interest did your National Bank pay on its immense circulation from 1797 to 1821, during which period that circulation was inconvertible, and for the time *repudiated?* How much of your National Debt has been incurred for money borrowed to meet the interest on it; thus avoiding delinquency in detail, by ensuring inevitable bankruptcy and repudiation in the end? And what sort of operation was that by which your present ministry recently expunged a handsome amount of that debt by substituting, through a process just not compulsory, one species of security for another? I am well aware that the faults of others do not excuse our own; but when failings are charged to slavery, which are shown to occur to equal extent where it does not exist, surely slavery must be acquitted of the accusation.

It is roundly asserted, that we are not so well educated nor so religious here as elsewhere. I will not go into tedious statistical statements on these subjects. Nor have I, to tell the truth, much confidence in the details of what are commonly set forth as statistics. As to education, you will probably admit that slaveholders should have more leisure for mental culture than most people. And I believe it is charged against them that they are peculiarly fond of power, and ambitious of honors. If this be so, as all the power and honors of this country are won mainly by intellectual superiority it might be fairly presumed that slave-holders would not be neglectful of education. In proof of the accuracy of this presumption I point you to the facts, that our Presidential chair has been occupied for forty-four out of fifty-six years by slave-holders; that another has been recently elected to fill it for four more, over an opponent who was a slave-holder also; and that in the Federal offices and both Houses of Congress considerably more than a due proportion of those acknowledged to stand in the first rank are from the South. In this arena the intellects of the free and slave States meet in full and fair competition. Nature must have been unusually bountiful to us, or we have been at least reasonably assiduous in the cultivation of such gifts as she has bestowed—unless indeed you refer our superiority to moral qualities, which I am sure *you* will not. More wealthy we are not; nor would mere wealth avail in such rivalry.

The piety of the South is unobtrusive. We think it proves but little, though it is a confident thing for a man to claim that he stands higher in the estimation of his Creator, and is less a sinner than his neighbor. If vociferation is to carry the question of religion, the North and probably the Scotch have it. Our sects are few, harmonious, pretty much united among themselves, and pursue their avocations in humble peace. In fact, our professors of religion seem to think—whether correctly or not—that it is their duty " to do good in secret" and to carry their holy comforts to the heart of each individual, without reference to class *or color*, for his special enjoyment, and not with a view to exhibit their zeal before the world. So far as numbers are concerned, I believe our clergymen, when called on to make a showing, have never had occasion to blush, if comparisons were drawn between the free and slave States. And although our presses do not teem with controversial pamphlets, nor our pulpits shade with excommunicating thunders, the daily walk of our religious communicants furnishes apparently as little food for gossip as is to be found in most other regions. It may be regarded as a mark of our want of excitability—though that is a quality accredited to us in an eminent degree—that few of the remarkable religious *isms* of the present day have taken root among us. We have been so irreverent as to laugh at Mormonism and Millerism, which have created such commotions farther North; and modern prophets have no honor in our country. Shakers, Rappists, Dunkers, Socialists, Fourrierists and the like keep themselves afar off. Even Puseyism has not yet moved us. You may attribute this to our Domestic Slavery if you choose. I believe you would do so justly. There is no material here for such characters to operate upon.

But your grand charge is that licentiousness in intercourse between the sexes is a prominent trait of our social system, and that it necessarily arises from slavery. This is a favorite theme with the Abolitionists, male and female. Folios have been written on it. It is a common observation, that there is no subject on which ladies of eminent virtue so much delight to dwell, and on which, in especial, learned old maids like Miss Martineau linger with such an insatiable relish They expose it in the slave States with the most minute observance and endless iteration. Miss Martineau, with peculiar gusto, relates a series of scandalous stories which would have made Boccaccio jealous of her pen, but which are so ridiculously false as to leave no doubt that some wicked wag, knowing she would write a book, has furnished her materials—a game too often played on tourists in this country. The constant recurrence of the female Abolitionists to this topic, and their bitterness in regard to it, cannot fail to suggest to even the most charitable mind, that

<blockquote>"Such rage without betrays the fires within."</blockquote>

Nor are their immaculate coadjutors of the other sex, though perhaps less specific in their charges, less violent in their denunciations. But recently in your island a clergyman has, at a public meeting, stigmatized the whole slave region as a "Brothel." Do these people thus cast stones being "without sin?" Or do they only

<blockquote>"Compound for sins they are inclined to
By damning those they have no mind to."</blockquote>

Alas that David and Solomon should be allowed to repose in peace—that Leo should be almost canonized, and Luther more than sainted—that in our own day courtesans should be formally licensed in Paris, and tenements in London rented for years to women of the town for the benefit of the Church, with the knowledge of the Bishop—and the poor Slave States of America alone pounced upon and offered up as a holocaust on the Altar of Immaculateness to atone for the abuse of natural instinct by all mankind; and if not actually consumed, at least exposed, anathematized and held up to scorn, by those who

<blockquote>"write
Or with a Rival's or an Eunuch's spite."</blockquote>

But I do not intend to admit that this charge is just or true. Without meaning to profess uncommon modesty, I will say that I wish the topic could be avoided. I am of opinion, and I doubt not every right-minded man will concur, that the public exposure and discussion of this vice, even to rebuke, invariably does more harm than good; and if it cannot be checked by instilling pure and virtuous sentiments, it is far worse than useless to attempt to do it by exhibiting its deformities. I may not, however, pass it over; nor ought I to feel any delicacy in examining a question to which the Slave-holder is invited and challenged by Clergymen and Virgins. So far from allowing, then, that licentiousness pervades this region, I broadly assert, and I refer to the records of our Courts, to the public press, and to the knowledge of all who have ever lived here, that among our white population, there are fewer cases of divorce, separation, crim. con. seduction, rape and bastardy, than among any other five millions of people on the civilized earth. And this fact I believe will be conceded by the Abolitionists of this country themselves. I am almost willing to refer it to them and submit to their decision on it. I would not hesitate to do so if I thought them capable of an impartial judgment on any matter where Slavery is in question. But it is said that the licentiousness consists in the constant intercourse between white males and colored females. One of your heavy charges against us has been that we regard and treat these people as brutes; you now charge us with habitually taking them to our bosoms. I will not comment on the inconsistency of these accusations. I will not deny that some intercourse of the sort does take place. Its character and extent, how ever, are grossly and atrociously exaggerated. No authority divine or human has yet been found sufficient to arrest all such irregularities among men. But it is a known fact, that they are perpetrated here, for the most part, in the cities. Very few mulattoes are reared on our plantations. In the cities a large proportion of the inhabitants do not own slaves. A still larger proportion are natives of the North or foreigners. They should share, and justly, too, an equal part in this sin with the slave-holders. Facts cannot be ascertained, or I doubt not it would appear that they are the chief offenders. If the truth be otherwise, then persons from abroad have stronger prejudices against the African race than we have. Be this as it may, it is well known that this intercourse is regarded in our society as highly disreputable. If carried on habitually it seriously affects a man's standing, so far as it is known; and he who takes a colored mistress—with rare and extraordinary exceptions—loses caste at once. You will say that *one* exception should damn our whole country. How much less criminal is it to take a white mistress? In your eyes it should be at least an equal offence. Yet look around you at home, from the cottage to the throne, and count how many mistresses are kept in unblushing notoriety, without any loss of caste. Such cases are almost unknown here, and down even to the lowest walks of life it is almost invariably fatal to a man's position and prospects to keep a mistress openly, whether white or black. What Miss Martineau relates of a young man's purchasing a colored concubine from a lady and avowing his designs, is too absurd even for contradiction. No person would dare to allude to such a subject in such a manner to any decent female in this country. If he did, he would be *lynched* —doubtless with your approbation.

After all, however, the number of the mixed breed in proportion to that of the black is infinitely small, and out of the towns next to nothing. And when it is considered that the African race has been among us for two hundred years, and that those of the mixed breed continually intermarry—often rearing large families—it is a decided proof of our continence that so few comparatively are to be found. Our misfortunes are twofold. From the prolific propagation of these mongrels among themselves, we are liable to be charged by tourists with delinquencies where none have been committed; while, where one has been, it cannot be concealed. Color marks indelibly the offence, and reveals it to every eye. Conceive that, even in your virtuous and polished country, if every bastard through all the circles of your social system was thus branded by nature and known to all, what shocking developments might there not be! How little indignation might your saints have to spare for the licentiousness of the slave region. But I have done with this disgusting topic. And I think I may justly conclude, after all the scandalous charges which tea-table gossip and long-gowned hypocrisy have brought against the slaveholders, that a people whose men are proverbially brave, intellectual and hospitable, and whose women are unaffectedly chaste, devoted to domestic life and happy in it, can neither be degraded nor demoralized, whatever their institutions may be. My decided opinion is, that our system of Slavery contributes largely to the development and culture of these high and noble qualities.

In an economical point of view—which I will not omit—Slavery presents some difficulties. As a general rule, I agree, it must be admitted that free labor is cheaper than Slave labor. It is a fallacy to suppose that ours is *unpaid labor*. The slave himself must be paid for, and thus his labor is all purchased at once, and for no trifling sum. His price was in the first place paid mostly to your countrymen, and assisted in building up some of those colossal English fortunes, since illustrated by patents of nobility and splendid piles of architecture—stained and cemented, if you like the expression, with the blood of kidnapped innocents, but loaded with no heavier curses than Abolition and its begotten fanaticisms have brought upon your land —some of them fulfilled, some yet to be. But, besides the first cost of the slave, he must be fed and clothed— well fed and well clothed—if not for humanity's sake, that he may do good work, retain health and life, and rear a family to supply his place. When old or sick he a clear expense, and so is the helpless portion of his family. No poor law provides for him when unable to work, or brings up his children for our service when we need them. These are all heavy charges on slave labor. Hence, in all countries where the denseness of the population has reduced it to a matter of perfect certainty that labor can be obtained whenever wanted, and the laborer be forced by sheer necessity to hire for the smallest pittance that will keep soul and body together and rags upon his back while in actual employment—dependent at all other times on alms or poor rates—in all such countries it is found cheaper to pay this pittance than to clothe, feed, nurse, support through childhood and pension in old age a race of slaves. Indeed, the advantage is so great as speedily to compensate for the loss of the value of the slave. And I have no hesitation in saying that, if I could cultivate my lands on these terms, I would without a word resign my slaves, provided they could be properly disposed of. But the question is, whether free or slave labor is cheapest to us in this country at this time, situated as we are. And it is decided at once by the fact that we cannot avail ourselves of any other than slave labor. We neither have nor can we procure other labor to any extent, or on anything like the terms mentioned. We must therefore content ourselves with our dear labor, under the consoling reflection that what is lost to us, is gained to humanity; and that inasmuch as our slave costs us more than your free man costs you, by so much is he better off. You will promptly say, emancipate your slaves, and then you will have free labor on suitable terms. That might be if there were five hundred where there now is one, and the continent, from the Atlantic to the Pacific, was as densely populated as your island. But until that comes to pass, no labor can be procured in America on the terms you have it.

While I thus freely admit that to the individual proprietor slave labor is dearer than free, I do not mean to admit as equally clear that it is dearer to the community and to the State. Though it is certain that the slave is a far greater consumer than your laborer the year round, yet your pauper system is costly and wasteful. Supported by your community at large, it is not administered by your hired agents with that interested care and economy—not to speak of humanity—which mark the management of ours by each proprietor for his own non-effectives; and it is both more expensive to those who pay, and less beneficial to those who receive its bounties. Besides this, Slavery is rapidly filling up our country with a hardy and healthy race, peculiarly adapted to our climate and productions, and conferring signal political and social advantages on us as a people to which I have already referred.

I have yet to reply to the main ground on which you and your coadjutors rely for the overthrow of our system of slavery. Failing in all your attempts to prove that it is sinful in its nature, immoral in its effects, a political evil, and profitless to those who maintain it, you appeal to the sympathies of mankind, and attempt to arouse the world against us by the most shocking charges of tyranny and cruelty. You begin by a vehement denunciation of " the irresponsible power of one man over his fellow men." The question of the responsibility of power is a vast one. It is the great political question of modern times. Whole nations divide off upon it and establish different fundamental systems of government. That "responsibility," which to one set of millions seems amply sufficient to check the government, to the support of which they devote their lives and fortunes, appears to another set of millions a mere mockery of restraint. And accordingly as the opinions of these millions differ, they honor each other with the epithets of "Serfs" or "Anarchists." It is ridiculous to introduce such an idea as this into the discussion of a mere Domestic Institution. But since you have introduced it, I deny that the power of the slave-holder in America is " irresponsible." He is responsible to God. He is responsible to the world—a responsibility which Abolitionists do not intend to allow him to evade—and in acknowledgment of which I write you this letter. He is responsible to the community in which he lives, and to the laws under which he enjoys his civil rights. Those laws do not permit him to kill, to maim, or to punish beyond certain limits, or to overtask, or to refuse to feed and clothe his slave. In short, they forbid him to be tyrannical or cruel. If any of these laws have grown obsolete, it is because they are so seldom violated that they are forgotten. You have disinterred one of them from a compilation by some Judge Stroud of Philadelphia, to stigmatize its inadequate penalties for killing, maiming, &c. Your object appears to be—you can have no other—to produce the impression that it must be often violated on account of its insufficiency. You say as much, and that it marks our estimate of the slave. You forget to state that this law was enacted by *Englishmen*, and only indicates *their* opinion of the reparation due for these offences. Ours is proved by the fact, though perhaps unknown to Judge Stroud or yourself, that we have essentially altered this law; and the murder of a slave has for many years been punishable with death in this State. And so it is, I believe, in most or all the slave States. You seem well aware, however, that laws have been recently passed in all these States making it penal to teach slaves to read. Do you know what occasioned their passage, and renders their stringent enforcement necessary? I can tell you. It was the Abolition agitation. If the slave is not allowed to read his Bible, the sin rests upon the Abolitionists; for they stand prepared to furnish him with a Key to it, which would make it, not a Book of hope and love and peace, but of despair, hatred and blood; which would convert the reader, not into a Christian, but a Demon. To preserve him from such a horrid destiny, it is a sacred duty which we owe to our slaves, not less than to ourselves, to interpose the most decisive means. If the Catholics deem it wrong to trust the Bible to the hands of ignorance, shall we be excommunicated because we will not give it, and with it the corrupt and fatal commentaries of the Abolitionists, to our slaves? Allow our slaves to read your writings, stimulating them to cut our throats! Can you believe us to be such unspeakable fools?

I do not know that I can subscribe in full to the sentiment so often quoted by the Abolitionists, and by Mr. Dickinson in his letter to me: "*Homo sum, humani nil a me alienum puto*," as translated and practically illustrated by them. Such a doctrine would give wide authority to every one for the most dangerous intermeddling with the affairs of others. It will do in poetry—perhaps in some sorts of Philosophy—but the attempt to make it a household maxim, and introduce it into the daily walks of life, has caused many a "Homo" a broken crown; and probably will continue to do it. Still, though a slave-holder, I freely acknowledge my obligations as a man; and that I am bound to treat humanely the fellow creatures whom God has entrusted to my charge. I feel therefore somewhat sensitive under the accusation of cruelty, and disposed to defend myself and fellow slave-holders against it. It is certainly the interest of all, and I am convinced that it is also the desire of every one of us, to treat our slaves with proper kindness. It is necessary to our deriving the greatest amount of profit from them. Of this we are all satisfied. And you snatch from us the only consolation we Americans could derive from the opprobrious imputation of being wholly devoted to making money, which your disinterested and gold-despising countrymen delight to cast upon us, when you nevertheless declare that we are ready to sacrifice it for the pleasure of being inhuman. You remember that Mr. Pitt could never get over the idea that self-interest would insure kind treatment to slaves, until you told him your woful stories of the Middle Passage. Mr. Pitt was right in the first instance, and erred, under your tuition, in not perceiving the difference between a temporary and permanent ownership of them. Slave-holders are no more perfect than other men. They have passions. Some of them, as you may suppose, do not at all times restrain them. Neither do husbands, parents and friends. And in each of these relations as serious suffering as frequently arises from uncontrolled passions as ever does in that of Master and Slave, and with as little chance of indemnity. Yet you would not on that account break them up. I have no hesitation in saying that our slave-holders are as kind masters, as men usually are kind husbands, parents and friends — as a general rule, kinder. A bad master—he who overworks his slaves, provides ill for them, or treats them with undue severity—loses the esteem and respect of his fellow citizens to as great an extent as he would for the violation of any of his social and most of his moral obligations. What the most perfect plan of management would be is a problem hard to solve. From the commencement of Slavery in this country, this subject has occupied the minds of all slave-holders, as much as the improvement of the general condition of mankind has those of the most ardent philanthropists; and the greatest progressive amelioration of the system has been effected. You yourself acknowledge that in the early part of your career you were exceedingly anxious for the *immediate* abolition of the Slave Trade, lest those engaged in it should so mitigate its evils as to destroy the force of your arguments and facts. The improvement you then *dreaded* has gone on steadily here, and would doubtless have taken place in the Slave Trade but for the measures adopted to suppress it.

Of late years we have been not only annoyed, but greatly embarrassed in this matter, by the Abolitionists. We have been compelled to curtail some privileges; we have been debarred from granting new ones. In the face of discussions which aim at loosening all ties between master and slave, we have in some measure to abandon our efforts to attach them to us and control them through their affections and pride. We have to rely more and more on the power of fear. We must in all our intercourse with them assert and maintain strict mastery, and impress it on them that they are Slaves. This is painful to us, and certainly no present advantage to them. But it is the direct consequence of the Abolition agitation. We are determined to continue Masters, and to do so we have to draw the rein tighter and tighter day by day to be assured that we hold them in complete check. How far this process will go on depends wholly and solely on the Abolitionists. When they desist we can relax. We may not before. I do not mean by all this to say that we are in a state of actual alarm and fear of our slaves; but under existing circumstances we should be ineffably stupid not to increase our vigilance and strengthen our hands. You see some of the fruits of your labors. I speak freely and candidly—not as a colonist who, though a slave-holder has a master; but as a free white man, holding, under God, and resolved to hold, my fate in my own hands; and I assure you that my sentiments and feelings and determinations are those of every slave-holder in this country.

The research and ingenuity of the Abolitionists, aided by the invention of runaway slaves—in which faculty, so far as improvising falsehood goes, the African race is without a rival—have succeeded in shocking the world with a small number of pretended instances of our barbarity. The only wonder is that, considering the extent of our country, the variety of our population, its fluctuating character, and the publicity of all our transactions, the number of cases collected is so small. It speaks well for us. Yet of these many are false, all highly colored, some occurring half a century, most of them many years, ago; and no doubt a large proportion of them perpetrated by foreigners. With a few rare exceptions the emigrant Scotch and English are the worst masters among us, and next to them our Northern fellow-citizens. Slave-holders born and bred here are always more humane to slaves, and those who have grown up to a large inheritance of them, the most so of any—showing clearly that the effect of the system is to foster kindly feelings. I do not mean so much to impute innate inhumanity to foreigners, as to show that they come here with false notions of the treatment usual and necessary for slaves, and that newly acquired power here, as everywhere else, is apt to be abused. I cannot enter into a detailed examination of the cases stated by the

Abolitionists. It would be disgusting and of little avail. I know nothing of them. I have seen nothing like them, though born and bred here, and have rarely heard of anything at all to be compared with them. Permit me to say that I think most of *your* facts must have been drawn from the West Indies, where undoubtedly slaves were treated much more harshly than with us. This was owing to a variety of causes, which might, if necessary, be stated. One was that they had at first to deal more extensively with barbarians fresh from the wilds of Africa; another, and a leading one, the absenteeism of Proprietors. Agents are always more unfeeling than owners, whether placed over West Indian or American slaves, or Irish tenantry. We feel this evil greatly even here. You describe the use of *thumb screws* as one mode of punishment among us. I doubt if a thumb screw can be found in America. I never saw or heard of one in this country. Stocks are rarely used by private individuals, and confinement still more seldom; though both are common punishments for whites, all the world over. I think they should be more frequently resorted to with slaves, as substitutes for flogging, which I consider the most injurious and least efficacious mode of punishing them for serious offences. It is not degrading and, unless excessive, occasions little pain. You may be a little astonished, after all the flourishes that have been made about "cart whips," &c., when I say flogging is not the most degrading punishment in the world. It may be so to a white man in most countries, but how is it to the white boy? That necessary coadjutor of the school-master the "birch" is never thought to have rendered infamous the unfortunate victim of pedagogue ire; nor did Solomon in his wisdom dream that he was counselling parents to debase their offspring, when he exhorted them not spoil the child by sparing the rod. Pardon me for recurring to the now exploded ethics of the Bible. Custom, which, you will perhaps agree, makes most things in this world good or evil, has removed all infamy from the punishment of the lash to the slave. Your blood boils at the recital of stripes inflicted on a man; and you think you should be frenzied to see your own child flogged. Yet see how completely this is ideal, arising from the fashions of society. You doubtless submitted to the rod yourself, in other years, when the smart was perhaps as severe as it would be now; and you have never been guilty of the folly of revenging yourself on the preceptor who in the plenitude of his "irresponsible power" thought proper to chastise your son. So it is with the negro, and the negro father.

As to chains and irons, they are rarely used; never, I believe, except in cases of running away. You will admit that if we pretend to own slaves they must not be permitted to abscond whenever they see fit; and that if nothing else will prevent it these means must be resorted to. See the inhumanity necessarily arising from slavery, you will exclaim. Are such restraints imposed on no other class of people given no more offence? Look to your army and navy. If your seamen, impressed from their peaceful occupations, and your soldiers, recruited at the gin shops—both of them as much kidnapped as the most unsuspecting victim of the Slave Trade, and doomed to a far more wretched fate—if these men manifest a propensity to desert, the heaviest manacles are their mildest punishment: it is most commonly death, after summary trial. But armies and navies you say are indispensable, and must be kept up at every sacrifice. I answer that they are no more indispensable, than slavery is to us—and to *you*; for you have enough of it in your country, though the form and name differ from ours.

Depend upon it that many things, and in regard to our slaves most things, which appear revolting at a distance, and to slight reflection, would on a nearer view and impartial comparison with the customs and conduct of the rest of mankind strike you in a very different light. Remember that on our estates we dispense with the whole machinery of public police and public Courts of Justice. Thus we try, decide and execute the sentences, in thousands of cases, which in other countries would go into the Courts. Hence, most of the acts of our alleged cruelty, which have any foundation in truth. Whether our Patriarchal mode of administering justice is less humane than the Assizes can only be determined by careful inquiry and comparison. But this is never done by the Abolitionists. All our punishments are the outrages of "irresponsible power." If a man steals a pig in England he is transported—torn from wife, children, parents and sent to the Antipodes, infamous and an outcast forever, though probably he took from the superabundance of his neighbor to save the lives of his famishing little ones. If one of our well-fed negroes, merely for the sake of fresh meat, steals a pig, he gets perhaps forty stripes. If one of your Cottagers breaks into another's house, he is hung for burglary. If a slave does the same here, a few lashes, or it may be a few hours in the stocks, settles the matter. Are our Courts or yours the most humane? If slavery were not in question you would doubtless say ours is mistaken lenity. Perhaps it often is; and slaves too lightly dealt with sometimes grow daring. Occasionally, though rarely, and almost always in consequence of excessive indulgence, an individual rebels. This is the highest crime he can commit. It is treason. It strikes at the root of our whole system. His life is justly forfeited, though it is never intentionally taken, unless after trial in our public Courts. Sometimes, however, in capturing, or in self-defence, he is unfortunately killed. A legal investigation always follows. But, terminate as it may, the Abolitionists raise a hue and cry, and another "shocking case" is held up to the indignation of the world by tender-hearted male and female Philanthropists, who would have thought all right had the master's throat been cut, and would have triumphed in it.

I cannot go into a detailed comparison between the penalties inflicted on a slave in our Patriarchal Courts, and those of the Courts of Sessions to which freemen are sentenced in all civilized nations; but I know well that if there is any fault in our criminal code, it is that of excessive mildness.

Perhaps a few general facts will best illustrate the treatment this race receives at our hands. It is acknowledged that it increases at least as rapidly as the white. I believe it is an established law, that population thrives in proportion to its comforts. But when it is considered that these people are not recruited by immigration from abroad as the whites are, and that they are usually settled on our richest and least healthy lands, the fact of their equal comparative increase and greater longevity, outweighs a thousand Abolition falsehoods, in favor of the leniency and providence of our management of them. It is also admitted that there are incomparably fewer cases of insanity and suicide among them than among the whites. The fact is, that among the slaves of the African race these things are almost wholly unknown. However frequent suicide may have been among those brought from Africa, I can say that in my time I cannot remember to have known or heard of a single instance of deliberate self-destruction, and but one of suicide at all. As to insanity, I have seen but one permanent case of it, and that twenty years ago. It cannot be doubted that among three millions of people there must be some insane and some suicides; but I will venture to say that more cases of both occur annually among every hundred thousand of the population of Great Britain than among all our slaves. Can it be possible, then, that they exist in that state of abject misery, goaded by constant injuries, outraged in their affections and worn down with hardships, which the Abolitionists depict, and so many ignorant and thoughtless persons religiously believe?

With regard to the separation of husbands and wives, parents and children, nothing can be more untrue than the inferences drawn from what is so constantly harped on by Abolitionists. Some painful instances perhaps may occur. Very few that can be prevented. It is and it always has been an object of prime consideration with our slaveholders to keep families together. Negroes are themselves both perverse and comparatively indifferent about this matter. It is a singular trait, that they almost invariably prefer forming connections with slaves belonging to other masters, and at some distance. It is therefore impossible to prevent separations sometimes, by the removal of one owner, his death, or failure, and dispersion of his property. In all such cases, however, every reasonable effort is made to keep the parties together, if they desire it. And the negroes forming these connections, knowing the chances of their premature dissolution, rarely complain more than we all do of the inevitable strokes of fate. Sometimes it happens that a negro prefers to give up his family rather than separate from his master. I have known such instances. As to wilfully selling off a husband or wife or child, I believe it is rarely, very rarely done, except when some offence has been committed demanding "transportation." At sales of estates, and even at Sheriffs' sales, they are always, if possible, sold in families. On the whole, notwithstanding the migratory character of our population, I believe there are more families among our slaves who have lived and died together without losing a single member from their circle, except by the process of nature, and in the enjoyment of constant, uninterrupted communion, than have flourished in the same space of time and among the same number of civilized people in modern times. And to sum up all, if pleasure is correctly defined to be in the absence of pain—which, so far as the great body of mankind is concerned, is undoubtedly its true definition—I believe our slaves are the happiest three millions of human beings on whom the sun shines. Into their Eden is coming Satan in the guise of an Abolitionist.

As regards their religious condition, it is well known that a majority of the communicants of the Methodist and Baptist churches of the South are colored. Almost everywhere they have precisely the same opportunities of attending worship that the whites have, and besides, special occasions for themselves exclusively, which they prefer. In many places not so accessible to clergymen in ordinary, missionaries are sent, and mainly supported by their masters, for the particular benefit of the slaves. There are none, I imagine, who may not, if they like, hear the Gospel preached at least once a month—most of them twice a month and very many every week. In our thinly settled country the whites fare no better. But in addition to this, on plantations of any size the slaves who have joined the church are formed into a class, at the head of which is placed one of their number, acting as deacon or leader, who is also sometimes a licensed preacher. This class assembles for religious exercises weekly, semi-weekly, or oftener, if the members choose. In some parts, also, Sunday schools for blacks are established, and Bible classes are orally instructed by discreet and pious persons. Now where will you find a laboring population possessed of greater religious advantages than these? Not in London, I am sure, where it is known that your churches, chapels, and religious meeting houses of all sorts, cannot contain one-half of the inhabitants.

I have admitted, without hesitation, what it would be untrue and profitless to deny, that slaveholders are responsible to the world for the humane treatment of the fellow-beings whom God has placed in their hands. I think it would be only fair for you to admit, what is equally undeniable, that every man in independent circumstances, all the world over, and every Government, is to the same extent responsible to the whole human family for the condition of the poor and laboring classes in their own country and around them, wherever they may be placed, to whom God has denied the advantages he has given themselves. If so, it would naturally seem the duty of true humanity and rational philanthropy to devote their time and labor, their thoughts, writings, and charity, first to the objects placed as it were under their own immediate charge. And it must be regarded as a clear evasion and sinful neglect of this cardinal duty, to pass from those whose destitute situation they can plainly see, minutely examine, and efficiently relieve, to inquire after the condition of others in no way entrusted to their care, to exaggerate evils of which they cannot be cognizant, to expend all their sympathies and exhaust all their energies on these remote objects of their unnatural, not to say dangerous benevolence, and, finally, to calumniate, denounce, and endeavor to excite the indignation of the world against their unoffending fellow-creatures for not hastening under their dictation to redress wrongs which are stoutly and truthfully denied, while they themselves go but little farther in alleviating those chargeable on them than openly and unblushingly to acknowledge them. There may be indeed a sort of merit in doing so much as to make such an acknowledgment, but it must be very modest if it expects appreciation.

Now I affirm that in Great Britain the poor and laboring classes of your own race and color, not only your fellow-beings, but your *fellow-citizens*, are more miserable and degraded, morally and physically, than our slaves; to be elevated to the actual condition of whom, would be to these your *fellow-citizens* a most glorious act of *emancipation*. And I also affirm that the poor and laboring classes of our older Free States would not be in a much more enviable condition but for our slavery. One of their own Senators has declared in the United States Senate "that the repeal of the Tariff would reduce New England to a howling wilderness." And the American Tariff is neither more nor less than a system by which the slave States are plundered to benefit those States which do not tolerate slavery.

To prove what I say of Great Britain to be true, I make the following extracts from the Reports of Commissioners appointed by Parliament, and published by order of the House of Commons. I can make but few and short ones. But similar quotations might be made to any extent, and I defy you to deny that these specimens exhibit the real condition of your operatives in every branch of your industry. There is of course a variety in their sufferings. But the same incredible amount of toil, frightful destitution, and utter want of morals, characterize the lot of every class of them.

Collieries. "I wish to call the attention of the Board to the pits about Brampton. The seams are so thin that several of them have only two feet head-way to all the working. They are worked altogether by boys from 8 to 12 years of age, on all-fours, with a dog belt and chain; the passages being neither ironed nor wooded, and often an inch or two thick with mud. In Mr. Barnes' pit these poor boys have to drag the barrows with one cwt. of coal or slack 60 times a day 60 yards, and the empty barrows back, without once straightening their backs, unless they choose to stand under the shaft and run the risk of having their heads broken by a falling coal."—*Rep. on Mines,* 1842, *p.* 71.

"In Shropshire the seams are no more than 18 or 20 inches."—*Ibid, p.* 67. "At the Booth pit," says Mr. Scriven, "I walked, rode and crept 1,800 yards to one of the nearest faces."—*Ibid.* "'Choke-damp,' 'Fire-damp,' 'Wild-fire,' 'Sulphur' and 'Water' at all times menace instant death to the laborers in these mines." "*Robert North,* aged sixteen : Went into the pit at 7 years of age, to fill up skips. I drew about 12 months. When I drew by the girdle and chain my skin was broken, and the blood ran down. I durst not say anything. If we said anything, the butty, and the reeve, who works under him, would take a stick and beat us."—*Ibid.* "The usual punishment for theft is to place the culprit's head between the legs of one of the biggest boys, and each boy in the pit—sometimes there are 20—inflicts 12 lashes on the back and rump with a cat."—*Ibid.* "Instances occur in which children are taken into these mines to work as early as 4 years of age, sometimes at 5, not unfrequently at 6 and 7, while from 8 to 9 is the ordinary age at which these employments commence."—*Ibid.* The wages paid at these mines is from $2,50 to $7,50 per month for laborers, according to age and ability, and out of this they must support themselves. They work 12 hours a day.—*Ibid.*

In *Calico printing.* "It is by no means uncommon in all the districts for children 5 or 6 years old to be kept at work 14 to 16 hours consecutively."—*Rep. on Children,* 1842, *p.* 59.

I could furnish extracts similar to these in regard to every branch of your Manufactures, but I will not multiply them. Everybody knows that your operatives habitually labor from 12 to 16 hours, men, women and children, and the men occasionally 20 hours per day. In lace making, says the last quoted Report, children sometimes commence work at 2 years of age.

Destitution.—It is stated by your Commissioners that 40,000 persons in Liverpool, and 15,000 in Manchester, live in cellars; while 22,000 in England pass the night in barns, tents, or the open air. "There have been found such occurrences as 7, 8 and 10 persons in one cottage, I cannot say for one day, but for whole days, without a morsel of food. They have remained on their beds of straw for two successive days, under the impression that in a recumbent posture the pangs of hunger were less felt."—*Lord Brougham's speech,* 11*th July,* 1842. A volume of frightful scenes might be quoted to corroborate the inferences to be necessarily drawn from the facts here stated. I will not add more, but pass on to the important inquiry as to

Morals and Education.—" *Elizabeth Barrett,* aged 14: I always work without stockings, shoes or trowsers. I wear nothing but a shift. I have to go up to the headings with the men. *They are all naked there.* I am got used to that."—*Report on Mines.* " As to illicit sexual intercourse it seems to prevail universally and from an early period of life." "The evidence might have been doubled which attests the early commencement of sexual and promiscuous intercourse among boys and girls." "A lower condition of morals, in the fullest sense of the term, could not I think be found. I do not mean by this that there are many more prominent vices among them, but that moral feelings and sentiments do not exist. *They have no morals.*" "Their appearance, manners and moral atures—so far as the word *moral* can be applied to them—are in accordance with their half-civilized condition"—*Rep. on Children.* "More than half a dozen instances occurred in Manchester, where a man, his wife, and his wife's grown up sister, habitually occupied the same bed."—*Rep. on Sanitary Condition.* Robert Cruchilow, *aged* 16: "I don't know anything of Moses—never heard of France. I don't know what America is. Never heard of Scotland or Ireland. Can't tell how many weeks there are in a year. There are 12 pence in a shilling, and 20 shillings in a pound. There are eight pints in a gallon of ale."—*Rep. on Mines.* Ann Eggly, *aged* 18: "I walk about and get fresh air on Sundays. I never go to Church or Chapel. I never heard of Christ at all."—*Ibid. Others:* "The Lord sent Adam and Eve on earth to save sinners." "I don't know who made the world, I never heard about God." "I don't know Jesus Christ—I never saw him—but I have seen Foster who prays about him." *Employer:* "You have expressed surprise at Thomas Mitchel's not hearing of God. I judge there are few colliers hereabout that have."—*Ibid.* I will quote no more. It is shocking beyond endurance to turn over your *Records* in which the condition of your laboring classes is but too faithfully depicted. Could our slaves but see it, they would join us in lynching Abolitionists, which, by the by, they would not now be loth to do. We never think of imposing on them such labor, either in amount or kind. We never put them to *any work* under ten, more generally at twelve years of age, and then the very lightest. Destitution is absolutely unknown—never did a slave starve in America; while in moral sentiments and feelings, in religious information, and even in general intelligence, they are infinitely the superiors of your operatives. When you look around you how dare you talk to us before the world of slavery? For the condition of your wretched laborers, you, and every Briton who is not one of them, are responsible before God and Man. If you are really humane, philanthropic and charitable, here are objects for you. Relieve them. Emancipate them. Raise them from the condition of brutes, to the level of human beings—of American slaves, at least. Do not for an instant suppose that the *name* of being freemen is the slightest comfort to them, situated as they are, or that the bombastic boast that "whoever touches British soil stands redeemed, regenerated and disenthralled," can meet with anything but the ridicule and contempt of mankind, while that soil swarms, both on and under its surface, with the most abject and degraded wretches that ever bowed beneath the oppressor's yoke.

I have said that slavery is an established and inevitable condition to human society. I do not speak of the *name*, but the *fact*. The Marquis of Normanby has lately declared your operatives to be "*in effect slaves*." Can it be denied? Probably, for such Philanthropists as your Abolitionists care nothing for facts. They deal in terms and fictions. It is the *word* "slavery" which shocks their tender sensibilities; and their imaginations associate it with "hydras and chimeras dire." The thing itself, in its most hideous reality, passes daily under their view unheeded—a familiar face, touching no chord of shame, sympathy or indignation. Yet so brutalizing is your iron bondage that the English operative is a byword through the world. When favoring fortune enables him to escape his prison-house, both in Europe and America he is shunned. With all the skill which 14 hours of daily labor from the tenderest age has ground into him, his discontent, which habit has made second nature, and his depraved propensities, running riot when freed from his wonted fetters, prevent his employment whenever it is not a matter of necessity. If we derived no other benefit from African slavery in the Southern States than that it deterred your *freedmen* from coming hither, I should regard it as an inestimable blessing.

And how unaccountable is that philanthropy which closes its eyes upon such a state of things as you have at home, and turns its blurred vision to our affairs beyond the Atlantic, meddling with matters which no way concern them—presiding, as you have lately done, at meetings to denounce the "iniquity of our laws" and "the atrocity of our practices," and to sympathize with infamous wretches imprisoned here for violating decrees promulgated both by God and man! Is this doing the work of "your Father which is in Heaven," or is it seeking only "that you may have glory of man?" Do you remember the denunciation of our Saviour, "Woe unto you, Scribes and Pharisees; Hypocrites! for ye make clean the outside of the cup and platter, but within they are full of extortion and excess?"

But after all, supposing that everything you say of slavery be true, and its abolition a matter of the last necessity, how do you expect to effect emancipation, and what do you calculate will be the result of its accomplishment? As to the means to be used, the Abolitionists, I believe, affect to differ, a large proportion of them pretending that their sole purpose is to apply "moral suasion" to the slaveholders themselves. As a matter of curiosity, I should like to know what their idea of this "moral suasion" is. Their discourses—yours is no exception—are all tirades, the exordium, argument, and peroration turning on the epithets "tyrants" "thieves," "murderers," addressed to us. They revile us as "atrocious monsters," "violators of the laws of nature, God and man," our homes the abode of every iniquity, our land a "brothel." We retort, that they are "incendiaries" and "assassins." Delightful argument! Sweet, potent "moral suasion!" What slave has it freed—what proselyte can it ever make? But if your course was wholly different—if you distilled nectar from your lips, and discoursed sweetest music, could you reasonably indulge the hope of accomplishing your object by such means? Nay, supposing that we were all convinced, and thought of slavery precisely as you do, at what era of "moral suasion" do you imagine you could prevail on us to give up a thousand millions of dollars in the value of our slaves, and a thousand millions of dollars more in the depreciation of our lands, in consequence of the want of laborers to cultivate them? Consider: were ever any people, civilized or savage, persuaded by any argument, human or divine, to surrender voluntarily two thousand millions of dollars? Would you think of asking five millions of Englishmen to contribute either at once or gradually four hundred and fifty millions of pounds sterling to the cause of Philanthropy, even if the purpose to be accomplished was not of doubtful goodness? If you are prepared to undertake such a scheme, try it at home. Collect your fund—return us the money for our slaves, and do with them as you like. Be all the glory yours, fairly and honestly won. But you see the absurdity of such an idea. Away, then, with your pretended "moral suasion." You know it is mere nonsense. The Abolitionists have no faith in it themselves. Those who expect to accomplish anything count on means altogether different. They aim first to alarm us: that failing, to compel us by force to emancipate our slaves, at our own risk and cost. To these purposes they obviously direct all their energies. Our Northern Liberty men have endeavored to disseminate their destructive doctrines among our slaves, and excite them to insurrection. But we have put an end to that, and stricken terror into them. They dare not show their faces here. Then they declared they would dissolve the Union. Let them do it. The North would repent it far more than the South. We are not alarmed at the idea. We are well content to give up the Union sooner than sacrifice two thousand millions of dollars, and with them all the rights we prize. You may take it for granted that it is impossible to persuade or alarm us into emancipation, or to making the first step towards it. Nothing, then, is left to try, but sheer force. If the Abolitionists are prepared to expend their own treasure and shed their own blood as freely as they ask us to do ours, let them come. We do not court the conflict; but we will not and we cannot shrink from it. If they are not ready to go so far; if, as I expect, their philanthropy recoils from it; if they are looking only for *cheap* glory, let them turn their thoughts elsewhere and leave us in peace. Be the sin, the danger and the evils of slavery all our own. We compel, we ask none to share them with us.

I am well aware that a notable scheme has been set on foot to achieve abolition by making what is by courtesy called "free" labor so much cheaper than slave labor as to force the abandonment of the latter. Though we are beginning to *manufacture with slaves*, I do not think you will attempt to pinch your operatives closer in Great Britain. You cannot curtail the rags with which they vainly attempt to cover their nakedness, nor reduce the porridge which barely, and not always, keeps those who have employment from perishing of famine. When you can do this, we will consider whether our slaves may not dispense with a pound or two of bacon per week, or a few garments annually. Your aim, however, is to cheapen labor in the tropics. The idea of doing this by exporting your "bold yeomanry" is, I presume, given up. Cromwell tried it when he *sold* the captured followers of Charles into *West Indian slavery*, where they speedily found graves. Nor have your recent experiments on British and even Dutch constitutions succeeded better. Have you still faith in carrying thither your Coolies from Hindostan? Doubtless that once wild robber race, whose highest eulogium was that they did not murder merely for the love of blood, have been tamed down, and are perhaps "keen for immigration," for since your civilization has reached it, plunder has grown scarce in Guzerat. But what is the result of the experiment thus far? Have the Coolies, ceasing to handle arms, learned to handle spades, and proved hardy and profitable laborers? On the contrary, broken in spirit and stricken with disease at home, the wretched victims whom you have hitherto kidnapped for a bounty, confined in depots, put under hatches and carried across the ocean—forced into "voluntary immigration," have done little but lie down and die on the *pseudo* soil of freedom. At the end of five years, two-thirds, in some colonies a larger proportion, are no more! Humane and pious contrivance! To alleviate the fancied sufferings of the accursed posterity of Ham, you sacrifice by a cruel death two-thirds of the children of the blessed Shem—and demand the applause of Christians—the blessing of Heaven! If this "experiment" is to go on, in God's name try your hand upon the Thugs. That other species of "Immigration" to which you are resorting I will consider presently.

But what do you calculate will be the result of emancipation, by whatever means accomplished? You will probably point me, by way of answer, to the West Indies—doubtless to Antigua, the great boast of abolition. Admitting that it has succeeded there—which I will do for the sake of the argument—do you know the reason of it? The true and only causes of whatever success has attended it in Antigua are, that the population was before crowded, and all or nearly all the arable land in cultivation. The emancipated negroes could not, many of them, get away if they desired; and knew not where to go, in case they did. They had practically no alternative but to remain on the spot; and remaining, they must work on the terms of the Proprietors, or perish—the strong arm of the mother country forbidding all hope of seizing the land for themselves. The Proprietors, well knowing that they could thus command labor for the merest necessities of life, which was much cheaper than maintaining the non-effective as well as effective slaves in a style which decency and interest, if not humanity, required, willingly accepted half their value, and at once realized far more than the interest on the other half in the diminution of their expenses, and the reduced comforts of the *freemen*. One of your most illustrious Judges, who was also a profound and philosophical Historian, has said "that Villeinage was not abolished, but went into decay in England." This was the process. This has been the process wherever (the name of) Villeinage or Slavery has been successfully abandoned. Slavery in fact "went into decay" in Antigua. I have admitted that under similiar circumstances it might profitably cease here—that is, profitably to the individual Proprietors. Give me half the value of my Slaves, and compel them to remain and labor on my plantation at 10 to 11 cents a day, as they do in Antigua, supporting themselves and families, and you shall have them to-morrow, and, if you like, dub them "free." Not to stickle, I would surrender them without price. No—I recall my words: My humanity revolts at the idea. I am attached to my Slaves, and would not have art or part in reducing them to such a condition. I deny, however, that Antigua, as a community, is or ever will be *as prosperous*, under present circumstances, as she was before abolition, though fully ripe for it. The fact is well known. The reason is that the African, if not a distinct, is an inferior Race, and never will effect, as it never has effected, as much in any other condition as in that of Slavery.

I know of no *Slave-holder* who has visited the West Indies since Slavery was abolished, and published *his* views of it. All our facts and opinions come through the friends of the experiment, or at least those not opposed to it. Taking these, even without allowance, to be true as stated, I do not see where the Abolitionists find cause for exultation. The tables of exports, which are the best evidences of the condition of a people, exhibit a woful falling off—excused, it is true, by unprecedented droughts and hurricanes, to which their free labor seems unaccountably more subject than slave labor used to be. I will not go into detail. It is well known that a large proportion of British Legislation and expenditure, and that proportion still constantly increasing, is most anxiously devoted to repairing the monstrous error of emancipation. You are actually galvanizing your expiring Colonies. The truth, deduced from all the facts, was thus pithily stated by the London Quarterly Review, as long ago as 1840: "None of the benefits anticipated by mistaken good intentions have been realized; while every evil wished for by knaves and foreseen by the wise has been painfully verified. The wild rashness of fanaticism has made the emancipation of the Slaves equivalent to the loss of one half of the West Indies, and yet put back the chance of Negro civilization." (*Art. Ld. Dudley's Letters.*) Such are the *real fruits* of your never-to-be-too-much-glorified abolition, and the valuable dividend of your twenty millions of pounds sterling invested therein.

If any further proof was wanted of the utter and well known though not yet openly avowed failure of West Indian emancipation, it would be furnished by the startling fact, that THE AFRICAN SLAVE TRADE HAS BEEN ACTUALLY REVIVED UNDER THE AUSPICES AND PROTECTION OF THE BRITISH GOVERNMENT. Under the specious guise of "Immigration" they are replenishing those Islands with Slaves from the Coast of Africa. Your colony of Sierra Leone, founded on that coast to prevent the Slave Trade, and peopled, by the bye, in the first instance by negroes stolen from these States during the Revolutionary War, is the Depot to which captives taken from Slavers by your armed vessels are transported. I might say returned, since nearly half the Africans carried across the Atlantic are understood to be embarked in this vicinity. The wretched survivors, who are there set at liberty, are immediately seduced to "immigrate" to the West Indies. The business is systematically carried on by Black "Delegates," sent expressly from the West Indies, where on arrival the "immigrants" are *sold into Slavery* for twenty-one years, under conditions ridiculously trivial and wickedly void, since few or none will ever be able to derive any advantage from them. The whole prime of life thus passed in bondage, it is contemplated, and doubtless it will be carried into effect, to turn them out in their old age to shift for themselves, and to supply their places with fresh and vigorous "Immigrants." Was ever a system of Slavery so barbarous devised before? Can you think of comparing it with ours? Even your own Religious Missionaries at Sierra Leone denounce it, "as worse than the Slave state in Africa." And your Black Delegates, fearful of the influence of these Missionaries, as well as on account of the inadequate supply of Captives, are now preparing to procure the able bodied and comparatively industrious Kroomen of the interior, by *purchasing from their Headmen* the privilege of inveigling them to the West India market! So ends the magnificent farce—perhaps I should say tragedy, of West India Abolition! I will not harrow your feelings by asking you to review the labors of your life and tell me what you and your brother Enthusiasts have accomplished for "injured Africa;" but, while agreeing with Lord Stowell that "Villeinage decayed," and admitting that Slavery might do so also, I think I am fully justified by passed and passing events in saying as Mr. *Grosvenor* said of the Slave Trade, that its *abolition* is "impossible."

You are greatly mistaken, however, if you think that the consequences of emancipation here, would be similar and no more injurious than those which followed from it in your little sea-girt West India Islands, where nearly all were blacks. The system of slavery is not in "decay" with us. It flourishes in full and growing vigor. Our country is boundless in extent. Dotted here and there with villages and fields, it is for the most part covered with immense forests and swamps of almost unknown size. In such a country, with a people so restless as ours, communicating of course some of that spirit to their domestics, can you conceive that anything short of the power of the master over the slave, could confine the African race, notoriously idle and improvident, to labor on our plantations? Break this bond, but for a day, and these plantations will be solitudes. The negro loves change, novelty and sensual excitements of all kinds, *when awake*. "Reason and order," of which Mr. WILBERFORCE said "liberty was the child," do not characterize him. Released from his present obligations his first impulse would be to go somewhere. And here no natural boundaries would restrain him. At first they would all seek the towns, and rapidly accumulate in squalid groups upon their outskirts. Driven thence by the "armed police" which would immediately spring into existence, they would scatter in all directions. Some bodies of them might wander towards the "free" States, or to the western wilderness, making their tracks by their depredations and their corpses. Many would roam wild in our "Big woods." Many more would seek the recesses of our swamps for secure covert. Few, very few of them could be prevailed on to do a stroke of work, none to labor continuously, while a head of cattle, sheep or swine could be found in our ranges, or an ear of corn nodded in our abandoned fields. These exhausted, our folds and poultry yards, barns and store-houses would become their prey. Finally, our scattered dwellings would be plundered, perhaps fired and the inmates murdered. How long do you suppose that we could bear these things? How long would it be before we should sleep with rifles at our bedside, and never move without one in our hands? This work once begun, let the story of our British ancestors and the aborigines of this country tell the sequel. Far more rapid however, would be the catastrophe. "Ere many moons went by," the African race would be exterminated, or reduced again to slavery, their ranks recruited, after your example, by fresh "Emigrants" from their father land.

Is timely preparation and gradual emancipation suggested to avert these horrible consequences? I thought your experience in the West Indies had at least done so much as to explode that idea. If it failed there, much more would it fail here, where the two races, approximating to equality in numbers, are daily and hourly in the closest contact. Give room for but a single spark of real jealousy to be kindled between them, and the explosion would be instantaneous and universal. It is the most fatal of all fallacies to suppose that these two races can exist together, after any length of time or any process of preparation, on terms at all approaching to equality. Of this, both of them are finally and fixedly convinced. They differ essentially, in all the leading traits which characterize the varieties of the human species, and color draws an indelible and insuperable line of separation between them. Every scheme founded upon the idea that they can remain together on the same soil, beyond the briefest period, in any other relation than precisely that which now subsists between them, is not only preposterous, but fraught with deepest danger. If there was no alternate but to try the "experiment" here, reason and humanity dictate that the sufferings of "gradualism" should be saved and the catastrophe of "immediate abolition" enacted as rapidly as possible. Are you impatient for the performance to commence? Do you long to gloat over the scenes I have suggested, but could not hold the pen to portray? In your long life many such have passed under your review. You know that *they* are not "*impossible.*" Can they be to your taste? Do you believe that in laboring to bring them about the Abolitionists are doing the will of God? No! God is not there. It is the work of Satan. The arch-fiend, under specious guises, has found his way into their souls, and, with false appeals to philanthropy, and foul insinuations to ambition, instigates them to rush headlong to the accomplishment of his diabolical designs.

We live in a wonderful age. The events of the last three quarters of a century appear to have revolutionized the human mind. Enterprise and ambition are only limited in their purposes by the horizon of the imagination. It is the transcendental era. In philosophy, religion, government, science, arts, commerce, nothing that has been is to be allowed to be. Conservatism in any form is scoffed at. The slightest taint of it is fatal. Where will all this end? If you can tolerate one ancient maxim let it be that the best criterion of the future is the past. That, if anything, will give a clue. And, looking back only through your time, what was the earliest feat of this same Transcendentalism? The rays of the new Moral Drummond Light were first concentrated to a focus at Paris, to illuminate the Universe. In a twinkling it consumed the political, religious, and social systems of France. It could not be extinguished there until literally drowned in blood. And then from its ashes rose that supernatural man, who for twenty years kept affrighted Europe in convulsions. Since that time its scattered beams, refracted by broader surfaces, have nevertheless continued to scathe wherever they have fallen. What political structure, what religious creed, but has felt the galvanic shock, and even now trembles to its foundations? Mankind, still horror-stricken by the catastrophe of France, have shrunk from rash experiments upon social systems. But they have been practicing in the East, around the Mediterranean, and through the West India Islands. And growing confident, a portion of them seem desperately bent on kindling the all-devouring flame in the bosom of our land. Let it once again blaze up to heaven and another cycle of blood and devastation will dawn upon the world. For our own sake, and for the sake of those infatuated men who are madly driving on the conflagration; for the sake of human nature, we are called on to strain every nerve to arrest it. And be assured our efforts will be bounded only with our being. Nor do I doubt that five millions of people, brave, intelligent, united, and prepared to hazard everything, will, in such a cause, with the blessing of God, sustain themselves. At all events, come what may, it is ours to meet it.

We are all well aware of the light estimation in which the Abolitionists, and those who are taught by them, profess to hold us. We have seen the attempt of a portion of the Free Church of Scotland to reject our alms, on the ground that we are "Slave-Drivers," after sending missionaries to solicit them. And we have seen Mr. O'Connell, the "irresponsible master" of millions of ragged serfs, from whom, poverty stricken as they are, he contrives to wring a splendid privy purse, throw back with contumely the "tribute" of his own countrymen from this land of "miscreants." These people may exhaust their slang and make black-guards of themselves, but they cannot defile us. And as for the suggestion to exclude slaveholders from your London clubs, we scout it. Many of us indeed do go to London, and we have seen your breed of gawky Lords, both there and here; but it never entered into our conceptions to look on them as better than ourselves. The American slave-holders, collectively or individually, ask no favors of any man or race who tread the earth. In none of the attributes of men, mental or physical, do they acknowledge or fear superiority elsewhere. They stand in the broadest light of the knowledge, civilization and improvement of the age—as much favored of Heaven as any of the sons of Adam. Exacting nothing undue, they yield nothing but justice and courtesy, even to royal blood. They cannot be flattered, duped, nor bullied out of their rights or their propriety. They smile with contempt at scurrility and vaporing beyond the seas, and they turn their backs upon it where it is "irresponsible;" but insolence that ventures to look them in the face, will never fail to be chastised.

I think I may trust you will not regard this letter as intrusive. I should never have entertained an idea of writing it, had you not opened the correspondence. If you think anything in it harsh, review your own—which I regret that I lost soon after it was received—and you will probably find that you have taken your revenge beforehand. If you have not, transfer an equitable share of what you deem severe to the account of the Abolitionists at large. They have accumulated against the slaveholders a balance of invective which, with all our efforts, we shall not be able to liquidate much short of the era in which your National debt will be paid. At all events, I have no desire to offend you personally, and, with the best wishes for your continued health, I have the honor to be,

   Your obedient servant,
      J. H. HAMMOND.

Thos. Clarkson, Esq.

Silver Bluff, S. C., March 24, 1845.

Sir:—In my letter to you of the 28th of January—which I trust you have received ere this—I mentioned that I had lost your circular letter soon after it had come to hand. It was, I am glad to say, only mislaid, and has within a few days been recovered.

A second perusal of it induces me to resume my pen. Unwilling to trust my recollection from a single reading, I did not in my last communication attempt to follow the course of your argument, and meet directly the points made and the terms used. I thought it better to take a general view of the subject which could not fail to traverse your most material charges. I am well aware however that, for fear of being tedious, I omitted many interesting topics altogether, and abstained from a complete discussion of some of those introduced. I do not propose now to *exhaust* the subject; which it would require volumes to do; but without waiting to learn—which I may never do —your opinion of what I have already said, I sit down to supply some of the deficiencies of my letter of January, and, with your circular before me, to reply to such parts of it as have not been fully answered.

It is, I perceive, addressed among others to "such as have never visited the Southern States" of this confederacy, and professes to enlighten their ignorance of the actual "condition of the poor slave in their own country." I cannot help thinking you would have displayed prudence in confining the circulation of your letter altogether to such persons. You might then have indulged with impunity in giving, as you have done, a picture of slavery drawn from your own excited imagination, or from those impure fountains, the Martineaus, Marryatts, Trollopes and Dickenses, who have profited by catering, at our expense, to the jealous sensibilities and debauched tastes of your countrymen. Admitting that you are familiar with the history of slavery and the past discussions of it, as I did, I now think rather broadly, in my former letter, what can *you know* of the true *condition* of the "poor slave" here? I am not aware that you have ever visited this country, or even the West Indies. Can you suppose that because you have devoted your life to the investigation of the subject—commencing it under the influence of an enthusiasm so melancholy at first and so volcanic afterwards as to be nothing short of hallucination—pursuing it as men of *one idea* do everything, with the single purpose of establishing your own view of it—gathering your information from discharged seamen, disappointed speculators, factious politicians, visionary reformers and scurrilous tourists—opening your ears to every species of complaint, exaggeration and falsehood that interested ingenuity could invent, and never for a moment questioning the truth of anything that could make for your cause—can you suppose that all this has qualified you, living the while in England, to form or approximate towards the formation of a correct opinion of the condition of slaves among us? I know the power of self-delusion. I have not the least doubt that you think yourself the very best informed man alive on this subject, and that many think so likewise. So far as facts go, even after deducting from your list a great deal that is not fact, I will not deny that probably your collection is the most extensive in existence. But as to the *truth* in regard to slavery, there is not an adult in this region but knows more of it than you do. *Truth* and *fact* are, you are aware, by no means synonimous terms. Ninety-nine facts may constitute a falsehood: the hundredth, added or alone, gives the truth. With all your knowledge of facts, I undertake to say that you are entirely and grossly ignorant of the real condition of our slaves. And from all that I can see, you are equally ignorant of the essential principles of human association revealed in history, both sacred and profane, on which slavery rests, and which will perpetuate it forever in some form or other. However you may declaim against it; however powerfully you may array atrocious incidents; whatever appeals you may make to the heated imaginations and tender sensibilities of mankind, believe me, your total blindness to the *whole truth*, which alone constitutes *the truth*, incapacitates you from ever making an impression on the sober reason and sound common sense of the world. You may seduce thousands—you can convince no one. Whenever and wherever you or the advocates of your cause can arouse the passions of the weakminded and the ignorant, and, bringing to bear with them the interests of the vicious and unprincipled, overwhelm common sense and reason—as God sometimes permits to be done—you may triumph. Such a triumph we have witnessed in Great Britain. But I trust it is far distant here: Nor can it from its nature be extensive or enduring. Other classes of Reformers, animated by the same spirit as the Abolitionists, attack the institution of marriage, and even the established relations of Parent and Child. And they collect instances of barbarous cruelty and shocking degradation which rival, if they do not throw into the shade, your slavery statistics. But the rights of marriage and parental authority rest upon truths as obvious as they are unchangeable—coming home to every human being—self-impressed forever on the individual mind, and cannot be shaken until the whole man is corrupted, nor subverted until civilized society becomes a putrid mass. Domestic slavery is not so universally understood, nor can it make such a direct appeal to individuals or society beyond its pale. Here, prejudice and passion have room to sport at the expense of others. They may be excited and urged to dangerous action, remote from the victims they mark out. They may, as they have done, effect great mischief; but they cannot be made to maintain, in the long run, dominion over reason and common sense, nor ultimately put down what God has ordained.

You deny, however, that slavery is sanctioned by God, and your chief argument is that when he gave to Adam dominion over the fruits of the earth and the animal creation he stopped there. "He never gave him any further right over his fellow men." You restrict the descendants of Adam to a very short list of rights and powers, duties and responsibilities, if you limit them solely to those conferred and enjoined in the first chapter of Genesis. It is very obvious that in this narrative of the creation Moses did not have it in view to record any part of the Law intended for the government of man in his social or political state. Eve was not yet created; the expulsion had not taken place; Cain was unborn; and no allusion whatever is made to the manifold decrees of God to which these events gave rise. The only serious answer this argument deserves, to say what is so manifestly true, that God's not expressly giving to Adam "any right over his fellow men" by no means excluded Him from conferring that right on his descendants; which he in fact did. We know that Abraham, the chosen one of God, exercised it and held property in his fellow man, and even anterior to the period when property in land was acknowledged. We might infer that God had authorised it. But we are not reduced to inference or conjecture. At the hazard of fatiguing you by repetition, I will again refer you to the ordinances of the Scriptures. Innumerable instances might be quoted where God has given and commanded men to assume dominion over their fellow men. But one will suffice. In the twenty-fifth chapter of Leviticus you will find *Domestic Slavery—precisely such as is maintained at this day in these States—ordained and established by God, in language which I defy you to pervert so as to leave a doubt on any honest mind that this institution was founded by Him, and decreed to be perpetual.* I quote the words:

Leviticus, xxv. 44: "Both thy Bondmen, and thy Bondmaids, which thou shalt have, shall be of the Heathen [Africans] that are round about you; of *them ye shall buy Bondmen and Bondmaids.*"

45: "Moreover of the children of the strangers that do sojourn among you, of them shall ye buy, *and of their families that are with you which they begat in your land;* [descendants of Africans?] and they shall be your possession."

46: "*And ye shall take them as an inheritance for your children after you, to inherit them for a possession.* THEY SHALL BE YOUR BONDMEN FOREVER."

What human Legislature could make a decree more full and explicit than this? What Court of Law or Chancery could defeat a title to a slave couched in terms so clear and complete as these? And this is the *Law of God*, whom you pretend to worship, while you denounce and traduce us for respecting it.

It seems scarcely credible, but the fact is so, that

you deny this Law so plainly written, and, in the face of it, have the hardihood to declare that "though slavery is not *specifically*, yet it is *virtually forbidden* in the Scriptures, because all the crimes which necessarily arise out of slavery, and which can arise from no other source, are reprobated there and threatened with divine vengeance." Such an unworthy subterfuge is scarcely entitled to consideration. But its gross absurdity may be exposed in few words. I do not know what crimes you particularly allude to as arising from slavery. But you will perhaps admit—not because they are denounced in the decalogue, which the Abolitionists respect only so far as they choose, but because it is the *immediate interest* of most men to admit—that disobedience to parents, adultery, and stealing are crimes. Yet these crimes "necessarily arise from" the relations of parent and child, marriage, and the possession of private property; at least they "can arise from no other sources." Then, according to your argument, it is "virtually forbidden" to marry, to beget children, and to hold private property! Nay, it is forbidden to live, since murder can only be perpetrated on living subjects. You add that "in the same way the gladiatorial shows of old, and other barbarous customs, were not specifically forbidden in the New Testament, and yet Christianity was the sole means of their suppression." This is very true. But these shows and barbarous customs thus suppressed, were not authorized *by God*. They were not ordained and commanded by God for the benefit of His chosen people and mankind, as the purchase and holding of Bondmen and Bondmaids were. Had they been, they would never have been "suppressed by Christianity," any more than slavery can be by your party. Although Christ came "not to destroy but fulfil the Law," he nevertheless did formally abrogate some of the ordinances promulgated by Moses, and all such as were at war with his mission of "peace and good will on earth." He "specifically" annuls, for instance, one "barbarous custom" sanctioned by those ordinances, where he says: "ye have heard that it hath been said, an eye for an eye and a tooth for a tooth; but I say unto you that ye resist not evil, but whosoever shall smite thee on the right cheek turn him the other, also." Now, in the time of Christ, it was usual for masters to put their slaves to death on the slightest provocation. They even killed and cut them up to feed their fishes. He was undoubtedly aware of these things, as well as of the Law and Commandment I have quoted. He could only have been restrained from denouncing them, as he did the "*lex talionis*," because he knew that, in despite of these barbarities, the institution of slavery was at the bottom a sound and wholesome as well as lawful one. Certain it is, that in His wisdom and purity he did not see proper to interfere with it. In your wisdom, however, you make the sacrilegious attempt to overthrow it.

You quote the denunciation of Tyre and Sidon, and say that "the chief reason given by the Prophet Joel for their destruction, was, that they were notorious beyond all others for carrying on the Slave Trade." I am afraid you think we have no Bibles in the slave States, or that we are unable to read them. I cannot otherwise account for your making this reference, unless indeed your own reading is confined to an expurgated edition, prepared for the use of the Abolitionists, in which everything relating to slavery that militates against their view of it is left out. The Prophet Joel denounces the Tyrians and Sidonians because "The children also of Judah and the children of Jerusalem have ye sold unto the Grecians." And what is the divine vengeance for this "notorious slave trading?" Hear it. "And I will sell your sons and daughters into the hands of the children of Judah, and they shall sell them to the Sabeans, to a people far off: for the Lord hath spoken it." Do you call this a condemnation of slave-trading? The Prophet makes God Himself a participator in the crime, if that be one. "The Lord hath spoken it," he says, that the Tyrians and Sidonians shall be *sold into slavery* to strangers. Their real offence was in enslaving the Chosen People; and their sentence was a repetition of the old Command, to make slaves of the "Heathen round about."

I have dwelt upon your scriptural argument because you profess to believe the Bible; because a large proportion of the Abolitionists profess to do the same, and to act under its sanction; because your Circular is addressed in part to "professing Christians;" and because it is from that class mainly that you expect to seduce converts to your anti-christian, I may say, infidel doctrines. It would be wholly unnecessary to answer you to any one who reads the Scriptures for himself, and construes them according to any other formula than that which the Abolitionists are wickedly endeavoring to impose upon the world. The scriptural sanction of slavery is in fact so palpable, and so strong, that both wings of your party are beginning to acknowledge it. The more sensible and moderate admit, as the organ of the Free Church of Scotland, the North British Review, has lately done, that they "*are precluded by the statements and conduct of the Apostles from regarding mere slave-holding as essentially sinful;*" while the desperate and reckless, who are bent on keeping up the agitation at every hazard, declare, as has been done in the Anti-Slavery Record, "If our inquiry turns out in favor of slavery, IT IS THE BIBLE THAT MUST FALL, AND NOT THE RIGHTS OF HUMAN NATURE." You cannot, I am satisfied, much longer maintain before the world, the Christian platform from which to wage war upon our Institutions. Driven from it, you must abandon the contest, or, repudiating REVELATION, rush into the horrors of NATURAL RELIGION.

You next complain that our slaves are kept in bondage by the "Law of force." In what country or condition of mankind do you see human affairs regulated merely by the law of love? Unless I am greatly mistaken you will, if you look over the world, find nearly all certain and permanent rights, civil, social, and I may even add religious, resting on and ultimately secured by the "law of force." The power of majorities—of aristocracies—of Kings—nay of priests, for the most part, and of property, resolves itself at last into "force," and could not otherwise be long maintained. Thus, in every turn of your argument against our system of slavery, you advance, whether conscious of it or not, radical and revolutionary doctrines calculated to change the whole face of the world, to overthrow all governments, disorganize society, and reduce man to a state of nature—red with blood, and shrouded once more in barbaric ignorance. But you greatly err, if you suppose, because we rely on force in the last resort to maintain our supremacy over our slaves, that ours is a stern and unfeeling domination at all to be compared in hard-hearted severity to that exercised, not over the mere laborer only, but by the higher over each lower order, wherever the British sway is acknowledged. You say that if those you address were "to spend one day in the South they would return home with impressions against slavery never to be erased." But the fact is universally the the reverse. I have known numerous instances; and I never knew a single one, where there was no other cause of offence and no object to promote by falsehood, that individuals from the non-slave-holding States did not, after residing among us long enough to understand the subject, "return home" *to defend our slavery*. It is matter of regret, that you have never tried the experiment yourself. I do not doubt you would have been converted, for I give you credit for an honest though perverted mind. You would have seen how weak and futile is all abstract reasoning about this matter; and that, as a building may not be less elegant in its proportions, or tasteful in its ornaments, or virtuous in its uses, for being based upon granite; so a system of human government, though founded on force, may develope and cultivate the tenderest and purest sentiments of the human heart. And our patriarchal scheme of domestic servitude is indeed well calculated to awaken the higher and finer feelings of our nature. It is not wanting in its enthusiasm and its poetry. The relations of the most beloved and honored chief, and the most faithful and admiring subjects, which from the time of Homer have been the theme of song, are frigid and unfelt compared with those existing between the master and his slaves—who served his father, and rocked his cradle, or have been born in his house-hold, and look forward to serve his children—who have been through life the props of his fortune, and the object of his care—who have partaken of his griefs, and looked to him for comfort in their own—whose sickness he has so frequently watched over and relieved—whose holidays he has so often made joyous by his bounties and his presence—for whose welfare when absent his anxious solicitude never ceases, and whose hearty and affectionate greetings never fail to welcome him home. In this cold, calculating, ambitious world of ours, there are few ties more heartfelt, or of more benignant influence, than those which mutually bind the master and the slave, under our ancient system, handed down from the Father of Israel. The unholy purpose of the Abolitionists is to destroy by defiling it; to infuse into it the gall and bitterness which rankle in their own envenomed bosoms; to poison the minds of the master and the servant; turn love to hatred, array "*force*" *against force*, and hurl all,

> "With hideous ruin and combustion down
> To bottomless perdition."

You think it a great "crime" that we do not pay our slaves "wages," and on this account pronounce us "robbers." In my former letter I showed that the labor of our slaves was not without great cost to us, and that in fact they themselves receive more in return for it than your hirelings do for theirs. For what purpose do men labor, but to support themselves and their families in what comfort they are able? The efforts of mere physical labor seldom suffice to provide more than a livelihood. And it is a well known and shocking fact, that while few operatives in Great Britain succeed in securing a comfortable living, the greater part drag out a miserable existence, and sink at last under absolute want. Of what avail is it that you go through the form of paying them a pittance of what you call "wages," when you do not, in return for their services, allow them what alone they ask—and have a just right to demand—enough to feed, clothe and lodge them, in health and sickness, with reasonable comfort. Though we do not give "wages" *in money*, we do this for *our slaves*, and they are therefore better rewarded than *yours*. It is the prevailing vice and error of the age, and one from which the Abolitionists, with all their saintly pretensions, are far from being free, to bring everything to the standard of money. You make gold and silver the great test of happiness. The American slave must be wretched indeed, because he is not compensated for his services *in cash*. It is altogether praiseworthy to pay the laborer a shilling a day and let him starve on it. To supply all his wants abundantly, and at all times, yet withhold from him *money*, is among "the most reprobated crimes." The fact cannot be denied, that the mere laborer is now, and always has been, everywhere that barbarism has ceased, enslaved. Among the innovations of modern times following "the decay of villeinage," has been the creation of a new system of slavery. The primitive and patriarchal, which may also be called the sacred and natural system, in which the laborer is under the personal control of a fellow-being, endowed with the sentiments and sympathies of humanity, exists among us. It has been almost everywhere else superseded by the modern artificial *money-power system*, in which man—his thews and sinews, his hopes and affections, his very being, are all subjected to the dominion of *Capital*—a monster without a heart—cold, stern, arithmetical—sticking to the bond—taking ever "the pound of flesh"—working up human life with Engines, and retailing it out by weight and measure. His name of old was "Mammon, the least erected spirit that fell from Heaven." And it is to extend his Empire, that you and your deluded coadjutors dedicate your lives. You are stirring up mankind to overthrow our Heaven-ordained system of servitude, surrounded by innumerable checks, designed and planted deep in the human heart by God and nature, to substitute the absolute rule of this "Spirit Reprobate," whose proper place was Hell.

You charge us with looking on our slaves "as chattels or brutes," and enter into a somewhat elaborate argument to prove that they have "human forms," "talk," and even "think." Now the fact is that, however you may indulge in this strain for effect, it is the Abolitionists, and not the Slave-holders, who practically, and in the most important point of view, regard our slaves as "chattels or brutes." In your calculations of the consequences of emancipation you pass over entirely those which must prove most serious, and which arise from the fact of their being *persons*. You appear to think that we might abstain from the use of them as readily as if they were machines to be laid aside, or cattle that might be turned out to find pasturage for themselves. I have heretofore glanced at some of the results that would follow from breaking the bonds of so many *human beings* now peacefully and happily linked into our social system. The tragic horrors, the decay and ruin that would for years, perhaps for ages, brood over our land, if it could be accomplished, I will not attempt to portray. But do you fancy the blight would, in such an event, come to us alone? The diminution of the sugar crop of the West Indies affected Great Britain only, and there chiefly the poor. It was a matter of no moment to Capital, that Labor should have one comfort less. Yet it has forced a reduction of the British duty on sugar. Who can estimate the consequences that must follow the annihilation of the cotton crop of the slave-holding States? I do not undervalue the importance of other articles of commerce, but no calamity could befall the world at all comparable to the sudden loss of two millions of bales of cotton annually. From the deserts of Africa to the Siberian wilds—from Greenland to the Chinese Wall, there is not a spot of earth but would feel the sensation. The Factories of Europe would fall with a concussion that would shake down castles, palaces and even thrones; while the "purse-proud, elbowing insolence" of our Northern monopolist would disappear forever under the smooth speech of the peddler, scouring our frontiers for a livelihood, or the bluff vulgarity of the South Sea whaler, following the harpoon amid storms and shoals. Doubtless the Abolitionists think we could grow cotton without slaves, or that at worst the reduction of the crop would be moderate and temporary. Such gross delusions show how profoundly ignorant they are of our condition here.

You declare that "the character of the people of the South has long been that of *hardened Infidels*, who fear not God, and have no regard for religion." I will not repeat what I said in my former letter on this point. I only notice it to ask you how you could possibly reconcile it to your profession of a Christian spirit, to make such a malicious charge—to defile your soul with such a calumny against an unoffending people?

> "You are old;
> Nature in you stands on the very verge
> Of her confines. You should be ruled and led
> By some discretion."—

May God forgive you.

Akin to this is the wanton and furious assault made on us by Mr. Macaulay in his late speech on the Sugar duties, in the House of Commons, which has just reached me. His denunciations are wholly without measure, and among other things he asserts "that Slavery in the United States wears its worst form; that, boasting of our civilization and freedom, and frequenting Christian Churches, we breed up slaves, nay, beget children for slaves, and sell them at so much a head." Mr. Macaulay is a Reviewer, and he knows that he is "nothing if not critical." The practice of his trade has given him the command of all the slashing and vituperative phrases of our language, and the turn of his mind leads him to the habitual use of them. He is an author, and as no copy-right law secures for him from this country a consideration for his writings, he is not only independent of us, but naturally hates everything American. He is the Representative of Edinburgh; it is his cue to decry our slavery, and in doing so he may safely indulge the malignity of his temper, his indignation against us, and his capacity for railing. He has suffered once for being in advance of his time in favor of Abolition, and he does not intend that it shall be forgotten, or his claim passed over to any crumb which may now be thrown to the vociferators in the cause. If he does not know that the statements he has made respecting the slaveholders of this country are vile and atrocious falsehoods, it is because he does not think it worth his while to be sure he speaks the truth, so that he speaks to his own purpose.

"Hic niger est, hunc tu, Romane caveto."

Such exhibitions as he has made may draw the applause of a British House of Commons, but among the sound and high-minded thinkers of the world they can only excite contempt and disgust.

But you are not content with depriving us of all religious feelings. You assert that our slavery has also "demoralized the Northern States," and charge upon it not only every common violation of good order there, but the "Mormon murders," the "Philadelphia riots," and all "the exterminating wars against the Indians." I wonder that you did not increase the list by adding that it had caused the recent inundation of the Mississippi, and the hurricane in the West Indies—perhaps the insurrection of Rebecca, and the war in Scinde. You refer to the law prohibiting the transmission of Abolition publications through the mail as proof of general corruption! You could not do so, however, without noticing the late detected espionage over the British Post Office by a Minister of

State. It is true, as you say, it "occasioned a general outburst of National feeling"—from the opposition; and a "Parliamentary inquiry was instituted"—that is moved, but treated quite cavalierly. At all events, though the fact was admitted, Sir James Graham yet retains the Home Department. For one, I do not undertake to condemn him. Such things are not against the laws and usages of your country. I do not know fully what reasons of State may have influenced him and justified his conduct. But I do know that there is a vast difference, in point of "national morality," between the discretionary power residing in your Government to open any letter in the public post office, and a well-defined and limited law to prevent the circulation of certain specified incendiary writings by means of the United States Mail.

Having now referred to everything like argument on the subject of Slavery that is worthy of notice in your letter, permit me to remark on its tone and style, and very extraordinary bearing upon other Institutions of this country. You commence by addressing certain classes of our people as belonging to "a nation whose character is *now so low* in the estimation of the civilized world;" and throughout you maintain this tone. Did the Americans who were "under your roof last summer" inform you that such language would be gratifying to their fellow-citizens "having no practical concern with slaveholding?" Or do the infamous libels on America, which you read in our Abolition papers, induce you to believe that all that class of people are, like the Abolitionists themselves, totally destitute of patriotism or pride of country? Let me tell you that you are grossly deceived. And although your stock brokers and other speculators, who have been bitten in American ventures, may have raised a stunning "cry" against us in England, there is a vast body of people here besides slave-holders, who justly

> "Deem their own land of every land the pride,
> Beloved by Heaven o'er all the world beside."

And who *know* that at this moment we rank among the First Powers of the world—a position which we not only claim, but are always ready and able to maintain.

The style you assume in addressing your Northern friends is in perfect keeping with your apparent estimation of them. Though I should be the last, perhaps, to criticise mere style, I could not but be struck with the extremely simple manner of your letter. You seem to have thought you were writing a Tract for benighted Heathen, and telling wonders never before suggested to their imagination, and so far above their untutored comprehension as to require to be related in the primitive language of "the child's own book." This is sufficiently amusing; and would be more so but for the coarse and bitter epithets you continually apply to the poor slave-holders—epithets which appear to be stereotyped for the use of Abolitionists, and which form a large and material part of all their arguments.

But perhaps the most extraordinary part of your letter is your bold denunciation of "*the shameful compromises*" of our Constitution, and your earnest recommendation to those you address to overthrow or revolutionize it. In so many words you say to them, "*you must either separate yourselves* from all political connexion with the South, and make your own laws; or, if you do not choose such a separation, you must break up the *political ascendancy which the Southern have had for so long a time over the Northern States.*" The italics in this as in all other quotations are your own. It is well for those who circulate your letter here, that the Constitution you denounce requires an overt act to constitute Treason. It may be tolerated for an American, by birth, to use on his own soil the freedom of speaking and writing which is guaranteed to him, and abuse our Constitution, our Union, and our people. But that a Foreigner should use such seditious language, in a Circular Letter addressed to a portion of the American people, is a presumption well calculated to excite the indignation of all. The party known in this country as the Abolition Party has long since avowed the sentiments you express, and adopted the policy you enjoin. At the recent Presidential election they gave over 62,000 votes for their own Candidate, and held the balance of power in two of the largest States—wanting but little of doing it in several others. In the last four years their vote has quadrupled. Should the infatuation continue, and their vote increase in the same ratio, for the next four years, it will be as large as the vote of the *actual slave-holders* of the Union. Such a prospect is doubtless extremely gratifying to you. It gives hope of a contest on such terms as may insure the downfall of Slavery or our Constitution. The South venerates the Constitution, and is prepared to stand by it forever, *such as it came from the hands of our fathers;* to risk everything to defend and maintain it *in its integrity.* But the South is under no such delusion as to believe that it derives any *peculiar* protection from the Union. On the contrary, it is well known we incur *peculiar danger*, and that we bear far more than our proportion of the burdens. The apprehension is also fast fading away that any of the dreadful consequences commonly predicted will necessarily result from a separation of the States. And, *come what may*, we are firmly resolved that OUR SYSTEM OF DOMESTIC SLAVERY SHALL STAND. The fate of the Union then—but thank God not of Republican Government—rests mainly in the hands of the people to whom your letter is addressed—the "professing Christians of the Northern States having no concern with slaveholding," and whom with incendiary zeal you are endeavoring to stir up to strife—without which fanaticism can neither live, move, nor have any being.

We have often been taunted for our sensitiveness in regard to the discussion of Slavery. Do not suppose it is because we have any doubts of our rights, or scruples about asserting them. There was a time when such doubts and scruples were entertained. Our ancestors opposed the introduction of Slaves into this country, and a feeling adverse to it was handed down from them. The enthusiastic love of liberty fostered by our Revolution strengthened this feeling. And before the commencement of the Abolition agitation here, it was the common sentiment that it was desirable to get rid of Slavery. Many thought it our duty to do so. When that agitation arose, we were driven to a close examination of the subject in all its bearings, and the result has been an *universal conviction* that in holding Slaves we violate no law of God—inflict no injustice on any of his creatures—while the terrible consequences of emancipation to all parties and the world at large, clearly revealed to us, make us shudder at the bare thought of it. The slaveholders are therefore indebted to the Abolitionists for perfect ease of conscience, and the satisfaction of a settled and unanimous determination in reference to this matter. And could their agitation cease now, I believe, after all, the good would preponderate over the evil of it in this country. On the contrary, however, it is urged on with frantic violence, and the Abolitionists, reasoning in the abstract—as if it were a mere moral or metaphysical speculation, or a minor question in politics—profess to be surprised at our exasperation. In their ignorance and recklessness they seem to be unable to comprehend our feelings or position. The subversion of our rights, the destruction of our property, the disturbance of our peace and the peace of the world, are matters which do not appear to arrest their consideration. When Revolutionary France proclaimed "Hatred to Kings and unity to the Republic," and inscribed on her banners "France risen against Tyrants," she professed to be only worshiping "Abstract Rights." And, if there can be such things, perhaps she was. Yet all Europe *rose* to put her sublime theories down. They declared her an enemy to the common peace; that her doctrines alone violated the "Law of Neighborhood," and, as Mr. Burke said, justly entitled them to anticipate the "damnum nondum factum" of the civil law. Danton, Barrere and the rest were apparently astonished that umbrage should be taken. The parallel between them and the Abolitionists holds good in all respects.

The rise and progress of this Fanaticism is one of the phenomena of the age in which we live. I do not intend to repeat what I have already said, or to trace its career more minutely at present. But the Legislation of Great Britain will make it historical; and, doubtless, you must feel some curiosity to know how it will figure on the page of the Annalist. I think I can tell you. Though I have accorded and do accord to you and your party great influence in bringing about the Parliamentary action of your country, you must not expect to go down to posterity as the only cause of it. Though *you* trace the progenitors of Abolition from 1516, through a long stream with divers branches, down to the period of its triumph in your country; it has not escaped contemporaries, and will not escape posterity, that England, without much effort, sustained the storm of its scoffs and threats until the moment arrived when she thought her colonies fully supplied with Africans; and declared against the Slave Trade only when she deemed it unnecessary to her, and when her colonies full of Slaves would have great advantages over others not so well provided. Nor did she agree to West India emancipation until, discovering the error of her previous calculation, it became an object to have slaves free throughout the Western world, and, on the ruins of the Sugar and Cotton growers of America and the Islands, to build up her great Slave Empire in the East; while her indefatigable exertions, still continued, to engraft the Right of Search upon the Law of Nations, on the plea of putting an end to the forever increasing Slave Trade, are well understood to have chiefly in view the complete establishment of her supremacy at sea.*

* On these points let me recommend you to consult a very able Essay on the Slave Trade and Right of Search by M. Jollivet, recently pub-

Nor must you flatter yourself that your party will derive historic dignity from the names of the illustrious British statesmen who have acted with it. Their country's ends were theirs. They have stooped to use you, as the most illustrious men will sometimes use the vilest instruments, to accomplish their own purposes. A few philanthropic common places and rhetorical flourishes, "in the abstract," have secured them your "sweet voices," and your influence over the tribe of mawkish sentimentalists. Wilberforce may have been yours, but what was he besides, but a wealthy county member? You must therefore expect to stand on your own merits alone before posterity, or rather that portion of it that may be curious to trace the history of the Delusions which from time to time pass over the surface of human affairs, and who may trouble themselves to look through the ramifications of Transcendentalism in this era of extravagances. And how do you expect to appear in their eyes? As Christians, piously endeavoring to enforce the will of God and carry out the principles of Christianity? Certainly not, since you deny or pervert the Scriptures in the doctrines you advance; and in your conduct furnish a glaring contrast to the examples of Christ and the Apostles. As Philanthropists, devoting yourselves to the cause of humanity, relieving the needy, comforting the afflicted, creating peace and gladness and plenty round about you? Certainly not, since you turn from

---

lished; and as you say, since writing your Circular Letter, that you "burn to try your hand on another little Essay if a subject could be found," I propose to you to "try" to answer this question, put by M. Jollivet to England: *"Pourquoi sa philanthropie n'a pas daigne, jusqu' a present, doubler le cap de Bonne-Esperance?"*

the needy, the afflicted; from strife, sorrow and starvation which surround you; close your eyes and hands upon them; shut out from your thoughts and feelings the human misery which is real, tangible, and within your reach, to indulge your morbid imagination in conjuring up woes and wants among a strange people in distant lands, and offering them succor in the shape of costless denunciations of their best friends, or by scattering among them " firebrands, arrows, and death." Such folly and madness—such wild mockery and base imposture, can never win for you, in the sober judgment of future times, the name of Philanthropists. Will you even be regarded as worthy citizens? Scarcely, when the purposes you have in view can only be achieved by revolutionizing governments and overturning social systems, and when you do not hesitate zealously and earnestly to recommend such measures. Be assured, then, that posterity will not regard the Abolitionists as Christians, Philanthropists, or virtuous citizens. It will, I have no doubt, look upon the mass of the party as silly enthusiasts, led away by designing characters, as is the case with all parties that break from the great, acknowledged ties that bind civilized man in fellowship. The leaders themselves will be regarded as *mere ambitious men;* not taking rank with those whose ambition is "eagle-winged and sky-aspiring," but belonging to that mean and selfish class who are instigated by "rival-hating envy," and whose base thirst is for *Notoriety;* who cloak their designs under vile and impious hypocrisies, and, unable to shine in higher spheres, devote themselves to Fanaticism as a trade. And it will be perceived that, even in that, they shunned the highest walk. Religious Fanaticism was an old established vocation, in which something brilliant was required to attract attention. They could not be George Foxes, nor Joanna Southcotes, nor even Joe Smiths. But the dullest pretender could discourse a jumble of pious bigotry, natural rights, and drivelling philanthropy. And, addressing himself to aged folly and youthful vanity, to ancient women, to ill-gotten wealth, to the reckless of all classes who love excitement and change, offer each the cheapest and the safest glory in the market. Hence, their numbers; and, from number and clamor, what impression they have on the world.

Such I am persuaded is the light in which the Abolitionists will be viewed by the posterity their history may reach. Unless, indeed—which God forbid—circumstances should so favor as to enable them to produce a convulsion which may elevate them higher on the "bad eminence" where they have placed themselves.

I have the honor to be
Your obedient servant,
J. H. HAMMOND.

THOMAS CLARKSON, Esq.

AN ORATION

DELIVERED BEFORE THE TWO SOCIETIES OF THE SOUTH CAROLINA COLLEGE ON THE FOURTH OF DECEMBER, 1849.

WE are accustomed to regard the age in which we live not only as the most enlightened which the world has known, but one of unprecedented progress. The rapidity with which ideas and events disseminated by the press, fly on the wings of steam and electricity around the globe, leads us to suppose that the sum total of human knowledge is far greater than it ever has been; and the discoveries in art and science, which are continually announced, induce the belief that human improvement is advancing at a pace beyond all former example. These two conclusions, so universally prevalent, are fast conducting us to others of much higher import, and of much more doubtful truth. "We," said Bentham, repeating an aphorism of Lord Bacon, "we are the ancients," and the whole school of Utilitarians—by far the most numerous of our day—declare that there was little wisdom in the past, and that nothing is venerable in antiquity. The present then and the future, we are taught, are alone worthy of our thoughts and cares.

Indeed a calm observer of mankind in our era might be led to think that the Utilitarians and most of the enthusiastic admirers of modern progress, believe that the seeds of it spontaneously germinated and could never fail; that discoveries and inventions are lucky accidents that will constantly recur; that the great events which influence the higher destinies of our species are the results of chance; and that the only task for man is to make the best use, each for himself, of whatever good fortune may throw in his way. But such absurd opinions no one will openly acknowledge that he entertains. All admit, when forced to reason, that there must be causes for effects. And, in general, the improvements of our age are attributed to the advance of physical and experimental philosophy, of which Lord Bacon is referred to as the founder.

The opinion that modern progress dates from the era of Bacon, and rests upon the philosophy with which his name is now most associated, has of late been so widely diffused, and so strenuously inculcated, that it is becoming, even among the most intelligent, a fixed belief; and, to look further back than to him and his doctrines, is deemed unnecessary for any useful purpose of the present day—all beyond being matters of curious inquiry and fit studies for elegant leisure, but of little value to the earnest and practical man of our enlightened age. And in the same spirit we are taught to pass lightly by all moral theories, and to treat with contempt all metaphysical discussion.

But the causes thus assigned for the progress of mankind, during the last two centuries, are wholly inadequate, and to a very great degree untrue. Whoever limits his views to the consideration of these causes only, cannot possibly comprehend the civilization he enjoys, and is, of course, not capable of performing thoroughly his own part in the important affairs of life—much less of promoting the welfare of those who are to come after us.

It is well known that the Novum Organum of Bacon was a sealed book to his contemporaries. Even Hobbes, his amanuensis, was not his disciple. The greatest admirers of this truly great man—to whom was vouchsafed the utmost intellectual capacity with which man can, so far as we know, be endowed—admit that this work has been more read within the present century than during the two previous—more since than before the time when Newton discovered the true theory of motion, when Lavoisier erected chemistry into a science, and Watt applied steam to useful purposes; while there is no reason to suppose that any of these illustrious men had been students of the new philosophy of Bacon. We owe a very large proportion of the discoveries and inventions of modern times to Italy, where this philosophy has not yet penetrated.

But Bacon himself lived in an age when progress had already made vast and rapid strides; when the grandest discoveries had been already effected in physics and verified by experiment; and when the foundations had been laid for nearly all the improvements which have been developed to the present day. Paper, Gunpowder, the Mariner's Compass, and the art of Printing had long been in use. The Copernican system, though probably unknown to Bacon, had been announced, and Galileo had made a Telescope and demonstrated the truth of it. Harvey had discovered the circulation of the blood; Paracelsus had, at least, rescued chemistry from the magicians; Agricola had commenced mineralogy; Leonardo had suggested the very theory of Geology now most in vogue; Columbus and De Gama had revealed two new worlds to astonished Europe, and Sir Francis Drake had sailed round the globe.

But the actual discoveries of Bacon were of little consequence; it is to his system of logic and his method of investigation that we owe, it is said, so much—to his Induction and "*experimentum crucis*." If Bacon was the first author and expounder of Inductive reasoning, and first suggested that nature should be put to the torture to disclose her facts, and modern improvements are due to these processes, to what do we owe the important discoveries before Bacon's time? Can it be that they were all accidents, and that there was no questioning of nature—no induction? Certainly not. Tubal Cain himself, if he discovered as well as wrought in metals, must have experimented in physics, and must have reasoned by strict induction on the results. Aristotle minutely examined and characterized almost every thing in animated nature, and, a century or more before the Novum Organum, Leonardo declared, in almost the same words, that the phenomena of nature were to be solved not by theories, but a rigid investigation of the facts.

It is not true then that Physical Philosophy and Inductive reasoning began with Bacon. He propounded a system and collected facts; but it was not until recently—not until men's minds had been illumined by the light shed abroad by actual improvement—that his facts were appreciated and his system comprehended—a system not wholly new in theory, and in some parts ancient in practice. The truth is that discovery has done more for Bacon than he has done as yet for it, since it is only now that we begin to look with astonishment and admiration at the vast range and wonderful foreshadowing of his mighty intellect. That he was himself, in some respects, overtaken and outrun by the progress of his own age is sufficiently illustrated by the melancholy fact that he was the first English judge tried and sentenced for receiving bribes—a practice which had been universal, and, until his case, notoriously tolerated.

The close inquirer will often be amazed to find how true it is, that, after all, there is little new under the sun; to perceive from what remote sources and for what a period, the greatest ideas, unrealized, unsystematized, almost unheeded, have floated down the mighty stream of time—now far out in the current, now driven near the shore, and finally thrown on some propitious headland where they found a genial soil and bear the most precious fruit. Thales attributed the formation of the earth to the action of water, and gave a hint of electricity. Pythagoras said the sun, and not the earth, was the centre of the universe, and that the planets moved round it in elliptical orbits. The Roman bakers stamped their bread. Aristotle believed that the explosive power of steam was sufficient to produce earthquakes. And Hero of Alexandria actually applied steam power to a toy machine, two centuries before the Christian Era. So, long ago, were laid the foundations for discoveries, which have, in some instances, been fully developed only in our age.

But if Physical and Experimental Philosophy is of much older origin than the seventeenth century, it is not less certain that it would have been utterly inadequate to produce the civilization we enjoy. The steam engine and power loom, printing, and the mariner's compass, have undoubtedly made vast additions to the comforts, conveniences and enjoyments of the whole human family; and it is common to say of them, and of other kindred inventions, that they have been great civilizers. But this is the language of metaphor—a language much too generally used, and too literally interpreted in our times. They have, indeed, been powerful instruments of civilization, and, in the hands of genius and enterprise, of men of refined and cultivated intellects, of pure and noble sentiments, they have been of incalculable service in improving and elevating the condition of mankind. But what service could even such mighty instruments have rendered, if there had not been hands strong enough and wise enough to wield them? What would a steam engine avail a Sioux? To what purpose would a Ghilanese apply a printing press? For unnumbered ages, nature, in her grandest aspects, has been familiar to those wild children of the sons of Noah. They have little else to study. Yet they have penetrated but few of her secrets—have appropriated but few of her blessings. What is it that has enabled the descendants of Japheth to conquer so many of her mysteries and to control, for *their* own ends, so many of their powers? To answer this question we must look back, and traverse a wide surface. We may, for the most part, readily tell who made this discovery, who was the author of that invention; but when we are asked what has brought the mind of the Caucasian race to its present high condition—what will keep it where it is—what will advance it still further in its glorious career; when these searching and necessary questions, on whose answers depend the whole solution of the great problem of human progress, are propounded, we cannot but see how puerile and absurd it would be to say, it is Physical and Experimental Philosophy—a philosophy essentially inert and dead itself, as matter, until life has been breathed into it by the cultivated intellect and refined imagination.

If we should say that it has taken all the past to make the present, we should state but the simple truth, and fall short of the whole truth if we said any thing less. It has required every event of the past, every teaching of philosophy in all its forms—every discovery of science, every work of art—every experiment whether in physics or morals, in politics or religion, on individuals or societies—to bring our race to its present improved and enlightened condition. Whatever men have done or spoken in the whole tide of time has produced effects, great or small, good or evil, which have contributed to bring about the existing state of things, in the midst of which it has been our fortune to be placed.

In looking back over the vast field through which the human family have made their long and momentous pilgrimage, it would be impossible to say that any incident of it could have happened otherwise than it did, without affecting *us*. If the route had been varied, if more or fewer obstacles had impeded the march of those who have gone before us, we could not now occupy the precise position that we do. The most successful culture of a single art or science would be utterly insufficient to account for any but the lowest grade of civilization. Nor could any combination of kindred arts and sciences, carried to the highest perfection, approximate to the production of the grand and infinitely varied results by which we find ourselves surrounded.

To know then where we are—to have any thing like a proper conception of the position that we really occupy, it is necessary for us to learn whence and how we came here, and to trace the mighty wanderings of our forefathers from the period when an offended Deity thrust our first parents from the gates of Eden —a task, beset with difficulties, from which utilitarianism shrinks. The voyager upon the shoreless ocean, and the traveller in the trackless desert, ascertain their situation by observation of the fixed and everlasting stars. But no such bright and steady lights shine out upon the boisterous sea of human affairs, or guide the adventurer through the wide waste of time. Truth, the only safe and certain guide, does not glitter from the heights, but casts up a feeble, though unerring ray, from the very depths of nature; and we must pass the prime of life in toilsome search for that, before we can read aright the dim traditions, and mutilated and discolored records which portray the wonderful career of man.

But it is only when we have conquered, sacked, and seized possession of the past, and all the past, that we have real knowledge, and may then, so far as we are permitted to do so, comprehend ourselves—our civilization and our mission. Yet, to fulfil that mission, we must not only know the past, but we must judge it. We must mark its errors and its follies, its crimes and wickedness. We must note where philosophy has gone astray; where superstition has betrayed its votaries; where ambition, bigotry, and ignorance have shed their blights; where that wholesome restraint, without which genuine liberty cannot exist, has been perverted into oppression, and where that just resistance to wrongs, which is the inherent right of all, has degenerated into factious warfare and ended in anarchy and ruin. And we must also ascertain what pursuits have most promoted the enlightened happiness and welfare of mankind.

Having thus armed ourselves with genuine knowledge, and learned these great and all important lessons from the past, we may be prepared to determine what our real state of progress is, and what shall be done to carry onward the mighty cause of civilization. And we cannot fail to perceive at once, and to denounce the shallow falsehood of those vulgar and narrow, but too common notions of utility, which, overlooking the great essential truths that man has passions as well as wants—sentiments and reason as well as appetites and muscles—attribute our present civilization to physical and experimental philosophy and inductive reasoning on their results, and teach that the highest objects of life, the most important duties to posterity are fulfilled by constructing steam engines, and railroads, and electric telegraphs. If, indeed, we are constrained to admit induction and experimental philosophy to be of paramount importance, it will be as applied on a higher, broader, and nobler scale, to the events of time—to the motives and actions of mankind. This, indeed, was the essential feature in Bacon's system, and that on which really rests all his usefulness and all his glory. He himself denounced experiments made for "productive rather than enlightening" purposes. He declared that "the duties of life were more than life itself"—that "the Georgics of the mind" were worthy of being celebrated in heroic verse; and, embodying profound truth in a striking metaphor, he said that "knowledges are as pyramids, whereof history is the basis."

It is perhaps given to no individual thoroughly to know himself; to bear in mind at all times the history of his own life, however obscure and short it may be; to comprehend precisely the exact position which he himself occupies in the drama of the world, or to anticipate all the consequences of his own acts, however well considered. Much less probable is it, therefore, that any single person shall be able to sift and to digest the whole history of the past, to understand all the relations of the men and nations who compose the existing generations of his race, or to look forward to their future destinies with any absolute certainty. The great Creator and Ruler of the universe alone knows all that has happened, all that is doing, all that shall come to pass. Such perfect knowledge He reserves for Himself, and holds fate in his mighty grasp. But he condescends to use His creatures as the instruments of his great works, and has not left them wholly blind. The genius of mankind has perhaps been equal, in all ages, and in all there have doubtless been wise men. The difference between our age and the ages which have preceded it is, that, while probably no individual may have greater capacity and knowledge than many of his predecessors, more minds are actively engaged in penetrating all the mysteries of creation, and ransacking all the archives of the past; while the facilities for disseminating knowledge which have never existed to any thing like the same extent before, and which we owe to various discoveries in the useful arts, spread it with unparalleled rapidity throughout the world. It strikes everywhere almost at the same time. Its effects are visible at once. No longer the night-blooming plant, which produces its blossom but once an age—knowledge now vegetates like the orange in its genial climes, to which springtime and autumn, flowers and fruits are ever present together. Thus action and re-action are almost instantaneous. Only two centuries ago, it required a thirty years' war to settle the religious and territorial disputes of a single empire. But we have ourselves just seen all Europe rise in arms; every government menaced, many shaken to the centre, some overthrown; and peace and order again apparently established within the space of twenty months. So swift has been the communication of intelligence that the people of two hemispheres have been actual spectators of the fields of conflict, and the public opinion of both has been heard and felt amid the storm of battle. And the combatants themselves on every side, not only thus influenced, but guided by the light of all the experience of other days, have promptly decided where to concede and how far to resist. How long this storm, which rose with bodings as terrific as any that has ever broken on the repose of man, is destined to subside, is known to none; but can be best conjectured, not by those who transmit facts, nor even those who govern trade and finance, but by those who have made themselves most familiar with the true state of human progress, and are accustomed to read the future in the past.

I have said that it is scarcely possible that any single individual can master all the past and thereby make himself completely conversant with all the present. Indeed it is impossible. Much that is valuable in history is lost to us forever—buried by the inscrutable dispensations of Providence in the impenetrable mist of time. The eager inquirers of the day have rescued something from oblivion—enough to excite the keenest curiosity, but scarcely any thing to satisfy it. The arch hitherto supposed to be a modern invention, has been recently exhumed from the mounds of Nimrod, which were once the palaces of the Assyrian Monarchs—where structures, which for unnumbered centuries have disappeared beneath their own dust, are found to have been reared on others, that had met the same fate before them. And hopes are entertained that if the arrow-headed characters still found on slabs, amid these ruins, can ever be deciphered, we shall recover glimpses of a thousand years, which have been hardly reckoned in chronology; and may learn something certain of that mighty Empire, which once overshadowed, according to tradition, all the East, and whose civilization we have now discovered to have been far higher than had ever been believed. The new world, as well as the old, has its mysteries too. We have as yet no clue to the builders of Palenque, nor to the hands that raised the extensive and well planned fortifications of the Scioto valley, both of which mark a degree of progress, to which the red man has never yet attained.

But still the diligent student will find more in the authentic annals of mankind than a single life can compass. And if we desire to continue to go forward in the career of improvement—if we even desire to remain stationary where we are—nay, if we do not desire to retrograde, the whole intellect of our time should be earnestly directed and incessantly stimulated to study the present and the future in the past; and to search through all its broad fields after knowledge, as after hidden treasure.

What is most desired by man is power. "I am famished," said Jason of Pheræ, "for want of empire." Such, no doubt, has been the secret feeling of every human heart—certainly, of every elevated soul. This it is that drives us onward in our various pursuits. But men for the most part follow shadows. The only real and substantial power, is the power of knowledge. He who famishes for empire—let him grasp at that. And if he would build for himself a pyramid for future ages to behold, he must be sure to lay its foundations upon history—history in the broad sense of Bacon.

I have already indicated that even the useful arts have a history, reaching back far beyond the era of this great philosopher, under the shadow of whose perverted reputation drivelling utilitarianism seeks a refuge. But whoever would analyze the framework of modern society, and the political and religious elements which are its pillars, must study the history of events—of the acts and institutions of our ancestors.

If he cannot trace the long wanderings of the grim Teuton, from his Bactrian cradle, through the deep forests and shaking morasses of the North, to the moment when he burst from darkness upon astonished Europe, he may, at least, take him up from the time when Alaric led him to the sack of Rome, overturned the decayed civilization of antiquity and rescued Christianity from a race, which, having failed to destroy it by persecution, would have entombed it with itself. Here commences modern history and Teutonic ascendency, though four dark and agonizing centuries elapsed before their birth can be said to have been fully accomplished; centuries of incessant action and experiment, in which a grand and terrible philosophy was at work—whose crucibles were heated by human passions, whose universal solvent was human blood, and whose *mortua capites* were the wreck of thrones and dynasties. If little that was great or lasting was established in this period, much was tried, and the results, both good and evil, contributed invaluable experience. The broader and milder light of the civilization to which he gave consistency, shines upon the era of the gigantic Charlemagne; and we clearly perceive that, when his powerful arm was withdrawn from it, the great experiment of Teutonic Monarchy failed in the hands of his successors, overwhelmed by the Feudal spirit of our ancestors. That spirit had yet to accomplish its mission of consecrating the hereditary principle, on the basis of indefeasible fealty, and compensating protection, from generation to generation, of the rulers and the ruled; and to foster still further, a lofty sense of personal dignity and honor, while it promoted patriotism, social sympathy, learning and religion. It is an invaluable lesson to us—a lesson which even to this day has not been fully learned in Europe—that this same Feudal system—slowly and naturally as it had been builded up, rich as were its fruits, indestructible as seemed the well wrought chain, which, stretching from prince to peasant, and penetrating all intermediate ranks, bound the whole structure of society in links of solid iron—fell beneath the bloodless blows of a despised *Bourgeoisie*. Two centuries of fanatical crusading had loosened many rivets, by sweeping off the flower of its chivalry; while the new and vast channels of commerce which those crusades opened and put in motion, and the golden flood of inestimable learning which poured in through them from the wise, old, superannuated East, awakened the middle classes to a knowledge of their rights, and gave them strength to strike these blows. And then commenced afresh the struggle and the movement, into which new and potent elements were introduced. The strife of knowledge was mingled with the strife of arms, and commerce and art unfurled their standards in the field. Schools, colleges and universities soon flourished, and broad and stable monarchies were founded. Philosophy and letters, inventions and discoveries, manufactures and trade, sound governments and the refining arts, all advanced, side by side, in the great march of progress. Religion lagged behind. The illustrious foster-mother saw all her glorious children pass before her, till Luther rose and broke the fetters that impeded her. The clogging abuses of the Old Church were in a measure reformed, and a New Church sprang into existence, which has proved the prolific parent of a hundred more. And here opens a chapter, which, perhaps above all others, requires the attention of those who who would fully understand our present condition. Religion has exercised more influence over the temporal affairs of man than all other causes combined, and, since the foundation of Christianity, no event has had greater influence on civilization than the Reformation. For more than a century after it broke out, religious wars and controversies assaulted every tradition and opinion, and shook every institution of the times. And from these wars and controversies, sprung modern civil liberty; all sides contributing in turn to its development. Suarez boldly announced the Jeffersonian creed, that all men were born equal, and that all political power was derived from the people. Buchanan, anticipating Locke, declared that government was founded on a voluntary compact; and honest John Bodin, as far in advance of Priestly and Bentham as he was elevated above the whole utilitarian school, proclaimed that the object of political association was the greatest good of the whole. These doctrines, promulgated before Bacon's era, first took deepest root in England, and soon bred that terrible conflict, in which, for a time, the people trod rough shod upon kings and nobles; and finally ended in making Great Britain what she is to our day, a Republic, governed under Monarchical forms. Our American forefathers left the old world in the very heat of this great struggle, and brought with them those religious and political principles, which have contributed much, very much more than any physical philosophy, or utilitarian code, to make us what we are.

But the earnest inquirer into our present state of

civilization, its causes and its prospects, would fall far short if he limited himself to filling out, however fully, the outline I have sketched. If Galileo was led to the study of astronomy by reading Ariosto, as he confessed he was, how much may we not, and do we not owe to Dante and Petrarch, to Shakspeare and Milton? If the inventor of the electric telegraph, and Fulton and Leonardo were painters, what inspiration may not have been derived from the immortal works of Raffaelle, and Michael Angelo? Whatever stirs the heart, or stimulates the imagination, will arouse the intellect and quicken it to action; and whoever fails to examine and estimate everything that influences to any extent the conceptions and emotions of mankind, must fail to comprehend the problem of their progress.

It is, as I have already said, the fashion of a large and prominent modern school to decry "the wisdom of the ancients," and account it folly to investigate antiquity. But, as thoroughly as the civilization of ancient times has been destroyed, and as essentially as it differed from our own, the debt we owe it is immense; and it would be impossible to trace to their sources, and fully understand, ideas and institutions familiar to our daily life, and deeply affecting our feelings and our interests, if we should close our vista of the past with Alaric and his barbaric followers. The revival of letters was due in a great measure to the renewed study of the classics. From their pages our immediate ancestors learned to love liberty, and we, ourselves, and our posterity in all future time, may still gather from them deepest wisdom.

Hume said, a century ago, that no portion of modern history was perhaps wholly new; and Dr. Arnold has recently remarked that ancient history affords political lessons more applicable to our times, than any part of modern history previous to the eighteenth century. These observations are profoundly true. So long as republics exist, the tragic story of the fall of Athens, as recited by the vigorous and eloquent Thucydides, will be looked to as the most pathetic and instructive example of the folly and insanity of faction; of the evils of ill regulated ambition; of the inevitable fate of every people who put their trust in demagogues. So long as empires shall survive, mankind may learn from Tacitus; may see with their own eyes, on his unfading canvass, the servility, the profligacy, the amazing treachery and appalling wickedness which surround despotic thrones, and crush the intellect and energy of the bravest and the best. So long as conspiracies shall flourish, the record of the keen and scrutinizing Sallust will expose their arts and crimes, and warn them of their end. So long as any government whatever shall be maintained, we must look to Aristotle for the principles on which to erect it, and the maxims by which it is to be conducted. That great philosopher, having examined and analyzed the constitutions of more than a hundred and fifty commonwealths, drew, from this treasury of experiments, results which enabled him to erect politics into a science. From his immortal work the whole host of modern writers on government, from Macchiavelli to Paley and those of the present day, have borrowed largely; and no one can pretend to real statesmanship who have not mastered it. The student of Aristotle will be surprised to find how few fundamental improvements have been effected in the science and practice of government, since his time. Even the compromise between wealth and population, so lately and so happily introduced into the Constitution of this State, and never, I believe, adopted any where before, was suggested and discussed by him.

In poetry, ancient genius exhausted every type of the ideal. It is impossible that Homer ever can be equalled, or that Horace can ever be surpassed. The Iliad, following Orpheus—perhaps, mounting higher—fixed the religion, and in a great measure formed the manners of the Greeks, and of the Romans, after them; and its influence is felt to this day. Demosthenes and Cicero are still the unrivalled masters of eloquence, whom we strive in vain to imitate. No second Venus or Apollo has ever been produced, and these yet stand the admiration and the models of the world of art. Few ambitious piles have been reared in modern times, that have not copied from the Pantheon or the Parthenon. Even our own State House, though so unlike it in materials and exterior ornaments, exhibits the precise dimensions of the latter.

It has been well and truly said, and generally admitted, that history is but an illustration of philosophy. Action is, in the main, the result of thought; and, to comprehend it thoroughly, we must penetrate the minds of men, and analyse their workings. To trace and understand our civilization, then, we must not only have the knowledge of the events of time, and of deeds, institutions, and experiments of mankind, and their ideal conceptions in poetry, and art, and oratory—but we must study the history of Thought. Metaphysical and moral philosophy have in all enlightened ages embodied the most important ideas of the present and the past, and developed the tendencies of men's minds in their varying but unremitted efforts to penetrate the future. But here, as in common history, we find, apart from revelation, but little new in modern times. The philosophers of antiquity made the first charts of the human mind, and so complete were they, that all inquirers since have been mainly guided by them. The great Sensual school, which has prevailed so extensively for the last century and a half, and of which Locke is called the founder, may be referred directly to Aristotle, who first boldly taught that all our knowledge comes through the senses. All other schools that deserve the name, are based on one portion or another of the ideal philosophy of Plato. All philosophic theories, even the wildest and most delusive broodings of the imagination, if made by subtle reasoning to assume a consistent shape, are replete with interest and instruction, since they teach the illusions of the ages and the races, and exhibit to us the weakness and blindness of our nature, and the absurdities to which we are forever prone. But the two great schools of the Lyceum and Academy were founded on imperishable elements in human nature; and, until the second advent shall shed perfect light, they will—after all the wheat is separated from the chaff—after the momentous truths of Revelation and the mighty facts which time developes, shall have been recorded over the acknowledged errors of philosophy—still, as they have so long done, divide between them a vast, unknown, and deeply interesting realm, through which all must travel, as all have travelled, to whom have been given reason, feeling, and imagination.

Whoever believes that all our ideas are derived from external sources through the senses, and all real knowledge from experiment—that God has given man the peculiar faculty of reason, as the only safe guide through the perilous paths of life; and that to do the right thing in the right place, "Το ΕΥ καὶ ΚΑΛΩΣ" is the highest human wisdom—he is a follower of Aristotle. Whoever, on the other hand, yields himself to a belief in innate ideas; whoever confides in the exalting faith that there is "a Divinity that stirs within us," and that, despite "this muddy vesture of decay that hems us in," the Author of our being holds direct communion with our souls, regulating our impulses, guiding our instincts, and infusing into us that "longing after immortality" which sustains the struggling spirit through the great "Μαχη Αθανατος," of the universe—he is a disciple of Plato the Divine.

The truly wise, the genuine christian, will perhaps endeavor in his practice to unite the virtues of both systems; and, in conformity with the Apostolic injunction, perfect his faith by works, and thus consummate the civilization of mankind.

After all that can be said for the progress of the last ten centuries—their brilliant epochs, their illustrious characters—it cannot be denied that we must still look to antiquity for the noblest deeds and grandest thoughts that illustrate the race of man. There were not only full-grown men, but giants in those days. And however the study of them may be decried, whosoever would become a statesman or philosopher, a poet, an artist, an orator, or a divine; whoever would understand the human character, its capacity and weakness, its failures and its triumphs, to what it has attained and what it may accomplish yet —must drink deep, and drink often, of the precious waters of those virgin fountains which were unlocked in Nature's first-known cycle. The solitary student, who seeks knowledge for the love of knowledge, and luxuriates in the rare felicity of a conscious expansion of the mind and elevation of the soul, will wander among them day and night, and make the converse of his life with those mighty spirits who yet hover around the Hill of Mars, and linger in the deep shadows of the Egerian Grove.

Our civilization is the civilization of Christianity. And Christianity, alone, made all the difference between the ancient and the modern mind and manners. The questions of the deepest and most abiding interest to man in every age have been—Whence came he? why is he here? whither is he going? who is the author of creation? and what is its design? To these questions ancient philosophy could give no satisfactory answer. And the great men, whose immortal ideas and achievements have come down to us, disgusted with the shallow mythology of the popular superstition, either wrought in ignorant and stern indifference to an accountability beyond the grave, or devoted their genius, in its prime of strength, to unavailing efforts to solve those mysteries of Being, which God in his providence still kept concealed. But when He came who brought life and immortality to light; the real "$\Lambda o \gamma o \varsigma$" whom Socrates and Plato sought so ardently to comprehend, all was changed: Not suddenly, but gradually; so gradually that we are yet in the very midst of the change, and it requires incessant study and consummate knowledge to know precisely where we are, and what it is that each and all of us should do to fulfil the purposes of our existence. While the utilitarian values the christian dispensation chiefly because it fosters peace, and has taught us to regard as honorable and cultivate assiduously those pacific arts which promote our temporal happiness— the truly wise, the genuine friend of progress takes a more exalted view, and reads, in the momentous Revelation of a Soul to Man, a Divine Command that all his earthly pursuits and aims, his social and political organizations, shall tend to the high and glorious end of Soul-development. The ancients endeavored to develope the soul without a Revelation and without a command. If they failed, the effort was a grand one, the means employed were noble, and the examples they have set are worthy of our study, our admiration, and, often of our imitation.

I have attempted to show that we do not owe our progress in improvement exclusively to the successful cultivation of physical and experimental philosophy, as is too generally believed; and that other causes infinitely numerous, infinitely varied, and vastly influential, have contributed, in just proportions, to the great results of which we are now enjoying the benefit. I have glanced in a hasty and imperfect manner at some of these causes, with a view to make it manifest that whoever would comprehend our civilization, and so comprehend it as to be able for any wise purpose to command the present, and, so far as permitted, shape the future, must sweep the whole circle of the past, and take, as Bacon himself did, "all learning for his province." And I may add, that, if like that great genius, he fails to accomplish all—as fail he must, since universal empire is impossible—he may, like him, accomplish much, and leave a name inwrought with flowers and fruits upon that peaceful ensign of the nations, under which we are taught that all shall one day lie down together in safety.

In looking around us upon the acting drama of life, we cannot but perceive how utterly contrasted these conclusions are with those by which a vast majority of the existing generations seem to be governed in their conduct. Action, not Learning, appears to be the watchword of this excited age, and its beau ideal is the Practical Man. Wealth and Office are the only sources of power that are generally acknowledged; and we are strenuously taught, by precept and example, from our cradle up, to clutch at gold and cater for popularity. The spirit of the age prescribes these means of improvement, of renown and happiness; and the strongest intellects, too rarely able to break from the bondage of custom and opinion, fall into the routine and succumb beneath it. The individual of high endowments—capable of what is great—who listens to such shallow and delusive counsels, and surrenders himself to such vulgar uses, must inevitably run a career of the sorest trials and bitterest disappointments. The people who erect no higher standards, must surely —no matter what for a time may be appearances—go backwards from the goal of progress.

Action is indeed the foundation of all greatness; but it must be action, curbed, and regulated, and directed, by profound knowledge and consummate judgment. Incessant and impulsive action is fatal to man and to society. Anarchy, exhaustion and premature decay, are its legitimate and necessary consequences.

It is no paradox to say that permanence—that permanence which is created by a just, and wholesome and somewhat stringent restraint of action—is the starting point of genuine progress, national and individual, and marks every footprint in the true line of march. That too restless spirit, which, in our day, sends almost half mankind roving to and fro upon the earth, and is breeding rash and rapid change through all its borders, can scarcely be the Spirit of Progress. If God, in his providence, intends it to prevail, it would rather seem that He means it as the instrument for breaking up the superstructure of our present civilization, as He did that of antiquity, to establish a broader and purer system in His own good time.

The practical man—who is, on the other hand, with no uncommon inconsistency, held up to admiration—is the type not merely of permanence, but of absolute fixity. The truly practical man is undoubtedly the greatest of all men. To thorough knowledge he adds well directed enterprise ; and works earnestly, manfully, and hopefully, for high and noble ends, with little thought of consequences to himself. He seeks no selfish reward, and immediate and personal success are no necessities to him. Socrates was a practical man, though he failed in his time to crush the Sophists, and forfeited his life by his attempt to overthrow the popular superstitions of Athens. Archimedes was a practical man, though he could not save Syracuse, and was slain while solving a problem amid the sack of the city. Galileo was a practical man, though imprisoned and persecuted for his discoveries, and compelled to renounce them. Bacon, too, was a practical man, though he fell from his high office and threw away his life in a trivial experiment. Yet all these men were regarded by most of their contemporaries as visionaries, as enthusiasts and dreamers; and so they would doubtless be regarded now, if they belonged to our era. What is generally meant by a practical man in these days—perhaps it was so in all days—is a successful man. But life is short; and truth and virtue bear fruits so slowly, that great immediate results are rarely achieved without a violation of their precepts. Intrigue, corruption, and force are the usual means by which practical men on a large scale advance themselves at the expense of others, and too often athwart the line of progress. The practical man of the more common and vulgar stamp—the genuine utilitarian—succeeds by dint of energetic selfishness. Distrustful, unfeeling and narrow, he cautiously and vigorously pursues his own ends, regardless of those of the rest of the world. He risks nothing in a cause not directly his own. While others less prudent, or more generous and brave, seek to make discoveries, to introduce improvements, and carry on the great warfare against ignorance, and prejudice, and vice—he but follows the camps; and, when a battle is fought, keeps aloof from the danger, and plunders the field. A thousand generations of such men would leave the world exactly where they found it.

But the accumulation of wealth, it is thought, is unquestionable progress, and a source of real power as well as happiness to individuals and nations. Of mere riches these things are by no means true. The treasures of India have always been proverbial, yet the civilization of India has been stationary from the dawn of history. She has again and again fallen a prey to conquest, and is at length perishing miserably under a foreign yoke. China has been for ages absorbing the precious metals of the world in exchange for luxuries that have been consumed; is the most populous now, and was once the most advanced nation of the earth. But China has been conquered too, is now insulted and trampled on within her own borders by invaders from the antipodes, and has made little or no progress for thousands of years. For its individual possessor wealth will secure comfort, will command the limited service of others, may win admiration from the weak, and may purchase the homage of parasites and flatterers. But all this confers no real power and little happiness, since it scarcely compensates for the cares and anxieties which riches impose, and the envy and hostility which they provoke. Wealth, as an instrument in the grasp of genius, learning and enterprise, may be made the means of accomplishing wonders. It may give vast power, and become a most effective agent in promoting the welfare and improvement of mankind. But then all that is achieved by it, must be referred directly to the wisdom which controls and designates its uses. In this the actual power resides, and no rational happiness can be derived from any other than a wise employment of wealth.

Bacon said that "men in great places were thrice servants: servants of the State, servants of fame, and servants of the people," and moreover that "the rising into place is laborious, the standing slippery, and the downfall a regress, or an eclipse at least." These are truths familiar to observers in all times, and perhaps more frequently exemplified in our own than any other. Yet men still continue anxious seekers after office. The noblest intellects and purest characters are still seduced by the idea that office confers power in proportion to its importance, and that by this means, "the servant of fame" may take a great and glorious part in promoting the welfare of his race. This has indeed happened, and may sometimes, though rarely, happen yet. But, wherever our civilization has shed its full light, public station, even if hereditary, and the possessor can be divested of it only by a revolution, enables him under ordinary circumstances, to exercise but a small portion of real power. Most of the Kings of Europe are now-a-days the merest cyphers; and hereditary legislators have become the foot-balls of the commons. And whoever holds office by the suffrage, and at the sufferance of that commons, has usually undergone such drudgery, and incurred such obligations, in rising into place, that he has neither strength, nor time, nor means to do more than prevent his own "downfall and eclipse," and may be esteemed most fortunate if he succeeds in that. In fact it is scarcely ever possible for him to sustain himself in office for any length of time against the storms which envious adversaries, self-seeking demagogues, and his own inevitable errors will surely raise against him, unless he seeks refuge in some faction, sinks the statesman in the partisan, and, instead of controlling and leading the people to a higher state of civilization, prostitutes himself to their caprices. But were it possible for an individual to attain high office without corruption or deception, and hold it without concessions—could he, like Macchiavelli's model patriot, consolidate all authority in his own hands—the power he could wield, the blessings he could confer on mankind and their posterity, and the renown he might achieve for himself beyond embalming his name in the catalogue of Kings, or Presidents, or Ministers, would depend entirely upon the greatness of his genius, and the knowledge and the wisdom he had acquired by its assiduous cultivation.

Thus, if we should pass in review all the pursuits of mankind, and all the ends they aim at, under the instigation of their appetites and passions, or at the dictation of shallow utilitarian philosophy, we shall find that they pursue shadows and worship idols, and that whatever there is that is good and great and catholic in their deeds and purposes, depends for its accomplishment upon the intellect, and is accomplished just in proportion as that intellect is stored with knowledge. And, whether we examine the present or the past, we shall find that Knowledge alone is real power—"more powerful," says Bacon, "than the Will, commanding the reason, understanding, and belief," and "setting up a Throne in the spirits and souls of men." We shall find that the progress of knowledge is the only true and permanent progress of our race, and that, however inventions, discoveries, and events which change the face of human affairs, may appear to be the results of contemporary efforts or providential accidents, it is in fact the Men of Learning who lead with noiseless step the vanguard of civilization, that mark out the road over which—opened sooner or later—posterity marches; and from the abundance of their precious stores sow seed by the wayside, which spring up in due season, and produce an hundred fold—casting bread upon the waters which is gathered after many days. The age which gives birth to the largest number of such men is always the most enlightened, and the age in which the highest reverence and most intelligent obedience is accorded to them, always advances most rapidly in the career of improvement.

And let not the ambitious aspirant to enrol himself with this illustrious band, to fill the throne which learning "setteth up in the spirits and souls of men," and wield its absolute power, be checked, however humble he may be, however unlikely to attain wealth or office, or secure homage as a practical man or man of action, by any fear that true knowledge can be stifled, overshadowed, or compelled to involuntary barrenness. Whenever or wherever men meet to deliberate or act, the trained intellect will always master. But for the most sensitive and modest, who seek retirement, there is another and a greater resource. The public press, accessible to all, will enable him, from the depths of solitude, to speak trumpet-tongued to the four corners of the earth. No matter how he may be situated—if he has facts that will bear scrutiny, if he has thoughts that burn, if he is sure he has a call to teach—the press is a tripod from which he may give utterance to his oracles, and if there be truth in them, the world and future ages will accept it. It is not Commerce that is King, nor Manufactures, nor Cotton, nor any single Art or Science, any more than those who wear the baubles-crowns. Knowledge is Sovereign, and the Press is the royal seat on which she sits, a sceptred Monarch. From this she rules public opinion, and finally gives laws alike to prince and people—laws framed by men of letters;

by the wandering bard; by the philosopher in his grove or portico, his tower or laboratory; by the pale student in his closet. We contemplate with awe the mighty movements of the last eighty years, and we held our breath while we gazed upon the heaving human mass so lately struggling like huge Leviathan, over the broad face of Europe. What has thus stirred the world? The press. The press, which has scattered far and wide the sparks of genius, kindling as they fly. Books, Journals, Pamphlets, these are the paixhan balls—moulded often by the obscure and humble, but loaded with fiery thoughts—which have burst in the sides of every structure, political, social and religious, and shattered too often, alike the rotten and the sound. For, in knowledge as in everything else, the two great principles of Good and Evil maintain their eternal warfare "Ο αγων αντί παντων αγωνων"—a war amid and above all other wars.

But, in the strife of knowledge, unlike other contests—victory never fails to abide with truth. The wise and virtuous who find and use this mighty weapon, are sure of their reward. It may not come soon. Years, ages, centuries may pass away, and the gravestone may have crumbled above the head that should have worn the wreath. But to the eye of faith, the vision of the imperishable and inevitable halo that shall enshrine the memory is forever present, cheering and sweetening toil, and compensating for privation. And it often happens that the great and heroic mind, unnoticed by the world, buried apparently in profoundest darkness, sustained by faith, works out the grandest problems of human progress—working under broad rays of brightest light—light furnished by that inward and immortal lamp, which, when its mission upon earth has closed, is trimmed anew by angel's hands, and placed among the stars of heaven.

AN ORATION

ON THE LIFE, CHARACTER AND SERVICES OF JOHN CALDWELL CALHOUN, DELIVERED ON THE 21st NOVEMBER, 1850, IN CHARLESTON, S. C., AT THE REQUEST OF THE CITY COUNCIL.

FAITH is an instinct of the human heart. Its strongest, its purest and its noblest instinct—the parent of love and of hope. In all ages and everywhere, mankind have acknowledged, adored, and put their trust in the great Creator and Ruler of the Universe. And, descending from the invisible and infinite, to the visible and finite, they have entertained the same sentiments, differing only in degree, for those of their own species, who have received from heaven an extraordinary endowment of intellect and virtue. The Ancient Heathen deified them. By the early Christians they were enrolled among the Saints. It is a shallow and a base philosophy which can see superstition only, in such customs, and fails to recognize the workings of a profound veneration for the attributes of God, as manifested through His favorite Creations. A better knowledge of the bounds which separate the natural from the supernatural, has taught us in our day to limit our homage; but still it is a deep and pure wisdom which counsels us to submit ourselves, in no grudging spirit, to the guidance of those great Minds that have been appointed to shed light and truth upon the world.

To the honor and praise of South Carolina it may be said that she has thus far recognized her prophets, and believed their inspiration. She has aided and sustained them in the performance of their missions, with a warm and steady confidence, and she has been faithful to their memory. Her loyal reverence for real greatness has ever been a deep—I might say a religious sentiment—untinged with superstition, but as profound as it is magnanimous and just.

For no one of her many noble sons has Providence permitted her to evince for so long a period her admiration, her affection and her confidence; for no one has she herself endured such trials; no one has she ever consigned to his last resting place in her bereaved bosom, amid such deep and universal grief, as him whose life and services we have assembled this day to commemorate. For more than forty years the name of Calhoun has never been pronounced in South Carolina without awakening a sensation. For nearly the same period it has been equally familiar and fraught with as deep an interest to every citizen of this widespread Union. Few of us here present can remembe the era when we heard it first. We have grown up from childhood under its mighty influence, and we feel that a spell was broken, a tie of life was sundered forever, when it ceased to be a living sound.

The Man is now no more. He has closed his career with us, to begin another in a better world. But what he did, and what he said, while here, still live, and will live forever in their consequences—as immortal as the Spirit which has returned to God. How he performed his part on earth it is ours now to consider. And drying our unavailing tears, and burying, for the moment, in the deepest recesses of our bosoms, the love and reverence we bore him, it is our duty to analyze his life with the strict impartiality of a distant posterity; and to bring the thoughts and actions he left behind him to the great standard of eternal Truth, that we may render complete justice to him, and gather for ourselves and our children the full measure of the lessons which he taught. The living Man scorned fulsome adulation; and his living Spirit, if permitted to hover over us now, and to hear our voices and perceive the pulsations of our hearts, will accept no offering that cannot bear the scrutiny of Time and the severest test of Truth.

Mr. Calhoun was born in the backwoods of South Carolina, near the close of the Revolutionary War. His early nurture was in the wilderness, and during the heroic age of the Republic. In youth he imbibed but a scant portion of the lore of books, but his converse with the volume of Nature was unlimited; and in the field and forest, by the stream and by the fireside, he was in constant intercourse with those rough but high-strung men, who had challenged oppression at its first step, and were fresh from the battles in which they had won their liberties with their swords. His father, too, was a wise and strong man. For thirty years in the councils of the State, he was as familiar with the strifes of politics, as of arms. In his rude way he penetrated to fundamentals—discovered that the true foundation of government is the welfare of the governed; denounced its excessive action; and opposed the Constitution of the Union because it placed the power of laying taxes in the hands of those who did not pay them. Amid such men and such scenes, there was little opportunity for what is commonly called education for the young Calhoun. But it may be doubted whether, having acquired the use of letters and figures, and been thus furnished with the two great keys of knowledge, there could have been a much better training for the future Statesman. Pericles and Alexander were, perhaps, taught but little more by Anaxagoras and Aristotle, than Calhoun learned from his few books, from nature and such men. In this School he learned to think, which is a vast achievement. And he was furnished with high and noble themes for thought, by those whose partial knowledge of facts led them to discuss chiefly essential principles, to unfold fundamental truths, and to build on them those lofty theories to which the exigencies of the times gave birth. He was thus taught, not only the sum and substance of elementary education, but was imbued with that practical philosophy, according to which human affairs are in the main conducted. It is true that thousands have received the same lessons and profited nothing. But we know that seed sown by the wayside and among stones and thorns, is gathered by the birds or is withered or choked up; and it is only when it falls on good ground that it springs up and produces fifty and a hundred fold. It is idle to deny the natural diversity of human intellects. It was due, after all, to the rich soil of Calhoun's mind that these noble seeds took root, and bore abundantly such precious fruits.

It was not until he had passed his eighteenth year

that he seriously embarked in the pursuit of Scholastic learning; and the event proved—as possibly it would in most cases—that no time had been really lost. Perhaps it seldom happens that the bud of the mind is sufficiently matured before this age, to expand naturally and absorb with benefit the direct rays of knowledge, so bright, so piercing and so stimulating. The tender petals eagerly opened at too early a period, often wither and die under the overpowering light. At eighteen years of age Mr. Calhoun went to the Academy; at twenty to College; at twenty-two he graduated at Yale; at twenty-five he was admitted to the Bar; at twenty-six he was elected to the Legislature; at twenty-eight to Congress. Thus, though apparently starting late, he nevertheless arrived at the goal far in advance of most of those who reach it. But when he went to the Academy he did not dream over books, any more than he did afterwards over the affairs of life. He had learned already what many never learn—to think; and to think closely—to the purpose—searching for the principle. Having acquired this mighty power—for it is a power, and the greatest of all—when he did start in his career, he strode onward like a conqueror. Difficulties were mere exercises. Valleys rose in his path and mountains sunk down to a level. First at School; first at College; he rose at once to the front rank at the Bar and in the Legislature; and was assigned a most distinguished position the moment he took his seat in Congress. His course was a stream of light. Men of all classes recognized its brilliancy, and hailed him, not as a meteor, but as a new star risen in the heavens, which had floated without effort into its appointed orbit, and promised long to shed the brightest and most beneficent beams upon the world.

What, we may properly ask, was the secret of this rapid and wonderful success? How was it that this young man, coming but a few years before from the wilderness, late in youth, without knowledge of books, unknown himself, and destitute of powerful friends, should, in so short a time, not only win his way into the Great Council of the Confederacy, but be at once conceded a place among the first, and draw to himself the admiration and the hopes of a people?

> "What should it be that thus their faith could bind?
> The power of Thought—the magic of the Mind!"

Mr. Calhoun first took his seat in Congress at the commencement of the Session of 1811. From that period may be dated his career as a Statesman. That career may be properly divided into several epochs, each of which is memorable in the history of our country, and was made memorable in no small degree by the parts which he performed. The first embraces his services in the House of Representatives. The great question of the Session of 1811-'12, was that of war with England. All Europe was then, and had been for twenty years, in arms, and that mighty conflict which terminated not long after in the overthrow of Napoleon, and the establishment of the Holy Alliance, was at its height. France and England were the two leading belligerents, and both of them, in utter disregard of neutral rights, had perpetrated unexampled outrages upon us. We had in vain resorted to embargoes and non-importation acts, and at length it became indispensably necessary to our maintaining any position among nations, that we should declare war against one or both of these powers. The direct pecuniary interests of the South had been but slightly affected by these outrages. She had but little commerce to be plundered—few seamen to be impressed. Her only great interest involved—and that she felt in every fibre—was the honor of our common country. To vindicate that she went for war, and went for it almost unanimously. South Carolina took the lead. Her illustrious Representatives Lowndes, Cheves, Williams and Calhoun, were the leaders of all those important Committees, whose province it is to propose war, and marshal the resources for carrying it on. And nobly and gloriously did they all perform their duty. Mr. Calhoun, placed second on the Committee of Foreign Relations, soon became its head by the retirement of the chairman, and, before the close of his first Session, he reported and carried through the House, a bill declaring war against Great Britain; and, throughout the momentous conflict, undaunted in courage and infinite in resources, he stood forward the leading champion of every measure for its vigorous prosecution. Young as he was, he shrunk from no opponent in that Congress, never before or since equalled for its assemblage of talent. He surrendered nothing and shunned no responsibility. In the darkest and most perilous hour of the war, when Napoleon had fallen, and England was free to turn the whole of her armament on us; when the Eastern States, not content with denouncing the war through their presses, and from their platforms and their pulpits, had assailed in every form the credit of the Government—had paralyzed all the financial operations of the country and caused a general suspension of the Southern Banks—had given valuable "aid and comfort to the enemy" by loans of specie, and were conspiring to withdraw from the Confederacy and make peace for themselves—in that desponding hour, when all seemed lost, he did not falter for an instant. "The great cause" he said "will never be yielded—no, never! never! I hear the future audibly announced in the past—in the splendid victories over the Guerriere, the Java, and the Macedonian. Opinion is power. The charm of British naval invincibility is gone."

Mr. Calhoun's course throughout the war can never fail of the admiration and applause of future times; and that war was a turning point in the history of the world. It established a competitor with England for the trident of the ocean, whose triumph is inevitable. And, just and necessary as it was and glorious as its result, it gave rise in the end to questions in this country, which no human sagacity could have anticipated—whose solution, yet in the womb of time, may be of far greater import than the dominion of the seas.

Mr. Calhoun entered Congress as a member of the Republican Party, as distinguished from the Federal, and throughout his service in the House, acted with it in the main. But he gave many and early proofs that his was a temperament which could never "give up to party what was meant for mankind." Following his illustrious Colleague*—who yet survives to our love and veneration, with his powerful intellect unimpaired, and his devotion to his native soil more ardent and self-sacrificing, if possible, than ever—he warmly advo-

* Hon. Langdon Chever.

cated a large addition to the navy, at an early period of warlike preparations, and, ever after, consistently and earnestly sustained this most important arm of defence and support of the State. The Republican Party, under Mr. Jefferson, had, with a narrow policy, condemned the navy. But amphibious man never attains half his national greatness, until his domain on the water equals that upon the land—until the terror of his prowess makes his home upon the deep as secure as on the mountains, and the products of his industry float undisturbed on every tide.

At this early period, also, Mr. Calhoun took his stand against the Restrictive System, which had been so great a favorite with Mr. Jefferson and Mr. Madison, as a substitute for war. He denounced it as unsound in policy, and wholly unsuited to the genius of our people; and he opposed it vigorously, until it fell beneath his blows. But it may well be questioned, whether, at that time, his opposition was at all enlightened by those great principles of Free Trade, then so little known, which it was the glory of his later life to develop and sustain under such trying circumstances. He then opposed the Restrictive System as a war measure, and demonstrated that it was not only inefficient, but injurious. Neither then, nor when the import duties were re-adjusted at the close of the war, did he appear to have perceived the dangers which lurked under the protection which this system gave to manufacturers, nor those which followed such protection when specifically given by the direct action of the Government. For, in the debate in 1814, while Mr. Webster, now the great champion of protection, declared "he was an enemy to rearing manufactures, or any other interest in a hot bed, and never wished to see a Sheffield or a Birmingham in this country," Mr. Calhoun said, " as to the manufacturing interest, in regard to which some fear has been expressed, the resolution, voted by the House yesterday, was a strong pledge that it would not suffer manufactures to be unprotected in case of a repeal of the Restrictive System. He hoped that, at all times, and under every policy, they would be protected with due care." And, again in 1816, he advocated, without any note or caution, the bill introduced by another distinguished Carolinian,* long since snatched from us by a premature death, but whose genius and virtues—-whose lofty character and inestimable services can never be forgotten—a bill which distinctly recognized the protective principle, and introduced perhaps its most oppressive feature. The truth is, that at that day, political economy was in its infancy. Free Trade was most commonly understood to mean merely the freedom of the seas. The most sagacious intellects of our country—Mr. Webster perhaps excepted—had, apparently no apprehensions of the evils of the false theory of protection as applied to us ; and that abominable system, since called " the American," it had entered into no man's imagination to conceive. Mr. Calhoun, at a later period, so far in advance of his age, was, at that epoch, the embodiment of the spirit of the times, and among its most able and effective expounders.

At the crisis of the war, when the credit of the Government was prostrate, an United States Bank was proposed by the administration, and supported by the

* Hon. William Lowndes.

Republican Party. This Mr. Calhoun opposed and defeated; though in a modified form, it would finally have passed the House, but for the casting vote of Mr. Cheves. It was, however, on account of the extraordinary character of the proposed Bank, that Mr. Calhoun resisted it, and not apparently from any doubt of the policy or constitutionality of a Bank chartered by Congress. In fact, he had himself previously proposed a Bank to be established in the District of Columbia, with the express view of getting rid of certain constitutional scruples felt by others; and he was the responsible author of the Bank of 1816, whose powerful efforts to prolong its own existence, so fiercely agitated the whole Union twenty years later, and ended in consequences so disastrous not only to its own stockholders, but to the country. From Mr. Calhoun's subsequent declarations, it is certain that, in his maturer years, he regarded the whole Banking system, as at present organized, as a stupendous evil; and he emphatically declared, that its power, "if not diminished, must terminate in its own destruction, or an entire revolution in our social and political system." And that of all Banks, he regarded a mere Government Bank as the most dangerous, may be safely inferred from the fact, that neither the ties of party, nor the entreaties of the administration, nor the exigencies of the most critical period of the war, could prevent him from vigorously opposing such an Institution, though not then hostile to an United States Bank. He advocated the Bank of 1816, as indispensably necessary for the restoration of the currency, and, to the last, he believed that no other expedient could have effected that great object. He avoided the constitutional question, by assuming that so long as the Government received Bank notes at all as money, it was bound to "regulate their value," and for that purpose a Bank was "necessary and proper." He said, however, even then, that "as a question *de novo*, he would be decidedly against a Bank;" and when in 1837, he thought it could be done with safety, he took an active and efficient part in excluding all Bank notes from the Treasury of the United States.

During the Session of 1816, arose another of those great questions, which may be said to have had their origin in the war, and which have since so divided and agitated our country. Mr. Jefferson had recognized the power of Congress to appropriate money for Internal Improvements in the case of the Cumberland Road, and, in 1808, Mr. Gallatin, his Secretary of war, had made a report, recommending a stupendous system. It was not until after the war, the expenses of which had been enormously increased by the cost of transportation, that the subject attracted the serious attention of the whole country. Mr. Calhoun brought forward and carried, in 1816, a bill appropriating the bonus and dividends of the United States Bank to Internal Improvements. This bill was vetoed as unconstitutional by Mr. Madison, to the surprise of all, and most especially of its author, who believed he was carrying out the views entertained by Madison, and suggested in his annual Message. In 1818, Mr. Calhoun, as Secretary of War, made a Report on Roads and Canals, embracing views and recommending measures fully as extensive as those of Mr. Gallatin. On none of these occasions did he express his opinion as to the constitutional power of the Federal Government to carry on Internal Improvements. But, if his opinions may be inferred from those of his most intimate and confidential friends—from the celebrated Message of Mr. Monroe in 1823, and the equally celebrated speech of Mr. McDuffie shortly after—it must be conceded that, at that time, he believed the power of the Government to lay taxes, and appropriate the proceeds, was limited only by the injunction that they should be applied to the "common defence and general welfare." This doctrine, in every way so fatal in our political system, has since received its severest blows from his hands; and, in 1838, he declared that one of the most essential steps to be taken, in order to restore our Government to its original purity—then the great and sole object of his political life—was to "put a final stop to Internal Improvements by Congress."

With the Session of 1816-17 closed Mr. Calhoun's services in the House of Representatives. Here also terminated an epoch in his career as a Statesman. He had more than fulfilled the high expectations entertained of him when he entered Congress. His reputation for talent had increased with every intellectual effort he had made. And his ability—now universally admitted to be of the very highest order—his well-tried patriotism, his unflinching moral courage, the loftiness and liberality of all his views and sentiments, and the immaculate purity of his life, gave him a position in the public councils and in the opinion of the country, second to no one of that illustrious band whom the greatest crisis in affairs since the revolution —"the second war of Independence"—had brought upon the stage.

In reviewing Mr. Calhoun's political course up to this period, if, with the sternness of the historian, we brush aside the splendid halo that surrounds it, and call to our aid the subsequent experience of a third of a century of rapid progress—above all, if we examine it by the effulgent light which he, himself, more than all other men, has since shed upon the Federal Constitution, and judge it by those rigid and severe tests which he has taught us, we cannot fail to perceive that brilliant, useful, and glorious, as it was, to his country and himself, his views, in many most important particulars, were essentially erroneous; and that he assisted powerfully in giving currency to opinions, and building up systems, that have proved seriously injurious to the South, and probably to the stability of the existing Union. These I have not hesitated to point out. It was due to truth, to history, and to him.

It has been customary to apologize for these errors, by saying that they were the errors of youth. But Mr. Calhoun had no youth, to our knowledge. He sprung into the arena like Minerva from the head of Jove, fully grown and clothed in armor: a man every inch himself, and able to contend with any other man. A severe moralist would point to them as conspicuous proofs of the fallibility of our nature, since the deepest devotion both to the Union and his native section, and the most perfect purity of purpose, combined with the subtlest intellectual acumen and the profoundest generalization, could not save him from them. There may be much truth and wisdom in this view. But there are reasons why Mr. Calhoun should have fallen at that time into the opinions that he held, which, properly considered, would remove every shadow of suspicion from his motives, if any has ever been seriously entertained, and almost wholly excuse the most sagacious of men who laid no claim to inspiration.

Although there were, from the commencement of the Government, two parties, one of whom contended for a strict and the other for a latitudinarian construction of the Constitution, a review of the practical questions which arose between them would show that few or none of them were of a sectional bearing. The Alien and Sedition Laws, which produced the greatest excitement of any internal question, had no such tendency. The Funding of the Domestic Debt might have been so accidentally; but no question, necessarily and permanently sectional, attracted serious notice until after the second war. In fact, under the administrations of the earlier Presidents, all those sectional jealousies which had displayed themselves so conspicuously during the Confederation, and which are so prominent in the debates of the Convention that framed the Constitution, had been lulled to sleep, and a large proportion of the ablest Southern men were Federalists. The great questions which did agitate the country, on which elections turned, and parties really, though not altogether nominally, divided off, were external, not internal questions. Our Colonial habits still predominated, and we looked abroad for our dangers, for our enemies and our friends. English, French and Spanish negotiations: Jay's Treaty: the squabble with the Directory: the acquisition of Louisiana: the terrible wars of Europe: the aggressions on our neutral rights: and finally the embargo, non-importation, non-intercourse laws, and war with England:—these were the great and deeply interesting subjects which absorbed men's minds and colored all their political opinions. The Constitution was overlooked and violated by both parties; and I believe it may be said that on no question of a constitutional character were party lines stringently drawn, after the election of Mr. Jefferson. Mr. Monroe declared, on his accession, that we were "all Federalists—all Republicans."

It was under these circumstances, and at a period when, above all others, an ardent and patriotic mind would be least disposed to contemplate sectional interests, or stickle about constitutional scruples, that Mr. Calhoun entered Congress. It was then, indeed, the imperative duty of the patriot to discard all mere sectional considerations; and, perhaps, to give the most liberal construction to the Constitution, to enable the ship of State to meet and ride out the storms which threatened to engulph it. The difficulties were immense. Mr. Calhoun, placed at once in a high and responsible position, and taking, as was said at the time, "the war upon his shoulders," was absorbed during his first three sessions, in devising measures to meet its pressing exigencies; and, during the last three, in endeavoring to dissipate its injurious effects upon the currency, commerce and industry of the country. And, considering the history of the past: the conduct of parties on internal constitutional questions: the habitual disregard of strict construction by the Republican leaders: the acquiescence of older and very able men of all sections in the constitutionality of the Bank, the Tariff and Internal Improvements, it is not at all to be wondered at, nor to be severely condemned, that in the universal confusion, and the burning glow of his broad patriotism, so fanned by current events, he should fail to look at the sectional bearing of propositions, or even of constitutional constructions. No man—not one in our wide confederacy—North or South—foresaw what was coming out of the convulsions of the war, and the measures adopted to ease down the country to a state of peace, and prepare her for a prosperous career, under circumstances so greatly different as were those of 1815-17 from any she had yet encountered. Carpings and croakings there were, of course, and prophecies of evil in abundance. But the results baffled all predictions: or at least verified so little of what any had foretold, as to place the wisest seer on no higher tripod than that of a lucky fortune-teller. Mr. Calhoun never croaked or carped. And if he erred in straying from the narrow, but only true path of rigid constitutional construction, he may well be forgiven for following precedents that were almost consecrated—the examples of nearly all with whom he acted—and the impulses of a generous, confiding, and wide-extended love of country.

Soon after Mr. Monroe's accession to the Presidency, Mr. Calhoun received the appointment of Secretary of War, and took his seat in the Cabinet in December, 1817, where he remained until March, 1825. This period embraced the second epoch of his career. The future biographer will find in it much that will be interesting to relate, but, on an occasion like this, it may be passed over without any minute examination. From the commencement of the war it had been discovered that the internal organization of the War Department was so defective, that it was impossible to conduct its affairs with due efficiency. It was in vain that three different Secretaries were in succession at its head during the war, and a fourth appointed at its close. When Mr. Calhoun took charge of it, nearly three years after, he found unsettled accounts to the amount of forty millions, and the greatest confusion in every branch. In a remarkably short period he introduced a perfect organization, in which all the details were so thoroughly and judiciously systematized, that no material changes have been made to this day. He reduced the unsettled accounts to a few millions, which were not susceptible of liquidation, and, against incessant and powerful opposition, curtailed the discretionary expenses nearly one half, while, at the same time, the efficiency of the army was greatly increased, and his own popularity in it grew with every reform, and to the last day of his administration.

Many of Mr. Calhoun's best friends had advised him not to accept this appointment. They knew the apparently insuperable difficulties of reorganizing that Department, which had baffled so many able men. They thought that his mind was of a cast too abstract and metaphysical to cope with the practical details of the Military System, and were apprehensive lest his brilliant reputation might be clouded. They did not remember that if real genius is not universal, both war and politics are but the concretes of Philosophy—that, in ancient times, these pursuits were almost invariably united; that the greatest of metaphysicians was the founder of the science of Politics, and trained the greatest warrior of antiquity; that Bacon presided in the House of Lords; that Carnot "organized victory;" that, in short, though politicians and soldiers may spring up every day, and strut their hour upon the stage, no one can be a statesman or a general who has not analyzed the structure of the human mind, and learned to touch the remotest springs of human action.

High as Mr. Calhoun's legislative talent had been rated, he had not been long in the War Department before his administrative talent was regarded as quite equal, if not superior; and he rose so rapidly in the estimation of his countrymen, that, early in Mr. Monroe's second term, when he was only forty years of age, and had been but little more than ten years in the Federal Councils, he was nominated for the Presidency by the large and influential State of Pennsylvania. He subsequently consented to have his name withdrawn in favor of Gen. Jackson. He was then nominated for the Vice-Presidency—was elected by a large majority, and took his seat as President of the Senate in 1825.

In regard to his direct connection with that body as its presiding officer, it is, perhaps, sufficient to say that on all occasions he fully sustained his reputation. No incident of lasting importance occurred to elicit any extraordinary display of peculiar qualities of mind or temperament, until near the close of his first term. But the period of that term constitutes a most important era in the annals of our country, and also in the life of Mr. Calhoun. And hence may be dated the third and last epoch in his career.

I have already adverted to the fact, that the Republican party had long strayed from the straight and narrow path of constitutional construction in which it first set out. The events of the war had so utterly prostrated and disgraced the Federal Party, that at its close, that party was dissolved, and the very name of Federalist almost universally repudiated. The check of opposition removed, the Republican party—with but few exceptions—fell headlong into the very slough in which their adversaries had foundered. They had everything in their own hands, and "feeling power they forgot right." A new party in the mean time grew up, which afterwards assumed the name of "National Republican," and more recently of "Whig," absorbing most of the old Federalists, and a portion of the old Republicans. Of this party was Mr. Adams —a converted Federalist—who was elected President in 1824, by the House of Representatives, through the instrumentality of Mr. Clay, who became his Secretary of State. The manner of Mr. Adams' election; the extreme Federal doctrines of his first Message; and, above all, perhaps, the exigencies of opposition, awakened the genuine Republicans to some consciousness of their great and long cherished errors. They united on General Jackson as their candidate for the Presidency. Their manifestoes breathed the true spirit of the Republicanism of '98; and the Constitution became apparently the favorite study of those who had come into public life subsequently to that period. Mr. Calhoun, it is said, avowed that, until this time, he had never fully analyzed and understood the Constitution. This may be readily believed, without referring to the instances already mentioned, in which he had departed from it. He had always been, up to that period, in the majority. Majorities do not rely on Constitutions. Their reliance is on numbers and the strong arm. It is not to be expected of them to study, and it seems to be almost impossible for them to comprehend Constitutions, the express purpose of which is to limit their power, and hedge in their privileges. It is minorities who look closely into Constitutions, for they are their shield and tower of safety. Mr. Calhoun had, doubtless, read the Constitution attentively, and mastered its general principles. But there were parts he had not scrutinized, and a deep and vital spirit running through the whole, which he had never yet imbibed, nor had any of the younger men up to that period. In fact, a new kind of constitutional questions now arose—or rather the progress of events had developed new and deeply important bearings in old questions. It now became manifest, for the first time since the Constitution had gone into operation, that it might be so construed as to oppress and ruin one section, for the benefit of another. And it was also clearly seen that the South was the doomed section, and that the chief instrument of destruction was a Protective Tariff.

It was well known that Mr. Hamilton, as early as 1791, had with great power advocated the protection of manufactures, and that duties had been imposed with that view; but they were so extremely moderate as to be of little benefit to that interest, and caused no alarm in others. The duties had been increased under every subsequent administration, for the sake of revenue, and had been doubled during the war. When, in 1816, it became necessary to reduce the war duties, the question arose to what extent they were to be retained for the protection of manufactures, and some of them were adjusted, for that purpose, at a high comparative rate, as I have already stated. These duties were increased in 1820; and, in 1824, the manufacturers again came forward with exorbitant demands, which were acceded to. Then, for the first time in thirty years, and by but a few voices, the constitutional power to protect manufactures was questioned in Congress. It was now obvious that the protected interest had "an appetite which grew from what it fed on;" and that, in this country, in every period of about four years, for reasons which it is unnecessary to dwell on here, it required new and enormous impositions.

Mr. Adams had warmly recommended the Protective Tariff, and Mr. Clay, giving it the *ad captandum* title of the "American System," claimed to be its first champion, and made it the leading question in the Presidential canvass, from 1825 to 1829. The South had opposed it with great vigor and much unanimity in 1824; because, on the principle of communism, it taxed the agricultural interest to support the manufacturing; and, inasmuch as we furnished two-thirds of the exports that paid for the imports on which the duties were levied, it was fully believed, and pretty clearly demonstrated, that our least populous section paid nearly two-thirds of the revenue of the Government, besides paying the manufacturers an enhanced price on the protected articles we consumed. Some of the Eastern States opposed it also, because it injured commerce and navigation, but they ultimately came in to its support. The Western and Middle States were decidedly for it. To secure their support, and yet retain that of the South, General Jackson gave the equivocal pledge that he would sustain a "Judicious Tariff," which in the South was construed to mean a constitutional Revenue Tariff; and elsewhere, to mean a Protective Tariff.

In 1828, at the end of four years, as was usual, a new tariff bill was brought forward in Congress. It was blotched and bloated with the corrupt bids of a majority of the Jackson party, itself, for manufacturers' votes, to be paid in gold wrung from the already overburdened South. And so extravagant were these bids that the protective interests hesitated to accept a bribe so monstrous, lest they should over-shoot the mark and fall under public odium. It was thought, at one time, that the vote in the Senate would be a tie, and the fate of the bill would depend on the casting vote of the presiding officer. Mr. Calhoun was then Vice-President, and a candidate for reëlection on the same ticket with Gen. Jackson, whose success depended entirely on the support of Mr. Calhoun's friends. It was confidently believed that, save Gen. Jackson, there was no one so popular throughout the Union as Mr. Calhoun; and his accession to the Presidency, on the retirement of Gen. Jackson, was considered almost certain. It was known that he was opposed to this bill, and he was now appealed to as the supporter of Gen. Jackson, and candidate of the Republican Party for the Vice-Presidency, and out of regard to his own future prospects, not to give his casting vote against it, but to leave the chair, as was not at all unusual, and allow the bill to take the chances of the Senate. Mr. Calhoun knew the full import of his reply to this appeal. If he not only refused to pledge himself to a "Judicious Tariff," but openly and unequivocally took his stand against the whole protective system, now overwhelmingly popular, he surrendered, in all human probability, every prospect of the Presidency, and must pass the remainder of his life in combating in a small and almost hopeless minority, not for power, not for glory, but for justice, and, in a measure, for the existence of the South. He was thus, in a critical moment, called on to make at once and forever, a decision which was to shape his destiny, and perhaps the destiny of a whole people. He did not hesitate. He had now mastered the Constitution; he also now saw clearly the fatal tendency of the prominent measures brought forward at the close of the war; and casting behind him all the glorious labors of the past, and all the brilliant prospects of the future— holding in one hand the Constitution, and in the other truth, justice, and the violated rights of his native land, he took his post with his little band, waged in the breach a truceless war of two and twenty years, and perished there.

Neither ancient nor modern annals furnish a nobler example of heroic sacrifice of self. Peel yielded to popular demands, and exchanged party for public gratitude and influence. Burke gave up friends, but power smiled upon him. Self-banished Aristides already had satiated his ambition. Cato and Brutus perished in the shock. But, in the early prime of life, midway his yet unchecked career—with the greatest of ambition's prizes but one bound ahead, Mr. Calhoun stopped and turned aside, to lift from the dust the Constitution of his country, trampled, soiled and rent; and bearing it aloft, consecrated himself, his life, his talents, and his hopes, to the arduous, but sacred task of handing it down to other ages as pure as it was when received from the Fathers of the Revolution.

Glorious and not bootless struggle. The Constitution has not been purified. It never will be; but its principles have been made immortal, and will survive and flourish, though it shall, itself, be torn to atoms and given to the winds.

The magnitude of Mr. Calhoun's sacrifice may be more readily appreciated than the difficulties of his undertaking. The diseases of the body politic had not only become deeply seated, but were complicated and peculiar. At the bottom was the now established doctrine that the majority had the unquestionable and the indefeasible right to place its own construction on the Constitution. On this arose not only the Tariff, but the Internal Improvement System, which had completely triumphed. Immense sums, the proceeds of high duties, were annually appropriated for the benefit of the Tariff States; while the United States Bank, by its control over the government funds, concentrated the exchanges at the North, and made the protected section the heart of the financial system of the Union. Thus was formed a combination of sectional interests, sustained by a sectional majority under a corrupted Constitution, all bearing with fatal and relentless aim on the devoted South, while behind them another question, purely sectional, and having nearly the same geographical lines, was easily to be discerned, rearing its monstrous crest, and portending dangers in comparison with which all others sunk to insignificance. Among a homogeneous people, majorities and minorities frequently change places. Indeed, it is natural, and, where discussion and free action are allowed, it is inevitable that they should. But, where they are sectional, even more than where they are founded on classes, vital and antagonistic interests make the change a Revolution, such as rarely happens without bloodshed. A sectional majority remote, arrogant, and fatally bent on maintaining its supremacy and promoting its peculiar interests, never listens to warning or to reason; and the minority, if it has not the courage or the strength to tender an issue of force, is soon corrupted, divided, and necessarily enslaved. Mr. Calhoun could not have failed to perceive all these difficulties, and in abandoning, under such circumstances, his high position in the majority, to unite his fortunes irrevocably with the weaker section, he exhibited an example, almost without parallel, of disinterested patriotism and lion-hearted courage, and of that "unshaken confidence in the Providence of God," which, in his latest moments, he declared to be his consolation and support.

Henceforth he is no longer to be viewed as the favorite child of genius and of fortune. His path is no longer strewed with garlands and his footsteps greeted with applause. Toiling in the deepest anxiety, yet, happily for himself, with the unfailing hopefulness of his nature, to accomplish his Herculean task, he encounters at every step the deadliest hostility. He is assailed on all sides and from every section—even from his own. Envy and malice shoot their long poisoned arrows, and ignorance and corruption shower every missile on him; and yet it remains to be decided, and depends in no small degree upon the issue of the great struggle now approaching its crisis, whether he shall go down to posterity portrayed in the colors of the Gracchi of the Patricians, or the Gracchi of the People.

The Tariff Bill of 1828 passed the Senate by a majority of one vote, and became a law. So exorbitant were its exactions, that out of an import of $64,000,000 it carried $32,000,000 into the Treasury. Mr. Calhoun, who had announced his intention to vote against it, was loud in his denunciations of it and of the protective system; and at the next succeeding Session of our State Legislature, an exposition was presented by the Committee of Federal Relations, drawn up by him, in which the whole subject was elaborately discussed. It was then that he suggested as the ultimate remedy, a resort to the State Veto—or nullification, as it is commonly called. It was not, however, Mr. Calhoun's opinion that the remedy should be immediately applied. It was certain that Gen. Jackson and himself would be elected President and Vice-President in a few months, for, as yet, war had not been openly declared against him—his support being essential to the success of the Jackson party. He thought it prudent to await a full explanation of Gen. Jackson's "Judicious Tariff;" and was not without hope that, through his influence, the protective system might be broken down. Besides, the period was near at hand when the Public Debt would be discharged, and no shadow of reason would remain for imposing high duties for revenue purposes. But the first Message of Gen. Jackson removed every doubt as to his policy, and showed clearly that he meant to sustain the Tariff interest. He also produced a breach between himself and Mr. Calhoun as soon as the prominent Executive appointments were confirmed, by reviving an old controversy supposed to have been settled many years before. It was evident that Mr. Calhoun had been doomed from the moment he had definitely taken ground against the

Protective System, and war was now made upon him without disguise.

Gen. Jackson did indeed denounce the Bank; and, early in his first term, he vetoed the Maysville Bill, and proposed a limit to appropriations for Internal Improvements—a limit, however, that was uncertain and discretionary with the President, and soon abandoned by himself. At the same time, he suggested a monstrous scheme for the permanent distribution among the States of the surplus revenue arising from the imposts; thus clearly showing that he would uphold Protection, even after the payment of the Public Debt, and perpetuate the system forever by corrupting the States.

Seeing, then, that there was no hope of any change in the action of the Federal Government, in regard to the Tariff, and its most objectionable cognate measures, the question as to what remedy a State could apply was seriously agitated in South Carolina. Mr. Calhoun proposed Nullification, and a considerable majority declared for it almost at once. But it required a vote of two-thirds in the Legislature to call a convention to enact a Nullifying ordinance. A warm and even bitter contest on this question was waged among the people of this State, until the October election in 1832, when the requisite majority was obtained. Gov. Hamilton immediately summoned the Legislature to assemble—a Convention was called, and in November of that year, all the Acts of Congress imposing duties, and especially the Acts of 1828 and 1832, were nullified and declared void and of no effect in the State of South Carolina. The Tariff Act of 1832 was named, because, as was customary every four years, the duties had been revised that year, and shortly before. They had been revised with special reference to the payment of the Public Debt, which was then virtually accomplished. The odious scheme of permanantly distributing the surplus revenue had not been carried, though there was every prospect that it would be ultimately; but while the amount of revenue, and average of duties were very slightly reduced, by a large increase of the free list—comprising articles most useful to the manufacturers—their particular interest was, in fact, much advanced, and the Tariff rendered more unequal and more oppressive than by the Act of 1828. Yet it was announced, authoritatively, that this was a final and permanent adjustment of the protective system, and that the South could never expect any amelioration of it.

Mr. Calhoun was still Vice-President of the United States, but Gen. Hayne having been recalled from the Senate and placed in the Executive Chair at this crisis, Mr. Calhoun was chosen in December to fill his place. Resigning his office, he took his seat in the Senate. Gen. Jackson had, immediately after the passage of the Ordinance, issued his famous proclamation, denouncing the proceedings of South Carolina as treasonable, nullification as unconstitutional and revolutionary, and even denying, for the first time, I believe, in the history of the country, the right of a State to secede. In fact, his doctrines went the full length of negativing all State Rights, and consolidating despotic power in the hands of the Federal Government. And this was followed by a message to Congress, demanding to be clothed with almost unlimited power to carry his views into effect by force of arms. The crisis was perillous. We were, apparently, on the verge of civil war, for South Carolina, on these hostile demonstrations, flew to arms. It was expected generally that Mr. Calhoun and most of the South Carolina Delegation would be arrested at Washington. But this was not done. A debate, however, arose in the Senate on the Bill embracing the recommendations of the President—commonly called the Force Bill—which will go down to future times, and live, an imperishable monument of the patriotism and courage, the wisdom and foresight, the genius and eloquence of Mr. Calhoun. His speech is not surpassed by any recorded in modern or in ancient times, not even by that of the great Athenian on the Crown.

This debate can never be read without its being seen, and felt, that Mr. Webster, his only opponent worthy to be named, gifted, as he is universally acknowledged to be, with talents of the highest order, and remarkable even more for his power of reasoning than for his brilliant declamation, was, on this memorable occasion, a dwarf in a giant's grasp. He was prostrated on every ground that he assumed. And if logic, building on undoubted facts, can demonstrate any moral proposition, then Mr. Calhoun made as clear as mathemathical solution, his theory of our Government and the right of each State to judge of infractions of the Constitution, and to determine the mode and measure of redress When the dust of ages shall have covered alike the men, the passions, and the interests of that day, this speech of Mr. Calhoun will remain to posterity, not merely a triumphant vindication of the State of South Carolina, but a tower-light to shed the brightest, purest, and truest rays upon the path of every Confederacy of Free States that shall arise upon the earth.

It is not probable that State Interposition will ever again be resorted to while this Union continues. More decisive measures will be preferred. But if the Federal Government was created by a Constitutional compact between Sovereign States, binding between those only that ratified it in Conventions: if only certain enumerated or defined powers were entrusted to it in its various departments, and all powers not granted to it, explicitly reserved to the States entering into the compact: and if that compact appointed no special tribunal to decide when the Government thus created transcended the powers granted to it, and trenched on those reserved by the States, it follows irresistibly that the States themselves must decide such questions: for if the Federal Government, by any or all of its Departments, assumes as an exclusive right this transcendant power, then is that Government sovereign over those by whom it was created—the Conventions of the people of the States; the limits to its powers, supposed to have been fixed in the most sacred and binding form, were only suggestions addressed to its discretion, and the whole mass of rights supposed to have been reversed absolutely to the States, have no existence save from its grace and will. If, however, the States have by virtue of their Sovereignty—and if it be historically true that at the time of the compact, each State was separately sovereign and remains so still—then if *each State* having the right to judge, in Convention, of infraction of the Constitution, it follows, with equal certainty, that each State must determine for itself the mode and measure of resistance to be applied to such infraction, or the right itself is a nullity. Two modes only of resistance are to be found. The one, to withdraw altogether from the violated compact; the other to nullify the unconstitutional act and compel the Federal Government to repeal it, or obtain a new grant of power from another Convention of the States. The Federal Government, or two-thirds of the States, may call a Convention for that purpose. A single State cannot. It must, therefore, surrender, not only its reserved rights, but its entire Sovereignty, or, resist if need be, singly and independently, as South Carolina did.

In recommending Nullification to the State of South Carolina in preference to Secession, which, at that time, it was almost universally agreed that a State had a clear right to resort to, Mr. Calhoun was mainly influenced by that deep, long cherished, and I might almost say superstitious attachment to the Union, which marked every act of his career from its commencement to its very close. For if there is one feature most prominent in Nullification as a remedial measure, it is that it is conservative of the Union—of that Constitutional Union, which is the only Union a patriot can desire to preserve. It was also recommended by the authority of the leaders and founders of the great Republican Party, Mr. Jefferson and Mr. Madison, who had proposed this identical measure to Virginia and Kentucky in the memorable crisis of 1798.

The Force Bill was passed, but was immediately nullified by South Carolina, and remains a dead letter in our State. In the mean time, however, both the Administration and Opposition in Congress, had become alarmed, and introduced bills for reducing the

Tariff, notwithstanding the loud declaration of finality by both, at the preceding Session. Ultimately, the famous Compromise Bill was proposed by Mr. Clay, the great leader of the Protectionists, and was accepted by Mr. Calhoun and his colleagues from South Carolina. It became a law and settled this perilous controversy. By this act, in consideration of nine years being allowed for a gradual reduction of the duties, the principle of Protection was forever surrendered, and it was provided that, at the end of that period, no more revenue should ever be collected than was necessary for the wants of an economical Government.

No pains have been spared by the majority to detract from the merit of the signal triumph achieved by South Carolina and Mr. Calhoun in his arduous and memorable contest. More, undoubtedly, might have been gained. The term of the reduction was a long one: the final enforcement of the Compromise was not, as was afterwards proven, sufficiently secured: and the Force Bill was passed—a monument of the subserviency and degradation of an American Congress. The triumph might have been more complete; but, shared with many, far less glorious, had South Carolina been sustained by her sister States of the South. Most of these had denounced the Protective System as unconstitutional and oppressive, and pledged themselves to resist it with as much show of indignation as South Carolina. But when the hour of actual conflict came, they shrunk from her side, and repudiated the remedy. She took her station in the breach alone, and, single-handed, won a victory whose renown can never fade, when she extorted from an over whelming and arrogant majority—in the teeth of declarations but a few months old—a full surrender of a formal and peculiarly solemn act of Congress.

Mr. Calhoun had now wholly devoted himself to the reformation of the Federal Government, and its first great step accomplished—although the struggle had so completely isolated him, that, out of the South Carolina delegation, he had scarcely a supporter in either House of Congress—he moved onward in his course, unbent and undismayed. His personal fortunes were apparently forever shipwrecked,

> ———"But he beat the surges under him,
> And rode upon their backs."

His broad vision swept the whole circle of the political system, and he noted every plague-spot of corruption on it. He made a powerful attack on Executive patronage in a Report to the Senate, of which an immense number of copies were printed by that body. He struck a fatal blow at Executive usurpation, by demonstrating that all the discretionary powers are vested in Congress, and that the other Departments can do nothing "necessary and proper to carry out" their constitutional powers, without the previous sanction of the law. He kept a steady eye on the Surplus Revenue, which, from various causes, accumulated beyond all expectation, notwithstanding the reduction of duties under the Compromise Act. As this Surplus must now be temporary, he thought it better to divide it among the States, than to keep it as a permanent fund, or to waste it in profligate and corrupting expenditures. It was a cordial maxim with him to keep the Government poor. History shows that the most fatal vices of all Governments originate in the command of too much money. To lessen the necessary amount of revenue by curtailing expenditures, was an essential feature of Mr. Calhoun's great scheme of reform. He did not fail to oppose every improper appropriation, and defeated many; and, finally, succeeded in carrying his proposition to relieve the dangerous plethora of the Treasury, by depositing the Surplus with the States—not to sustain tariffs as Jackson's recommendation of a similar substitution was intended, and to be permanently maintained, but to arrest the general waste of money, until the Compromise Act materially reduced the revenue.

Some of the diseases of the Government Mr. Calhoun thought it would be dangerous to heal too suddenly. One of these was the United States Bank, whose charter expired in 1836. Gen. Jackson had, in 1832, vetoed a recharter of it; and in October, 1833, he removed the Government funds from its coffers, and deposited them in the State Banks without any authority from Congress.

Mr. Calhoun condemned this high-handed and unconstitutional measure, and, believing that the Bank could not be closed immediately, without producing a financial convulsion—so completely had it brought the whole financial and mercantile system under its power—proposed to give it twelve years more to wind up its affairs. But he did not let the occasion pass, without clearly indicating his views of the Banking system. He said that the Government ought, at a proper time, to be entirely divorced from all connection with Banks. "I have great doubts," he said, "if doubts they may be called, of the soundness and tendency of the whole system, in all its modifications. I have great fears that all will be found hostile to liberty, and the advance of civilization—fatally hostile to liberty in our country, where the system exists in its worst and most dangerous form." His proposition failed, however, and the Bank fell headlong into ruin, dragging thousands of victims after it, and spreading deep gloom over the whole country. It is but just, however, to say, that this disastrous catastrophe, which did not occur until some years later, was due more to its own violent and reckless efforts to extend its influence and operations, to maintain its existence, and to revenge its defeat, than to the measures of the Government, unfair as they had been.

Early in 1837, shortly after Mr. Van Buren's elevation to the Presidency, the financial crisis which Mr. Calhoun had long predicted, came. In the crash, the Banks suspended payments almost everywhere, and among them, the deposit Banks. By a joint resolution, introduced by Mr. Calhoun in 1816, the notes of suspended Banks could not be received into the Treasury, and by a clause in the recent Deposit Act, such Banks could not be used as fiscal agents. Thus, suddenly, and in a most unexpected manner, the divorce between the Government and Banks was fully effected; and believing that no injury could now result from keeping them separate forever, Mr. Calhoun cordially and powerfully supported Mr. Van Buren's recommendation, at the extra session of 1837, to reorganize the Treasury Department on the Sub-Treasury plan. To the Bill introduced, Mr. Calhoun moved an amendment, that specie only should be received in public dues, and made this the *sine qua non* of his support.

After many defeats and great difficulties in a contest that lasted six or seven years, this Sub-Treasury system, with the specie feature, finally prevailed, and has been found to work admirably. It has put an end to every prospect of the recharter of the United States Bank, and that once alarming source of danger to our Institutions, may be said to be extinct.

For the part which Mr. Calhoun took on this occasion, he was subjected to a new and tremendous torrent of abuse and calumny. His course, since 1833, had led him to act mostly with the Opposition, who were endeavoring to check the march of Executive usurpation. This Opposition was composed chiefly of the surviving Federalists, and the recruits they had made from time to time, and now assumed the name of the Whig party, and on this very question received a large accession of State Rights men, and even Nullifiers, whose attachments and hostilities to men, and to subordinate measures, blinded them apparently to principles. With all these, Mr. Calhoun parted, when he took his ground in favor of the Sub-Treasury. He was charged with deserting his Party, though he had refused openly in the Senate to be called a Whig, and had, again and again, declared that he did not belong to either of the leading parties, but would act indifferently with whichever might be promoting his views of the Constitution and true policy of the Country. The charge of inconsistency, now so warmly urged against him, had been incessantly reiterated from 1828, and was continued, more or less, to the hour of his death. It is surprising, that, in an enlightened age like this, such narrow notions of consistency should so extensively prevail. The situation of public affairs is ever shifting, and the wise and patriotic Statesman must necessarily vary his own course to conform to, or oppose every altered state of circumstances. New truths are daily developed, not only in the scientific world, but in the workings of political systems, and especially in our own. Those only who are ignorant of these discoveries, can remain without change in their opinions; and to change opinions, and not avow and act upon them, is to be basely and dangerously false. Cicero, when accused of inconsistency in having sided with almost every party to which the convulsions of his times had given birth, fully admitted the fact that he had done so, but nobly vindicated himself by showing, that, in every change, he had in view one consistent object—the good of Rome. Thus Cato, after years of warm hostility to Pompey, advised his countrymen to put all power in his hands. Thus Aristides volunteered to serve under Themistocles; thus Solon became the counsellor of Pisistratus, who had overthrown his Constitution. Mr. Calhoun himself, as long ago as his speech on the repeal of the Embargo, had very properly defined inconsistency to be "a change of conduct without a change of circumstances to justify it." Tried by this standard, he was never liable to any imputation of inconsistency. He never moved, in any direction, without giving such cogent reasons for it, as must satisfy every impartial mind, if not of the propriety, at least of the reality of his convictions. Influenced by the highest and most patriotic considerations, and scorning the false and vulgar cry of inconsistency, he did not hesitate a moment in magnanimously extending the thorough and effective support of his powerful intellect, in the hour of their greatest need, to the man who had been, he believed, his most zealous enemy, and to the party which had excluded him from its ranks with the most violent anathemas.

He was now gladly welcomed back; and, in the high and commanding position in the Republican Party, which, through the severest trials, he had a second time won for himself, it is difficult to over-estimate what he might have achieved, had that party been able to sustain itself in power at that time. But, the name of Mr. Van Buren was not associated in the minds of the people, with any brilliant talents or illustrious services. Magician, as he was said to be among his partisans, he could cast no spell upon the masses, excited by the wide-spread financial troubles of the times, all of which were naturally attributed by the ignorant, and not without much justice, to the errors and corruptions of the party then in power. He was overthrown in the election of 1840, and the Whigs came into the Presidency with a majority in both Houses of Congress. An extra Session was immediately called and held in the spring of 1841, but before it met, Gen. Harrison died, and the Vice-President, Mr. Tyler, who, fortunately for the country, though a Whig, had been bred a State Rights Republican, succeeded to the vacant Chair.

The Whigs, elated with victory, rushed to Washington, resolved to secure all its fruits without delay. Banks, Tariffs, Distributions of Revenue, the most prodigal expenditures for individual and sectional benefit, and Bankrupt Laws to wipe off the embarrassment of past extravagance and speculation, swam in delightful confusion before their excited vision. Measures were promptly brought forward, and pressed on the minority with unequalled energy and arrogance. Mr. Calhoun was the leader of the Republican Party in the Senate. He penetrated every design, and met every movement of the Whigs. To all the measures that could not be defeated, conditions were proposed and sustained with such unanswerable arguments, that the reaction of public opinion compelled the majority to pause, to waver, and finally to give way—and the close of that Session, which had been called by the Whigs to consolidate their power, found them not only a dispirited, but virtually a defeated Party; results which were due in great measure, to the activity and firmness, the powerful logic and profound Statesmanship of Mr. Calhoun.

In that Session, however, and the two succeeding, during which the Whigs remained in power, several unconstitutional and dangerous measures were forced through. The Bankrupt Law, which was soon repealed. The distribution of Revenue, arising from sale of public lands, which expired under the condition imposed on it. The recharter of the Bank, which was vetoed by Mr. Tyler. The Tariff Act of 1842, which was equally stringent with that of 1828. This Act, which was passed in open violation of the Compromise Act of 1833—a violation which should forever put an end to all faith in Legislative Compromises by Congress, was justified on the ground that a larger revenue was indispensable to the Government. A justification deliberately prepared before-hand by the unconstitutional distribution of a portion of the Revenue, and the prodigal expenditures which so many corrupt interests had fastened on the Government.

A resort to State action to resist this oppressive act,

was again proposed by some in South Carolina. But Mr. Calhoun resisted it, because he believed that the next Congressional Elections would bring the Republicans into power, and that they would repeal the law. They obtained majorities, but did not repeal; and in 1844, a more strenuous effort was made to excite State iuterposition. But Mr. Calhoun resisted still. There was one hope left. The approaching election for President would give the Republicans complete control of the Federal Government, and he desired to await that event. The fact was, that after the experience of 1833, —the consolidation principles then avowed by all parties and the growing alienations of the different sections since—he believed the Union could not survive the decisive resistance of a State on points of vital interest, and his attachment to it was so deep that he was averse to putting it to hazard, while any reasonable hope was left of redress by other means. A Republican President was elected, and in 1846, the Tariff of 1842 was so materially modified as to forbid extreme resistance. But, after all the struggles of more than a quarter of a century, the Protective System, though somewhat weakened in opinion and narrowed in action, still flourishes in violation of every principle of free and equal Government—a gross infraction of the Constitution, and a deadly injury to the South.

During the Session of 1843, Mr. Calhoun again strikingly displayed his devotion to his country, and the impossibility of surrendering his serious convictions and his patriotic sense of duty to party considerations, by strenuously and successfully opposing, in common with the Whigs, a proposition from the Republican ranks to take possession of the whole of Oregon, without necessity, under doubtful title, and at imminent hazard of a war with England. At the close of that Session he resigned his seat in the Senate, and retired from public life.

His health, which, although his constitution had been considered diseased and ultimately proved to be so, had been almost perfect throughout his long service, began now to exhibit some symptoms of decay. And well it might—and well might he be wearied out. For ten—in fact for fourteen successive years, he had been engaged in a contest that taxed to their uttermost all his physical and mental powers. Body and spirit, he had devoted himself without a moment's respite to the arduous and perilous task of restoring a violated Constitution and a corrupted Government. It had been one long, raging storm, with scarce a single intermission. A storm such as none but the most hopeful and the bravest would have dared to defy, and in which none but the most prudent, the most hardy, the most skilful—endowed with the rarest intellect, strengthened by every resource upon which genius can make a requisition, and held to the encounter by an unconquerable will—could have outrode a second blast. But he stood in the centre of the vortex, unblenched, immoveable

"As a tower, that firmly set,
Shakes not its top for any wind that blows."

For the first time a clear expanse was now visible above the political horizon. The Federalists, tracked through all their disguises, were again beaten to the ground. They lay prostrate, and the Republicans, after the salutary experience of a great reverse and many years of desperate warfare, all brought on by their own departure from the Constitution, were about to resume, in full, the reins of power, made wiser not only by the events of the past, but by the brilliant light which his clear and profound intellect had shed and concentrated around the principles of Constitutional Government; and Mr. Calhoun, with the entire approbation of his friends, seized this apparently propitious moment to retire and recruit after his long and arduous labors.

The State of South Carolina in May, 1843, nominated Mr. Calhoun for the Presidency. But in December following, he withdrew his name, when it became apparent that the Convention, to be held at Baltimore to nominate the candidate of the whole Republican Party, was not to be constituted on principles analogous to the Constitution. He could not, with his views, accept a nomination, if tendered, by a Convention formed in any other manner, and he did not wish to embarrass the Party from mere personal considerations.

He was not permitted, however, to enjoy his repose for any length of time. In the spring of 1844, he was nominated as Secretary of State, by Mr. Tyler, without his previous knowledge; and the nomination being instantly and unanimously confirmed, he could not do otherwise than obey the call. Two critical and eminently important negotiations were then on foot. One to adjust the Oregon question with England; the other to secure the annexation of Texas. In the latter, his success was complete, and to him, perhaps, more than to any other, we owe that important and invaluable acquisition. The Oregon negotiation was not closed when Mr. Polk came into office. He did not tender to Mr. Calhoun the reappointment as Secretary, but offered and urged on him an Embassy to England, to continue that negotiation. But believing his post of duty was, if anywhere, on this side of the Atlantic, he declined the Embassy, and returned once more to his Plantation.

In the hands of Mr. Calhoun's successor, the Oregon negotiations completely failed. The President was pledged by his party to claim the whole of the Territory, and the fulfilment of that pledge was now demanded. Should Congress sustain the claim, war was inevitable, and, as the Republican Party had majorities in both Houses, there seemed to be no escape. The whole country became alarmed. In this exciting crisis, the eyes of all parties, all interests, all classes, were turned instinctively to Mr. Calhoun—the pilot who had weathered so many storms—the sagacious and patriotic Statesman who had been found equal to every emergency. His return to the Federal Councils was called for from every quarter, and his successor in the Senate, Judge Huger, with a rare magnanimity, offered to give way for him. There was no resisting such appeals, and Mr. Calhoun returned to Washington late in December, 1846. When he took his seat, it was so fully understood that the Executive, backed by a majority in Congress, was resolved to assert our right to the whole of Oregon, and to attempt to take immediate possession of it, that the Opposition was paralyzed in despair. He did not lose a moment in taking a clear, decided, and open stand against the Administration he had contributed so largely to bring into power. He rallied the dispirited Opposition, composed chiefly of Whigs, with whom he had lately been so violently contending. He appealed to the country against the

Republican Party. The sound common sense of the people sustained him: and the tide of public opinion set in so strongly in favor of a compromise with England, that negotiations were resumed with fresh vigor, and in a few months the whole question was adjusted to the entire satisfaction of the great body of every party in the two countries. In his whole public career, Mr. Calhoun had never rendered a more conspicuous —perhaps never a more substantial—service to his country; and it was appreciated and acknowledged throughout the Union. To him, and almost to him alone, was justly and universally accredited the distinguished merit of having saved the United States from a war with the most powerful nation in the world, about a matter so insignificant as to be almost frivolous, and in which neither the honor nor the interests of either were seriously involved. Thousands of such wars disfigure the pages of history, and have often been the most bloody and disastrous.

But this affair had hardly been placed in a sure train of settlement before another difficulty arose, in appearance far less formidable, but in its results likely to prove much the most important in our annals, since the Revolution. A sudden, and to the great body of our people, most unexpected war broke out with Mexico. Pending negotiations with that Republic concerning the western boundary of Texas, a portion of our Army had been, contrary to the usual courtesy of nations, marched into the disputed Territory. The Mexicans attacked it. Battles ensued, and a flame was kindled, which spread instantaneously over both countries. Congress was called on to declare, or rather to recognize the existence of war, and to make the most extensive provisions for its vigorous prosecution. Mr. Calhoun did not hesitate to take his stand against the war. He condemned the invasion of disputed territory; but as it had been done and battles fought, he was for voting such supplies as would enable our army to maintain its position, and without recognizing a state of war, to renew negotiations. But he stood alone—literally alone—abandoned by all parties in the Senate. Yet he did not waver. He knew that peace was the fundamental policy of our country. That war was disastrous to all its real interests, and was only to be waged to maintain that most vital of all interests—its honor. And that could never be involved in a contest with so weak a power as Mexico. He saw, too, that all his hopes of reforming the Government and resuscitating the Constitution must vanish when the sword was drawn. Other fatal consequences were also apparent to his keen vision. But he could not see all. No human sagacity could penetrate them then, or can penetrate them now. Mr. Calhoun declared that though he foresaw much evil, for the first time in his whole public life, he could not form a rational conjecture of the end—that an impenetrable curtain had fallen betwixt him and the future. For the first time, too, he was sunk in gloom. And that great heart, which had never before felt fear, was stricken with terror—almost with despair. Hostilities were carried on with vigor. Victory crowned every effort of our arms; and an imperishable wreath of military glory was won for our flag—South Carolina contributing some of the brightest and most unfading flowers. Mr. Calhoun steadily interposed, on every opportune occasion, to arrest the progress of the war, brilliant as it was; and hailed with delight the Treaty of Peace, which was ratified early in 1848.

The first important consequence of the war was an immense expenditure—far exceeding the ordinary revenues, and entailing on the country a heavy debt, which has put an end to all prospect of an early reduction of the Protective Duties. The next was the overthrow of the political party which conducted it, by the elevation of one of its successful Generals to the Presidency; an event not due so much to the errors committed by the one, or the wisdom and patriotism displayed by the other party, as to the disgust felt by a large portion of the people for both, and their desire to establish for once an administration that would not be governed by party considerations—a desire which has been altogether disappointed. The third great consequence of the war has been the unparalleled excitement occasioned by the attempt and failure to make a fair division between the Slaveholding and non-Slaveholding sections of this confederacy, of the immense territory acquired from Mexico—an excitement in the midst of which we now are, and the result of which it is not given us to foresee.

I have omitted thus far to do more than incidentally allude to a question of the highest and most vital interest, which has long and deeply agitated our country, in the conduct of which Mr. Calhoun has acted throughout a conspicuous and leading part. At the period of the Declaration of Independence, African Slavery was established in every Colony, and, as late as the formation of the Constitution, slaves were still held in every State. But it was a decaying institution everywhere save in the Plantation States, and great apprehensions existed among the Southern members of the Convention that the other States would combine to emancipate all the Slaves immediately, or gradually. They therefore refused absolutely to enter into any union with them without a distinct agreement on this essential matter. One great object in so constructing the Federal Government that it should have no powers not clearly conferred upon it, reserving all others to the States, was to prevent legislation on this subject. But beyond this the Southern Delegates required a Constitutional obligation from all the other States, to assist them in maintaining their authority over their slaves in case of necessity, by restoring fugitives and aiding to put down insurrections. They also demanded a recognition of slaves as a permanent element of political power and a fixed caste, by assigning them a representation, though a restricted one, in Congress. From the adoption of the Constitution up to 1819, the harmony between the North and South was never for a moment seriously disturbed by the Slave question. At that period, when Missouri applied for admission into the Union, the North, where African Slavery was now almost wholly extinct, opposed her application, on the ground that Slaveholding was permitted by her Constitution. A deeply exciting controversy immediately arose, which was finally adjusted by the concession from the South that, thereafter, no Slaveholding State should be admitted into the Union North of 36° 30' N. latitude.

For many years after this contest there was no open agitation of this exciting topic, and public men in every section generally concurred in frowning upon all attempts to bring it forward. It was not until 1834-'35, that it again made its appearance on the political stage, when petitions were poured in upon Congress to legislate upon it. It was then discovered that, without attracting much attention, a great many Abolition Societies had been formed in the Northern States, who had set up presses and printed books, pamphlets, newspapers and engravings in immense numbers, and disseminated them North and South for the purpose of arousing the people to what were termed the horrors of African Slavery. Public lecturers were also employed and sent everywhere. The excitement increased rapidly. The people of the non-Slaveholding States seemed ripe for it. But lately they had been apparently baffled in their attempt to make us the overseers of our slaves for their benefit. No longer having it in prospect to reap the harvest of our fields and gather into their own granaries, by virtue of their legislation, one half of the net produce of the labor of the slaves, they were eager, in their rage and disappointment, to deprive us of the slaves themselves, and blast our prosperity forever. Both branches of Congress were soon flooded with petitions, full of the vilest abuse and slander of the South, and praying for the Abolition of Slavery and the Slave Trade in the District of Columbia. Others followed asking the Abolition of Slavery in the Territories, Forts, Dockyards, &c., and of the trade between the States. Some demanded the Abolition of Slavery in the States; and finally it was petitioned that the Union should be dissolved to save the North from the sin of slaveholding. Warm and, at length, the most angry debates in Congress were brought about by these petitions. At first, few or none professed to be in favor of them, yet the non-Slaveholding majority never would permit the South to adopt any decisive measure to exclude them from the Halls of Congress. In no long while, however, there was a complete change. The Abolitionists were soon strong enough to enter fully into the political field. They nominated candidates for President and Vice-President, and exhibited the startling fact, that, in that election, they held the balance of power between the parties in several of the largest States. From that moment they were courted, openly or secretly, by nearly every aspiring politician in the non-Slaveholding States. They soon sent members to Congress as their especial Representatives, and struck down every public man in the North who dared to defend the institutions of the South.

Against this violent crusade on the South, Mr. Calhoun took his stand at the very first, and combated it with all his powers, at every step, and to the latest moment of his life. He succeeded in arresting the circulation of Abolition publications through the mail, and, for a long time, he kept their petitions at the threshold of the Houses of Congress. In fact, Abolition petitions were formally received in the Senate for the first time, on the last day that he appeared there. From the beginning he predicted the progress of this agitation through all its stages, and declared that it must inevitably bring about a dissolution of the Union, if not put down early and forever.

While the Abolitionists have directed their attacks against specific parts of the Slave system, they have never made any secret of what indeed was perfectly apparent, that, from the first, their object was the entire emancipation of all the African race in the United States, without removal and without compensation to their owners, since removal or compensation are known to be utterly impossible. They proclaimed that by the laws of nature all men are free and equal; and that African Slavery is a social and political evil, and a deadly sin against God. Mr. Calhoun contended that, if our Slavery was a social evil and sin, we alone would be the sufferers and should be allowed to deal with it ourselves. Politically he claimed for it only the fulfilment of the solemn guaranties of the Constitution. But he thought it could not be a sin, since God had expressly ordained it; nor an evil, since both the white and black races had improved in every point of view under the system. He scouted the idea of natural freedom and equality. Men were born helpless, and owed life, liberty and everything to those who nurtured them. A state of complete natural liberty was inconceivable. Even the wildest savages placed severe restraints upon it. And so far from men being created equal, no two men, and in fact no two things, were ever yet created precisely equal. Inequality is the fundamental law of nature, and hence alone the harmony of the universe. But it was useless to attempt to reason with enthusiastic Abolitionists, or with the masses of the non-Slaveholders, equally bigoted in their abstract notions of morality, freedom and equality. It was still more useless to attempt to reason with politicians who existed only in the breath of such a people. A majority influenced by such ideas, and led on, some by a fanatical zeal to enforce what they believed to be truth, others by the love of power, and all by the hope of spoil, has never yet been effectually checked except by force.

It has not, however, yet become the plan of the Abolitionists to carry their purposes by a direct and decisive exertion of the political power they possess. They wish first to acquire a more overwhelming power, both political and physical. And, to effect this, they have aimed steadily to enlarge their own domain and to narrow down that of the Slaveholders, while they have endeavored to divide the South by appeals to the consciences of all, and to the supposed interests of the non-Slaveholders among us. And the two great political parties of the North have skilfully aided them in dividing and lulling the South for the purpose of keeping up their own connections with their respective allies here. They have united in denouncing, and have taught many to denounce as ultraists, disunionists and traitors, all those who have attempted to awaken the Southern people to a sense of the dangers that environed them. And more did they denounce than all the rest Mr. Calhoun, whose sagacity could not be deluded—whose virtue was incorruptible, and whose constant exposure of their designs, and effective opposition to them, was apparently the greatest obstacle to their success. Listening to no compromises, and snapping instantly every party tie where this transcendent question was involved, he waged mortal combat on every issue, open or concealed. The great difficulty with the Abolitionists was to identify their cause with some of the great practical political questions of the country. The pretended infringement of the much abused right of petition could not be made to serve them materially, for it was too absurd to contend that Congress was bound to receive and treat respectfully all sorts of petitions—petitions frivolous, unconstitutional and destructive of law, order and society. When the annexation of Texas was brought forward, they fastened upon that measure, and opposed it with great zeal and much effect, upon the ground that it extended the area of Slavery. But there were too many interests, even in the North, in favor of annexation, and Mr. Calhoun was enabled to defeat them signally. But when the Mexican war was declared, a new and vast field was opened to them. It was certain that a large territory would be gained by that war: and it was scarcely begun before it was moved in Congress and carried in the House, and almost carried in the Senate, to prohibit Slavery in the domain that might be acquired.

The alarm was immediately sounded, and the South appeared for once to be fully roused. A number of Southern States declared, through their Legislatures, that if this Prohibition was enacted they would not submit to it. While, on the other hand, a still larger number of Northern States made Legislative declarations in favor of it, and instructed their Senators to support it. Thus, at length, the Abolition question, always purely sectional, became again, as in the case of Missouri, but under far more ominous circumstances, the chief element in the most important practical political issue of the day. From 1846 up to near the close of the late memorable Session of Congress, this contest was carried on in various forms with deepening import, until at length it entirely absorbed the public mind, and occupied the Federal Government to the almost total exclusion of all other business. Early in the last Session it came up on the proposition to admit California into the Union. A band of adventurers having assembled in that distant region in unknown numbers, and, to a great extent, of unknown origin—scarcely any with legal titles to lands, and still fewer with fixed residences—after calling a Convention without proper authority, formed a government and demanded admission, as a Sovereign State, into the Union, with boundaries embracing the whole Pacific Coast to Oregon, and a Constitution, which, for the express purpose of securing the support of the non-Slaveholding majority, prohibited Slavery.

Mr. Calhoun's health, which had been failing rapidly for a few years past, had at length become so feeble that it was evident to his friends he could not long survive; and during the previous summer it was considered scarcely possible that he could return again to Washington. To almost any other man it would have been impossible. But when he saw the great battle which he had so long led had reached, as he believed, its final crisis; and that the fate of his country hung on the momentous movement which was about to be made, he discarded all thoughts of self-preservation, and hastened to the field, resolved to spend his last breath in striking one more blow for the great cause of the South—the cause of Justice and of the Constitution.

Arrived at Washington, his health was so feeble that he was soon compelled to remain most of his time at his lodgings, and went only occasionally to the Senate. In the mean while the conflict went fiercely on; and numerous plans for adjusting it were set afloat. Mr. Calhoun committed his views to paper, and on the 4th of March, after a long interval, appeared with it in the Senate. But he was not able even to read it, and transferred the task to his friend, Mr. Mason, a Senator from Virginia. In that speech he traced the territorial history of the United States, showing that the non-Slaveholding States, who originally owned but one fourth of the territory of the Union, were about to succeed, by the action of the Government and the concessions of the South, in getting possession of nearly three-fourths of it: that, by the system of revenue and expenditure which had been adopted, much the larger portion of the taxes were paid by the South, while the disbursements were made chiefly at the North: and that while these measures destroyed the equilibrium between the two sections, the Federal Government had concentrated all power in itself, and interpreted the Constitution and ruled the country according to the will of a majority, responsible only to the Northern section, by which it is elected. The result of all, he said, was that "what was once a Constitutional Federal Republic, is now converted, in reality, into one as absolute as that of the Autocrat of Russia, and as despotic in its tendencies as any absolute Government that ever existed." He showed that the California adventurers had no right to attempt to form a State without previous permission from Congress, and that what they had done was "revolutionary and rebellious in its character, anarchical in its tendency, and calculated to lead to the most dangerous consequences." He gave a succinct history of Abolition from its origin; showed how it had gained strength year by year, and declared that, "if something decisive was not now done to arrest it the South would be forced to choose between Emancipation and Secession." He denounced the childish idea of preserving the Union by continually crying "Union! Union! the glorious Union!" and expressed his conviction that there was no other way to save it, but by an amendment to the Constitution, "which would restore to the South in substance the power she possessed of protecting herself, before the equilibrium between the two sections was destroyed by the action of the Government."

No speech ever pronounced in Congress produced a more profound sensation there and in the country than this did. The deep and incalculable importance of the questions in issue; and the fact that this was generally regarded as the last effort of an illustrious statesman, who had, for almost half a century, led in the councils of the Confederacy, scarcely heightened the intensity of the interest created by the novel and startling, yet sound and prophetic views which had been developed with a force and clearness rarely equalled. Mr. Calhoun, himself, intended it rather as a preliminary speech. He still hoped that he could, by his iron will, baffle and repel the advances of disease, and that God would spare him to consummate this last task. He had only laid down his groundwork, and reserved ample materials for reply, after all had exhibited their positions, and his had been sufficiently attacked. He did not even announce what amendments to the Constitution he intended to propose. Whatever they were—for he afterwards said that several were necessary—the suggestion of them manifested his undiminished anxiety for the preservation of a Constitutional

Union; and the latest offering of his life was laid upon that altar at which he had so long worshipped. It is scarcely to be regretted that he did not specify them, for nothing is more certain than that no amendments to the Constitution can ever be carried that will give the South the express power of self-protection. They would not receive a single vote from that Northern majority, which will ere long be large enough to amend the Constitution without the South, if it shall choose to regard forms in perpetrating its oppressions. But such amendments, if passed, would not avail the South, for her action under them would soon be denounced as revolutionary, as the clearly Constitutional right of Secession is now denounced.

In fact, neither this Union nor any Union or Government can exist long by virtue of mere paper stipulations. "Written Constitutions," said Anacharsis to Solon, "are but spiders' webs, which hold only the poor and weak, while the rich and powerful easily break through." Solon thought otherwise, but lived to see the Government he established completely overthrown. Lycurgus, more wise, forbade written laws. His principles were durably impressed, by training from childhood, on the minds and manners of his people, and interwoven with the whole social fabric. And they governed the Spartans for six centuries or more. In modern France no enacted Constitution has survived five years; while the Constitution of England, resting on traditions and occasional Acts and Charters, appears to bid defiance to time and progress. Those Governments only can endure which spring naturally from the social system, and are habitually sustained by it. And written—artificial Constitutions are, indeed, but "spiders' webs," if they do not continually draw their vital breath from the same living source. For more than twenty years the Federal Constitution has been a dead letter, or a snare to the minority. It has, for that length of time, had no material influence in maintaining the Union of these States. They have been held together by habit; by the recollections of the past, and a common reverence for the patriots and heroes of the Revolution; by the ties of political parties, of religious sects, and business intercourse. But the events of these twenty years, and mainly the developments of Abolitionism, have clearly revealed to us that we have at least two separate, distinct, and in some essential points, antagonistic social systems, whose differences can never be reconciled and subjected to one equal and just Government, unless our respective industrial interests are left free from every shackle, and the fell spirit of Abolitionism crushed and entirely eradicated. Many of the cords which once bound these two systems together have been, as Mr. Calhoun pointed out in his last speech, already snapped asunder. The religious bonds have been nearly all ruptured; party ties are going fast; those of business are seriously endangered. It is vain to hope to preserve the Union by any common sentiment of reverence for the past, or even by amending the Constitution, unless these severed chains can be relinked together, and that brotherly love which mingled the blood of our fathers in the battle fields of the Revolution can be restored, by providential interposition, to its ancient fervor. It is, however, the province and the sacred duty of the statesman, whatever may be the ultimate result, to point out the diseases of the Constitution and the Government, and to propose the best remedies he can. This was the great object of Mr. Calhoun for the last two and twenty years of his career. For this he lived: and to this his last efforts and his latest thoughts were consecrated.

Consecrated in vain! for already the disease has passed a fatal crisis, and there is no longer a remedy that can save. California has been admitted, and the equilibrium of this Government has been destroyed forever. The edict has gone forth that no new Slaveholding State shall ever enter the Union: and the South, deprived at last, and finally, of her equality in the Senate, the only safe hold she ever had in this Confederacy, and from which she has so long and so nobly battled for her rights, is now condemned to a minority that can know no change, in every department of the Federal Government. The Slaveholding States have become emphatically the Provinces of a great Empire, ruled by a permanent sectional majority, unrelentingly hostile to them, and daring, as it is despotic. If they submit to continue thus, their history is already written —in the chronicles of Poland, of Hungary, and of Ireland—perhaps of St. Domingo and Jamaica.

After the 4th of March, Mr. Calhoun went but two or three times to the Senate Chamber. His last appearance there was on the 13th of that month; and as if the political storms which had pursued him so long were fated to pursue him to the last, he had, on that day, a warm debate, in which he was compelled to maintain the expediency of his proposition to amend the Constitution; and to defend himself from the charge of aiming to dissolve the Union. He retired exhausted, and returned no more. But still his thoughts were there, and his anxious interest for his distracted country lent its excitement to every pulsation of his heart. "If I could have," he said, as his end drew near, " If I could have one hour more to speak in the Senate, I could do more good than on any past occasion of my life."

He expired tranquilly on the morning of the 31st of March.

The deep and poignant grief which pervaded our State on the announcement of this event, although it was not unexpected, I will not attempt to depict. Your own hearts retain and cherish a recollection of it, more vivid and more durable than could be recalled, or impressed by any words of mine. The same feelings seemed to penetrate almost every portion of the Union. Since the death of Washington, no similar event, it is generally agreed, has produced a sensation so profound and universal. Envy and malice, sectional hostility and party persecution, seemed to be instantly extinguished. His real greatness was at once fully acknowledged, and all united in paying the highest honors to his memory.

Mr. Calhoun's moral character, as exhibited to the public, was of the Roman stamp. Lofty in his sentiments, stern in his bearing, inflexible in his opinions, there was no sacrifice he would not have made without a moment's hesitation, and few that he did not make, to his sense of duty and his love of country. As a Consul, he would have been a Publicola,—as a Censor, Cato—as a Tribune, Gracchus. He was often denounced for his ambition, but his integrity was never questioned. "Ambition is," as Mr. Burke justly said, "the malady of every extensive genius." Mr. Calhoun's enemies believed that it infected him to an extraordinary and dangerous degree. But the enemies of every distinguished man have said the same. He undoubtedly desired power. But there is no evidence to be found, either in his conduct or in his words, that he ever stooped to any mean compliance to obtain it, or that, when obtained, he ever used it but in the purest manner and for the welfare of his whole country. The nature of his ambition was well tested. Eight years Vice-President; for as long a period a Minister of State; six years in the House of Representatives, and fifteen in the Senate of the United States, he enjoyed all the power of the highest offices of our Government, save the very highest, and that he would in all human probability have attained, but that his aspirations were subordinate to his principles, and these led him to repudiate his party, and throw himself into opposition to its corruptions when it was at the zenith of its power.

That he did not reach the Presidency, and that no other statesman of the first rank has had the slightest prospect of reaching it for the last five and twenty years, are among the most striking proofs of the downward tendency of our Federal Institutions.

In private life Mr. Calhoun was remarkably accessible. Open, unsuspicious, mild in his manners and uniformly warm, cheerful, and hopeful, he was interesting, instructive and agreeable to all who had the happiness to know him. While in every domestic relation his conduct approached as near perfection as we can suppose human nature capable of doing.

The intellect of Mr. Calhoun was cast in the Grecian mould: intuitive, profound, original—descending to the minutest details of practical affairs; and soaring aloft, with balanced wing, into the highest heavens of invention. He appreciated wit and humor, the flights of fancy and the keen shafts of sarcasm; but he either did not possess, or entirely failed to cultivate the faculties which lead to distinction in these lines. He admired and valued high-toned declamation on appropriate occasions; and sometimes, though rarely, attempted it himself, and not without success. The force of his imagination, his command of language, his nobility of sentiment, and his enthusiastic temperament eminently qualified him for declamation of the highest order, and his themes were as well adapted to it as those of Demosthenes himself. But the audience to which he commonly addressed himself could not hear his voice or see his action, or decide his cause under the spell of eloquence. It covered millions of square miles, and reached far down the stream of time. And his keen judgment and deep earnestness would not often permit him to use weapons that could strike effectively those only who were near at hand. The intellectual power of Mr. Calhoun was due mainly to the facility and accuracy with which he resolved propositions into their elementary principles, and the astonishing rapidity with which he deduced from these principles all their just and necessary consequences. The moment a sophism was presented to him he pierced it through and through, and plunging into the labyrinth, brought truth from the remote recesses where she delights to dwell, and placed her, in her native simplicity, before the eyes of men. It was in these preëminent faculties that Mr. Calhoun's mind resembled the antique and particularly the genuine Greek mind, which recoiled from plausibilities and looked with ineffable disgust on that mere grouping of associated ideas which so generally passes for reasoning. It was in conformity with these great intellectual endowments that he created all his speeches and State papers. It was commonly said of his productions that they were characterized by extraordinary condensation. But Mr. Calhoun was often careless in his diction, and habitually so in the construction of his sentences. He sought only the words that most clearly expressed his meaning, and left their arrangement apparently to chance. What he did do was to go straight to the bottom of his subject, following the slender plummet line of truth until he reached it. Then he built up in a manner equally direct, discarding all extraneous materials; and erected a structure, simple, uniform and consistent, decorated with no ornament for the sake of ornament, and occupying no more space than was necessary for the purposes in view.

The faculty of Invention—which is the highest characteristic of genius—is the necessary result of rapid and correct analysis and synthesis. To the possession of these powers, then, is also due the aknowledged originality of Mr. Calhoun, which gave such a peculiar charm to every one of his productions, as led the public invariably to pronounce his latest to be the best. The common mind never looks beneath the surface, and draws its conclusions from the facts and arguments that float around it. Even rather uncommon minds seldom penetrate very deep or very quickly. From whatever subject, therefore, upon which such extraordinary powers of analysis and generalization were brought to bear, they would necessarily extract ideas lying far beyond the range of others, and so new and startling as to overwhelm ordinary intellects and obliterate their confused remembrances of past productions, in which he had carried them delighted through equally unaccustomed regions.

Hence, also, arose and was received the charge, worn thread-bare by reiteration, that Mr. Calhoun's mind was too metaphysical and speculative for conducting the affairs of Government. A charge which, if it was not absurd in itself, was signally refuted by his conduct of the War, by his organization of the War Department, by his negociations as Secretary of State, by his frequent, minute, and accurate, and powerful elucidations of all the financial, commercial, manufacturing and agricultural operations of the country—in short, by the whole course of his labour, from the commencement to the close of his career. It was the remarkable characteristic of the Greek mind, now too little appreciated, to be at once practical and speculative, as in fact it ever has been of all really great minds. In the palmiest days of Greece her Philosophers were Statesmen, her Poets and Historians were Warriors. The Astronomer who first predicted an eclipse made a fortune by dealing in olives. To a successful Usurper we owe the collection of the scattered songs of Homer. The mere practitioner is, necessarily, a quack in medicine, a pettifogger in law, and a charlatan in politics.

The colloquial powers of Mr. Calhoun have been highly lauded. In this there is a mistake. Strictly speaking he had no uncommon endowment of this sort. It is true that he entered readily and easily into any conversation, and there were few subjects on which he did not throw new light, or at least dissipate some of the darkness that might surround them. But he exhibited no sparkling wit, no keen retort, none of that liveliness of fancy which so delightfully season and refine familiar conversation. Nor was he anything of a *raconteur*. All these things he occasionally enjoyed with much zest, but rarely attempted them himself. The conversation in which he really shone was but a modified species of Senatorial debate. And, in that, no one approached to an equality with him. In the Senate, where time is given for preparation, and the conflict of intellect is conducted, for the most part, like a cannonade, by heavy discharges at considerable intervals, his opponents might make a show of vigorous combat with him. But, in the close encounter of informal discussion, there was no one who could stand before him. The astonishing rapidity of his intellectual operations enabled him to anticipate every proposition before it was half stated, to resolve it into all its parts, and not only to answer his opponent without an instant's hesitation, but to take up his whole train of argument, run through it in advance of him, and so turn all his points as to convince, or at least, to silence him. At these times there was a fascination about him which none could resist. It was not merely his warmth, his earnestness, his deep sincerity that charmed, but his reasoning—commencing so far back, and disentangling the first elements, the facts and principles—moved forward with such simplicity and ease, such clearness and connection, with a sweep so graceful, yet so broad and powerful, that you felt as though you were listening rather to a narrative than to an argument. There were rarely any tropes or figures, or learned illustrations, but your very passions were enlisted by the ardor and intenseness of his logic, and you were carried unresistingly along, as well by the force of your imagination as by the convictions of your judgment. The power which he thus exercised was so transcendant that, could he have seen and conversed with every individual in the Union, he would have reigned supreme over public opinion.

The fame of Mr. Calhoun will rest chiefly on his character as a Statesman. Posterity, with a knowledge of events yet concealed from us, will analyse it closely. It is believed that it will stand the most rigid scrutiny.

So many qualifications are necessary to the formation of Statesmen, and so rare a combination of all the highest moral and mental qualities is requisite to constitute one of the first order, that they are usually rated rather by degrees of ability, than by the peculiarities of talent. Such peculiarities, however, do exist, and so color their current opinions, that they are in all countries classed, at least temporarily, according to the domestic parties whose views they favor for the time. In this country, where every thing is so new and variable; where not only our political institutions are experimental, but our civilization has not attained a permanent standard, there is great difficulty in appropriating distinctive names to our Statesmen—a difficulty enhanced by the fact that nearly or quite all of our eminent men have, in the course of their careers, radically changed some of their opinions; changes which, indeed, few of the great Statesmen of any country, in the last eighty eventful years, have escaped.

Coming into the public councils at a period when twenty years of successful experiment had, it was thought, fully tested our Federal Constitution, and established the permanence of the Federal Government—when a vigorous effort to convert it into a central despotism had been signally defeated, and all sectional jealousies and apprehensions had been lulled, Mr. Calhoun devoted himself wholly, and enthusiastically, to the grand purpose of developing all the mighty resources of his country, and raising her to the highest pitch of prosperity and greatness. His views were large—far reaching—noble. And his measures were in full accordance with them. Whenever in war or in peace, an exigency occurred, his active and inventive genius promptly suggested a provision for it, always ample, and usually the best that could be adopted. Whenever favoring circumstances invited a forward movement, or a wider exertion of energy, he was ever ready with plans, thoroughly digested, and fully adapted to accomplish all the ends in view. While close in his calculations, and careful of details, there was nothing low or narrow in any thing he ever proposed. He had an ineffable scorn for whatever was mean or contracted in legislation; and having an abiding confidence, not only in truth and justice, but in the power of reason, and the capacity of the people to appreciate what was right and comprehend the arguments in favor of it, he never for a moment yielded to the current popular opinion, when it differed from his own. He expected to restrain it by his logic, and ultimately reverse it by the benefits his measures would confer. As a progressive Statesman, leading ardently, during the first part of his career the very van of Progress, Mr. Calhoun may be considered a perfect model.

When, however, a few years of peace had developed in this new and rapidly growing country—what it has taken thirty centuries to make manifest in older and more closely cemented social fabrics—that Governments and Constitutions are more severely tried by the conflicts of domestic than of foreign interests, and ambition; and it became evident that our Government was to be perverted and our Constitution set aside, to enable one section of this Confederacy to despoil another—then Mr. Calhoun became a Conservative Statesman. He saw that, in common with the founders of the Republic, he had been deceived in his belief that the Constitution had been consecrated by a quarter of a century of successful operation, and that all danger of a central despotism had passed by. He saw, what many in all countries have been too slow in seeing, that there is a Progress which, like "vaulting ambition, overleaps itself." He recoiled from the operation of machinery he had himself helped to put in motion; and he now ardently devoted all his talents and all his energy to arrest the march of usurpation and corruption, and to preserve the liberties and institutions inherited from our fathers.

But merely negative and stolid conservatism did not at all suit the genius of Mr. Calhoun, which was essentially active and ever looking forward to the improvement of mankind. He sought, therefore, earnestly, to discover the principles and theory of Movement that might be onward and unfailing—yet regular and safe. In accomplishing this task, he sounded anew the depths of human nature; he reviewed the whole science of politics; he analysed the Constitution word by word—its letter and its spirit; and he studied thoroughly the workings of our Government. The result was that he lifted himself above all parties, and became a Philosophical Statesman—the only true and real Statesman. And it was in the wide and exhaustless field now opened to him, that he gathered those immortal laurels, whose verdure shall delight, whose blossoms shall refresh, whose fruit shall be the food of the latest posterity.

The example of his noble efforts to reform the Government and to restore the Constitution of his country, distinguished by the display of the vastest resources and the most masterly powers of intellect—though like Agis, and Conon and the younger Brutus, he failed in his glorious designs—will live forever. But his speeches and writings will constitute a new epoch in the science of Politics. Our Federal Constitution, he often said, was in advance of the wisdom of those who framed it; and he it was who first thoroughly explored, comprehended, and expounded it. He found in it nearly all that was requisite to establish, on the firmest foundations, a free and popular Government, which was his beau ideal of Government; and which, though it has had many friends and many martyrs, and has been illustrated by patriots and heroes, has scarcely before had a genuine Apostle. He laid down, for the first time, its true principles and marked out its true limits; and has shown how it might, and unless vigilantly watched, eventually would depart from those principles and limits, and produce all those evils which have so long made it odious to the best and wisest men. He has shown on the other hand how capable it is of unlimited expansion, to meet all the exigencies and reap all the benefits of real progress—if its power is confided to the proper majorities and their suffrages collected in the proper manner; and how its harmony may be kept undisturbed and its duration made perpetual, by securing to the minorities the sacred and all-important right of self-protection. In short, he has so thoroughly elucidated all the checks and balances of Free Constitutions—simple and confederated—that henceforth, in the long tide of time, no Republic will be erected or reformed on a durable foundation, without a constant recurrence to the theories he has discussed, and the measures he has proposed; and a profound observance of the precepts he has taught.

I have endeavored to point out the most prominent events in the life of Mr. Calhoun: the parts he took in public affairs; the services he rendered his country; the policy and views by which he was at various periods influenced. I have also endeavored to pourtray the most striking features of his moral and intellectual character; and have briefly reviewed his Statesmanship. My task is executed, however feebly and imperfectly. It would be vain to attempt to fathom the Divine Will, and seek to learn why, in this most eventful period of our history, our Great Leader has been snatched away, leaving no one behind who can fill his place. What we do know is, that high and sacred duties have devolved on us; and imitating his illustrious example, we should go forward in the performance of them with "unshaken confidence in the Providence of God."

SPEECH

ON THE ADMISSION OF KANSAS, UNDER THE LECOMPTON CONSTITUTION. DELIVERED IN THE SENATE OF THE UNITED STATES, MARCH 4, 1858.

THE Senate, as in Committee of the Whole, having under consideration the bill for the admission of the State of Kansas in the Union—Mr. HAMMOND said:

Mr. President: In the debate which occurred in the early part of the last month, I understood the Senator from Illinois (Mr. Douglas) to say that the question of the reception of the Lecompton Constitution was narrowed down to a single point. That point was, whether that constitution embodied the will of the people of Kansas. Am I correct?

Mr. Douglas. The Senator is correct, with this qualification: I could waive the irregularity and agree to the reception of Kansas into the Union under the Lecompton Constitution, provided I was satisfied that it was the act and deed of that people, and embodied their will. There are other objections; but the others I could overcome, if this point were disposed of.

Mr. Hammond. I so understood the Senator. I understood that if he could be satisfied that this Constitution embodied the will of the people of Kansas, all other defects and irregularities could be cured by the act of Congress, and that he himself would be willing to permit such an act to be passed.

Now, sir, the only question is, how is that will to be ascertained, and upon that point, and that only, shall we differ. In my opinion the will of the people of Kansas is to be sought in the act of her lawful convention elected to form a Constitution, and no where else; and that it is unconstitutional and dangerous to seek it elsewhere. I think that the Senator fell into a fundamental error in his report dissenting from the report of the majority of the territorial committee, when he said that the convention which framed this Constitution was "the creature of the Territorial Legislature;" and from that one error has probably arisen all his subsequent errors on this subject.

How can it be possible that a convention should be the creature of a Territorial Legislature? The convention was an assembly of the people in their highest sovereign capacity, about to perform their highest possible act of sovereignty. The Territorial Legislature is a mere provisional government; a petty corporation, appointed and paid by the Congress of the United States, without a particle of sovereign power. Shall such a body interefere with a sovereignty—inchoate, but still a sovereignty? Why, Congress cannot interfere; Congress cannot confer on the Territorial Legislature the power to interfere. Congress itself is not sovereign. Congress has sovereign powers, but no sovereignty. Congress has no power to act outside of the limitations of the Constitution; no right to carry into effect the Supreme Will of any people, and, therefore, Congress is not sovereign. Nor does Congress hold the sovereignty of Kansas. The sovereignty of Kansas resides, if it resides anywhere, with the sovereign States of this Union. They have conferred upon Congress, among other powers, that to administer such sovereignty to their satisfaction. They have given Congress the power to make needful rules and regulations regarding the Territories, and they have given it power to admit a State—"*admit*," not *create*. Under these two powers, Congress may first establish a provisional territorial government merely for municipal purposes; and when a State has grown into rightful sovereignty, when that sovereignty which has been kept in abeyance demands recognition, when a community is formed there, a social compact established, a sovereignty born as it were on the soil, then to Congress is granted the power to acknowledge it, and the Legislature, only by mere usage, sometimes neglected, assists at the birth of it by passing a precedent resolution assembling a convention.

But when that convention assembles to form a Constitution, it assembles in the highest known capacity of a people, and has no superior in this Government but a State sovereignty; or rather only the State sovereignties of all the States, acting by their established Constitutional agent the General Government, can do anything with the act of that convention. Then if that convention was lawful, if there is no objection to the convention itself, there can be no objection to the action of the convention; and there is no power on earth that has a right to inquire, outside of its acts, whether the convention represented the will of the people of Kansas or not, for a convention of the people is, according to the theory of our Government, for all the purposes for which the people elected it, the people, *bona fide*, being the only way in which *all* the people can assemble and act together. I do not doubt that there might be some cases of such gross and palpable frauds committed in the *formation* of a convention, as might authorize Congress to investigate them, but I can scarcely conceive of any. And when a State knocks at the door for admission, Congress can with propriety do little more than inquire if her Constitution is republican. That it embodies the will of her people must necessarily be taken for granted, if it is their lawful act. I am assuming, of course, that her boundaries are settled, and her population sufficient.

If what I have said be correct, then the will of the people of Kansas is to be found in the action of her constitutional convention. It is immaterial whether it is the will of a majority of the people of Kansas *now*, or not. The convention was, or might have been, elected by a majority of the people of Kansas. A convention, elected in June, might well frame a Constitution that would not be agreeable to a majority of the people of a new State, rapidly filling up, in the succeeding January; and if Legislatures are to be allowed to put to vote the acts of a convention, and have them annulled by a subsequent influx of immigrants, there is no finality. If you were to send back the Lecompton Constitution, and another was to be framed, in the slow way in which we do public business in this country, before it would reach Congress and be accepted, perhaps the majority would be turned the other way. Whenever you go outside of the regular forms of law and constitutions to seek for the will of the people you are wandering in a wilderness—a wilderness of thorns.

If this was a minority constitution I do not know that that would be an objection to it. Constitutions are made for minorities. Perhaps minorities ought to have the right to make constitutions, for they are administered by majorities. The Constitution of this Government was made by a minority, and as late as 1840 a minority had it in their hands, and could have altered or abolished it; for, in 1840, six out of the twenty-six States of the Union held the numerical majority.

The Senator from Illinois has, upon his view of the Lecompton Constitution and the present situation of affairs in Kansas, raised a cry of "popular sovereignty." The Senator from New York (Mr. Seward) yesterday made himself facetious about it, and called it, "squatter sovereignty." There is a popular sovereignty which is the basis of our Government, and I am unwilling that the Senator should have the advantage of confounding it with "squatter sovereignty." In all countries and in all time, it is well understood that the numerical majority of the people could, if they chose, exercise the sovereignty of the country; but for want of intelligence, and for want of leaders, they have never yet been able successfully to combine and form a stable, popular government. They have often attempted it, but it has always turned out, instead of a popular sovereignty, a *populace* sovereignty; and demagogues, placing themselves upon the movement, have invariably led them into military despotism.

I think that the popular sovereignty which the

Senator from Illinois would derive from the acts of his Territorial Legislature, and from the information received from partisans and partisan presses, would lead us directly into *populace*, and not popular sovereignty. Genuine popular sovereignty never existed on a firm basis except in this country. The first gun of the Revolution announced a new organization of it which was embodied in the Declaration of Independence, developed, elaborated, and inaugurated forever in the Constitution of the United States. The two pillars of it were Representation and the Ballot-box. In distributing their sovereign powers among various Departments of the Government, the people retained for themselves the single power of the ballot-box; and a great power it was. Through that they were able to control all the Departments of the Government. It was not for the people to exercise political power in detail; it was not for them to be annoyed with the cares of Government; but, from time to time, through the ballot-box, it was for them—enough—to exert their sovereign power and control the whole organization. This is popular sovereignty, the popular sovereignty of a legal constitutional ballot-box; and when spoken through that box, the "voice of the people," which for all political purposes, "is the voice of God;" but when it is heard outside of that, it is the voice of a demon, the *tocsin* of a reign of terror.

In passing I omitted to answer a question that the Senator from Illinois has, I believe, repeatedly asked; and that is, what were the legal powers of the Territorial Legislature after the formation and adoption of the Lecompton Constitution? The Kansas Convention had nothing to do with the Territorial Legislature, which was a provisional government almost without power, appointed and paid by this Government. The Lecompton Constituton was the act of a people, and the sovereign act of a people legally assembled in convention. The two bodies moved in different spheres and on different planes, and could not come in contact at all without usurpation on the one part or the other. It was not competent for the Lecompton Constitution to overturn the territorial government and set up a government in place of it, because that Constitution, until acknowledged by Congress, was nothing; it was not in force anywhere. It could well require the people of Kansas to pass upon it or any portion of it; it could do whatever was necessary to perfect that Constitution, but nothing beyond that, until Congress had agreed to accept it. In the mean time the territorial government, always a government *ad interim*, was entitled to exercise all the sway over the Territory that it ever had been entitled to. The error of assuming, as the Senator did, that the convention was the creature of the territorial government, has led him into the difficulty and confusion resulting from connecting these two governments together. There was no power to govern in the convention until after the adoption by Congress of its Constitution, and then it was of course defunct.

As the Senator from Illinois, whom I regard as the Ajax Telamon of this debate, does not press the question of frauds, I shall have little or nothing to say about them. The whole history of Kansas is a disgusting one, from the beginning to the end. I have avoided reading it as much as I could. Had I been a Senator before, I should have felt it my duty, perhaps, to have done so; but not expecting to be one, I am ignorant, fortunately, in a great measure, of details; and I was glad to hear the acknowledgement of the Senator from Illinois, since it excuses me from the duty of examining them.

I hear, on the other side of the Chamber, a great deal said about "gigantic and stupendous frauds;" and the Senator from New York, in portraying the character of his party and the opposite one, laid the whole of those frauds upon the pro-slavery party. To listen to him, you would have supposed that the regiments of immigrants recruited in the purlieus of the great cities of the North, and sent out, armed and equipped with Sharpe's rifles and bowie knives and revolvers, to conquer freedom for Kansas, stood by, meek saints, innocent as doves, and harmless as lambs brought up to the sacrifice. General Lane's lambs! They remind one of the famous "*lambs*" of Colonel Kirke, to whom they have a strong family resemblance. I presume that there were frauds; and that if there were frauds, they were equally great on all sides; and that any investigation into them on this floor, or by a commission, would end in nothing but disgrace to the United States.

But, sir, the true object of the discussion on the other side of the Chamber, is to agitate the question of slavery. I have very great doubts whether the leaders on the other side really wish to defeat this bill. I think they would consider it a vastly greater victory to crush out the Democratic party in the North, and destroy the authors of the Kansas-Nebraska bill; and I am not sure that they have not brought about this imbroglio for the very purpose. They tell us that year after year the majority in Kansas was beaten at the polls! They have always had a majority, but they always get beaten! How could that be? It does seem, from the most reliable sources of information, that they have a majority, and have had a majority for some time. Why has not this majority come forward and taken possession of the government, and made a free-State constitution and brought it here? We should all have voted for its admission cheerfully. There can be but one reason: if they had brought, as was generally supposed at the time the Kansas-Nebraska act was passed would be the case, a free-State constitution here, there would have been no difficulty among the northern Democrats; they would have been sustained by their people. The statement made by some of them, as I understood, that that act was a good free-State act, would have been verified, and the northern Democratic party would have been sustained. But Kansas coming here a slave State, it is hoped will kill that party, and that is the reason they have refrained from going to the polls; that is the reason they have refrained from making it a free State when they had the power. They intend to make it a free State as soon as they have effected their purpose of destroying by it the Democratic party at the North, and now their chief object here is, to agitate slavery. For one, I am not disposed to discuss that question here in any abstract form. I think the time has gone by for that. Our minds are all made up. I may be willing to discuss it—and that is the way it should be and must be discussed—as a *practical thing*, as a thing that *is*, and *is to be;* and to discuss its effect upon our political institutions, and ascertain how long those institutions will hold together with slavery *ineradicable*.

The Senator from New York entered very fairly into this field yesterday. I was surprised, the other day, when he so openly said "the battle had been fought and won." Although I knew, and had long known it to be true, I was surprised to hear him say so. I thought that he had been entrapped into a hasty expression by the sharp rebukes of the Senator from New Hampshire; and I was glad to learn yesterday that his words had been well considered—that they meant all that I thought they meant; that they meant that the South is a conquered province, and that the North intends to rule it. He said that it was their intention "to take this Government from unjust and unfaithful hands, and place it in just and faithful hands;" that it was their intention to consecrate all the Territories of the Union to free labor; and that, to effect their purposes, they intended to reconstruct the Supreme Court.

The Senator said, suppose we admit Kansas with the Lecompton constitution—what guarantees are there that Congress will not again interfere with the affairs of Kansas? meaning, I suppose, that if she abolished slavery, what guarantee there was that Congress would not force it upon her again. So far as we of the South are concerned, you have, at least, the guarantee of good faith that never has been violated. But what guarantee have we, when you have this Government in your possession, in all its departments, even if we submit quietly to what the Senator exhorts us to submit to—the limitation of slavery to its present territory, and even to the reconstruction of the Supreme Court—that you will not plunder us with tariffs; that you will not bankrupt us with internal improvements and bounties on *your* exports; that you will not cramp us with navigation laws, and other laws impeding the facilities of transportation to southern produce? What guarantee have we that you will not create a new bank, and concentrate all the finances of this country at the North, where already, for the want of direct trade and a proper system of banking in the South, they are ruinously concentrated? Nay, what guarantee have we that you will not emancipate our slaves, or, at least, make the attempt? We cannot rely on your faith when you have the power. It has been always broken whenever pledged.

As I am disposed to see this question settled as soon as possible, and am perfectly willing to have a final and conclusive settlement *now*, after what the Senator from New York has said, I think it not improper that I should attempt to bring the North and South face to face, and see what resources each of us might have in the contingency of separate organizations.

If we never acquire another foot of territory for the South, look at her. Eight hundred and fifty thousand square miles. As large as Great Britian, France, Austria, Prussia and Spain. Is not that territory enough to make an empire that shall rule the world? With the finest soil, the most delightful climate, whose staple productions none of those great countries can grow, we have three thousand miles of continental sea-shore line so indented with bays and crowded with islands, that, when their shore lines are added, we have twelve thousand miles. Through the heart of our country runs the great Mississippi, the father of waters, into whose bosom are poured thirty-six thousand miles of tributary rivers; and beyond we have the desert prairie wastes to protect us in our rear. Can you hem in such a territory as that? You talk of putting up a wall of fire around eight hundred and fifty thousand square miles so situated! How absurd.

But, in this territory lies the great valley of the Mississippi, now the real, and soon to be the acknowledged seat of the empire of the world. The sway of that valley will be as great as ever the Nile knew in the earlier ages of mankind. We own the most of it. The most valuable part of it belongs to us now; and although those who have settled above us are now opposed to us, another generation will tell a different tale. They are ours by all the laws of nature; slave-labor will go over every foot of this great valley where it will be found profitable to use it, and some of those who may not use it are soon to be united with us by such ties as will make us one and inseparable. The iron horse will soon be clattering over the sunny plains of the South to bear the products of its upper tributaries of the valley to our Atlantic ports, as it now does through the ice-bound North. And there is the great Mississippi, a bond of union made by Nature herself. She will maintain it forever.

On this fine territory we have a population four times as large as that with which these colonies separated from the mother country, and a hundred, I might say a thousand fold stronger. Our population is now sixty per cent. greater than that of the whole United States when we entered into the second war of independence. It is as large as the whole population of the United States was ten years after the conclusion of that war, and our own exports are three times as great as those of the whole United States then. Upon our muster-rolls we have a million of men. In a defensive war, upon an emergency, every one of them would be available. At any time, the South can raise, equip, and maintain in the field, a larger army than any Power of the earth can send against her, and an army of soldiers —men brought up on horseback, with guns in their hands.

If we take the North, even when the two large States of Kansas and Minnesota shall be admitted, her territory will be one hundred thousand square miles less than ours. I do not speak of California and Oregon; there is no antagonism between the South and those countries, and never will be. The population of the North is fifty per cent. greater than ours. I have nothing to say in disparagement either of the soil of the North, or the people of the North, who are a brave and energetic race, full of intellect. But they produce no great staple that the South does not produce; while we produce two or three, and these the very greatest, that she can never produce. As to her men, I may be allowed to say, they have never proved themselves to be superior to those of the South, either in the field or in the Senate.

But the strength of a nation depends in a great measure upon its wealth, and the wealth of a nation, like that of a man, is to be estimated by its surplus production. You may go to your trashy census books, full of falsehood and nonsense—they tell you, for example, that in the State of Tennessee, the whole number of house-servants is not equal to that of those in my own house, and such things as that. You may estimate what is made throughout the country from these census books, but it is no matter how much is made if it is all consumed. If a man possess millions of dollars and consumes his income, is he rich? Is he competent to embark in any new enterprise? Can he long build ships or railroads? And could a people in that condition build ships and roads or go to war without a fatal strain on capital? All the enterprises of peace and war depend upon the surplus productions of a people. They may be happy, they may be comfortable, they may enjoy themselves in consuming what they make; but they are not rich, they are not strong. It appears, by going to the reports of the Secretary of the Treasury, which are authentic, that last year the United States exported in round numbers $279,000,000 worth of domestic produce, excluding gold and foreign merchandise re-exported. Of this amount $158,000,000 worth is the clear produce of the South; articles that are not and cannot be made at the North. There are then $80,000,000 worth of exports of products of the forest, provisions and breadstuffs. If we assume that the South made but one third of these, and I think that is a low calculation, our exports were $185,000,000, leaving to the North less than $95,000,000.

In addition to this, we sent to the North $30,000,000 worth of cotton, which is not counted in the exports. We sent to her $7 or $8,000,000 worth of tobacco, which is not counted in the exports. We sent naval stores, lumber, rice, and many other minor articles. There is no doubt that we sent to the North $40,000,000 in addition; but suppose the amount to be $35,000,000, it will give us a surplus production of $220,000,000. But the *recorded* exports of the South now are greater than the whole exports of the United States in any year before 1856. They are greater than the whole average exports of the United States for the last twelve years, including the two extraordinary years of 1856 and 1857. They are nearly double the amount of the average exports of the twelve preceding years. If I am right in my calculations as to $220,000,000 of surplus produce, there is not a nation on the face of the earth, with any numerous population, that can compete with us in produce *per capita*. It amounts to $16 66 per head, supposing that we have twelve millions of people. England with all her accumulated wealth, with her concentrated and educated energy, makes but sixteen and a half dollars of surplus production per head. I have not made a calculation as to the North, with her $95,000,000 surplus; admitting that she exports as much as we do, with her eighteen millions of population it would be but little over twelve dollars a head. But she cannot export to us and abroad exceeding ten dollars a head against our sixteen dollars. I know well enough that the North sends to the South a vast amount of the productions of her industry. I take it for granted that she, at least, pays us in that way for the thirty or forty million dollars worth of cotton and other articles we send her. I am willing to admit that she sends us considerably more; but to bring her up to our amount of surplus production—to bring her up to $220,000,000 a year, the South must take from her $125,000,000; and this, in addition to our share of the consumption of the $333,000,000 worth introduced into the country from abroad, and paid for chiefly by our own exports. The thing is absurd; it is impossible; it can never appear anywhere but in a book of statistics, or a Congress speech.

With an export of $220,000,000 under the present tariff, the South organized separately would have $40,000,000 of revenue. With one-fourth the present tariff, she would have a revenue with the present tariff adequate to all her wants, for the South would never go to war; she would never need an army or a navy, beyond a few garrisons on the frontiers and a few revenue cutters. It is commerce that breeds war. It is manufactures that require to be hawked about the world, and that give rise to navies and commerce. But we have nothing to do but to take off restrictions on foreign merchandise and open our ports, and the whole world will come to us to trade. They will be too glad to bring and carry us, and we never shall dream of a war. Why the South has never yet had a just cause of war except with the North. Every time she has drawn her sword it has been on the point of honor, and that point of honor has been mainly loyalty to her sister colonies and sister States, who have ever since plundered and calumniated her.

But if there were no other reason why we should never have war, would any sane nation make war on cotton? Without firing a gun, without drawing a sword, should they make war on us we could bring the whole world to our feet. The South is perfectly competent to go on, one, two, or three years without planting a seed of cotton. I believe that if she was to plant but half her cotton, for three years to come, it would be an immense advantage to her. I am not so sure but that after three years' entire abstinence she would come out stronger than ever she was before, and better prepared to enter afresh upon her great career of enterprise. What would happen if no cotton was furnished for three years? I will not stop to depict what every one can imagine, but this is certain: England would topple headlong and carry the whole civilized world with her, save the South. No, you dare not make war on cotton. No power on earth dares to make war upon it. Cotton *is* king. Until lately the Bank of England was king; but she tried to put her screws as usual, the fall before the last, upon the cotton crop, and was utterly vanquished. The last power has been conquered. Who can doubt, that has looked at recent events, that cotton is supreme? When the abuse of credit had destroyed credit and annihilated confidence; when thousands of the strongest commercial houses in the world were coming down, and hundreds of millions of dollars of supposed property evaporating in thin air; when you came to a dead lock, and revolutions were threatened, what brought you up? Fortunately for you it was the commencement of the cotton season, and we have poured in upon you one million six hundred thousand bales of cotton just at the crisis to save you from destruction. That cotton, but for the bursting of your speculative bubbles in the North, which produced the whole of this convulsion, would have brought us $100,000,000. We have sold it for $65,000,000, and saved you. Thirty-five million dollars we, the slaveholders of the South, have put into the charity box for your magnificent financiers, your "cotton lords," your "merchant princes."

But, sir, the greatest strength of the South arises from the harmony of her political and social institutions. This harmony gives her a frame of society, the best in the world, and an extent of political freedom, combined with entire security, such as no other people ever enjoyed upon the face of the earth. Society precedes government; creates it, and ought to control it; but as far as we can look back in historic times we find the case different; for government is no sooner created than it becomes too strong for society, and shapes and moulds, as well as controls it. In later centuries the progress of civilization and of intelligence has made the divergence so great as to produce civil wars and revolutions; and it is nothing now but the want of harmony between governments and societies which occasions all the uneasiness and trouble and terror that we see abroad. It was this that brought on the American Revolution. We threw off a Government not adapted to our social system, and made one for ourselves. The question is, how far have we succeeded? The South, so far as that is concerned, is satisfied, harmonious, and prosperous, but demands to be let alone.

In all social systems there must be a class to do the menial duties, to perform the drudgery of life. That is, a class requiring but a low order of intellect and but little skill. Its requisites are vigor, docility, fidelity. Such a class you must have, or you would not have that other class which leads progress, civilization, and refinement. It constitutes the very mud-sill of society and of political government; and you might as well attempt to build a house in the air, as to build either the one or the other, except on this mud-sill. Fortunately for the South, she found a race adapted to that purpose to her hand. A race inferior to her own, but eminently qualified in temper, in vigor, in docility, in capacity to stand the climate, to answer all her purposes We use them for our purpose, and call them slaves. We found them slaves by the common "consent of mankind," which, according to Cicero, "*lex naturæ est*." The highest proof of what is Nature's law. We are old-fashioned at the South yet; slave is a word discarded now by "ears polite;" I will not characterize that class at the North by that term; but you have it; it is there; it is everywhere; it is eternal.

The Senator from New York said yesterday that the whole world had abolished slavery. Aye, the *name*, but not the *thing;* all the powers of the earth cannot abolish that. God only can do it when he repeals the *fiat*, "the poor ye always have with you;" for the man who lives by daily labor, and scarcely lives at that, and who has to put out his labor in the market, and take the best he can get for it; in short, your whole hireling class of manual laborers and "operatives," as you call them, are essentially slaves. The difference between us is, that our slaves are hired for life and well compensated; there is no starvation, no begging, no want of employment among our people, and not too much employment either. Yours are hired by the day, not cared for, and scantily compensated, which may be proved in the most painful manner, at any hour in any street in any of your large towns. Why, you meet more beggars in one day, in any single street of the city of New York, than you would meet in a lifetime in the whole South. We do not think that whites should be slaves either by law or necessity. Our slaves are black, of another and inferior race. The *status* in which we have placed them is an elevation. They are elevated from the condition in which God first created them, by being made our slaves. None of that race on the whole face of the globe can be compared with the slaves of the South. They are happy, content, unaspiring, and utterly incapable, from intellectual weakness, ever to give us any trouble by their aspirations. Yours are white, of your own race; you are brothers of one blood. They are your equals in natural endowment of intellect, and they feel galled by their degradation. Our slaves do not vote. We give them no political power. Yours do vote, and, being the majority, they are the depositaries of all your political power. If they knew the tremendous secret, that the ballot-box is stronger than "an army with banners," and could combine, where would you be? Your society would be reconstructed, your government overthrown, your property divided, not as they have mistakenly attempted to initiate such proceedings by meeting in parks, with arms in their hands, but by the quiet process of the ballot-box. You have been making war upon us to our very hearthstones. How would you like for us to send lecturers and agitators North, to teach these people this, to aid in combining, and to lead them?

Mr. Wilson and others. Send them along.

Mr. Hammond. You say send them along. There is no need of that. Your people are awaking. They are coming here. They are thundering at our doors for homesteads, one hundred and sixty acres of land for nothing, and Southern Senators are supporting them. Nay, they are assembling, as I have said, with arms in their hands, and demanding work at $1,000 a year for six hours a day. Have you heard that the ghosts of Mendoza and Torquemada are stalking in the streets of your great cities? That the inquisition is at hand? There is afloat a fearful rumor that there have been consultations for Vigilance Committees. You know what that means.

Transient and temporary causes have thus far been your preservation. The great West has been open to your surplus population, and your hordes of semi-barbarian immigrants, who are crowding in year by year. They make a great movement, and you call it progress. Whither? It is progress; but it is progress towards Vigilance Committees. The South have sustained you in a great measure. You are our factors. You fetch and carry for us. One hundred and fifty million dollars of our money passes annually through your hands. Much of it sticks; all of it assists to keep your machinery together and in motion. Suppose we were to discharge you; suppose we were to take our business out of your hands;—we should consign you to anarchy and poverty. You complain of the rule of the South; that has been another cause that has preserved you. We have kept the Government conservative to the great purposes of the Constitution. We have placed it, and kept it, upon the Constitution; and that has been the cause of your peace and prosperity. The Senator from New York says that that is about to be at an end; that you intend to take the Government from us; that it will pass from our hands into yours. Perhaps what he says is true; it may be; but do not forget—it can never be forgotten—it is written on the brightest page of human history—that we, the slaveholders of the South, took our country in her infancy, and, after ruling her for sixty out of the seventy years of her existence, we surrendered her to you without a stain upon her honor, boundless in prosperity, incalculable in her strength, the wonder and the admiration of the world. Time will show what you will make of her; but no time can diminish our glory or your responsibility.

SPEECH

DELIVERED AT BARNWELL C. H., S. C., OCTOBER 29, 1858.

I thank you very sincerely for this kind and cordial reception. To stand here and speak to the people of Barnwell reminds me of times long gone by. I have addressed you, I believe, but once in more than twenty years. But those were stirring times, when, a quarter of a century ago, I so often spoke to you here of the Constitution and the Union—of your rights and wrongs in this Confederacy. No, not you, but your fathers. I am, indeed, happy to recognize in this assemblage many who were actors in those scenes; but many, many more, have been summoned hence, while you, my young friends, have grown up to supply their places. The gallant spirits who then surrounded me here, and whose kindling eyes and heaving bosoms animated and responded to my speech, have for the most part passed away, but the theme is still the same; and it is my part to-day, adhering with unchanged conviction and unabated zeal to every principle I then maintained, to discourse upon the same great topics. Our battle then was for the Constitution and our rights, in the Union, if possible—out of it, if need be. And this is our battle now.

The lapse of thirty years has brought much experience to the survivors of those who enlisted for this great cause in South Carolina. The veil of what was then the future—a future covered with angry clouds and doubts and darkness—has been removed, and looking back, we now see the events of long years which were then unknown to us. The hard-fought fields; our chequered fortunes; our victories, our defeats; the dead; the living—all then deep buried in the womb of time, are now all clear and palpable. And to those of us who have been spared to make this retrospect, it is a proud satisfaction to know that time and events have proved that our principles were true and our cause just; to recognize the unflinching courage and wonderful ability with which they have been so long maintained, and to feel renewed assurance that they must finally and fully triumph.

Your fathers confided in me from the first moment that we met upon this spot. They took me in their arms and lifted me into all the high places that were within their reach; and I have had many proofs that they taught you to confide in me as they had done. For this great and generous and abiding confidence and trust, I never knew but one reason, and that was that I always told them the truth, according to my best knowledge and belief. And as I dealt with them, I shall deal with you.

The last Legislature of the State conferred on me the high honor of a seat in the Senate of the United States; and during the late stormy session of Congress, I in part represented you there. You will expect me to give you some account of the proceedings there, and most especially of those which occupied four-fifths of time of the session, and produced such great excitement throughout the country—I allude to the Kansas question. And as no exception has been taken, so far as I know, to any act of mine, save my course on that, I will take this occasion to give my views in full upon it.

When, four years ago, the Kansas and Nebraska act was passed, giving governments to those Territories, I was, like most of you, a private citizen. I was earnestly engaged in renovating old lands, and creating new out of morasses hitherto impenetrable, and I had as little desire or expectation of ever again taking a part in public affairs, as the least ambitious of you here present. I made up my mind that this bill was fraught with delusion and trouble to the South, and so expressed myself on all suitable occasions.

The bill had two leading features in it. It enacted that every Territory, in forming its constitution for the purpose of applying for admission into the Union, should have the right to establish its own organic or constitutional laws, and come in with its own institutions, with the single condition that they should be republican. Why, unless our constitution is mere waste paper, all our institutions shams, and our theory of self-government a fallacy, this principle and privilege is their essence—lies at the bottom of the whole, and constitutes the corner-stone. It is the very right for which our fathers fought and made a revolution. I might not have refused to reaffirm it, but it was supererogatory; it might well weaken the whole structure of the Government to dig up, for the mere purpose of verification, its foundation.

The other feature of the bill was the repeal of the Missouri Compromise line. That was already repealed;

it had long fulfilled its mission; it had calmed the troubled waters for a time; it was obsolete until the annexation of Texas, when we acceded to the demand to extend it through the northern deserts of that State. But when California came—California that should have been and may yet be a slave State—and we demanded to extend that line to the Pacific and thus secure for the South a portion of the magnificent territory purchased in great part by her blood and treasure, it was refused. Then that line was blotted out everywhere and forever. To repeal it was a mere formality. The Supreme Court has recently pronounced it unconstitutional, and so the repeal was in no respect of any importance.

But this bill, with these two features, neither of them of any practical importance, magnified and exaggerated by orators and newspapers into a great Southern victory, led the South into the delusion that Kansas might be made a slave State, and induced it to join in a false and useless issue, which has kept the whole country in turmoil for the last four years, and gave fresh life and vigor to the Abolition party.

Through the most disgusting as well as tragic scenes of fraud and force, the Territory of Kansas at length came before Congress for admission as a State, with what is known as the Lecompton Constitution, embodying slavery among its provisions. But at the same time the Convention, by an ordinance, demanded of the United States some twenty-three millions of acres of land, instead of the four millions usually allowed to new States containing public lands. It was almost certain that a majority of the people of Kansas were opposed to this constitution, but would not vote on it;

and this additional nineteen millions (which, if allowed, would probably have kept them again from the recent polls) was what the South was expected to pay for that worthless slavery clause, which would have been annulled as soon as Kansas was admitted. I confess my opinion was that the South herself should kick that Constitution out of Congress. But the South thought otherwise. When the bill for its adoption was framed, with what is called the *Green Proviso*, I strenuously objected to it, and felt very much disposed to vote against the whole, but again gave way to the South, which accepted it by acclamation. If that proviso meant nothing, (and so I finally interpreted it,) it was nonsense, and had no business there, being without precedent. If it could be made to mean anything, it must have been something wrong and dangerous. But, as I said, the South, far and wide, took that bill. The House rejected it. They passed then the Crittenden substitute, which proposed to submit the Lecompton Constitution to a vote of the people of Kansas, and to accept it, if ratified by them. The Senate had previously refused that substitute, and did so a second time. It then asked a committee of conference. That committee reported what is called the "English Bill." By that bill Congress accepted the Lecompton Constitution, pure and simple, without proviso. The land ordinance of the Lecompton Constitution (which was in no wise a part of the constitution, but a separate measure) demanded, as I have said, a donation of some twenty-three millions of acres of land, being nineteen millions more than had been given to any other land State. The "English Bill" cut this down to the usual amount of four millions of acres, and required that the people of Kansas should ratify this modification, and surrender all claim to the remainder of the lands, as the condition of her final admission. Such a requisition has been made on every new State, carved out of the public lands, that has been admitted into this Union—sometimes in the enabling act, and, where there was none, always after accepting the constitution. Go to the statutes of Congress, and you will find it in every one of them. It is the custom—it is necessary—and this feature in the "English Bill" was in accordance with strict precedent. The only difference is this: that, usually, the Legislature of the State has been required to accept this compact by an irrevocable act, but in this case it was referred to the people of Kansas directly. In this there was no sacrifice of principle whatever, nor was it without precedent altogether; for in the case of the State last before admitted, (Iowa,) this question had been submitted to the Legislature or the people, as Iowa might prefer. This is the whole sum and substance of this "English Bill," except that it further declared that unless the people of Kansas accepted this modified ordinance, they should not be admitted as a State until they had a population that would entitle them to one Representative under the Federal apportionment. I voted for this bill; I voted properly; I voted no compromise; I sacrificed no particle of principle or Southern interest. It is true, its phraseology is halting and bungling; it was drawn up hastily and in great excitement. I objected to the wording of it in several passages, but I assured myself that nothing sinister was designed, and I voted for it, leaving its authors responsible for its diction on the statute book. I thought it preferable to the first bill the

Senate passed, and voted for it more willingly. It is true, some Northern Democrats who voted against the Senate bill voted for this, and thus it was carried. But was that a reason why I should not vote for it? Does that prove that I sacrificed any principle? They found themselves wrong, and perhaps wanted some excuse to retrace their steps. I was happy to assist in giving it to them without cost to ourselves. I was particularly pleased to get rid of the mysterious proviso of the first bill, and to require a solemn compact in regard to the public lands, which had not been properly provided for in that bill.

The only principle involved in this whole Kansas affair—if an affair so rotten, from beginning to end, can have a principle at all—was this: Would Congress admit a slave State into the Union? The Senate said yes. The House, by adopting the Crittenden substitute, said yes, if we are assured that a majority of the people of the State are in favor of it. For this substitute all the opposition voted in both Houses, so that every member of Congress, of all parties, first and last, committed themselves to the principle and policy that a State should be admitted into the Union, with or without slavery, according to the will of its own people—thus re-enacting one feature of the Kansas and Nebraska bill. I should myself have been willing to rest there, and let Kansas rest also. Whatever there was of principle or honor in the matter was secured by the votes already given. The English bill, however, came up in due course, and I voted for it cheerfully, believing that it was better calculated than any that had been offered to close up this miserable business, which has furnished much the most disgraceful chapter, so far, in our history.

But it is said that in submitting this land ordinance to a vote of the people of Kansas, Congress submitted also the Lecompton Constitution with its pro-slavery clause. If so, the passage in which it was done can surely be pointed out. Badly drawn up as the bill is, I should like to see the clause or the words that will justify such an assertion. If there was such a clause, why did not Judge Douglas and his friends vote for it? Why did not the black republicans and all who voted for the Crittenden substitute which also submitted the constitution, vote for this bill? It was the very point they made, yet to a man they voted against it. That, I think, should be conclusive.

But, then, it is said it was a virtual submission of the constitution to the people, because, if they refused to ratify the modified land ordinance, the admission of Kansas under the Lecompton Constitution was defeated. Well, the facts are so; I cannot and do not deny them. But I should like to know how that could by any possibility have been avoided or remedied. Suppose Congress had admitted Kansas without modifying anything, yielding even to her enormous "land grab," which embraced many more acres than there are in all South Carolina, I should like to know if the Lecompton Constitution would not still have been submitted to the people as virtually as it was by the English bill; that is, not submitted at all, but left with them—an inevitable necessity. Congress could do no more, no less, no other way. The constitution belonged to the people of Kansas. Congress could not withhold it from them a moment, nor could it make them organize under it, assemble their Legislature, assume the position of a State, and send Senators and Representatives to Congress against their own will. Can Congress coerce a State into the Union? Then Congress can coerce a State to remain in the Union, or drive a State out of it. Congress is omnipotent. But where are, then, the rights of the States? Fortunately for us, the Constitution of every State and of every Territory asking to be a State, is not only virtually but actually in the hands of its people at all times and under all circumstances, and they cannot be divested of that control without the utter destruction of the Federal Constitution and an entire revolution. The whole power of Congress in the premises is exhausted when it accepts the Constitution without condition.

There are some who go still further, and assert that, although there might be no way to avoid a submission of the Lecompton Constitution to the control of the people of Kansas, yet that the conference bill was a compromise of principle, inasmuch as it specifically required them to act, and it made for them the definite opportunity to defeat the constitution as well as the ordinance. Now this is true as a fact, yet the inference is absurd upon its very face. If Congress could not take the Lecompton Constitution out of the hands of the people of Kansas, what difference did it make whether they voted on the ordinance in August, under the direction of Congress, or any other time, whether fixed by Congress or themselves? August was agreed upon, because it was very well to set a time and let things end. But from August to August, again and forever, this constitution was in the hands of the people of Kansas, and they could do with it what they pleased.

True, Congress might have avoided that specific occasion and August vote by swallowing the land ordinance and all, and asking no security for the remainder of the public lands; but Kansas could still have refused to organize as a State, and no power under our Constitution could have interfered. It is all words, and nothing more. Congress was charged with bribing Kansas to become a slave State. But the bribe was by the conference bill, four millions of acres of land instead of twenty-three millions. If we had given her the whole twenty-three millions for her useless slavery clause, there might have been some ground for the charge. Yet it would have been of no avail, for Kansas could, under no bribe or coercion known to our Government, have been compelled to accept the constitution or ordinance, or become a State against her own will at any period whatever. I will not presume that any one is less proficient in Constitutional lore, or is less conversant with the history of Congressional proceedings in the admission of new States than myself. But I will say that I am incapable of comprehending them at all if in this conference bill there was any "compromise" of southern principle or interests, any concession whatever by the South, any departure from the strictest construction of the Constitution, or any material deviation from the usual practice of the Government.

The people of Kansas have, by an overwhelming majority, rejected the land ordinance as modified by Congress, and refused to come into the Union on such terms. Be it so. It is what I expected—what I rather desired. It sorts precisely with what I felt when I saw Kansas thrust herself into Congress and demand—reeking with blood and fraud—to be enrolled among the States. Let her stay out. I am opposed to her coming in before she has the requisite population; not because she will be a free State, but because I fully approved of the prohibitory clause of the conference bill, and for that reason voted against the admission of Oregon. Unless in exceptional cases, such as that of Kansas was last winter, I do not think that a State should be admitted with less population than would entitle her to a member of the House. It is not just to the other States, and is not consonant with the theory of our government.

But I will not detain you longer with what belongs to the past. The present and the future are what concerns us most. You desire to know my opinion of the course the South should pursue under existing circumstances. I will give you frankly and fully the results of my observation and reflection on this all-important point.

The first question is, do the people of the South consider the present union of these States as an evil in itself, and a thing that it is desirable we should get rid of under all circumstances? There are some, I know, who do. But I am satisfied that an overwhelming majority of the South would, if assured that this government was hereafter to be conducted on the true principles and construction of the Constitution, decidedly prefer to remain in the Union, rather than incur the unknown costs and hazards of setting up a separate government. I think I state what is true when I say that, after all the bitterness that has characterized our long warfare, the great body of the southern people do not seek disunion, and will not seek it as a primary object, however promptly they may accept it as an alternative, rather than submit to unconstitutional abridgments of their rights. I confess that, for many years of my life, I believed that our only safety was the dissolution of the Union, and I openly avowed it. I should entertain, and without hesitation express the same sentiments now, but that the victories we have achieved and those that I think we are about to achieve, have inspired me with the hope, I may say the belief, that we can fully sustain ourselves in the Union and control its action in all great affairs. It may well be asked how I can entertain such views and expectations, when within these few years the South has lost her equality in the Senate, and the free States have at length a decided majority in both Houses of Congress, while this unfortunate Kansas contest has swept into their political graves so many of our ancient friends in those States, that it may be doubted whether they have at this moment, after the recent elections—the finale of the disastrous Kansas abortion—a majority in a single one of them; and there seems to be at present no prospect of our extending the area of slavery in any quarter.

These facts are true, and if you will bear with me I will place them all in the strongest light I can before you—for it is of the utmost importance that we should at least see clearly how we stand, and what are our resources, in order to form an idea of what we can do, and how to avoid wasting our strength on what cannot be accomplished. The equality of the free and slave States has long been lost in the House; by the admission of California it was lost in the Senate. Since then another free State has been admitted, and another yet has passed the Senate, and in a few years more we shall have Kansas, Nebraska, Washington, New Mexico, and perhaps others, on our roll. The emigration from Europe to the North, is sufficient to form one or more new States every year. To the South there is literally no emigration. We have, since the closing of the slave trade, added to our population mainly by the natural increase of our people, and we have no surplus population, white or black, to colonize new States. We lost Kansas partly by our inability to colonize it, and we are perhaps yet to have a struggle for a portion of Texas. The idea then of recovering the equality of the two sections, even in the Senate, seems remote indeed. We have it proposed to re-open the African slave trade, and bring in hordes of slaves from that prolific region to restore the balance. I once entertained that idea myself, but on further investigation I abandoned it. I will not now go into the discussion of it, further than to say that the South is itself divided on that policy, and, from appearances, opposed to it by a vast majority, while the North is unanimously against it. It would be impossible to get Congress to re-open the trade. If it could be done then it would be unnecessary, for that result could only be brought about by such an entire abandonment by the North and the world of all opposition to our slave system, that we might safely cease to erect any defences for it.

But if we could introduce slaves, where could we find suitable territory for new slave States? The Indian Reserve, west of Arkansas, might make one. But we have solemnly guaranteed that to the remnants of the red race. Everywhere else, I believe, the borders of our States have reached the great desert which separates the Atlantic from the Pacific States of this confederacy. No where is African slavery likely to flourish in the little oases of that Sahara of America. It is much more likely, I think, to go to the Pacific slope, and to the north in the great valley, than anywhere else outside of its present limits. Shall we, as some suggest, take Mexico and Central America to make slave States? African slavery appears to have failed there. Perhaps, and most probably, it will never succeed in those regions. If it might, what are we to do with the seven or eight millions of hardly semi-civilized Indians, and the two or three millions of Creole Spaniards and mongrels who now hold these countries? We would not enslave the Indians. Experience has proven that they are incapable of steady labor, and are therefore unfit for slavery. We would not exterminate them, even if that inhuman achievement would not cost ages of murder and incalculable sums of money. We could hardly think of attempting to plant the black race there, superior for labor as it is, though inferior perhaps in intellect, and expect to maintain a permanent and peaceful industry, such as slave labor must be, to be profitable, amid those idle, restless, demoralized children of Montezuma, scarcely more civilized, perhaps more sunk in superstition than in his age, and now trained to civil war by half a century of incessant revolution. What, I say, could we do with these people or these countries to add to Southern strength? Nothing. Could we degrade ourselves so far as to annex them on equal terms, they would be sure to come into this Union free States all. To touch them in any way is to be contaminated. England and

France, I have no doubt, would gladly see us take this burthen on our back, if we would secure for them their debts and a neutral route across the Isthmus. Such a route we must have for ourselves, and that is all we have to do with them. If we cannot get it by negotiation or purchase, we must seize and hold it by force of arms. The law of nations would justify it, and it is absolutely necessary for our Pacific relations. The present condition of those unhappy States is certainly deplorable, but the good God holds them in the hollow of his hand, and will work out their proper destinies.

We might expand the area of slavery by acquiring Cuba, where African slavery is already established. Mr. Calhoun, however, from whose matured opinions, whether on constitutional principles or southern policy, it will rarely be found safe to depart, said that Cuba was "forbidden fruit" to us, unless plucked in an exigency of war. There is no reasonable ground to suppose that we can acquire it in any other way; and the war that will open to us such an occasion will be great and general, and bring about results that the keenest intellect cannot now anticipate. But if we had Cuba, we could not make more than two or three slave States there, which would not restore the equilibrium of the North and South; while, with the African slave trade closed, and her only resort for slaves to this continent, she would, besides crushing out our whole sugar culture by her competition, afford in a few years a market for all the slaves in Missouri, Kentucky and Maryland. She is, notwithstanding the exorbitant taxes imposed on her, capable now of absorbing the annual increase of all the slaves on this continent, and consumes, it is said, twenty to thirty thousand a year by her system of labor. Slaves decrease there largely. In time, under the system practiced, every slave in America might be exterminated in Cuba, as were the Indians. However the idle African may procreate in the tropics, it yet remains to be proven, and the facts are against the conclusion that he can, in those regions, work and thrive. It is said Cuba is to be "Africanized" rather than the United States should take her. That threat, which, at one time was somewhat alarming, is no longer any cause of disquietude to the South. What have we lost by that? I think we reaped some benefit; and, if the slaves of Cuba were turned loose, a great sugar culture would grow up in Louisiana and Texas, rivalling that of cotton, and diverting from it so much labor that cotton would rarely fall below its present price.

You must not suppose, for a moment, that I am opposed to "the expansion of the area of African slavery." On the contrary, I believe that God created negroes for no other purpose than to be the "hewers of wood and drawers of water"—that is, to be the slaves of the white race; and I wish to see them in that capacity on every spot on the surface of the globe where their labor is necessary or beneficial. Nor do I doubt that such will be the final result. Much less would I oppose the acquisition of territory that would place the slave States on a numerical equality, and more, with the free States in the Union. But this review and scrutiny of the resources of the South shows, I think, pretty conclusively, that we have not now the surplus population, nor suitable territory, within our present reach, to create any number of slave States; that to attempt it by costly, yet impracticable and abortive, enterprises, will be to waste our strength to no purpose; and that the idea of recovering the equality in voting of the slave and free States, whether on the floors of Congress or elsewhere, is vis'onary. We had better, then, I think, at once make up our minds, according to the facts, and giving up all bootless efforts, look every consequence of our position full in the face. For one, I can do so without dismay—without the slightest trepidation. Why, the South, numbering twelve millions of people, possesses already an imperial domain that can well support an hundred millions more. What does she need to seek beyond her borders, or what has she to fear? With such a sea-coast and harbors; such rivers, mountains and plains; so full of all the precious metals, so fertile in soil, so genial in climate, producing in such unparalleled abundance the most valuable agricultural staples of the world; capable of manufacturing to any extent; and possessing the best social and industrial systems that have ever yet been organized—she might have sunk into sloth from excess of prosperity had she not been kept on the alert by the fierce assaults of an envious world. Assaults which, at one time alarming, it has been in fact scarcely more than wholesome exercise to repel; an exercise which has made us the most virtuous and one of the most enlightened and most powerful people who now flourish on the globe. The South has long been undervaluing and doing great injustice to herself. She has been lamenting her weakness, and croaking about the dangers that beset her, when she might glory in her strength and hurl defiance to her enemies.

But it is said that with a fixed and overwhelming free State majority against us in this Union, we must, in spite of all our natural advantages, dissolve the connection to insure our present safety and accomplish our proper destiny. Perhaps so. But permit me to suggest, not yet. The dissolution of the Union is an alternative that we have always at command, and for which we should be ever ready; but a peaceful, prosperous and powerful people may not challenge Fate a day too soon. The question still remains, can the free States be brought to concur permanently in any line of policy that will subvert the Constitution, and seriously damage the South in this confederacy? I do not believe that they can. Reckless as is political ambition, and insane as fanaticism ever is, I have no idea that the free States can be consolidated on the wild project of ruling the slaveholders by mere brute numbers, either through the ballot-box or by force of arms; whether to emancipate our slaves, or strip us of the fruits of their labor; or to govern us with the mildness and paternal care due to inferiors. The nervous in the South, and the abolition demagogues of the North, may believe it. But when it comes to the actual test, if neither sober sense nor patriotism should prevail, the sense of danger and the love of cotton and tobacco would, with our northern brethren, in every crisis over-ride their love of negroes. On this I think you may depend, despite the insolent boasts of the abolitionists of what they will do when they get the government in their hands. The North has only to be made clearly sensible how far she can go, and what the South will not submit to. She will not trespass beyond that, but will content herself with the glory of carrying the alternate biennial elections, as she has just done—always leaving it to the democracy to carry that which makes the President.

But I am making mere assertions. Allow me, then, to refer to facts to show the past power of the South in this Union, and the present state of the great questions in which she is most deeply interested. When, thirty years ago, we began this arduous conflict for the constitutional reform of this government and the security of the South, the South herself was thoroughly divided. The tariff, the bank, the internal improvement system, nay, even abolition itself, all had the sanction of a large number of our most prominent Southern men. If they did not all originate, they were all resuscitated, in that era of infatuation, when a southern President proclaimed that we were "all federalists, all republicans;" when Southern Statesmen sneered at State rights, and the Constitution became for the time a dead letter.

The tariff of 1828 levied average duties of more than forty per cent. on all of our imports. By the tariff of 1857 the average of duties was reduced below twenty per cent. We have accomplished that much; and, besides, the principle of free trade is pretty generally conceded now throughout the Union. It cannot be denied that this is a great success. I think the duties should be reduced still lower; and particularly that the discriminations against the agricultural interests should be abolished. But it is supposed that there will be a demand for their increase at the next session. If so, it will of course be resisted, and I trust successfully. Free trade is the test, the touchstone of free government, as monopoly is of despotism. I have no hesitation in saying that the plantation States should discard any government that made a protective tariff its policy. They should not submit to pay tribute for the support of any other industrial system than their own, much less to make good the bubble speculations of another section of the Union. Unequal taxation is, after all, what we have most to fear in this Union, and against that we must be always ready to adopt the most decisive measures.

The internal improvement system was in full vigor in 1828. Inaugurated also by southern men, it absorbed all the surplus of the treasury, and being in its nature unlimited, it was capable of absorbing all the revenue that could be extorted by the highest possible tariff. That too, if not destroyed, has been checked and crippled by southern action. It is true that it still appears annually in Congress—but the once haughty brigand is now little more than a sturdy beggar.

We had then, also, in full operation, a Bank of the United States, with branches in all our principal cities. It received and speculated on all the revenues of the government, and controlled and concentrated in the North all the exchanges, thus levying a per centage upon every commercial transaction of the South. That has been annihilated. It sleeps the sleep that knows no waking. But let me say that the system which it established still exists. Despite of its destruction by the Federal Government and the collection of the revenue in specie, our exchanges still centre in the North, and our otherwise stable industry is still compelled to participate more or less in all the reckless speculations of that fanatical section—more fanatical in its love of money than even in its devotion to negroes. But this is a self-imposed vassalage. Through the privileges which our southern legislatures have granted to our innumerable banks, we are made tributary to New York, which is itself tributary to London, the great world centre of exchanges in our age. Thus, by our own acts, we pay double tribute, though nearly all the trade of the United States with England is based on southern products.

Thus has the South, by her energy and ability, disposed of the capital grievances against which she protested—with almost half her public men against her—in 1828. During this time our opponents have twice wrested the government from us, and inflicted other injuries, but they were soon stripped of their power and their acts repealed. Only four times since the organization of this government has the North had possession of it, and in each case only for one term. The North has never united long on any policy. The injuries inflicted on the South have been mainly inflicted by her own ambitious, factious and divided public men, and our history proves that no man and no measure has yet been strong enough to stand against the South when united. I believe none ever will.

But it is thought that the abolitionists will inevitably get the power of this government permanently into their hands, and, backed by the opinion of the world, use it for our destruction. Let us consider the facts. From the time that the wise and good Las Casas first introduced into America the institution of African slavery—I say institution, because it is the oldest that exists, and will, I believe, survive all others that flourish—it has had its enemies. For a long while they were chiefly men of peculiar and eccentric religious notions. Their first practical and political success arose from the convulsions of the French Revolution, which lost to that empire its best colony. Next came the prohibition of the slave trade—the excitement of the Missouri Compromise in this country, and the then deliberate emancipation of the slaves in their colonies by the British government in 1833-4. About the time of the passage of that act, the abolition agitation was revived again in this country, and abolition societies were formed. I remember the time well, and some of you do also. And what then was the state of opinion in the South? Washington had emancipated his slaves. Jefferson had bitterly denounced the system, and had done all he could to destroy it. Our Clays, Marshalls, Crawfords, and many other prominent southern men, had led off in the colonization scheme. The inevitable effect in the South was, that she believed slavery to be an evil—weakness—disgraceful—nay, a sin. She shrank from the discussion of it. She cowered under every threat. She attempted to apologize, to excuse herself, under the plea—which was true—that England had forced it on her; and in fear and trembling she awaited a doom that she deemed inevitable.

But a few bold spirits took the question up; they compelled the South to investigate it anew and thoroughly, and what is the result? Why, it would be difficult now to find a southern man who feels the system to be the slightest burthen on his conscience; who does not, in fact, regard it as an equal advantage to the master and the slave, elevating both; as wealth, strength and power; and as one of the main pillars and controlling influences of modern civilization; and who is not now prepared to maintain it at every hazard. Such have been for us the happy results of this abolition discussion. So far, our gain has been immense from this contest, savage and malignant as it has been. Nay, we have solved already the question of emancipation by this re-examination and explosion of the false theories of religion, philanthropy and political economy which embarrassed our fathers in their day. With our convictions and our strength, emancipation here is simply an impossibility to man, whether by persuasion, purchase or coercion. The rock of Gibraltar does not stand so firm on its base as our slave system. For a quarter of a century it has borne the brunt of a hurricane as fierce and pitiless as ever raged. At the North and in Europe they cried "havoc," and let loose upon us all the dogs of war. And how stands it now? Why, in this identical quarter of a century our slaves have doubled in numbers, and each slave has more than doubled in value. The very negro who, as a prime laborer, would have brought four hundred dollars in 1828, would now, with thirty more years upon him, sell for eight hundred dollars. What does all this mean? Why, that for ourselves we have settled this question of emancipation against all the world, in theory and practice, and the world must accept our solution. The only inquiry is, how long this new found superstition will survive, and how far it may carry its votaries elsewhere? What changes in production, in commerce, society or government, it may effect? For production, commerce, society and government, must yield and change whenever they come in contact with the great fundamental principle of the subordination of the inferior to the superior man—as made by God; and especially of the colored to the white races. It is, I say, only through the evils that this superstition may bring upon other peoples, and especially on those of the North and of Europe, with whom we are so closely connected, that the South can be materially damaged by it, standing as she now does, firm, assured, united. How, then, is it with others?

Permit me to say that, in my opinion, the tide of abolition fanaticism has begun to ebb everywhere, and will never rise again. When the English freed the negroes in their colonies, it was not wholly a sentimental movement, dictated by political radicals and the saints of Exeter Hall. Her statesmen, in their ignorance, thought that what was called free labor— that is, "wages slavery"—would succeed in tropical culture as well or better than slave labor. In their arrogance they believed also that all the world must follow their example in this silly scheme of abolition; and that from her great wealth and world-encircling colonies, the monopoly of cotton and sugar culture would fall into the hands of England. Nature, and the indomitable spirit and intellect of the South, have disappointed all their calculations. The South still flourishes, and cotton and sugar, and coffee and rice and tobacco, are still the heritage of the slaveholders.

Galled by their utter dependence upon us for cotton, without the free use of which they would both tumble into ruin in a day, England, and France, who, in her frequent frenzies, at length destroyed all her colonies by emancipation, have ransacked the universe to find climes and soils adapted to the cheap growth of this great staple. They have failed everywhere. It is not that the soils and climates do not exist; but that this and the other great agricultural staples, sugar, rice, tobacco, coffee, can never be produced as articles of wide extended commerce, except by slave labor. This they at length found out. But such labor they had repudiated everywhere. No, not everywhere. Not in France nor in Great Britain, where they still hold as sacred splendid thrones and palmy aristocracies amid starving laborers. Only for outside barbarians they ordained freedom and equality. But failing in all their schemes, and finding that, with all their costly expenditures and high sounding manifestoes, they had simply ruined their own colonies, and made themselves the vassals of the slaveholders, what have they done? Why, renewed the slave trade. Not in name. Oh, no! Exeter Hall and the Parliament Houses still thunder execrations against that; while the colonists, under governmental protection, and with English money, wrung by taxation from her "wages slaves," are importing by hundreds of thousands Chinese and Hindoo Coolies, under conditions compared with which the Algerine slavery of the last century was merciful. They do not hold and support them as we do our slaves, for better, for worse, in sickness and health, in childhood and old age. No; in their prime of life they seduce them from their homes, transport them to distant and unwholesome climes; for the merest pittance of wages, consume their best years in the severest labors, and then turn them out to die—the direst slavery that brutal man has ever instituted. France, less sensitive—having no Exeter Hall—embracing the same scheme, resorts to Africa, and openly makes purchases, for so they may be called, from slave catchers; nay, she buys from the President of Liberia, the far-famed settlement of our own Colonization Society; buys the colonists, our own emancipated slaves, who, sick of freedom, prefer any form of slavery, and in their desperation do not hesitate to make their pious patrons in this country the laughing-stock of the whole world.

Thus these two nations—France and England, whose adoption of this abolition crotchet alone made it respectable and influential—have thoroughly renounced it, practically, and almost in theory. The press of England, perhaps the greatest power of the world, sustains these movements; while in France the newspapers are openly discussing the question of importing negro slaves, by name, in Algeria. I think it may be fairly said that in Europe abolition has run its course. Brougham, Palmerston, Russell, and all the old political agitators, are hanging their harps upon the willows. Even the son of Wilberforce, the Fanatic, approves of coolie slavery, which we abhor. But recently the British government openly surrendered its claim to the right of search—a claim set up mainly to put down the African slave trade, and without which all attempts to do it by force will probably be idle. And there is nothing to surprise us in all this, if we are correct in our views of African slavery. If it be sustained by the religion of the Bible; if neither humanity nor sound philosophy oppose it; if, as we are convinced, it is a social, political, and economical benefit to the world, then it was inevitable that, sooner or later, the abolition crusade must die out—and why not now?

If there is truth in what I have stated to you—if the abolition fever has nearly or quite exhausted itself in Europe—if time and facts have proved there, that it is an absurdity—it seems to me we should not doubt that its career is about to close here. Such is my opinion, however differently those may think who judge only by appearances, or take their cues from agitating politicians. I ask any one to tell me upon what measure or upon what man the abolitionists of this country can ever again muster their legions as they did in 1856? Kansas is squeezed dry. It stinks in the nostrils of all people. They can do no more there. Will they attempt a "cry" against the Supreme Court for the Dred Scott decision? What is there in that to inflame popular sentiment? It is always uphill business to agitate against a judiciary, but especially against the Supreme Court of the United States, which the northern people have been taught to revere as the bulwark of their liberties. Will they demand the abolition of slavery in the District of Columbia? They have never been able to do much with that, though they have often tried. That issue is a little too practical and too dangerous. Not many are bold enough to embark in it. They might as well make the question of disunion nakedly. Will they take up the abstract, and, probably, never again to be other than abstract, proposition of "no more slave States?" They have done that. They have already split upon it. The northwest will not take it, and the free States, at bottom, all want Cuba. They love molasses, and hanker after free trade with that rich island. Where, then, are they to go? I cannot see. They do not appear to see themselves. Will any one state the practical question, if we offer them none,—and we have none to offer,—on which they are next to rally for the conquest of the South? The measure or the man? It does seem to me that this great fire is dying out from want of fuel. That this crusade, as many crusades before, has exhausted itself, and that there is no argument or leader that can keep it alive. They have had their Peter Hermits, but their Godfreys, their Baldwins, their lion-hearted Richards, where are they? It seems that they will scarcely agree even on their Louis IX., who shall lead their last pious campaign and enjoy martyrdom.

And let me say that if the abolitionists cannot unite the free States as a purely anti-slavery party in the presidential election of 1860, and fail again in 1864, we shall never hear more of them as a political party; and it is only as a political party that they are worthy of our notice. There always will be abolitionists—for fools, enthusiasts, men of morbid imaginations, bent on mischief or ambitious of notoriety, always will exist. But the abolition party in the free States is now almost wholly political. Do you suppose that the Sewards, Hales, Wades, Wilsons, Chases, and their associates, care anything for African slavery, or are really hostile to our system of labor, any more than is the President, Dickinson, Bright, Pugh, or Douglas? I do not. Their object is political power. They have placed themselves on this spring-tide of fanaticism to obtain it. If it fails them—if, at the next presidential election, assuredly if at the two next —we beat them, all this party machinery will fall to the ground, and the Smiths, Tappans, Garrisons, and Parkers, will be left alone to their glory.

But if I am all wrong—if my facts and reasonings are false, and my hopes delusive—if, in 1860, they beat us—what then? These are questions that may well be asked. And the answer is obvious. We must be prepared; and the very efforts we must make to prevent such results will better prepare us than any course we can pursue that I can see. We must be prepared, I say, to take care of ourselves, whatever may come. It is clear that the slaveholding States of this confederacy, whatever hazards they may choose to incur by remaining in alliance with a majority of non-slaveholders now so inflamed against them, must ever and at all times hold, under God, their destinies in their own hands. They can never permit any foreign or hostile power to legislate in reference to their peculiar industrial system, whether to abolish or modify, or impose undue burdens on it. Such legislation must be resisted with all our means, and without regard to any consequences. If it should so happen that the free States of this Union, being now, and always to be, in a majority, do establish a political line between the two sections, and the two systems of labor, legislate upon it and maintain it, then they will constitute a power as foreign to us as any nation in the world, and we cannot submit to it. Whatever the weak and defenceless colonies of other countries may have submitted to, before these southern States will be placed in the condition of St. Domingo or Jamaica, or one at all approximating to it, they will rend this Union into fragments and plunge the world in ruin. It is in their power to do both, for the world cannot get on without them; and, if ruthless fanaticism and brute force combine, under whatever names, and with whatever authority, to ride them down, they will carry with them the pillars of the temple of civilization, and force a common fate on all mankind.

There are many who believe that some such catastrophe is inevitable. It cannot be denied that from appearances here and elsewhere, that it is entirely possible, and it may not be unwise for all of us to suppose it probable. Although I think that the ranks of our enemies are broken and the moral victory won, I am far from proclaiming that the battle is over, and that we have now only to gather the fruits of our success. Many a battle has been won and lost again, by overweening confidence, by reckless pursuit, or by turning aside for the sake of spoil. Let us fall into none of these errors, for we are still in the very heat and turmoil of this great conflict, and all may yet be lost. What I wish to impress upon you is that there is hope for effort—triumph for union, energy and perseverance.

It has fallen upon the slaveholders of the South to conduct this question of African slavery to its final conclusion. Such is our fate. It is inevitable. Let us cheerfully accept and manfully perform our destined parts, and do it with no distrust of God; with no misgivings of our cause or of ourselves; with no panic; no foolish attempt to fly from dangers which cannot be avoided, which have not been proven to be insurmountable, and which I for one believe that we can conquer. After what has been achieved by a divided South, now that it is almost thoroughly united —now that we have a President and his Cabinet—a majority in both Houses of Congress—a Supreme Court of the United States, and still hosts of allies in the free States, all substantially concuring with us in our construction of the Constitution, and under its obligations earnestly battling with us for the maintenance of our rights and interests; we owe it to our country, to ourselves, to the world and to posterity, to cast aside all weak fears—all petty or impracticable issues—all mere wrangling and vituperation, personal and sectional, and move forward with the dignity of conscious strength and the calmness of undoubted courage, to the overthrow of every false theory of government, and every sentimental scheme for organizing labor; carrying with us the Constitution of our fathers, and if we can, their Union.

But the slave States constituting, and as I think forever to constitute, a numerical minority, can however accomplish nothing in this Union, without the aid of faithful allies in the free States. It has been of late too much the habit in the South to mistrust all such allies—to disparage, to denounce, and drive them from us. Nothing could be more unwise or more unjust. It is distrusting the truth and justice of our own cause, or calumniating human nature, to doubt that there are in the free States thousands of sound-thinking, true-hearted and gallant men, who concur essentially in our views, and are ready to make common cause with us. Nay, it is falsifying history and fact. During the late session I saw men acting cordially and vigorously with us against the positive instructions of their excited constituents, at the hazard of political martyrdom; and in two instances, that martyrdom was consummated before the adjournment. Shall we do no honor to such men? Shall we pay no tribute to such heroic devotion to truth, to justice, and the Constitution? Shall we revile them in common with all northern men, because many revile and some have betrayed us? To be truly great, we must be not only just, but generous and forbearing with all mankind. Let us place ourselves in the situation of northern public men in this great contest, consider their dangers and responsibilities, and making every allowance for human weakness, do homage to the brave and faithful.

And this leads me to say that, having never been a mere party politician, intriguing and wire-pulling to advance myself or others, I am not learned in the rubric of the thousand slang, unmeaning, and usually false party names to which our age gives birth. But I have been given to understand that there are to be two parties in the South, called "National" and "State Rights Democrats." The word "national" having been carefully excluded from the Constitution by those who framed it, I never supposed it applicable to any principle or policy of our government, and having been surrendered to the almost exclusive use, in this country, of the federal consolidationists, I have ever myself repudiated it. But if a southern "National Democrat" means one who is ready to welcome into our ranks with open arms, and cordially embrace and promote according to his merits every honest free State man who reads the Constitution as we do, and will coöperate with us in its maintenance, then I belong to that party, call it as you may, and I should grieve to find a southern man who did not.

But, on the other hand, having been all my life, and being still, an ardent "State rights" man—believing "State rights" to be an essential, nay, the essential element of the Constitution, and that no one who thinks otherwise can stand on the same constitutional platform that I do, it seems to me that I am, and all those with whom I act habitually, are, if democrats at all, true " State rights democrats." Nothing in public affairs so perplexes and annoys me as these absurd party names, and I never could be interested in them. I could easily comprehend two great parties, standing on the two great antagonistic principles which are inherent in all things human: the right and the wrong, the good and the evil, according to the peculiar views of each individual, and was never at a loss to find my side, as now, in what are known as the democratic and republican parties of this country. But the minor distinctions have, for the most part, seemed to me to be factitious and factious, gotten up by cunning men for selfish purposes, to which the true patriot and honest man should be slow to lend himself. For myself, and for you while I represent you, I shall go for the Constitution strictly construed and faithfully carried out. I will make my fight, such as it may be, by the side of any man, whether from the North, South, East, or West, who will do the same, and I will do homage to his virtue, his ability, his courage, and—so far as I can—make just compensation for his toils and hazards, and sacrifices. As to the precise mode and manner of conducting this contest, that must necessarily, to a great extent, depend upon the exigencies that arise; but of course I could be compelled, by no exigency, by no party ties or arrangements, to give up my principles, or the least of those principles which constitute our great cause.

If the South has any desire to remain in the

Union, and control it, as her safety requires that she should, in some essential particulars, if she does remain in it, she must conciliate her northern allies. She must be just, kind and true to all who are true to truth and to her. But if she determines, and whenever she determines, to throw off her northern friends and dissolve this Union, I need scarcely say that I shall, without hesitation, go with her fully and faithfully. I do not for a moment doubt that, in or out of this Union, she can sustain herself among the foremost nations of the earth. All that she requires is the union of her own people, and happily they never were at any former period so united and harmonious as now. A homogeneous people, with our social and industrial institutions the same everywhere, and all our great interests identical, we should always have been united in our moral and political opinions and policy. The ambitious dissensions of the host of brilliant men whose names adorn our annals, have heretofore kept us apart. The abolitionists have, at length, forced upon us a knowledge of our true position, and compelled us into union—an union not for aggression, but for defence; purely conservative of the Constitution and the constitutional rights of every section and of every man. The union of these States, from the Canadas to the Rio Grande, and from shore to shore of the two great oceans of the globe, whatever splendor may encircle it, is but a policy and not a principle. It is subordinate to rights and interests. But the union of the slaveholders of the South is a principle involving all our rights and all our interests. Let that union be perfect and perpetual. It constitutes our strength, our safety and prosperity. Let us frown down every proposition that might seriously divide us, and present to our assailants from every quarter a solid and impregnable phalanx. Let us also give to the winds every thought of fear, every feeling of despondency, and fully comprehending, and temperately but resolutely asserting our great power in this confederacy and throughout the world, let us develop and consolidate our resources, and devote ourselves manfully and hopefully to the accomplishment of the magnificent future that is within our reach.

SPEECH

ON THE RELATIONS OF THE STATES, DELIVERED IN THE SENATE OF
THE UNITED STATES, MAY 21, 1860.

The Senate having under consideration the resolutions submitted by Mr. Davis on the 1st of March, relative to the relations of the States, and the rights of persons and property in the Territories, and the duty of protecting slave property in the Territories, when a necessity for so doing shall exist—Mr. Hammond said:

MR. PRESIDENT: I feel reluctant to trespass on the time of the Senate, and to follow up with a dry constitutional argument the able, eloquent, and stirring speech of the Senator from Georgia; but I have a few words to say, and may as well go on this afternoon.

If I understand it aright, the precise question before the Senate is simply this: Have the territorial governments established by Congress, the power to define and declare what shall be and what shall not be property within the territorial boundaries? Those who advocate the resolution offered by the Senator from Mississippi, deny that the Territories have such power. Those who oppose the resolutions maintain that they have. Both parties will agree, of course, that the power to define and declare what is property is supreme, and uncontrollable; in short, what we call sovereign. Certainly no other power can do it; since, in that case, the really supreme power could at once reverse any such declaration, and without a proper definition of property agreed upon by the controlling power of a Government, there could be no civil Government at all; for civilized government, however far it may reach, is organized property, and never has existed, and never can exist long without defining by law or established usage what is property.

We have no history of the origin of human association and political government that affords us any full or clear account. The Bible and other ancient books give us hints, which suggest thoughts, that enable us to form such conceptions of these matters, which are, perhaps, sufficient for all our practical purposes. A roving family, grown into a tribe, finding pleasant waters, fine soil, and sweet air, that have not been appropriated, arrests its wanderings, drives down its stakes, claims this delightful region as its own, constitutes it property, and, dividing it out, organizes a government, and, by the right of eminent domain, of usage, and its physical power, establishes a sovereignty. That sovereignty is good so long as it can be maintained against all assaults. If it sustains itself, in time it grows great; it becomes over-populous; it sends out emissaries to discover other similarly-endowed lands; it obtains them by first discovery, by purchase, or by conquest; it colonizes them with its surplus population, but, holding the eminent domain, it holds its colonies in strict subordination to its own will, and maintains sovereignty over them. The colonies also grow. In time they demand sovereignty for themselves.

It is wisely conceded, or by a successful rebellion, it is conquered by the colonies, and each becomes sovereign. Such, I take it, has been the almost unvarying history of the origin and progress of human association and political organization.

Thus the thirteen colonies, which became the United States of America in 1787, were planted long previously by Great Britain. In 1776, they severally proclaimed themselves to be sovereign and independent States. Great Britain refused to concede to their demands; but after a long and bloody war, they achieved their independence, and were acknowledged as sovereign States.

When the present constitutional Union was established, many States were entitled, by charters and grants from the former mother country, to large areas of territory still wild and unpeopled. These they all surrendered to the new General Government, for the purpose, mainly, of creating a fund to pay off the war debt of the Revolution. Subsequently we have acquired by purchase, Louisiana and Florida; by annexation, Texas; and by conquest and purchase our Pacific coast. To every one of these large acquisitions, every inch of which, Texas excepted, became the common property of each and all of the States—of whom the General Government was the trustee—large numbers of our citizens flocked, seeking to better their fortunes, not only unrestrained, but very rightly encouraged, by this Government. By the Constitution of the United States, Congress was empowered "to dispose of and make all needful rules and regulations respecting the territory and other property of the United States." This was a very vague and indefinite grant of power; but it was, by unanimous consent, construed to mean that Congress might establish a suitable provisional government for each Territory as soon as the number of inhabitants required that law and order should be enforced, and the property of the United States, as well as peace and justice, preserved there, by the intervention of the Federal Government. It was considered a "needful regulation," and nothing more.

Yet these adventurers, few or more, squatting on land they do not own, but which belongs to all the States, and of which they do not squat on more than a small portion within the limits assigned them, are those, into whose hands the opponents of these resolutions demand that *sovereignty* throughout their whole border shall be surrendered. Why, they are but voluntary exiles who have been allowed to seek homes in a wilderness not discovered, purchased, or conquered by them, but still the property of the States, whereon these tenants by sufferance, in their yet unfinished term of social infancy and political pupilage, the great agent of the States has kindly undertaken to protect; giving them judges, Governors, and a sort of Legislature—all subject, however, to be withdrawn at any moment—and the whole system supported from the Treasury of the States. Yet it is said that such Territories are sovereignties, and such people sovereigns, and that such an organization can assume the high and sovereign function of defining and declaring what is and what is not property, and thereby forbid a large proportion of the citizens of the States, who really own the lands, from entering such Territories with their rightful property.

It is said here, by those who advocate this extraordinary doctrine, that adventurers going, for instance, to Pike's Peak, Nevada, or Arizona, and organizing for themselves provisional governments, without recognition from this government, would not be entitled to the rights of sovereigns. To this the Senator from Mississippi (Mr. Davis) very pointedly and justly answered, that perhaps they were the very people who, from the absolute necessity of the case, would be justified in exercising, for a time, sovereign power. And I will add, that if they could sustain themselves in their organization against all attacks, they would become permanently and rightfully sovereign. But that gangs of adventurers, intruding into a domain that belongs to others, squatting on its choicest lands, and when increased to such numbers that they can no longer keep the peace among themselves, petitioning then to the agent of the true owners of the soil, and receiving, at the owners' charge and cost, ample protection, should immediately thereafter proceed to exercise the high and supreme sovereign right of deciding what is and what is not property on that domain, and exercise it in a way to exclude the people of nearly half the States from their own Territory, is as monstrous as it is absurd. It is a proposition not merely anomalous in every feature, not only unknown to history, but utterly opposed to truth, to reason, to justice, to honor, and to common honesty. It is called "squatter sovereignty." The name describes it. It can never achieve a more respectable designation.

I have endeavored to show, rather by statement than by argument, that our territorial organizations—called governments by courtesy, but which really are only corporations, that may be dissolved at the will of the Federal Government—cannot declare what is property in the Territories, and are not sovereign. It is said, nevertheless, that they are sovereign, because of a certain natural and inherent right of any population organized under any form of government to regulate their own affairs. Nothing could be more vague, uncertain, metaphysical, and shadowy, than such a proposition as this. If any man has any natural or inherent rights—which I deny—regarding all the rights to which a being born so helpless as man, may attain, to be purely conventional, and such as other men allow him—I should suppose that those rights belong to him as an individual, rather than as a member of any social or political system. It seems to me clear that we must be born with whatever is natural or inherent to us, and that we can receive no accession of rights of that character from any social or political organization; but that, on the contrary, such rights, whatever they may be, must be in no small degree restrained and diminished by any organization formed for the good of the whole. Such, in fact, is the case. Individual rights—no individual pretensions, passions, and desires, mistaken for rights—are just what governments are instituted to control and regulate. But if any such natural or inherent rights could possibly exist, they are conceded when the settler on the public domain, asking the protection of this Government, agrees to be governed by such an organic law as Congress may offer him—which he does for the substantial consideration of protection. If he, by himself, or in conjunction with his fellow-settlers, had any such rights, they are entirely surrendered when they come under the Constitution and the laws of this Confederation. Their immediate local governments have no other foundation than the vague power of Congress to make "needful rules and regulations;" that such a population should set itself up as a sovereign people and such a corporation claim to exercise any sovereign power, especially the great central sovereign power of declaring what is property, is, I repeat it, with due deference, simply absurd, and would, I think, be agreed to by no human being of ordinary intelligence who was not misled by his passions, prejudices, or interests. Why, the Federal Government itself, save in one or two instances where the power has been specifically conferred on it, cannot declare what is or what is not property. That is a power reserved by the sovereign States, and by them alone can it be exercised; and it is by this reservation that they prove their sovereignty. What each State declares to be property, the General Government is bound, in all its departments, to regard as property, and protect as property; and so under the Constitution, every other State is bound to regard and protect it; and each and every State has a right to demand that, whatever it has, by its sovereign fiat, declared to be property, shall most fully be recognized and protected as such on the Territorial soil of which it is part owner.

But another great power has been granted to Congress which bears directly on this question. Though it can only make "needful rules and regulations for the territory," &c.,—you will note that the word is "territory," not *territories*—showing that the whole scope of the grant of power was to regulate property only—yet this Government, not sovereign itself, can, as it were, create a sovereign, by the expressly and constitutionally recorded will of the sovereign States. It is authorized to "admit new States." All "STATES" are sovereign. They can define and establish property, and your Territories, when they are admitted as States, may do it also. In this we all agree. And it seems to me very strange that the Territories, when a few short years will enable them to attain the high position of sovereign States in this Confederation, should wish to snatch at sovereignty before their time. It was not so of old. It can only be explained by referring to the progress of demagogueism in these degenerate days of the Republic, and to the insane desire to destroy one section of this Union. But this is beside the argument.

If the framers of the Constitution had supposed that in granting the power to the General Government "to dispose of, and make needful rules and regulations, respecting the territory and other property of the United States," they conferred the power to establish in such Territory political governments, endowed with the sovereign power to define what is and what is not property, then they would have stultified themselves by the additional grant of power to "admit new States." The Territories would be States at once, and with, perhaps, great advantage over the other States. The power "to make needful rules," &c., has from the first been stretched so far as to authorize each Territory to send a Delegate to the House of Representatives. What obstacle is there then, but the mere will of Congress, to a Territory sending one also to the Senate—nay, two—and to the House as many as the different political and other interests of the different sections of the Territory might be supposed to require? Thus it would have ample opportunity to attend to all its wants here, and share in all the honors of the Government except the very highest, while its government, in all its branches, would be carried on at the cost of the General Government, and its people would be protected by the arms of the United States. More than this: as the Federal Constitution does not authorize Congress to define property, if the definition given to it by each sovereign State is not to prevail in the Territories, then, if they can exclude or confiscate one kind of property, they can exclude or confiscate any kind of property. Thus the coal and iron of Pennsylvania, the cotton and woolen manufactures of New England, the grain and provisions of the Northwest, in short, the staples and manufactures, and even shipping of every section, might be declared not to be property in a Territory, and as the major includes the minor proposition, might be confiscated or heavily taxed. And if it be agreed that the Territories shall not be bound to consider as property what the sovereign States, or any one of them, declares to be property, then much less will the States themselves be bound to respect it; and that agreed on, this "more perfect Union" of these States will subside into a condition not at all better than that of the old Confederacy, if, in fact, half so good.

I will not pursue the subject farther. The Senate is weary of it, the country is weary of it, and I, myself, am so weary of it that I have not listened or read, when it was the topic, for months. I have presented it now briefly, and in only one point of view; and even that I do not fully carry out. I have said enough, and probably nothing not familiar to every one who has heard all that has been said here, which I have not. In every aspect of this new doctrine—and there are many I have not touched—it has appeared to me an illegitimate and dangerous excrescence on our republican system—the offspring of an unsound, morbid, and licentious spirit of mobocracy, well calculated, in fact, if successfully persisted in, sure—to destroy the genuine spirit of our political institutions—nay, to destroy the confederacy.

It was not my intention to have intruded upon the Senate any remarks upon the subject; but the Senator from Illinois, in his speech the other day, made some allusion to my State which I thought should be corrected. He asked not to be interrupted, and afterwards promised to make the correction in the report of his speech. I do not doubt that he has done so; but what he said has gone forth from the reporters, and cannot be fully corrected by any omission from his speech. On this account I felt bound to make the corrections myself; and could not refrain from saying something more.

When South Carolina voted for General Cass, in 1848, after his celebrated letter to Judge Nicholson, she put upon that letter the interpretation then universal in the South; she assumed him to mean, in what he said, that a Territory, when it came to frame a constitution, and ask admission as a State, might declare what should be property within its limits. South Carolina did not intend by her vote to sustain squatter sovereignty.

The compromise measures of 1760, which the Senator says contained this doctrine, had not a friend, so far as I know, in South Carolina. The proposition was that the State should secede in consequence of these very measures. The issue only made was whether the State should secede alone, or refuse to do so without the coöperation of one or more other States. Mr. Rhett, who took his seat in the Senate some months after the passage of those measures, led the party in favor of a separate secession of the State. He was defeated. Not by those in favor of the compromise act or of squatter sovereignty, which never had the slightest foothold in South Carolina, but by the coöperationists, who would not go out of the Union without some other State approving and sustaining.

The Kansas and Nebraska act, of which the Senator claims to be the author, and I believe was, met the approbation of South Carolina; but it was interpreted in the same way with the Nicholson letter. So far, therefore, as South Carolina has acted, she has not done the least thing to support these new doctrines in regard to sovereignty; and I think I can assure the Senator from Illinois she never will.

EXPLANATORY NOTES

REPORT AT A MEETING OF THE STATE RIGHTS AND FREE TRADE PARTY

7.15 "the two Judges": David Johnson (1782–1855) and John Belton O'Neall (1793–1863), two of the three members of the South Carolina Court of Appeals, had declared the "test oath" unconstitutional with William Harper dissenting. The Court of Appeals was abolished in 1835. In addition to his judicial offices O'Neall was an author and temperance advocate. Johnson was Governor of South Carolina during 1846–1848.

9.2 "O'Neale": A common misspelling of John Belton O'Neall's surname.

13.23 "the express reservation": The Tenth Amendment of the U.S. Constitution.

SPEECH ON THE JUSTICE OF RECEIVING ABOLITION PETITIONS

15.heading: This speech was delivered in the U.S. House of Representatives on February 1, 1836.

15.1 "Mr. Cushing": Caleb Cushing (1800–1879), at this time Representative from Massachusetts. He subsequently held numerous public offices as Whig, Democrat, and Republican, including U.S. Attorney General and Minister to China.

16.6 "concur in every principle which he laid down": In his speech on January 25 Cushing had deprecated abolitionism but defended the right of petition.

24.7 "P.M.": Postmaster.

29.3 "Dr. Channing has softened the asperity of his remarks": William Ellery Channing (1780–1842), Unitarian theologian, had in his work *Slavery* (1835) criticized abolitionists as

370   EXPLANATORY NOTES

"enthusiasts." In *The Abolitionists* (1837) he was more sympathetic to them.

29.4 "Thompson": George Thompson (1804–1878) was a British abolitionist who had toured the United States with William Lloyd Garrison during 1834–1835 and had been forced to flee from a mob in Boston.

30.6 "Mr. Granger and Mr. Lee": Francis Granger and Gideon Lee, Representatives from New York.

31.2 "Jay's Inquiry": William Jay, *An Inquiry into the Character and Tendency of the American Colonization, and American Antislavery Societies* (1835).

32.5 "it has been said by a distinguished Virginian": Remarks attributed to John Randolph of Roanoke.

32.26 "one serious insurrection": The Nat Turner revolt in Southampton County, Virginia, August, 1831.

36.23 "Mr. Adams": John Quincy Adams, the former President, was at this time a Representative from Massachusetts and was active in presenting abolitionist petitions to the House.

37.20 "unfortunate occurence (*sic*) at Southampton": See note 32.26.

40.10 "Toussaint, or Boyer": Toussaint L'Ouverture (1743–1803) and Jean Pierre Boyer (1773–1850) were black leaders on the island of Hispaniola.

44.10 "The hounds of Acteon": Actaeon, because he observed Artemis, goddess of the hunt, bathing, was turned into a stag and thereupon was torn to pieces by his own hunting dogs.

47.18 "They indicted Peltier": Jean Gabriel Peltier, a French emigré in London, called for the assassination of Napoleon in an article published in 1803. Suit was brought against Peltier in the British courts on initiative of the French ambassador.

48.4 "Tappan and Garrison": Arthur Tappan, William Lloyd Garrison, and Gerrit Smith were early abolitionists.

MESSAGE AS GOVERNOR, 1843

54.table "Benefit of Mrs. Randolph": In 1826 the South Carolina General Assembly had voted $10,000 in state bonds, payable in annual installments to 1850, for the relief of Martha Jefferson Randolph, daughter of Thomas Jefferson.

54.table "L.C. & C.R.R. Co.": The Louisville, Cincinnati, and Charleston Railroad Company, in which the state of South Carolina had invested heavily in the interest of establishing commercial links with the Ohio Valley.

55.16 "the funds of the State now committed to the management of the bank": The Bank of the State of South Carolina, usually

EXPLANATORY NOTES 371

called the State Bank, was a private corporation chartered in 1802. By a plan analogous of the arrangement between Congress and the second Bank of the United States, the South Carolina General Assembly subscribed part of the stock, elected one-fifth of the board of directors, and allowed the State Bank the exclusive privilege of holding deposits of state and city funds.

58.6 "the Governor's consent": Presumably Pierce Manning Butler, Governor of South Carolina during 1836–1838. He was subsequently killed in action commanding the Palmetto Regiment in the Mexican War. Butler and Hammond were joint owners of Argyle, one of the famous race horses of the day.

67.19 "amonnt": Misprint for "amount."

68.20 "my immediate predecessor": John P. Richardson, Governor of South Carolina during 1840–1842.

69.10 "the present incumbent": Robert Q. Pinckney, Secretary of State of South Carolina 1842–1846.

70.13 "compromises of the Constitution": Hammond refers to the balance of power between the Upcountry and Lowcountry established by the South Carolina constitution of 1790, as amended in 1808.

74.32 "1860": Misprint for "1680."

75.14 "Edmund Ruffin": Edmund Ruffin (1794–1865), agricultural experimenter and publicist, produced in 1843 his *Report of the Commencement and Progress of the Agricultural Survey of South Carolina.*

75.23 "the Act of 1840": This law penalized banks for any suspension of payment in hard money and required all banks to incorporate it as a part of their charters.

76.21 "the Bank of South Carolina": This institution should not be confused with the Bank of the State of South Carolina.

77.5 "English Minister for Foreign affairs": George Hamilton-Gordon, 4th Earl of Aberdeen, in the ministry of Sir Robert Peel.

MESSAGE AS GOVERNOR, 1844

83.30 "the President of that institution": Franklin Harper Elmore (1799–1850) was president of the Bank of the State of South Carolina during 1839–1850. He strongly defended that Bank against Hammond's efforts to curtail its involvement in state finances.

88.2 "efficient Adjutant General": James W. Cantey was Adjutant General of South Carolina 1841–1853.

93.3 "Mount Dearborn lands": Mount Dearborn, located in present Chester County, had been purchased by the federal government in 1802 as the site for a proposed arsenal. The arsenal was never constructed, and the land was reacquired by the state.

93.16 "M. Tuomey, Esq.": Michael Tuomey (1805–1857) produced a *Report on the Geological and Agricultural Survey of the State of South Carolina* (1844).

94.23 "the Compromise Act": The tariff law of 1833, passed by Congress as a part of the resolution of the nullification controversy, provided for step-by-step reduction in the rates of the tariff on imported goods.

97.17–19 "the Electors of President and Vice-President are chosen by the people, in all the Southern States except our own": According to the Constitution of the United States, presidential electors are to be selected in each state "in such manner as the Legislature thereof may direct." By 1844 South Carolina was the only state in which electors were still chosen by the legislature itself rather than by some form of popular vote.

99.26 "the female sovereign of a petty island at the antipodes": Queen Pomari of Tahiti was intimidated by a gunboat into accepting a French protectorate over her domain in 1842.

99.30 "kingdom on the Musquito shore": In 1840 the king of the Moskitos made a will naming a British official at Belize, Honduras, as regent of his territory.

101.17–18 "a pious Bishop of the South": James O. Andrews, Bishop of Georgia, was suspended by the General Conference of the Methodist Episcopal Church in 1844. In the aftermath of this incident the church split into northern and southern organizations.

102.1–2 "the organized Abolition vote might decide the pending Presidential election": This prediction was accurate. James G. Birney, presidential candidate of the Liberty Party, diverted sufficient votes from Henry Clay, the Whig candidate, in New York to give that state by plurality to James K. Polk, Democrat. Polk defeated Clay by the margin of the New York electoral votes. Thus, in effect, the Liberty Party held the balance in the national election and was able to penalize the Whigs for being insufficiently responsive.

LETTER TO THE FREE CHURCH OF GLASGOW

105.1 "Sir": The letter is addressed to "the Rev. Thomas Brown, D.D., Moderator of the Free Church of Glasgow, and to the Presbytery thereof," as is made clear on page 113.

EXPLANATORY NOTES 373

105.14 "Brown had no criminal design in what he did": Hammond may refer to the contemporary report that the slave that John L. Brown was convicted of aiding to escape was his mistress. Brown professed himself not to be an abolitionist.

108.23 "Middle Passage": In the international slave trade the voyage from West Africa to America (usually the West Indies) was called the Middle Passage because it fell between the slave ship's voyage from home port in Europe or New England to Africa, and the voyage from America, after sale of the slaves, to home port.

FIRST LETTER TO THOMAS CLARKSON

114.4 "your Circular Letter": Thomas Clarkson, *Letter to Such Professing Christians in the Northern States of America, as Have Had No Practical Concern with Slave-Holding . . .* (London: 1844).

116.11 "your pious King": An ironic reference to George III, who in 1807 gave assent to the Parliamentary act outlawing the slave trade in the British Empire.

116.22 "Mr. Grosvenor": Perhaps Richard Grosvenor, 1st Earl Grosvenor (1731–1802).

118.32 "Peter the Hermit": The itinerant preacher credited with instigating the First Crusade in 1095.

119.4 "tortious": Legally wrongful.

124.12 "1 Peter ii, 20": The verse reads, in the King James version: "For what glory is it, if, when ye be buffeted for your faults, ye shall take it patiently? but if when ye do well, and suffer for it, ye take it patiently, this is acceptable with God."

124.16 "Ex[odus] xxi, 6": The verse reads, in the King James version: "Then his master shall bring him unto the judges; he shall also bring him to the door; or unto the door post; and his master shall bore his ear through with an aul; and he shall serve him forever."

126.13 "Gov. M'Duffie": George McDuffie (1790–1851), Representative from S.C. 1821–1834, Governor 1834–1836, and Senator 1842–1846, was a passionate orator, strong opponent of the tariff, and ally and friend of John C. Calhoun.

129.14 "apprenticeship": An ironic reference to the apprenticeship system of labor for blacks which had been employed in the British colonies as a part of the emancipation program in 1833–1838. It was ostensibly a transitional phase from slavery to freedom.

129.27 "But so are our taxes": The U.S. Constitution provided that in determining representation in the House of Representatives and in apportioning direct taxes to the states, three-fifths of the slave population was to be counted.

133.8–9 "another has been recently elected . . . over an opponent who was a slave-holder also": James K. Polk of Tennessee defeated Henry Clay of Kentucky in the election of 1844.

134.15 "Millerism": An Adventist sect organized by William Miller in New York state had acquired a large following in the North. Miller's prediction of the second coming of Christ no later than March, 1844, had just recently failed to materialize.

134.17 "Shakers": A communal religious sect founded in England in 1770 by "Mother" Ann Lee, who emigrated to America in 1774. Shakers practiced celibacy and regarded God as an androgynous being.

134.17 "Rappists": A religious sect with mystical and communist doctrines which was transferred from Germany to Pennsylvania in 1803.

134.17 "Dunkers": A common name for the Church of the Brethren, a primitivist communal sect originating in Germany but established in Pennsylvania in the eighteenth century.

134.18 "Fourrierists": Charles Fourier (1772–1837) was a French utopian socialist who advocated the organization of society into communal bodies called "phylansteries." So organized, society would progress materially and spritually to perfection on earth.

134.19 "Puseyism": Edward Bouvier Pusey (1800–1882) was one of the initiators of the Oxford Movement, an attempt to revive sacramentalism in the Anglican Church. In 1843 Pusey had been tried for heresy and suspended from clerical offices for two years.

134.31 "Miss Martineau": Harriet Martineau (1802–1876), a British writer, had toured America during 1834–36. Her *Society in America* (1837) was notoriously harsh in criticism of Americans.

135.20 "Leo should be almost canonized": Apparently a reference to the Renaissance Pope Leo X, a worldly Medici.

136.18 "crim. con.": Crimonious conversation, i.e., adultery.

142.10–11 "Judge Stroud of Philadelphia": George McDowell Stroud (1795–1875), author of *Sketch of the Laws Relative to Slavery in the Several States* (1827).

143.14 "*Homo sum, humani nil a me alienum puto*": I am a man; all that touches mankind is my concern.

144.7 "Mr. Pitt": William Pitt, the younger (1759–1806), was converted to support for Parliamentary suppression of the slave trade.

EXPLANATORY NOTES   375

157.33 "atures": Misprint for "natures."
159.21 "Marquis of Normanby": Constantine H. Phipps, 1st Marquis (1797–1863), a leading Whig Parliamentarian.
164.10 "Thugs": Members of an Indian religious organization who robbed and murdered in the service of Kali, a god of destruction.
165.3 "One of your most illustrious Judges": William Scott, Lord Stowell (1745–1836).
166.20 "(Art. Ld. Dudley's Letters)": Hammond attributes the immediately preceding quotation to an article in the London Quarterly Review for 1840 concerning a book published that year: John William Ward, Earl of Dudley, Letters to the Bishop of Llandoff.
168.24 William Wilberforce (1759–1833), along with Clarkson among the best-known of the British abolitionists.
171.9 "Drummond Light": A limelight invented by Thomas Drummond (1797–1840), a British engineer, had been a scientific and popular sensation when first displayed in the 1820's.
172.12 "Mr. O'Connell": Daniel O'Connell (1775–1847), a leader of the Irish Catholic party in the British Parliament.

SECOND LETTER TO THOMAS CLARKSON

174.28 "Martineaus, Marryatts, Trollopes and Dickenses": Harriet Martineau, Frederick Marryat (sic), Mrs. Frances Trollope, and Charles Dickens were all English writers who had published unflattering travel accounts of the United States.
180.19 "lex talionis": The law of retaliation.
182.2 "as . . . the North British Review, has lately done": The article quoted, titled "The United States of America," appeared in the North British Review, vol. III, 1844. The sentiments reproduced by Hammond were ascribed to "the great mass of clergy in the Free States," who, while believing slavery inconsistent with natural rights and the general spirit of Christianity, did not believe that a crusade against "mere slave-holding" was justified.
182.7 "the Anti-Slavery Record": A monthly magazine published in New York by the American Anti-Slavery Society.
184.24–25 "With hideous ruin and combustion down . . .": Milton, Paradise Lost, I, 46.
188.10–13 "You are old. . . . You should be ruled and led by some discretion": Shakespeare, King Lear, II, iv.
188.16 "Mr. Macaulay": Thomas Babington Macaulay, British historian, essayist, and official.

189.13 "Hic niger est, hunc tu, Romane caveto": From Horace: That man is a knave, Roman, beware of him.
189.22 "Mormon murders": Antagonism between Mormon settlers at Nauvoo, Illinois, and non-Mormons led to riots in which the Mormon leader Joseph Smith and his brother were murdered in June, 1844.
189.22-23 "the Philadelphia riots": Anti-Catholic, anti-Irish rioting took place in May and again in July, 1844.
189.27 "the insurrection of Rebecca": A series of riots against toll roads in Wales which continued from 1839 to 1844, so called because rioters often disguised themselves in women's clothes.
189.28 "war in Scinde": The First Afghan War, 1839-1841, between Britain and the Moslem rulers of Afghanistan, which led to the conquest of the Sind (sic) region by Britain.
189.31-32 "late detected espionage": Sir James Robert Graham, British Home Secretary, had been exposed as having ordered the opening of private mail by postal authorities.
192.18 "recent Presidential election": See note 102.1-2.
194.26 "Mr. Burke": Edmund Burke (1729-1797), statesman active in mobilizing British opinion against the French Revolution.
194.27 "damnun nondum factum": The "damage not yet done" (but so certain as to warrant response).
195-196.note "M. Jollivet": Adolphe Jollivet (1799-1848) was a member of the French Chamber of Deputies for the West Indian island of Martinique and one of the leading spokesmen against emancipation in the French colonies. The question he put to England translates as: "Why has your philanthropy, up to now, not reached beyond the Cape of Good Hope?"
198.3 "George Fox": The founder of the English Quakers.
198.4 "Joanna Southcote": An English mystic and religious fanatic (1750-1814) who assumed the right to certify those who were to be saved in the next life.
198.4 "Joe Smith": Joseph Smith (1805-1855), founder of the Mormons.

ORATION BEFORE THE TWO SOCIETIES
OF SOUTH CAROLINA COLLEGE

199.heading "Two Societies": The Clariosophic and Euphradian Societies were student organizations. They were partly social and partly assumed functions later undertaken by student body governments, but their primary function was training in debate and oratory. Hammond had been president of the Euphradian Society in 1825.

EXPLANATORY NOTES 377

200.16 "Lord Bacon": Francis Bacon (1561–1626), English statesman and philosopher who attacked reliance on authority for knowledge and proposed instead inductive inquiry.
202.2 "Paracelsus": Phillipus Aureolus von Hohenheim (1493–1541), Swiss alchemist, physician, and pharmacologist.
202.3 "Agricola": Georg Bauer (1494–1555) classified minerals by their physical properties in his *De Natura Fossilium* and also studied mining and smelting.
202.12 "*experimentum crucis*": Test of torture, i.e., test by use or experimentation.
202.20 "Tubal Cain": According to *Genesis*, Tubal Cain was the first bronzeworker and blacksmith.
204.24 "Ghilanese": Ghilan was a Persian province on the Caspian Sea.
204.30 "descendants of Japheth": Japheth was the youngest and most blessed son of Noah and the proverbial progenitor of Western Europeans.
208.8 "the Georgics of the mind": Virgil's *Georgics* idealize the labors and experiences of agriculture and rural life.
209.20 "seen all Europe rise in arms": A reference to the revolutions of 1848.
210.17 "mounds of Nimrod": These marked the site of Nineveh, capital of the Assyrian Empire in the 8th century B.C. The city was excavated by Henry Layard during 1845–1851.
210.32 "Palenque": A Mayan city that flourished in the 7th century A.D.
211.1 "fortifications of the Scioto valley": A series of burial mounds constructed by pre-Columbian Indians in Ohio. The structures were in the 19th century commonly attributed to a lost race.
211.15 "Jason of Pherae": A minor tyrant of the 4th century B.C. who dreamed of leading all Greece against the Persian Empire.
212.17 "*mortua capites*": Literally: dead heads; that is, relics, or symbols of terror.
214.13 "Suarez": Francisco Suarez (1548–1617), Spanish scholastic philosopher, argued that people should choose their own governments and approved tyrannicide.
214.15–16 "Buchanan": George Buchanan (1506–1582), Scottish scholar.
214.18 "Bodin": Jean Bodin (1530–1596), French political philosopher.
215.33 "Dr. Arnold": Thomas Arnold (1795–1842), English schoolmaster and classical scholar. He was the father of Matthew Arnold.
216.29 "Paley": William Paley (1743–1805), professor at Cambridge, was the author of *Evidences of Christianity* (1794) and

Natural Theology (1802), works that were famous in the 19th century.
219.16 Greek: Immortal struggle.
220.10–11 "Hill of Mars" and "Egerian Grove": Hallowed spots within ancient Rome.
220.29 Greek: Logos.
229.11 "paixhan balls": In 1824 General Henri Paixhan, a French artillerist, substituted gunpowder-filled exploding projectiles for solid shot.

ORATION ON JOHN C. CALHOUN

232.30 "The Man is now no more": Calhoun had died on March 31, 1850.
237.10 "Lowndes, Cheves, Williams": William Lowndes, Langdon Cheves, and David R. Williams of South Carolina were considered among the most able "War Hawk" members of the House of Representatives. Lowndes was nominated for President by the South Carolina legislature in 1821 but died the next year. Cheves was Speaker of the U.S. House of Representatives and the able President of the Bank of the United States. Williams became Governor and a pioneer cotton manufacturer.
237.29 "the Eastern States": That is, New England.
238.9 "The Guerriere, the Java, and the Macedonian": British vessels subjected to unprecedented defeats by American ships during the War of 1812.
238.note: "Chever": Misprint for "Cheves."
241.13–14 "so fiercely agitated": Hammond refers to the controversy during the 1830's between President Andrew Jackson and the second Bank of the United States and to the Panic of 1837 which ensued.
242.16 "Mr. Gallatin": Albert Gallatin was Secretary of the Treasury 1801–1814, not Secretary of War.
243.4 "Message of Mr. Monroe": In 1822 President James Monroe had vetoed the Cumberland Road Bill on the ground that appropriations for internal improvements were not within the constitutional power of Congress. However, he stated that he approved the general idea of internal improvements if a constitutional amendment were passed granting the power to Congress. In his annual message to Congress in 1823, Monroe suggested that several canal projects, being clearly national in scope, might be the proper subjects of Congressional legislation.
243.5 "celebrated speech of Mr. McDuffie": In a speech on February 4 and 5, 1824, George McDuffie, a close associate of

EXPLANATORY NOTES 379

Calhoun and then a member of the U.S. House of Representatives, had supported the constitutional power of Congress to subsidize internal improvements.

245.30 "the squabble with the Directory": The "XYZ Affair" between the United States and the French government in 1797.

246.7–9 "Mr. Monroe declared, on his accession, that we were 'all Federalists—all Republicans'": The words were actually used by Thomas Jefferson in his first inaugural address in 1801. Hammond is literally wrong but perhaps correct in spirit in attributing the words to Monroe, a mistake he makes again on page 341.

248.29 "greatest of metaphysicians": Aristotle, teacher of Alexander the Great.

252.12 "*ad captandum*": The Latin phrase is "ad captandum vulgus"—to catch the mob.

256.30–32 "whether he shall go down to posterity portrayed in the colors of the Gracchi of the Patricians, or the Gracchi of the People": That is, as a conspiratorial rebel or a patriotic hero.

258.4 "the Maysville Bill": An appropriation for internal improvements, specifically for a federal investment in a turnpike company in Kentucky.

258.26 "Gov. Hamilton": James Hamilton, Jr. (1786–1857), Governor of South Carolina during 1830–1832.

259.18 "Gen. Hayne": Robert Young Hayne (1791–1839) resigned as Senator from South Carolina in December, 1832, to become Governor.

260.11 "His speech": Calhoun's speech on the Force Bill, February 15–16, 1833.

260.13 "that of the great Athenian on the Crown": Demosthenes' *On the Crown*, which summed up his opposition to the Macedonian monarchy.

261.25 "reversed": Misprint for "reserved."

263.3 "Compromise Bill": The compromise tariff law of 1833 provided for gradual reduction of the tariff rates.

264.12–13 "But he beat the surges under him . . .": Shakespeare, *The Tempest*, II, 1.

270.2 "the leader of the Republican Party": Here and in many other places Hammond uses the term "Republican" to describe what was then and later called the Democratic Party. Hammond's terminology is both conventional and deliberate. For Hammond, the "Republican Party" is the State rights party of Jefferson, as opposed to the Federalist-Whig Party descended from Hamilton. He obviously does not mean the Republican Party of Abraham Lincoln, which had not come into existence at the time Hammond spoke.

380   EXPLANATORY NOTES

271.18–19 "A Republican President was elected": That is, James K. Polk, Democrat. See the immediately preceding note.

273.13–16 "the Convention . . . was not to be constituted on principles analogous to the Constitution": Calhoun in effect wanted each State's delegation to the national convention to reflect the distribution of viewpoints within that state, rather than allowing a simple majority to elect all of the state's delegates.

274.6 "Mr. Calhoun's successor": James Buchanan succeeded Calhoun as Secretary of State.

274.20 "Judge Huger": Daniel Elliott Huger (1779–1854), Senator from South Carolina 1843–1845.

277.9 "elevation of one of its successful Generals": Zachary Taylor, elected President as the Whig candidate in 1848.

280.9 "in that election, they held the balance of power": See note 102.1–2.

285.5 "Mr. Mason": James Murray Mason, Senator from Virginia 1847–1861, later Confederate Minister to Great Britain.

287.17 "Anacharsis": An advisor to the Athenian lawgiver Solon. His alleged maxims were often quoted by Cicero.

290.27–28 "he would have been a Publicola . . . Cato . . . Gracchus": Exemplary performers of the different major offices of republican Rome.

294.23 "The Astronomer": Anaxagoras.

294.25 "successful Usurper": The earlist written versions of Homer date from the reign of Peisistratus who usurped the government of Athens during 560–510 B.C.

299.15 "Agis, Conon and the younger Brutus": Agis IV, King of Sparta in 230 B.C., attempted to restore the ancient law codes of Lycurgus, but was captured and executed by his co-king, Leonidas. Marcus Junius Brutus, one of the assassins of Julius Caesar, failed to restore the Roman republic. Conon (died 392 B.C.) was an Athenian general who failed to defeat the Spartans. However, it is not impossible that "Conon" is a misprint for Cimon, a much better known Athenian (died 449 B.C.) who failed in opposing damaging changes to the constitution.

SPEECH ON THE ADMISSION OF KANSAS

301.6 "the Senator from Illinois": Stephen A. Douglas, who had broken with the Democratic majority in the Senate to oppose the admission of Kansas under the Lecompton (pro-slavery) constitution.

EXPLANATORY NOTES 381

305.17 "the Senator from New York": William H. Seward, Republican and leading spokesman for the free-soil position.
307.28 "Ajax Telamon": One of the Greek heroes at the siege of Troy. After the death of Achilles, Ajax and Odysseus competed for Achilles' armor. When he lost, Ajax in a rage slaughtered a flock of sheep, then killed himself in shame. In this case, Hammond suggests, Douglas is competing with Buchanan for the Presidential nomination.
308.17 "General Lane's lambs!": The forces of James Henry Lane, an anti-slavery leader in the Kansas guerrilla war.
308.18 "Colonel Kirke": Percy Kirke (1646?–1691), notorious for his cruelty to prisoners in the suppression of the Monmouth Rebellion.
308.26 "other side of the Chamber": The Republicans.
310.19 "they intended to reconstruct the Supreme Court": Seward had suggested this on March 3 in a speech attacking the Dred Scott decision.
312.30 "second war of independence": The War of 1812.
317.7 "Until lately the Bank of England was king": Hammond refers to the panic of 1857 during which many American banks and mercantile houses had folded and the Bank of England had saved itself by issuing two million pounds in notes unbacked by the necessary reserves.
318.1–2 "Society precedes government": An echo of the opening passage of Calhoun's "A Disquisition on Government."
319.2–3 "*lex naturae est*": Literally: "is the law of nature."
320.22 "Mr. Wilson": Henry Wilson, Senator from Massachusetts and later Vice-President under Grant, a leading Republican who had begun life as a laborer.
320.31 "Mendoza and Torquemada": Major figures of the Spanish Inquisition.

SPEECH DELIVERED AT BARNWELL COURT HOUSE

323.2–3 "the people of Barnwell": In accordance with customary South Carolina usage, Hammond means the people of Barnwell District, not just the town of Barnwell Court House.
323.5–6 "stirring times, when, a quarter of a century ago, I so often spoke to you here": That is, during the Nullification crisis.
325.33 "Missouri Compromise line": Congress in 1820 had excluded slavery from the territories north of 36°30'. That provision had applied specifically to the Louisiana Purchase, not to later acquisitions of territory.

382 EXPLANATORY NOTES

326.12 "The Supreme Court has recently pronounced it unconstitutional": A reference to the Dred Scott decision of 1857.
327.9 "*Green Proviso*": Senator James S. Green of Missouri had managed the efforts of the James Buchanan administration to secure approval of the Lecompton Constitution in the Senate. By the "Green Proviso" Hammond apparently means the provision of the original Senate bill granting 23 million acres of public lands to the Kansas legislature.
327.18–19 "Crittenden substitute": Proposed by Senator John J. Crittenden of Kentucky, a Whig, and Representative William Montgomery of Pennsylvania, a Democrat.
327.24 "English Bill": Introduced by Representative William H. English of Indiana, Democrat, with the backing of the Buchanan administration.
330.10 "Judge Douglas": See note 301.6.
333.4 "prohibitory clause": The provision mentioned on page 328, lines 20–25.
341.2 "the democracy": The Democratic Party.
341.16–17 "all federalists, all republicans": See note 246.7–9. Hammond clearly means to ascribe Jefferson's words to James Monroe, as the preceding reference to "thirty years ago" makes clear.
343.16 "only four times": The administrations of John Adams, John Quincy Adams, Martin Van Buren, and Millard Fillmore.
343.29–30 "wise and good Las Casas": Bartolomeo De Las Casas (1474–1566), Bishop of Chiabas, at the same time opposed the enslavement of Indians by the Spanish and advocated the use of African slaves in the New World.
344.16 "Clays, Marshalls, Crawfords": Henry Clay, John Marshall, and William Harris Crawford of Georgia, with many other prominent Southerners, had supported the colonization of freed slaves outside the United States prior to the appearance of abolitionism in the 1830's.
346.15 "the saints of Exeter Hall": Exeter Hall was a London meeting place for evangelical societies, notably the Clapham Group whose membership included many prominent British abolitionists. The Parliamentary members of the Clapham Group were often referred to as "saints."
346.30–31 "France, who, in her frequent frenzies": Slavery was abolished temporarily during the French Revolution, reinstated by Napoleon, and finally abolished in French colonies in 1848.
347.23 "Algerine slavery": The enslavement of Christians by the Barbary pirates of North Africa. Such slaves could hope only

EXPLANATORY NOTES 383

to be employed in the galleys or treated as commodities for sale.

348.18 "Brougham": Henry Peter Brougham, Lord Brougham and Vaux (1778–1868), had been a leader of the Parliamentary abolition forces.

348.18 "Palmerston": Henry John Temple, 3rd Viscount Palmerston (1784–1865), was another Parliamentary supporter of emancipation. He was Secretary of State for Foreign Affairs 1830–1841 and 1846–1851. As Prime Minister during the American Civil War he was unsympathetic to the Confederate cause.

348.18 "Russell": Lord John Russell, 1st Earl Russell (1792–1878), British Prime Minister 1846–1851.

348.20 "son of Wilberforce": Samuel Wilberforce (1803–1873), son of the abolitionist William Wilberforce, was, as Bishop of Oxford and Winchester, a member of the House of Lords.

350.8 "Peter Hermits": See note 118.32.

350.8–9 "their Godfreys, their Baldwins, their lion-hearted Richards": Military leaders of the First and Second Crusades in the 11th and 12th centuries: Godfrey of Bouillon, three generations of Baldwins who were kings of Jerusalem, and Richard I of England.

350.11 "Louis IX": St. Louis, King of France, who died leading a crusade in 1270.

350.23 "Sewards, Hales, Wades, Wilsons, Chases": William H. Seward of New York, John P. Hale of New Hampshire, Benjamin F. Wade of Ohio, Henry Wilson of Massachusetts, and Salmon P. Chase of Ohio, all free-soil politicians.

350.26–27 "the President, Dickinson, Bright, Pugh, Douglas": President James Buchanan, former Senator Daniel S. Dickinson of New York, Senators Jesse D. Bright of Indiana, George E. Pugh of Ohio, and Stephen A. Douglas of Illinois, all Democratic politicians usually sympathetic to the South.

350.32–33 "Smiths, Tappans, Garrisons, and Parkers": Abolitionists like Gerrit Smith, Arthur and Lewis Tappan, William Lloyd Garrison, and Theodore Parker, as distinct from the free-soil politicians mentioned in 350.23.

353.31 "martyrdom was consummated before the adjournment": Perhaps a reference to Democratic Senators George W. Jones of Iowa and William Wright of New Jersey who were replaced by Republicans in the 1858 elections.

354.22 "federal consolidationists": The term carries intimations of the Federalist Party.

384   EXPLANATORY NOTES

SPEECH ON THE RELATIONS OF THE STATES

358.2 "Mr. Davis": Senator Jefferson Davis of Mississippi had introduced resolutions calling for federal protection of slave property in the territories up to the point when a territory became a State and decided for itself whether to permit slavery or not.

358.10 "speech of the Senator from Georgia": Robert A. Toombs, Senator from Georgia during 1853–1861, had just finished speaking on Davis' resolution.

367.12–13 "the Senator from Illinois, in his speech the other day": Stephen A. Douglas, leader of the Northern Democrats, was to be nominated for President in June, 1860. His speech on Davis' resolutions, delivered on May 17, can be found in *Congressional Globe*, 36th Congress, 1st Session, columns 2151–2156.

367.23 "General Cass": Lewis Cass of Michigan, the Democratic nominee for President in 1848.

367.24 "letter to Judge Nicholson": In a letter to Alfred O.P. Nicholson of Tennessee during the 1848 campaign, Cass had expressed his opposition to the Wilmot Proviso, which forbade slavery in the territories, and his willingness to leave that issue to the citizens directly concerned.

367.32 "1760": Misprint for "1850."

368.6 "Mr. Rhett": Robert Barnwell Rhett (1800–1876), leading advocate of secession in South Carolina.

368.15 "Kansas and Nebraska Act": See pages 325–326.

INDEX

Aberdeen, Earl of: 77, 371.
Abolitionism: *See* Antislavery movement; Free Soil movement.
Adams, John Quincy: 36, 48, 250, 252, 370.
Afghanistan: 189, 376.
Africa: 38–39, 99, 112, 115–18, 151, 166–68, 187, 347–48, 373.
Agis: 299, 380.
Agricola: 202, 377.
Agriculture: 34, 38–39, 62, 75, 79, 93–95, 109, 140, 252, 341.
Alaric: 212, 215.
Alexander the Great: 234, 248.
Allegiance, political: 8–12.
American Revolution: 12, 27, 42, 47, 54, 103–04, 126, 167, 193, 214, 233, 254, 277, 306, 312, 318, 360.
Anacharsis: 287, 380.
Anaxagoras: 234, 294, 380.
Andrews, James O.: 101, 372.
Antigua: 164–65.
Antislavery movement: 15–50, 77, 100–98, 255, 277–90, 343–48, 352–57, 369–70, 372–76, 382–83. *See also* Free Soil movement.
Anti-Slavery Record: 22–24, 182, 375.
Archimedes: 223.
Ariosto, Lodovico: 215.
Aristides: 254, 268.
Aristocracy: 42–45, 71, 110–11, 127, 132–33, 139, 141, 172, 182, 226.
Aristotle: 202–03, 216, 218–19, 234, 248, 379.
Arnold, Thomas: 215, 377.
Assyria: 210, 377.

Bacon, Francis: 199–230, 248, 377.
Banking: 55–67, 75–76, 82–85, 238, 241, 265–69, 370–71. *See also the four succeeding entries.*
Bank of England: 132, 317, 381.
Bank of South Carolina: 75–76, 85, 371.
Bank of the State of South Carolina: 55–67, 75–76, 82–85, 370–71.
Bank of the United States: 63, 240–42, 246, 255, 258, 265–67, 270, 311, 341–42, 371, 378.
Baptists: 152.
Barnwell District, S.C.: 5–14, 323–24, 381.
Barrere, Bertrand: 194.
Bentham, Jeremy: 189, 214.
Bible, references to: 37–38, 107–08, 113, 120–25, 135, 142–43, 148, 152–53, 160, 170, 172, 176–82, 202, 204, 206, 373, 377.
Boccaccio, Giovanni: 135.
Bodin, John: 214, 377.
Borgia, Cesare: 226.
Boyer, Jean Pierre: 40, 370.
Bright, Jesse D.: 350, 383.
British Empire: *See* Great Britain; India; Ireland; West Indies.
Brougham, Henry, Lord: 157, 348, 383.
Brown, John L.: 105–13, 373.
Brown, Thomas: 105, 113, 372.
Brutus: 254, 299, 380.
Buchanan, George: 214, 377.
Buchanan, James: 274, 350, 352, 380–83.
Burke, Edmund: 194, 254, 290, 376.
Butler, Pierce Manning: 58, 371.
Buxton, Thomas Fowel: 117.

385

386 INDEX

Calhoun, John C.: 231–300, 337, 378–81.
California: 284–85, 289, 313, 326, 334.
Cantey, James W.: 88, 371.
Capitalists: 26, 45–46, 51–52, 60, 62, 186–87, 210, 213, 224, 317–22, 340, 342–43, 349. *See also* Banking; Industry; Speculation.
Carnot, Lazare: 248.
Cass, Lewis: 367, 384.
Catawba Indians: 74–75.
Cato: 254, 268, 290, 380.
Central America: 99, 210, 336–37, 372, 377.
Channing, William Ellery: 29, 369–70.
Charlemagne: 42, 212.
Charles I, of England: 163.
Charleston, S.C.: 54–58, 68, 72, 75, 86, 93, 231.
Chase, Salmon P.: 350, 383.
Cherokee Indians: 74.
Chester County, S.C.: 372.
Cheves, Langdon: 237–38, 378.
China: 187, 225, 347.
Christian religion: 20, 24, 29, 42, 45, 50, 78, 89, 101, 105–13, 114, 118–25, 133–36, 141–43, 152–54, 158–60, 164, 167, 172, 176–88, 193, 196–98, 207–08, 212–14, 219–21, 231, 256, 288, 300, 319, 338, 343, 346, 347, 351, 359, 372, 374–75, 377. *See also* Bible.
Cicero: 217, 268, 319, 380.
Cimon: 299, 380.
Clarisophic Society of South Carolina College: 199ff., 376.
Clarkson, Thomas: 114–98, 373, 375.
Classics: *See* Greece, ancient; Rome, ancient.
Clay, Henry: 133, 250, 252, 263, 344, 372, 374, 382.
Colonization: 26, 344, 348, 382.
Columbia, S.C.: 68, 70, 75, 86, 91.
Columbus, Christopher: 202.
Compromise of 1850: 284–85, 289, 367.

Compromise Tariff of 1833: 94–96, 263–65, 270, 372, 379.
Comptroller General of South Carolina: 82–83.
Conon: 299, 380.
Constitution of South Carolina: 6, 14, 70, 217, 228, 371–72.
Convention of the people: 261–62, 301–07, 330–32. *See also* Social compact; Sovereignty.
Corporations: 60.
Cotton: 79–80, 117, 187, 195, 228, 314–16, 340, 346.
Crawford, William H.: 344, 382.
Crittenden, John J.: 327, 329–30, 382.
Cromwell, Oliver: 163.
Cuba: 77, 337–38, 349.
Currency: 51–52, 79, 242.
Cushing, Caleb: 15–16, 18, 48, 369.
Dante Alighieri: 215.
Danton, Georges: 194.
Davis, Jefferson: 358, 362, 384.
Death penalty: 49, 107, 142, 150.
Debt, British national: 131–32, 173.
Debt, South Carolina public: 54–66, 82–85.
Declaration of Independence: 126, 277, 306.
Democratic Party: 95–97, 249–52, 267, 270–90, 301–02, 330, 341, 350–55, 367, 372, 379–84.
Democratic-Republican Party: 236–50, 262, 379, 382.
Demosthenes: 217, 260, 292, 379.
Dickens, Charles: 174, 375.
Dickinson, Daniel S.: 350, 383.
Dickinson, Willoughby M.: 114, 143.
District of Columbia, slavery in: 15, 17–18, 20, 349.
Douglas, Stephen A.: 301–22, 330, 350, 367–68, 380–84.
Drake, Sir Francis: 202.
Dred Scott decision: 310, 326, 349, 381–82.
Drummond Light: 171, 375.
Dudley, Earl of: 166, 375.
Duelling: 130–31.

INDEX

Dunkers: 134, 374.
Dutch colonies: 163.

Earle, Baylies John: 76.
Education, South Carolina public: 70–74, 87–90, 133, 228, 234–35. *See also* South Carolina College.
Electricity: 199, 207, 215.
Elmore, Franklin Harper: 63, 83, 371.
Empiricism: 199–230.
England: *See* Great Britain.
English Bill: 327–30, 382.
Euphradian Society of South Carolina College: 199ff., 376.
Exeter Hall: 346–47, 382.

Federalist Party: 12, 238, 245–46, 249–50, 267, 272, 341, 354, 379, 382–83.
Force Bill: 260, 263, 379.
Fourierism: 134, 374.
Fox, George: 198, 376.
France: 32, 47, 99, 109, 130, 135, 171, 194–96, 236–37, 245, 287, 337, 346–48, 376, 379, 382. *See also* French Revolution.
Free labor: 20, 28, 32–34, 36, 108–10, 128, 139–41, 154–60, 163–70, 184–87, 318–20, 373, 381.
Free Soil movement: 283, 283–89, 301–22, 325–41, 349, 368, 380–84.
Free trade: 52–53, 80, 96–97, 239–40, 341, 349. *See also* Tariff.
French Revolution: 41–45, 132, 171, 194, 344.
Frontier: 130–31, 233.
Fulton, Robert: 215.

Galileo Galilei: 201, 215, 223.
Gallatin, Albert: 242, 378.
Gama, Vasco da: 202.
Garrison, William Lloyd: 48, 350, 370, 383.
George III: 116, 373.
Gracchi: 256, 290, 379–80.
Graham, Sir James Robert: 189–90, 376.
Granger, Francis: 30, 48, 370.

Great Britain: 11–12, 22, 29, 32–33, 35, 42, 44, 47, 52–53, 57, 77, 79–80, 99, 102, 104–98, 203, 214, 240, 287, 317, 336, 343–44, 346–48, 360, 370–73, 375–76, 382. *See also* War of 1812.
Greece, ancient: 44, 128, 181, 183, 199–230, 234, 244, 248, 254, 260, 268, 287, 291–94, 299, 307, 370, 377–81.
Green Proviso: 327, 329, 332–33, 382.
Grosvenor, Richard, 1st Earl: 116–17, 168, 373.

Hale, John P.: 310, 350, 383.
Hamilton, Alexander: 251.
Hamilton, James, Jr.: 258, 379.
Harper, William: 369.
Harrison, William H.: 269.
Harvey, William: 202.
Hayne, Robert Y.: 259, 379.
Hero of Alexandria: 203.
Hobbes, Thomas: 201.
Homer: 183, 217, 294.
Horace: 189, 217, 376.
Huger, Daniel Elliott: 274, 380.
Hume, David: 125, 215.

India: 99, 163–64, 171, 189, 195, 224, 347, 375.
Indians: 39, 74–75, 119, 169, 189, 204, 210–11, 335–38, 377.
Industry: 155–60, 163, 228, 339.
Inquisition: 27, 320, 381.
Insanity: 151.
Internal Improvements: 54–57, 70, 82, 242–43, 246, 255, 258, 341–42, 378–79.
Interposition: *See* Nullification.
Iowa: 328.
Ireland: 32, 108, 147, 158, 172, 289, 375.
Italy: 201.

Jackson, Andrew: 21, 249–53, 257–62, 265, 378.
Jay, John: 31, 245.
Jay, William: 31, 117, 370.

Jefferson, Thomas: 27, 126, 214, 239, 242, 246, 262, 344, 370, 379, 382.
Johnson, David: 6–9, 369.
Jollivet, Adolphe: 195–96, 376.
Jones, George W.: 353, 383.
Judiciary: 5–14, 75, 82, 91–92, 105, 150, 203, 310, 326, 349, 369.

Kansas question: 301–22, 325–41, 349, 368, 380–82, 384.
Kirke, Percy: 308, 381.
Knapp, Isaac: 28.

Labor: *See* Free labor.
Lancaster District, S.C.: 93.
Lane, James H.: 308, 381.
Las Casas, Bartolomeo de: 343, 382.
Lavoisier, Antoine: 201.
Lecompton Constitution: *See* Kansas question.
Lee, Gideon: 30, 370.
Leo X: 135, 374.
Liberty Party: 102, 162, 192, 280, 372.
Limestone Springs, S.C.: 70.
Locke, John: 214, 218.
London Quarterly Review: 166, 375.
Louis IX of France: 350, 383.
Louisville, Cincinnati, and Charleston Railroad: 54, 56, 59, 62, 370.
Lowndes, William: 237, 240, 378.
Luther, Martin: 135.
Lycurgus: 287.

Macaulay, Thomas Babington: 188, 375.
Machiavelli, Niccolo: 216, 227.
Machinery: 43, 171, 186. *See also* Steam power.
Madison, James: 239, 242, 262.
Magistrate's courts in South Carolina: 91–92.
Marryat, Frederick: 174, 375.
Marshall, John: 344, 382.
Martineau, Harriet: 134–35, 137, 174, 374–75.
Maryland: 17.

Mason, James M.: 285, 380.
Massachusetts: 15–16, 21, 24, 27–28, 36, 48, 100, 128, 370, 381.
McDuffie, George: 126, 243, 373, 378–79.
Mendoza, Pedro Gonzales de: 320.
Methodists: 101, 152, 372.
Mexican War: 275–77, 283, 371.
Mexico: 98–99, 336.
Michelangelo Buonarroti: 215.
Middle Ages: 42, 118, 212–13, 350, 373, 383.
Militia: 37, 67–68, 75, 85–88, 127–28, 168, 313, 371.
Millerism: 134, 374.
Milton, John: 184, 215, 375.
Miscegenation: 136–38.
Missouri Compromise: 278, 283, 325–26, 344, 381.
Mobs: 27, 32, 43, 128, 131, 169, 171, 320–21, 367, 376.
Monarchy: 8, 10, 25, 42–43, 104, 172, 182, 214, 216, 226, 228.
Monroe, James: 243, 246–47, 249, 341, 378–79, 382.
Mormonism: 134, 189, 198, 376.
Morse, Samuel F.B.: 215.
Mount Dearborn, S.C.: 93, 371–72.
Mudsill class: 318–19.

Napoleon I: 47, 171, 236–37, 370, 382.
Nativism: 32, 189, 376.
Navy, U.S.: 238–39.
New England: 20, 27–28, 41, 45, 119, 155, 187, 237–38, 252, 366, 373, 378. *See also* Massachusetts.
Newton, Isaac: 201.
New York: 20, 24, 29, 30–31, 47, 97, 128, 319, 343, 372, 374.
Nicholson Letter: 367–68, 384.
Normanby, Marquis of: 159, 375.
North British Review: 182, 375.
North Carolina: 74.
Notaries public in South Carolina: 91–92.
Nullification: 5–14, 94–96, 98, 257–64, 267, 270–71, 323–24, 369, 372, 381.

INDEX

Obedience, political: 8–12.
O'Connell, Daniel: 172, 375.
Ohio: 25, 38–39, 128.
O'Neall, John Belton: 6–9, 105, 369.
Oregon: 271–75, 313, 333.

Paixhan balls: 229, 378.
Paley, William: 216, 377.
Palmerston, 3rd Viscount: 348, 383.
Panama, Isthmus of: 337.
Panic of 1837: 51–52, 79–80, 131–32, 266, 378.
Panic of 1857: 317, 381.
Paracelsus: 202, 377.
Parker, Theodore: 350, 383.
Peel, Sir Robert: 254, 371.
Peisistratus: 268, 294, 380.
Peltier, Jean Gabriel: 47, 370.
Pennsylvania: 20, 97, 128, 131, 142, 189, 249, 366, 374, 376.
Pericles: 234.
Peter the Hermit: 118, 350, 373, 383.
Petition, right of: 16, 48, 282–83, 369.
Petitions, abolitionist: 15–50, 279–80, 369–70.
Petrarch: 215.
Pinckney, Robert Q.: 69–70, 90–91, 371.
Pitt, William, the younger: 144, 374.
Planter class: 25–28, 34, 62, 95, 140, 321–322.
Plato: 218–20.
Polk, James K.: 133, 271, 273–74, 372, 374, 380.
Pompey: 268.
Presbyterians: 105–13, 172, 182, 372.
Presidential elections: 97–98, 102, 133, 192, 249–50, 252, 254, 269, 271, 273, 277, 280, 343, 350, 351, 367, 372, 381.
Press, freedom of: 46–48.
Press, power of: 228–29.
Priestly, Joseph: 214.
Public debt: *See* Debt.
Publicola: 290, 380.

Pugh, George E.: 350, 383.
Puseyism: 134, 374.
Pythagoras: 203.

Railroads: 43, 54, 56, 59, 62, 68, 86, 207, 314, 370.
Randolph, John: 32, 370.
Randolph, Martha Jefferson: 54, 370.
Raphael: 215.
Rappists: 134, 374.
Reformation: 42, 135, 213–14.
Renaissance: 201–04, 213–27, 374, 377.
Representation: *See* Three-fifths rule.
Republican Party: 305–22, 330, 350, 354–55, 379, 381–83.
Revolutions of 1848: 209–10, 377.
Rhett, Robert Barnwell: 368, 384.
Richardson, John P.: 68, 371.
Rome, ancient: 128, 189, 199–230, 254, 256, 268, 290, 299, 319, 376–80.
Ruffin, Edmund: 75, 93, 371.
Russell, John, 1st Earl: 348, 383.
Russia: 99, 187, 285.

Sallust: 216.
Santo Domingo: 29, 40, 107, 289, 351.
Science: 93, 199–230, 268, 371–72, 377.
Scotland: *See* Great Britain.
Secession: 13, 35, 49, 100, 103, 162, 191–93, 259–62, 286–87, 289, 333–34, 342, 351, 355–56, 368.
Secretary of State of South Carolina: 69–70, 90–91, 371.
Serfdom: 33, 165, 185.
Sensualist philosophy: 218.
Seward, William H.: 305, 308, 310, 319, 321, 350, 381, 383.
Sex: 134–38, 157–58, 161, 179.
Shakers: 134, 374.
Shakespeare, William: 188, 215, 264, 375, 379.
Sierra Leone: 166–67.
Silver Bluff, S.C.: 114, 173.
Slave family: 36, 108, 139, 151–52.

Slave insurrection: 26–27, 29–30, 32, 35–37, 40, 49, 102, 107, 128–29, 145–46, 150, 168–69, 197, 370.
Slavery: *See* Antislavery movement.
Slaves, punishment of: 147–50, 373.
Slave trade: 15, 17, 18, 20, 31, 108, 115–18, 139, 144–45, 148, 163–64, 166–67, 193, 195–96, 335, 337, 347–48, 373–74.
Smith, Gerrit: 48, 350, 370, 383.
Smith, Joseph: 198, 376.
Social compact: 10–12, 303–04, 359–60, 362–65.
Socialists: 134, 374.
Socrates: 220, 223.
Solon: 268, 287.
South America: 131, 343. *See also* Central America.
South Carolina College: 71–73, 88–89, 199–230, 376.
South Carolina Constitution: *See* Constitution of South Carolina.
South Carolina Court of Appeals: 5–14, 105, 369.
Southcote, Joanna: 198, 376.
South West Railroad Bank: 54, 58, 62.
Sovereignty: 8, 10–12, 301–22, 330–32, 358–68, 384.
Speculation: 51–52, 62–63, 191, 269–70, 317, 321, 342.
Steam power: 43, 117, 199, 201, 203–04, 207.
Stowell, Sir William Scott: 165, 168, 375.
Stroud, George M.: 142, 374.
Suarez, Francisco: 214, 377.
Suffrage: 97, 126–27.
Sugar: 187–88, 195.
Suicide: 151.
Surveyor-General of South Carolina: 69, 91.

Tacitus: 216.
Tahiti: 99, 372.
Tappan, Arthur: 23, 48, 350, 370, 383.
Tariff: 52–53, 79–80, 94–98, 102, 155, 240, 251–59, 263, 269–71, 277, 316, 341–42, 372, 379.
Taylor, Zachary: 277, 380.
"Test Oath" controversy: 5–14, 369.
Texas: 77, 98–101, 273–75, 283, 326, 338, 360.
Thales: 203.
Themistocles: 268.
Three-fifths rule: 25–26, 40, 129, 278, 374.
Thompson, George: 29, 36, 370.
Thucydides: 216.
Toombs, Robert A.: 358, 384.
Torquemada: 320.
Toussaint L'Ouverture: 40, 370.
Transcendentalism: 124, 170, 196.
Trollope, Frances: 174, 375.
Tuomey, Michael: 93, 372.
Turner, Nat: 32, 37, 370.
Tyler, John: 269–70, 273.

Utilitarianism: 199–230.

Van Buren, Martin: 266, 269.
Vinci, Leonardo da: 202, 215.
Virgil: 208, 377.
Virginia: 17, 32, 37, 75, 93, 370.
Voltaire: 125.

Wade, Benjamin F.: 350, 383.
War Department, Calhoun in: 247–49.
War of 1812: 236–39, 243–46, 251, 378, 381.
Washington, George: 104, 290, 344.
Watt, James: 201.
Watts, Beaufort T.: 79.
Webster, Daniel: 239–40, 260.
Wertenbaker, William: 24.
West Indies: 29, 35, 40, 77, 107, 116, 129, 147, 163–69, 171, 175, 187, 189, 195, 289, 337–38, 349, 351, 370, 373.
Whig Party (American): 250, 267, 269–72, 274, 277, 372, 379–80, 382.

Wilberforce, Samuel: 348, 383.
Wilberforce, William: 168, 196, 375, 383.
Williams, David R.: 237, 378.
Wilson, Henry: 320, 350, 381, 383.

Wright, Elizar, Jr.: 23–24.
Wright, William: 353, 383.

XYZ Affair: 245, 379.

www.ingramcontent.com/pod-product-compliance
Lightning Source LLC
Chambersburg PA
CBHW051240300426
44114CB00011B/830